# TRACKS IN EUROPE

# Tracks in Europe

Captain C. J. Boardman

Published by City Press Services
Chapel House, 172 Chapel Street, Salford M3 6BG



ISBN 0 9515822 0 8 Tracks in Europe. (hbk)



Typeset and printed by
John Roberts & Sons Printers (Salford) Ltd., Chapel Street, Salford M3 6BG.

KENSINGTON PALACE

As Colonel-in-Chief of the 5th Royal Inniskilling Dragoon Guards, I am delighted that Jim Boardman has been able to produce his new book, "Tracks in Europe", about the last war. It is most important to have recorded the personal experiences of those who fought in that conflict. Their stories provide us with relevant lessons for the present and encourage us to emulate their courage and endeavour. The authors of the collected stories fought most gallantly for their country and their Regiment. This book will be an inspiration to others.

Charles

# Contents

# FOREWORD

by

## General Sir Cecil H Blacker GCB, OBE, MC

This is, so to speak, a regimental history of the Second World War seen from the worm's eye view, and it achieves an effect which no official account could do. Jim Boardman has conceived the idea of a narrative serving chiefly to link together a series of personal accounts, some extremely vivid, of the wartime experiences of regimental members. He begins with those far-off days of 1939 and the ensuing withdrawal to Dunkirk, continues through the frustrations and disappointments of the middle war years and then on to Normandy and the advance to Schleswig Holstein.

Official histories unavoidably have occasionally to use such phrases as 'the advance continued against opposition', 'a fire-fight followed', or 'some casualties were suffered'. Here we can read what actually happened to those at the sharp end.

The book succeeds in its declared intention of serving as a tribute to all concerned, and their relatives and friends. It is more than that; it is fascinating reading. It portrays war as it was, with its sense of comradeship, its humorous and lighter moments—and its boredom and frustration—only serving to mask and to mitigate the tragedies, the suffering, and the waste of young lives. Some accounts are harrowing and some moving; some, particularly the experiences of those wounded and made POW in 1940, leave one marvelling at the fortitude displayed in conquering pain and despair.

The book is written with compassion and with the kindness and deep affection which has characterised Jim Boardman's attitude towards the regimental family. Since he joined as a boy soldier fifty years ago he has made an altogether outstanding contribution to the Regiment, and for this, his latest offering, we owe him our warmest thanks.

# An Appreciation

I suspect that few books are written without a supporting cast of proof-readers, typists and considerable tolerance from the close family who surrender a room to be completely taken over and made uninhabitable and uncleanable for months. Such has been my experience. My own typing is limited to one index finger on each hand supported by several erasers and pots of correcting fluid which cover the keyboard and wall with splashes.

After completing the first phase, I submitted the drafts to General 'Monkey' Blacker and Major General Henry Woods and awaited their reactions. General Monkey was most encouraging and enjoyed the experience of mind reverberance. General Henry who entered the active stage of war a little later, was more cautious but kind enough not to tell me to give it all up. I thank them both. Pat Whitmore became so involved that I have considered making the writing a joint venture. Without his tutorial corrections to my home work and guidance throughout, the book would not have been published. These three people gave me sufficient encouragement to continue something which was to become a greater task than orginally foreseen.

I thank all those who have contributed to the memories and thank the descendents of those who have since died. I hope that by recording their information, I have left a memorial to them. I hope that those who survive and the relatives of those already departed will share the satisfaction which I feel. One of my friends commented that the project has been like a long pregnancy . . . thank you happy fathers.

The typing expertise of Christine Thompson at Home Headquarters in Chester transformed my original rough drafts into readable material before presentation to David Tattersall and Ian Redford of City Press Services and Jim Lewis who have added the final professional touches. Major 'Bill' Spiegelberg, the Association Treasurer has given his total support by handling the finances and as a proof-reader. Friend and neighbour, Ann Billington has kindly added valuable advice as a non-military reader. The final work is now left with my successor at Home Headquarters, Major John Etherington and my friend and colleague while I held the appointment, Rita Robertshaw. I thank every one of them.

# Introduction

During the thirteen years I held the post of Regimental Secretary to the 5th Royal Inniskilling Dragoon Guards, I was privileged to hear war stories from past members spanning the years from the Boer War to present times. I was also fortunate in having free access to the Regimental Archives where old reports and records have been stored for years. My service with the Regiment and subsequent employment as Secretary to the Association brought me into close contact with those who had served during the early actions of World War Two and I gathered first class and personal experience from 1942 onwards. Many of the reports were used by Major General Roger Evans to cover the history of the Regiment from the amalgamation of the 5th Dragoon Guards and the 6th Inniskilling Dragoons in 1923 and some were included in the history written by General Sir Cecil Blacker and Major General Henry Woods, *'Change and Challenge'*, covering the years from 1928 to 1978.

Both are excellent records and recommended reading.

However, for those men who were involved in this campaign they have a different meaning. There was often no mention at all of particular incidents most outstanding in one's personal memory. I was myself wounded in Normandy, not seriously, but sufficient to cause me to be evacuated to UK for four months. In that action the War Diary and subsequently both histories record this incident in which two of my very close friends were killed and three others wounded, by recording the tragedy in the following words:

"On the morning of 26th August 1944; the Regiment were held up by mines. The Recce Squadron met with some opposition and there were some casualties."

It is impossible to record every incident on a front sometimes spread over three or more miles—and indeed, many incidents were never known to Regimental Headquarters. For this reason I have spent six years encouraging friends to write their own experiences and permit me to include them into a new account of that eventful period of our lives. There are many stories still untold because the tellers are too old or cannot remember but I have sufficient to give a better picture of life at that time and make the task more than worthwhile. I dedicate this book to my friends and particularly those who contributed to this period of the Regiment's history.

# PART I

# Colchester and France 1939 – June 1940

Readers who are not old enough to remember 1939 may not easily understand the technical and emotional trauma in Cavalry regiments brought about by mechanisation in that year. Germans now had a leader who they believed could restore their economy and avenge their downfall in 1918. Even if it is accepted that the average German did not seek world domination, there is no doubt that Adolf Hitler did and had prepared well for the coming conflict.

Attacks upon neighbouring countries, he proclaimed, were only to reclaim territory taken from Germany after the Great War. Whether we believed this or not, we had not the force to prevent it. Neville Chamberlain, though appearing naïve, carried a tremendous burden and, waving his piece of paper on returning from the Munich conference, proclaimed "Peace in our time!" He had at least bought us some time in which to re-arm and strengthen our forces.

Young men were conscripted into the army in June, 1939, and became known as the "June Militia!" The Regiment absorbed about 30 who were intended to train and then return to civil employment as reservists. Supplementary Reserve Officers were called up and given basic training, while those men serving on the reserve were placed on the alert. Swords, bandoliers, pants, puttees and spurs were withdrawn along with the horses, which had long been our faithful and efficient servants and symbols of pride for which a tank was no substitute.

Territorial regiments were also given a more serious period of training, particularly the Royal Artillery regiments charged with anti-aircraft defence. The powerful beams of searchlights made patterns across the sky in search of the lonely target aircraft. Our bombers were few and slow. The predictor-controlled beams soon picked up the intruder and followed it.

In my own village of Groombridge, on the Kent-Sussex border, a meeting was held to discuss what should be done about air defence. Those present concluded that the hills to the north of us, some 150 feet high, would force pilots to fly so high that they would not see the village at all. Those same villagers were soon to witness the savage air conflicts of the Battle of Britain and, later, to find themselves under the flight path of the flying bombs aimed at London.

There was an air of confidence, born of ignorance and swelled by rumours of the poor state of the German forces. There were tales of cars colliding with tanks which were found to be made of wood, and aircraft whose uneven drone was caused by badly tuned engines. The general public believed that any war started by the Germans would be over in a matter of months.

The cavalry regiments were equipped with the Mark VIB light tank and made the most of the few months available for retraining. Many men were too old to adapt and could hardly be blamed for their lack of enthusiasm. They were posted to other duties where their years of experience with the horse could still be of use: mule teams for the Middle East, Pioneers for ammunition stores, and road construction units. Some were fortunate to be absorbed by the Royal Scots Greys who still clung to their horses.

Small cadres of men from the Royal Tank Corps were posted in to assist with armoured training. Interestingly, the question of leadership was never in doubt. Officers trained to lead on a horse would be well able to cope with a tank. Leadership qualities remained unchanged even though there were new technical considerations. This judgment proved to be absolutely correct.

The Mark VIB tank, with armour only a quarter of an inch thick and equipped with two Vickers machine guns, one .303 and the other .5 of an inch, was to prove no match against the heavier German tanks then in service. Its communication system worked well with well trained operators. Crews could communicate by speech over a range of four miles, and there was a Morse capability over a range of some twenty miles if the set could be sited properly. The internal link between the commander and driver was through the old type of speaking tube.

The tank's lightness gave it a speed advantage, and both officers and men believed themselves a match for the German Panzer divisions. What they lacked in firepower and protection was compensated for by courage and determination to uphold the traditions of our army and, in particular, the Regiment.

* * * * *

*Lieutenant Andrew Craig-Harvey*, a young troop leader described that eventful day, 3rd September, 1939—The day war broke out:

"The Regiment occupied Gujarat Barracks, Colchester, having moved from the Cavalry Barracks. The mess was overcrowded with the regular members, reservists and some cross postings. Over forty officers made a fine sight at dinner. Many reserve officers had fought during the Great War and were still subalterns whilst their contemporaries who had served on had become the senior officers of the Regiment.

"The previous evening there had been what could be called an unfortunate incident: two of the elderly subalterns announced that they were going to "roll 'Lucy' up in the hearth rug"—a frequent after-dinner prank. With some difficulty they were dissuaded as Lucy now happened to be Major Jack Anstice, the Second-in-Command of the Regiment. They still thought it unreasonable to abandon what had been a ritual.

"At eleven o'clock there was a gathering in the ante-room to listen to the Prime Minister's broadcast when the outcome of an ultimatum to the Germans would be given. In the doorway, Michael Maude and Alec Scott were deep in a seemingly acrimonious conversation on some matter obviously more important than the impending declaration of war.

"Mr Chamberlain ended the broadcast with the dramatic announcement, 'and so we are at war with Germany'. Immediately, and above the many comments in the mess, was heard 'All right, Alec, all I can say is that if I can't have a three-tonner then I simply can't get the mess silver down to the bank.'

"That evening the main guard was mounted in the usual dress, white sword slings and bandolier, but carrying a pick-helve instead of a sabre. We believed that acts of sabotage might be carried out or that the locals might start looting. This strange weapon had to be scrubbed and carried in a uniform manner. RSM Maurice Peters was tasked to devise a drill. Being a fine figure of a man, he did so with ease.

"The first day had proved to be uneventful; nobody knew quite what to expect. The officers, having had a late and fully licenced evening, retired to bed. Corporal Barber, the mess corporal, disapproved strongly of officers sharing rooms. He had served the mess for many years and sharing was unthinkable.

"Soon after midnight the air raid siren was sounded, having picked up the alarm from the next town. A German aircraft had crossed the coast at high altitude and was making for London. The duty trumpeter took up the message by sounding 'General Alarm' and continued to do so from every vantage point he could find. The officers, reluctant to dress and vacate their rooms, heard the supernumerary trumpeter knocking loudly on the front door of the mess and shouting 'Air raid warning, red'. This he repeated over and over again. Then Corporal Barber's indignant voice could be heard, 'A trumpeter coming to the front door, you young * * *. Go round to the servants' entrance.' Then the more gentle tones of the same Corporal Barber are heard outside each door, 'Gentlemen, there is an air raid warning. Your servants have been warned and are coming up with tea and to enquire which uniform you require'.

"In total darkness we emerged to join others of the Regiment who were milling about trying to get to their appointed places. The trumpeter is having a heyday and is still blowing the 'General Alarm', for it's not often in a trumpeter's life that he can blow this call without the immediate follow-up of 'As you were'.

"The Commanding Officer, the much loved and highly respected Lieutenant Colonel 'Ugly' Martin, who had moved from his own country house into a quarter next to the mess then appeared shouting into the darkness for the Second-in-Command. 'Jack, tell that boy to stop blowing his bloody trumpet, he's already woken Margaret and the children'!"

Thus it was, and with no real premonition of the seriousness of events to follow, that the 5th Royal Inniskilling Dragoon Guards entered World War II.

Captain Neville Ussher, a Supplementary Reserve officer holding the rank of Second Lieutenant, recalls his short-lived military career. Called up on 1st September, 1939, having joined the Regiment from Cambridge seven months earlier, he relates his initiation:

*2nd Lieutenant N A Ussher:*

"I was reading agriculture and in my second year, privileged to be among friends of the same age and interests. We all felt that the storm clouds of war were gathering and little time should be wasted in getting ourselves organised for what seemed a certainty.

"Gilbert Monckton, later to become Major-General the Viscount Monckton of Brenchley, was a fellow student and already responsible for getting a few of us up to Colchester for a week-end on a familiarisation visit. This gave the opportunity for the Commanding Officer to look at us and we to look at the Regiment.

"It was a splendid weekend. Everyone was very kind, helpful and friendly. I was accepted and kitted myself out with service dress, blues, mess kit, sword and Sam Browne, two pairs of breeches and a pair of corduroys from the regimental tailor. I remember it costing much more than the miserable clothing allowance.

"In June, 1939, I was called to join the Regiment at Colchester for six weeks' annual training. In addition to the Supplementary Reserve officers of the Regiment there were many others from other cavalry regiments stationed abroad. Thirty very junior officers and very green young officers were put through their paces. I parked my £12 second-hand Armstrong Siddeley car as far from the mess as I could. It seemed so very out of keeping with the standard of my brother officers. (The poor old car was later used by the Home Guard as a road block. I found it in 1943 and recovered the clock which I still have—in working order).

"It was made very clear that we were in for a very intensive six weeks. The Commanding Officer spoke to us in the mess and, in the nicest possible way, left us in no doubt about the standard expected. 'The Regiment does nothing by halves. It's going to be six weeks of flat-out training and to the top. Second best is not acceptable'. We were each allocated to a Regular junior officer who was responsible for teaching us the ropes. Michael Maude took me under his wing and put me completely at ease.

"Things soon began to fall into place. We were thrown in at the deep end and, of course, being watched all the time by either a senior officer or NCO. I think it was Michael who said, 'Never look as if you are doing nothing, even if you are doing nothing. You must at all times be going to or returning from somewhere'.

"The physical activity included a crash course in drill and there wasn't a lot of time to cover the syllabus. Early morning drill was under Sergeant Gower, who was in turn watched over by RSM Peters. Maurice was a charming man but could put fear and dread into any young subaltern. After four weeks we were thought to be just—but only just—good enough to be examined by the Adjutant, Captain Bill Bovill.

"There had been repeated threats of 'Not good enough, gentlemen, we'll do it again'. Poor Otter-Barry was one of those unfortunates who had difficulty in co-ordinating leg and arm movement—there is usually one in every squad!—and Sergeant Gower could express his annoyance in a most forthright manner!

"Came the day of the passing-out parade and someone forgot his gloves. The parade was cancelled and we were arrayed the following day, properly dressed. Those who had been properly turned out were furious and, of course, passed on their annoyance to the culprit. Had we been passed out on the first occasion we'd have been permitted a day off. Hard but effective discipline.

"The afternoons were absorbed with gunnery, driving and maintenance, tactics, lectures, the rôle of a divisional cavalry regiment (now armoured, but still thinking cavalry), means of supply and a hundred and one other things. One's power of concentration was never permitted to lapse for a second.

"The mess was a friendly place. We soon got to know and talk to the senior officers, who went out of their way to be helpful. And although they were apt to come down on us like the proverbial ton of bricks during working hours, it was all forgotten over a drink later. Life was punctuated by trumpet calls which we all had to learn.

"Orderly officer duty came up with great regularity but the orderly sergeant was always there to help and advise. There was always the dread of a complaint at meal time. Old soldiers were well aware of the failings and lack of knowledge of young officers and ready to take full advantage. I was no exception.

"In the dining hall on my first day of duty, the orderly sergeant struck a table with his whip and announced loudly: 'Orderly officer. Any complaints?' A trooper stood up immediately and said, 'Sir, the liver tastes very bitter and we all think the same.' I tasted it, found it to be quite horrid, and knew from my agricultural training that the cook had failed to remove the gall bladder before cooking. I placed the unfortunate cook on a charge for spoiling several pounds of best liver, and he was given seven days' C.B. (Confined to Barracks, commonly known as Jankers). The news quickly spread and, since the cook was a fairly unpopular man, I gained considerable respect at his expense.

"The training progressed into night driving without lights, and pretty hazardous it was for ourselves and other road-users. The CO was far from satisfied with the first attempt and ordered a repeat performance the following night. Two night' loss of sleep and a pounding during the day also added to my training which was to be put into effect so very soon.

"At the end of the six weeks the Commanding Officer addressed us and said he had no doubt that we would be recalled very quickly and that all our training would be put into effect. He informed us that we still had much to learn but had made a satisfactory beginning. Leave followed.

"My university summer vacation was put to good use at helping to take blackout precautions and distributing gas masks to civilians. Gas had been used extensively only twenty years earlier and the increased range of aircraft made a gas attack a much stronger possibility than a heavy bombing raid. Air raid wardens were appointed and sirens installed.

"During the last days of August the German Army was concentrated on the Polish border—for 'annual maneouvres'. Contingency plans were made to evacuate children from our cities. On Friday, September 1st, the BBC announced that Germany had invaded Poland and added: 'All TA and reservists in possession of instructions as to action to take on mobilisation should act on those instructions forthwith'. In the afternoon a telegram arrived to confirm this.

"I telephoned Kenneth Woods and we agreed to catch the next train, meet in London, and go down to Colchester together. So off I went after cancelling the first partridge day, which had promised to be good!

"In the officers' mess, where we gathered in the evening, there were new faces—those of First World War Reserve officers, some with two rows of medals. We very junior officers liked what we saw and seemed to take to them at once. (Father to son?).

"Saturday, September 2nd, brought much to do. I was sent off to receive the Regular Reservists who were pouring in from all over the country. I had to take down their particulars. Some were AA and RAC patrol men. The majority had finished their services as horsed cavalrymen and had no mechanical training for the new Armoured Cavalry Regiment. But they were splendid chaps, and to me, a twenty-year-old second lieutenant, they were the backbone of the Army we had heard so much about. They were tough, experienced and dedicated to duty. And they had left their wives and children and their settled homes to rejoin the colours.

"We were issued with 'wartime equipment'—Pistol .38 (but no ammunition), field dressings, and a lot of other kit we had not seen before. It was a full day and we were glad to be back in the mess for drinks and dinner."

* * * * *

Another memory of this period comes from *Trumpeter Syd Shepherd*, one of those bandsmen who had joined as a boy soldier in 1929 and had served as a despatch rider (a duty for which many of the band had been trained). "For me, this period was a grand reunion with old friends recalled to the Colours, all of whom had served a minimum of six years—and many twelve or more years—before transferring to the Reserve. The NAAFI manageress, in a real panic, accepted an offer from a few old soldiers to help out. This resulted in much free and cheap drinking by helpers who returned to the barrack rooms with their pockets bulging! Takings, it later turned out, were well down in consequence."

# REGIMENTAL COMMAND STRUCTURE as at 23 SEPTEMBER 1939

| | |
|---|---|
| **Regimental Headquarters** | |
| Lieutenant Colonel J H Anstice | Commanding Officer |
| Major M P Ansell | Second in Command |
| Captain J E Swetenham | Adjutant |
| Captain T C Williamson | Technical Adjutant |
| Lieutenant C H Blacker | Signals Officer |
| 2nd Lieutenant F V Beaufort | Intelligence Officer |
| Captain W Barnes | Quartermaster |
| RQMS D Spridell | Regimental Quartermaster Sergeant |
| RSM M Peters | Regimental Sergeant Major |
| **Headquarters Squadron** | |
| Captain W Barraclough MC | Squadron Leader |
| 2nd Lieutenant W R S Turner | Troop Leader DRs |
| Lieutenant Ginn RAOC | Ordnance Mechanical Officer |
| SSM R Rushton | Squadron Sergeant Major |
| **A Squadron** | |
| Major W F Bovill | Squadron Leader |
| Captain C P D Legard | Second in Command |
| Lieutenant H F Philips | Troop Leader |
| Lieutenant E G B Oates | Troop Leader |
| SSM Hall | Squadron Sergeant Major |
| **B Squadron** | |
| Major A B J Scott | Squadron Leader |
| Captain A Carr | Second in Command |
| Lieutenant The Marquess of Kildare | Troop Leader |
| 2nd Lieutenant B C Fleury-Teulon | Troop Leader |
| SSM Lee | Squadron Sergeant Major |
| **C Squadron** | |
| Major C R P Walker | Squadron Leader |
| Captain J D Anderson | Second in Command |
| 2nd Lieutenant M W V Maude | Troop Leader |
| 2nd Lieutenant G W R Monckton | Troop Leader |
| SSM J Burrows | Squadron Sergeant Major |

# The British Expeditionary Force

The Regiment's orders came through: a small advance party, under command of Captain Arthur Carr, was to be off to France at once. Supplementary Reserve officers were not on the regimental list for overseas duty with the BEF and orders came through that they were to go to Bovington or Lulworth, driving and gunnery schools respectively.

The Regiment moved to France in September, 1939, and was still referred to as Divisional Cavalry, 4 Division, and under the command of Major General D G Johnson, VC, CB, DSO, MC. The precious months between then and May 10th, 1940, when active operations commenced were well spent in individual training, developing initiative and making the men as comfortable as circumstances would allow. These endeavours were crowned with a fair measure of success, as *Lieutenant C H Blacker* writes:

"There were frequent moves and changes of formation—an irksome experience at the time but conducive to adaptability which was to prove invaluable to all ranks at a much later stage. Towards the end of April, 1940, having survived the spring crisis, we reverted to our own division and moved into summer quarters We were billeted in considerable comfort in the Roubaix area, conveniently near but not too close to Divisional HQ at Croise-Laroche on the north-west outskirts of Lille.

"The weather was favourable during the early part of May. Days had lengthened, the sun shone with a pleasant warmth, trees were green with new leaf and only a road here and there damaged by frost remained to remind us of the extremely severe winter we had survived.

"Training, of course, remained with us still, but was none too arduous owing to the unsuitability of the local countryside and the overriding necessity to preserve the life of our tracks for more serious use. To add to the pleasure of life, there were seats in the gardens after dinner, tennis, an abundance of cafés, ENSA productions round the corner, and even a whisper that there might be polo later on.

"The prevailing atmosphere was one of restrained gaiety. Memories of a longish period of rural calm, broken only by intensive training at Vimy in the early spring, followed by weeks of grime in the slums of Lille prior to our move to Roubaix, became imperceptibly lost, slowly fused with those of camp at St-Nazaire, rain at Magnicourt, Christmas at Virlinghem, New Year at Béthune, and hockey on the ice at Mouvaix.

"There were few of us who did not in some measure realise that we were in Roubaix for a reason. Nor was it far to seek, for it was plain to all that during the intermittent periods of alarm we had experienced in the past, the Regiment, together with many other units of the BEF, had been rushed to places on or near the frontier considered suitable as starting points for a German attack on Belgium."

* * * * *

While this activity and training was going on, Neville Ussher was at Bovington learning about the mechanics of the Mk V1B tank and the Bren Carrier. He recalls two noteworthy incidents from that twelve-week course: someone accidentally fired half a belt of .303 through the roof of the hangar, which called for some explanation; and his greyhound had a fight in the mess with Randolph Churchill's bulldog. Randolph blamed his dog for starting it.

After this training he was posted to Perham Down and Tidworth to complete a PT course. Just as memorable as September 3rd is the severity of that 1939-40 winter, and he found cross-country runs particularly uncomfortable. In February, having completed three courses, he was ready for posting back to the Regiment. To his utter dismay he found himself posted to the 12th Lancers, but at least it was to France to join the British Expeditionary Force. His story continues and shows that his initiative training was paying off:

"On February 24th. I left Southampton by overnight boat to Cherbourg. This was my first experience of leaving the country. There was a lot of hanging about on arrival, and no one gave directions. Suddenly the RTO (Railway Transport Officer) appeared: 'What's your regiment?' On telling him it was the 5th Royal Inniskilling Dragoon Guards, I was ordered to 'Get on this train quickly.' As I did so, I realised that I should have replied 12th Royal Lancers but the chance to join my own regiment and friends was too good to miss!

"On arrival at the railhead in Northern France I was asked the same question and gave the same reply. So I arrived with the Regiment at Mouvaux.

"In the morning I reported to Bill Bovill, the Second in Command, who took me to the Colonel, now Jack Anstice. 'Whatever are you doing here? I didn't send for you.' So, explanation was given! 'You'd rather stay here I suppose than go to the 12th Lancers?' 'Yes Colonel, please.' 'I'll talk to Herbert Lumsden and see what I can do. You've broken a lot of rules you know.' I stayed and was delighted to be among friends. I was given a troop of carriers in 'B' Squadron, commanded by Major Perry Harding.

"All through March and April the Regiment were training hard—day and night exercises. There were a number of 'flaps' and, in April, we were moved at a moment's notice to the Belgian frontier.

At first we were billeted in Vimy and I was now in 'C' Squadron under Major Tom Williamson. Training was intense but we did have a bit of time off to go to Lille for dinner when things were quiet. Then, on April 9th, when Germany invaded Norway, we were moved to Lille—a smelly, dirty quarter of the town. Nothing happened and leave was reopened, and normal life resumed.

"On April 17th I celebrated my 21st birthday and out to dinner we went, borrowing the car of our French liaison officer Jacques Ozanne. We had an excellent dinner—lobster I think. Afterwards to Madame Coco, and all the girls were left in no doubt whose birthday it was! I think Tom Williamson told me to report sick next day—at least until lunchtime!"

* * * * *

*Trumpeter Syd Shepherd* recalls this period in France, too:

"Over Christmas the Regiment was billeted in the village of Pérenches. Lieutenant 'Monkey' Blacker and Major Bill Barraclough produced a very excellent play entitled 'The Monkey's Paw'. There was an inter-squadron boxing match, too. The DRs were placed under command of Lieutenant John Ward-Harrison and were well established in an 'estaminet'.

"I remember the Commanding Officer visiting on Christmas Day and predicting that everyone would be home for Christmas the following year. His prediction proved to be partly true, of course, though the circumstances were not those which the Colonel had in mind."

The exchange rate of 200 francs to the pound made for high standards of living during those months of waiting and there was plenty of sport. Rum and coffee before breakfast was a frequent luxury.

Major Mike Ansell arranged a boxing match against the South Lancashire Regiment. (Corporal Griffiths, one of our outstanding boxers, was to be killed later, during the withdrawal). Sport and recreation included hunting, but without well trained hounds. A Breton driving whip presented by Colonel J R W (Mick) Muirland is now on display in our Regimental Museum in Chester, with the inscription which emphasises the ingenuity employed to keep both officers and men active, fit and alert.

*Lieutenant J R W Muirland:*

"The whip, bought in a small shop in Guérande in October 1939, was used by a whipper-in to Lieutenant John Ward-Harrison, when he and his 'pack' were hunting anything that stirred from the ground in the surrounding countryside. Assorted dogs had been rounded up at random in Guérande. Their owners eventually co-operated, though the first round-up resulted in some—ultimately amicable—discussion with the local gendarmerie.

"The pack leader was an ancient basset-hound who started to give tongue as soon as he was collected in the town and continued to do so without pause throughout the proceedings. He was known to the hunt followers as 'Monsieur Le Brun', this from his colour and not with any reference to the then President of France. Needless to say, no Frenchman who heard the animal so addressed believed this. Another participant was a terrier-like creature called 'Kike', the property of a large lady at the local boulangerie. He was imortalised in her benediction whenever he departed for the hunt. 'Ah! le petit Kike, il aime beaucoup le sport'.

* * * * *

"The whole enterprise centred on J W-H's skill and enthusiasm. It provided both a welcome relief from boredom and some much needed exercise for the cavalry reinforcements at the base depot. The quarry, mostly rabbits and an occasional cat, invariably escaped, but that was of small importance. A short report of these activities appeared in either *The Field* or *Country Life* towards the end of 1939, but it has not been possible to check the exact reference."

# Into Action

*Lieutenant C H Blacker* continues:

"The British Expeditionary Force had been placed under the command of the French, and accordingly the C-in-C, General Lord Gort, VC, KCB, CBE, DSC, MVC, MC, received his orders from the Commander of the French North-eastern Front, General Georges. During the winter, plans of a highly secret nature had been prepared by General Georges for an advance into Belgium in the event of a request being made for military assistance. The BEF was allotted this rôle, since much of our training had been designed to prepare us to carry it out.

"That we would eventually advance and fight in Belgium none of us doubted. It is just possible, too, that a few may have foreseen that the action we would be called upon to fight would be of a rearguard nature. Such a view was never expressed, but the emphasis properly placed on this type of action during collective training may well have been noted by the more observant. It is certain, however, that had anyone in the calm of the late evening of Thursday, May 9th, made so bold as to wager that the British columns would once again be winding their way along Belgian roads, lightless in the dark and within twenty-four hours, the Regiment to a man would have offered fantastic odds.

"Early next morning, it was evident that something unusual was afoot. Enemy aircraft were active overhead and the sound of anti-aircraft fire floated through our bedroom windows and we learned from the eight o'clock news bulletin from London of the German invasion of Holland and Belgium. We heard, too, that the King of the Belgians, our Colonel-in-Chief, had invoked allied assistance.

"Shortly afterwards came the expected warning order and the intimation that the Regiment had been placed under command of 3 Division, whose commander summoned the Commanding Officer to a conference in his Lesquins headquarters. A few minutes after 2130 hours, the Regiment swung into its appropriate place in the column moving east. RHQ led, followed by 'C' Squadon under the command of Major T C Williamson, 'B' Squadron commanded by Major A B J Scott, and Headquarters Squadron under the command of Captain W Barraclough MC.

"The night was dark and rather cold and the atmosphere tense, but, once the column had shaken itself out, the march proceeded without incident till dawn. There were desultory cheers from time to time from gaping villagers—cheers that were all but drowned out by the clatter of our steel tracks over their cobbled streets.

"Shortly before first light we were told by an officer at a traffic control point west of Alost that the town had been heavily bombed, with some damage to the bridges which were its exits eastwards. The extent of this damage was unknown to him but he believed we would be able to pass. We entered Alost in half-light and saw for the first time what the Luftwaffe could do.

"The damage seemed considerable at the time, but we were soon to see far more thorough examples than this. Nevertheless, the progress of the column was considerably affected and traffic control, which until now had been excellent, broke down. Movement was intermittent and our speed reduced to a slow walking pace, with all vehicles head to tail. Dawn was breaking and every other onlooker, of whom there were many, shouted good natured advice which seemed tinged with hysteria but may well have been merely Flemish.

"An undamaged bridge was eventually found and the Regiment gradually got clear of the burning town. Since it was now broad daylight, it seemed reasonable to suppose that enemy bombers would soon return. This bridge was slightly south of the one we had intended to use and brought us out on the main Alost-Brussels road, from which we turned left to regain our route at the village of Moorsel. The remainder of the march was uneventful.

"Enemy bombers were active throughout the morning but the Regiment, though not ignored, sustained no casualties. We experienced, however, for the first but by no means the last time, how difficult and unpleasant it was to advance on narrow roads in tanks when faced with closed columns of resolute allied soldiery, equally determined, for reasons which were somewhat obscure, to proceed in the contrary direction. No doubt the same was thought of us.

"At about 0730 hours on Saturday, May 11th, we reached our objective and the Regiment halted and collected itself in the shade afforded by the tall trees which lined either side of the straight road between Cortenburg and Louvain. The Colonel reported himself to Headquarters, 3 Division, which had been established in a spacious but exposed château standing in wooded parkland near Everberg. He learned that we were to billet ourselves in the area Erps-Querps—Olmenhoek—Veltham-Beyssem. This we proceeded to do and, by the early afternoon, all ranks had fed themselves and settled into their new quarters.

"Belgian withdrawals from forward positions had necessitated the immediate occupation by 3 Division on its line astride Louvain. On the evening of Saturday, May 11th, a squadron was also required to cover the crossings over the Dyle Canal to the left of the British position. The bridges in question were in fact the responsibility of Belgian troops, who were already in position, but it was considered expedient to give them the support of armoured troops.

"Major Alec Scott was ordered to deploy his squadron along the canal between the Wijomael crossing and that at Over de Vaart, both inclusive. He placed a carrier troop at each of the four bridges in his sector and retained his tank troops at Squadron headquarters at Doren, a hamlet about a mile due north of Herent. In the meantime, A and C Squadrons were resting in the villages of Olmenhoek and Erps-Querps, respectively. RHQ with B Echelon passed a quiet night at Velthem-Beyssem.

"Already a constant stream of refugees choked the roads which led westward. Traffic control on the main Brussels road soon became impossible after dark. Indeed, it became a vehicular adventure to cross the road, as was necessary to visit our Divisional Headquarters. An ominous sign, too, was the ever increasing trickle of Belgian soldiery from the front now swelling the civilian stream. The 15/19th Hussars were at this time still forward of the river but not yet in contact with the enemy.

"All ranks improved their ability to live off the country, which was not difficult because every other house had been evacuated. Eggs, beer and chickens were abundant. By Monday, May 13th, there were ominous signs that the Belgian Army was not faring too well. It was decided that the Coldstream Guards should move and take over the Belgian sector left of the Grenadiers.

"Difficulties arose because the Belgians had no intention of leaving and indeed refused to do so. It was nevertheless decided to duplicate the defence at this point. Similarly, two tank troops from 'B' Squadron under command of Lieutenant Robert Crockett and TSM Holt were moved forward to the Dyle Canal and to the entrance of an anti-tank obstacle which prolonged the canal defences to the north. This was a formidable affair in iron, about eight feet high and manned by Belgian troops. The morale of these troops was above reproach and permitted our tanks to be withdrawn at dusk.

"A tank patrol led by Lieutenant Humphrey Philips from 'A' Squadron was sent to investigate rumours that the Germans had made a break-through at Hasselt and Diest and a further troop under Lieutenant Michael Maude joined from 'C' Squadron. Both returned without making contact. Early on the morning of May 14th, Lieutenant Gilbert Monckton led a tank troop from 'C' Squadron with an 'A' Squadron troop under command of TSM Ted Imms and repeated this reconnaissance, again without making contact. They had barely returned, however, before definite information was received of a breakthrough at Tiremont, twelve miles south east of Louvain. Contact would surely not be much longer delayed."

* * * * *

*Lieutenant Andrew Craig-Harvey*, who describes events in the Regiment on the outbreak of war, had not been so fortunate as Neville Ussher after his training and found himself posted to the headquarters of an armoured brigade and was appointed intelligence officer to Brigadier Charles Norman, an ex-9th Lancer. He recorded this short-lived career:

"I reported to the Brigadier in April, 1940, and informed him of my lack of experience and qualifications to fill this exalted post. I was told to read it up in Field Service Regulations and to do my best. We were quartered in a charming hotel in the village of Ivry-la-Bataille, south of the Seine. We were alone with no troops to command as they were further north in the Lille area.

"On May 10th, when the Germans struck across the Belgian frontier, the Brigade headquarters consisted of eight officers and 130 men with two trucks and the Brigadier's car. We were ordered to move 130 miles north to Lille and rendezvous with the regiments in the brigade. My task was to travel to Arras and obtain as much transport as possible from the depot there.

"I set off with the two trucks and as many men as they would carry. The roads were already being bombed and were packed with refugees. I collected all the vehicles I could, consonant with the drivers I had. New vehicles with stiff gear-boxes and steering added to the hazards of the journey by night. Our French liaison officer had informed my Brigadier that I had little or no chance of getting the vehicles back because of the bombing and refugee problem and that some other route would be necessary to get the brigade to Lille.

"Incidentally, our liaison officer was none other than Prince Murat, a direct descendant of Napoleon's Marshal. He was a man of large stature, enormous charm and ability. He enquired from the station master how they could get to Lille by train. 'Somewhat complicated but possible' said the station master. 'You take the slow train to Pontoise, where you will have to wait an hour, then catch the local train to Beauvais, wait another hour and then catch the Paris-Lille express. You should get to Lille in about five hours'. Pierre Murat booked eight first-class seats and 130 second-class singles for the following day, but by then I had arrived with the transport.

"A sequel to this is not without interest. Pierre had come to war in his Delage car with chauffeur-valet in attendance. When we set off for Lille, he suggested that we might as well travel together. His valet and my servant were put together in a small car which I had purloined for personal use. Nothing untoward happened until we were north of the Seine when Stukas attacked the road.

"We were now in some of the best shooting country in France, where Pierre had often shot. All too frequently we stopped while he explained the best drives and places where he had stood to obtain a bag of 120 brace per day—quite undeterred by the bombs falling while we lay in a ditch.

"After this guided tour of the partridge shoots, we eventually arrived at a very comfortable château near Lille. The previous residents, the 1st Grenadiers, had signed the visitors' book on the hall table. We added our names. A few days after arrival, and during the confusion of the battle for Belgium, I was travelling with the

Brigade Major. 'Stop', he ordered. We looked northward up the road. 'Well, Andrew, we have considerable distinction. We are the rearguard of the British Army. You realise that we have nobody between us and the German Army.' We withdrew quickly.

"On another occasion, a Gunner major appeared at Brigade headquarters and said that he had just fought on the field of Waterloo but had unfortunately lost his entire battery as he was in the position once occupied by Napoleon.

"My final downfall was a very ordinary incident. We were running very short of petrol. The tanks in the brigade had no auxiliary engine, and the wireless had to be powered by the main engine. As the engines could not be run continually, the main communication had to be by DR. I became the Brigade DR, conveying messages verbally. I set off to contact the East Riding Yeomanry in a location last reported. To my dismay, the Germans were occupying that position. Naturally enough, they greeted me with a shot. I lay on the ground and was soon found by a German officer who demanded my revolver. He spoke perfect English and we had a brief conversation. We discovered that he had been at Oxford while I had been at Cambridge.

"The following day, when being marched along with other prisoners, he passed by in his car, recognised me and told the officer in charge that as a fellow cavalry officer, he was going to give me a lift to the POW cage. He was the only decent German officer I ever encountered."

* * * * *

*Neville Ussher* had been roused from his comfortable bed in a wool merchant's house by his faithful servant, Priestly, and was told: "It's a fine warm day at 6 am. The Germans have invaded Holland and Belgium and have bombed Rotterdam. Battle-dress as usual, Sir?" Ussher was up in a flash and down to Squadron headquarters, where the Colonel had called a conference. The Regiment would move across the Belgian frontier at 2130 hours. Baggage was packed for sending back and the day spent preparing for the move.

I feel it is important to record here the words written by Major-General Roger Evans in his history of the regiment which so perfectly described this moment:

"We may regard the Regiment as it moved off that night from Roubaix as the embodiment of the old order of Cavalry: officers made supple in mind and body by the exertions and hazards of the hunting field, the polo ground and the racecourse; trained to take responsibility and to think and act for themselves in carrying out their commanders' intention; men schooled to use initiative, to act offensively, to ride down their enemy in the same spirit as they had shown when their weapons were horses and the sword. Officers and men lived together, trained together, played together in their years of peace; each was inspired by the spirit of the Regiment—a pride in their great traditions, and a determination to do whatever had to be done with might and main.

"We now used our experience of night driving to effect. There was just the glimmer of the tail light, well hidden from the air, to follow. We arrived at Alost at dawn. Here for the first time was war in all its horror. Now quite suddenly we saw what it was all about. The smoke, the smell, the frightened populace rushing about and not knowing what to do. The Regiment was moving forward fast now. I remember being confused to see Belgian troops, horsed transport in particular, coming to meet us and travelling west! We were moving east to meet the Germans invading their country.

"We travelled through the suburbs of Brussels, found some cover from the air, halted and made a meal. During the early afternoon of May 11th, we arrived at our destination. We rested, each taking turn for duty. We were all very tired, having had no sleep for 36 hours. We were to remain ready to move at a moment's notice. When my turn came to rest I found a farmhouse and requested a bed for a few hours. I was joined by another officer but I forget who it was. We were shown an enormous bed covered with a large feather mattress. Boots off only, we got on to the bed and to sleep, but were awakened after only an hour. It was not an emergency, but the arrival of two, three or perhaps four enormous Belgian women, presumably farm workers, who had returned to their bed. They were surprised, to say the least, to find it occupied by two fully-dressed British officers. We left hurriedly!"

* * * * *

*Lieutenant Blacker* describes the regimental move forward:

"Our infantry had consolidated their positions while the Belgian Army poured back over the temporary bridges and through Louvain. There were dense columns of horse-drawn artillery, cavalry and infantry on every road leading west. Refugees of all ages added inextricable complications. Roads and bridges were being heavily bombed.

"The dejected appearance of the retreating troops and their obvious confusion was most disturbing. There were rumours that gas was being used. Some of these rumours may have been deliberately originated by German parachutists and fifth-column agents. At 1700 hours the 15/19th Hussars reported contact with the enemy on the Tirlemont road. Shortly afterwards they were withdrawn into a reserve position behind us. At about 2230 hours Major Scott reported that his right-hand troop, led by Lieutenant Turner, was being attacked and was in action against the enemy. Later that evening, the Commanding Officer decided to relieve B Squadron, which had had an anxious time. Major Perry Harding led his Squadron to take over at 2100 hours."

# REGIMENTAL COMMAND STRUCTURE as at 10 MAY 1940

| | |
|---|---|
| **Regimental Headquarters** | |
| Lieutenant Colonel J H Anstice | Commanding Officer |
| Major W F Bovill | Second in Command |
| Lieutenant C H Blacker | Adjutant |
| Lieutenant J R W Muirland | Technical Adjutant |
| 2nd Lieutenant B C Fleury-Teulon | Signals Officer |
| Lieutenant F A Stockdale | Intelligence Officer |
| Major W Barnes | Quartermaster |
| RQMS D Spridell | Regimental Quartermaster Sergeant |
| RSM M Peters | Regimental Sergeant Major |
| **Headquarters Squadron** | |
| Captain W Barraclough MC | Squadron Leader |
| Lieutenant E G B Oates | Liaison Officer |
| Captain H Nicholl | Ordnance Mechanical Officer |
| The Reverend A Saunderson | Padre |
| Lieutenant M Chamberlain | Medical Officer |
| SSM R Rushton | Squadron Sergeant Major |
| TSM McCullough | Troop Leader Despatch Riders |
| **A Squadron** | |
| Major R P Harding | Squadron Leader |
| Captain J E Swetenham | Second in Command |
| Lieutenant H F Philips | Troop Leader |
| 2nd Lieutenant C H Terrot | Troop Leader |
| TSM E Imms | Troop Leader |
| TSM Crawley | Troop Leader |
| TSM Crouch | Troop Leader |
| TSM Adams | Troop Leader |
| SSM Hall | Squadron Sergeant Major |
| **B Squadron** | |
| Major A B J Scott | Squadron Leader |
| Captain A Carr | Second in Command |
| Lieutenant A. C. Gibson | Troop Leader |
| Lieutenant J R Crockett | Troop Leader |
| 2nd Lieutenant W R I Turner | Troop Leader |
| TSM Holt | Troop Leader |
| TSM R A Baker | Troop Leader |
| TSM Bevington | Troop Leader |
| SSM Lee | Squadron Sergeant Major |

**C Squadron**

| | |
|---|---|
| Major T C Williamson | Squadron Leader |
| Captain D Gregson | Second in Command |
| Lieutenant M W V Maude | Troop Leader |
| Lieutenant G W R Monckton | Troop Leader |
| TSM J Robinson | Troop Leader |
| Sgt Catley | Troop Leader |
| SSM J Burrows | Squadron Sergeant Major |
| Lieutenant E N Barran | ADC to GOC 4 Division |

* * * * *

*2nd Lieutenant Turner*, of Third Troop, 'B' Squadron gave his own account of this action:

"At about midnight on May 11-12th, I was ordered to take my troop to a bridge near Louvain and to give assistance to the Belgians holding it. I arrived in pitch darkness and with difficulty found the Belgian officer in charge and informed him of my presence. He asked me to position two of my Bren carriers to cover the far side of the river.

"He informed me of a small pontoon bridge, some 400 yards to the right and towards Louvain, which was being used by about a hundred Belgians who were occupying a position in a factory on the far side. He said the bridge was already prepared for demolition and that, if his troops were driven from the factory, they would cross and destroy it.

"The following morning I took a look at this pontoon and noticed that, although there were pillboxes all along the bank, nothing really covered the bridge. Since it was to be blown up, however, there was no reason for concern. I made a closer inspection of the pontoon and, to my real concern, found that no preparation had been made to demolish it. A Belgian corporal, who said he was in charge of the demolition, explained that the necessary material was at his company's headquarters, but assured me that it would be brought along that morning. I was to learn later that I should never have accepted this assurance.

"I then visited a number of pillboxes and found the occupants to be in good heart and confident that they could hold the river position, though they did appear a lot of poor soldiers. At lunchtime we were recalled to proceed with three other troops of the squadron to the town of Haecht, where we were to help the Belgians to search for reported parachutists. We had quite an enjoyable day which included a meal with a Belgian regiment who, I believe, were the 5th Chasseurs, a cavalry regiment who had only just lost their horses.

"At about 1800 hours on returning to the Squadron headquarters, we were given fresh instructions by wireless. My troop was to return to the original position on the bridge. We were not too happy about this change. It was already getting dark and we had looked forward to a well deserved rest. On arrival at the bridge, at about 2200 hours, I went to sleep. We had averaged about two hours' sleep during the past five days and were feeling very tired.

"May 13th dawned quietly enough until a German plane flew over us at about 40 feet. We threw ourselves to the ground. I landed in a manure heap! Smoke was pouring from the plane, which narrowly missed some trees before crashing. I learned later that one of our cooks had claimed it with a burst from his Bren gun.

"My instructions included an order that any civilian approaching from the far side was to be halted by a shot in the air and to turn him or her back. It was expected that they might bring Germans with them. I heard the soldier on duty fire a single shot but took little notice as this had become a frequent event. After about five minutes he fired another shot and this was followed by a long burst from the Belgians.

"I found on investigation that a man had approached the bridge on three separate occasions. On the first approach he was on a bicycle, with a red blanket around him. The second approach was without the bicycle, but still wearing the blanket. On the third approach he was again mounted on his bicycle and had drawn fire which killed him. I at first blamed the Belgians for this but, on searching him and finding only a letter in German and some Polish money, I accepted that our man had bagged him!

"My sleep that night was again disturbed by the Belgians who changed their troops over at 0200 hours. The 14th dawned quietly and slowly broke into a nice, sunny day. We made friends with our new Belgians and, as on previous days, I visited my little pontoon bridge to find out what progress had been made with the demolition plans. As ever, nothing had been done. The corporal was still there and assured me that the gun-cotton was on its way. As soon as it arrived, he would prepare it. This was becoming a real thorn in my side and I told him in my best French that it was high time that something was done. At 1730, Robert Crockett arrived on a motorcycle and informed me that the Germans were reported some twenty kilometres away. We were to remain very alert!

"In addition, I was to open up on my wireless set at 1800 hours. When I did so, my Squadron Leader informed me that the enemy was in fact nine kilometres away. I made for the bridge with all haste and, to my horror, found the situation unchanged. The corporal was still sitting there waiting for something to turn up! I was not alone in my concern for the demolition of this bridge and had been asked many times to give a progress report.

"I grabbed the corporal's bicycle and rode down the towpath to the Coldstreams, who were by then in action. I borrowed, without hope of returning, six Mills grenades. I returned and gave the corporal three of them. Then I noticed an 8 cwt truck which had been left for a time by the forward observation officer of the Gunners. He was, I discovered, in the highest part of the factory which was on the far side of the river. I took it, and the corporal, to his company headquarter—where after what seemed hours but was in fact about fifteen minutes—we were given a supply of gun cotton and fuses but, alas, no detonators!

"On being assured that these would be brought along the moment they arrived from the battalion headquarters, we hurried back through a maze of barbed wire road blocks now placed in position. All had to be moved and replaced. Fortunately, only days previously, I had watched some of our own engineers prepare and demolish the remains of the main bridge which had been hit by a 500lb bomb. On arrival at the bridge, star shells were bursting almost overhead and the Belgian corporal refused to work on the far side.

"My short experience with the REs was to pay dividends, for I had to prepare the far side myself. Whilst this was going on, a star shell landed plumb in the middle of the room in which the OP officer had been only minutes earlier and only just before I had returned his truck. Just as we had completed the demolition preparation, the electric detonators arrived and I breathed a heavy sigh of relief. I came off that bridge with shrapnel landing in the water so close that I felt the splashes.

"I returned to the troop who were very keen to have a go at the advancing Germans. It was after dark when we made our first contact with the enemy, who had by now occupied the houses on the opposite bank. There was sudden firing all along the bank on our side. This caused the Germans to pause and make a new plan. At 2230 hours came my first real experience of war when our artillery put down a barrage on to the far bank positions. Shells passed over our heads. We were very tense during the first ten minutes but were well protected in our positions and had no qualms about our safety.

"After fifteen minutes, one of the drivers came forward to join me, I think mainly for some company. He was able to assure me that our wireless was working well. I was positioned with one of the machine-gunners and about one hundred yards from the set. Half of that distance was open country. There was a very full moon and I knew I would make a wonderful target. I had to make a dash for it. Two tracer bullets were fired at me from the direction of the factory, which helped speed me up. One of the older soldiers in the troop reassured me by informing me that the firing of tracer at a man was against the rules of war. 'Tracer rounds were intended for firing at planes' he informed me! I sent back a message forgetting all procedures and call signs and reporting simply: 'I am being attacked'.

"Our own barrage had only just ceased when the Germans opened up. I believe they call it 'counter-fire'. Once again it passed over our heads but making a completely different noise. Our shells sounded like someone whistling with too much air in his mouth. The German shells reminded me of the sound of a tracked vehicle going flat out over a paved road. While this hate session was going on, there was some intermittent firing at us from the opposite bank of the river. Then our artillery really got angry and put down a barrage which landed near the opposite bank and slowly worked away from us, pushing the Germans with it. They never fired another shot that night.

"Soon after the barrage had ceased, I received a message over the wireless that my Squadron Leader, Major Alec Scott, was coming up to see me. As the second Belgian line of defence in our rear continued to fire I knew this would pose some danger for Alec, who would have to travel through it. My operator volunteered to return to the Belgian line to warn them, but soon returned saying that he couldn't make himself understood. Off he went for the second time, met Alec, and returned. Of course by this time the Germans had retreated and I had nothing to show him!

"Dawn broke the following day with the Germans back in the factory but, apart from a little firing, the day was quiet with the exception of two periods, each of about half an hour's duration, when the Germans shelled us with high explosives timed to explode over our heads. This was done very accurately but after a few rounds we were able to recognise the sound of the gun firing and the shells' approach. This gave us plenty of time to get under cover.

"Throughout the day our own artillery fired with great success. At 1930 hours a message was received that we were to be relieved at 2100 hours. This was wonderful news for we were very tired. But they were 35 minutes late and we were beginning to think we would have to remain there for another night. We were told to return to Velthem-Beyssem—a route which took us through our own gun positions where, at five second intervals, guns fired at very close proximity. In the five days of this action, the best sleep I had experienced had been in the seat of the Bren carrier. In Velthem-Beyssem we were able to sleep in proper beds. What luxury!"

# The Beginning of the Withdrawal

The Regiment was by now engaged all along the front, the main task being to cover the infantry withdrawal. Final abandonment of the position was ordered at 2100 hours on May 16th. The withdrawal was to be through Herent and Velthem-Beyssem. All went according to plan, but was interrupted by isolated snipers who laid up in the woods and shot at DRs as they moved from troop to troop. German parachustists were blamed, but it is more probable that these incidents were the handiwork of fifth columnists or isolated Belgians who mistook us for Germans. One DR was shot at by one of our own Boyes anti-tank riflemen. The bullet penetrated the rider's steel helmet and left a slight cut on his head. He was indeed fortunate to suffer no other injury.

On May 17th the Regiment drove through Brussels. It was a clear spring day, the streets were crowded, and civil police directed the traffic. Fair damsels thrust cake, chocolate and other sweetmeats into the grateful hands of our hungry men. The Bren carrier crews fared better than the tank crews because they were easier to reach. The population seemed unaware that they were about to be overrun by the Germans.

The bridges over the canals had been prepared for demolition and were being held by men of our old division whom we had not seen since May 10th. Immediately we were across, the bridges were blown, leaving the inhabitants to their fate on the wrong side. One pathetic woman, wiser than the others, pale and distraught, implored us to take her across with us, but this could not be. With a hopeless shrug she returned to await her fate, her dusky dress drab in the brilliant sunshine . . .

Trumpeter Syd Shepherd was one of those DRs who had experienced the snipers. He was working with 'A' Squadron under the command of Major Perry Harding. During one of the halts during the retreat through Belgium he took a walk into a wood and to his surprise found a complete regiment of Belgian Cavalry. The horses were unattended and some were loose. On closer inspection he found an old friend with 5DG clearly marked on its hoof. Sounds of merriment issued forth from a local café indicating that the occupiers were making the most of the deserted premises.

Much later on he remembered seeing Trooper Lionel Rudd, a fellow DR, riding a cavalry horse in the direction of Dunkirk. He had lost his motor-cycle. Syd was given a message to convey to the officer responsible for the demolition of a bridge in Oudenarde. He was to tell the officer that one of our troops was still on the other side and that the bridge was not be be blown until it crossed. The agitated officer gave poor Syd some stick, demanding to know who the hell he thought he was and did he realise that he was putting the whole of the BEF in jeopardy. "I was more than relieved when Major Harding appeared in his tank and took the steam out of the situation," said Syd.

* * * * *

*Lieutenant Ussher* relates his experience in this withdrawal:

"On May 15th I was on the Dyle Canal opposite a blown railway bridge. We were on the left of the Coldstreams, who were fully engaged with the enemy. In front of me was a Belgian pillbox from which occasional bursts of fire were aimed at the enemy on the opposite bank. I made contact with the occupants, four rather scruffy soldiers. We had a glass of wine and they gave me a large box of grenades. Just as I arrived back with the troop, I saw one of the Belgians I had been talking to leave the pillbox and start to swim across the canal. He was about half way across when his comrades in the pillbox opened fire and killed him. I supposed that he had deserted.

"I organised my night fire positions to cover the broken bridge and the railway track on the opposite bank. There was a lot of shooting but I thought the enemy were firing at random and had not picked out our position. The Coldstreams were very heavily engaged on my right and stretcher parties were passing through my position making their way to the rear. I remember a Guards sergeant in charge of two or three parties, who on seeing me, an officer, ordered 'Eyes right—eyes front!' Surely no-one but a guardsman would do that in the middle of a battle.

"The main German attack came upon my position at Wyjael at 2100 hours. We also experienced the use of tracer against us. We returned the fire. Many bullets struck our vehicles but we suffered no casualties. I hoped our fire was being effective but it was too dark to see. At 2300 hours, enemy fire ceased and the night sky was lit with fires all round our positions. I could not tell whether the enemy had crossed the canal, so we could only continue to fire at the opposite bank and hope. At midnight two tank troops commanded by Michael Maude and Gilbert Monckton arrived to help me out. The Coldstreams, though now suffering many dead and wounded, continued to fight on gallantly.

"As we withdrew, carrying the surviving Coldstreams, the Germans managed to get rafts across the canal just in front of our position. This, the first action my troop had experienced, was accentuated by the smell of explosions, noise and sweat, dust, and heat of battle. We had done our bit by holding our position for a few hours but the odds were against us. The whole front was being overrun by sheer weight of numbers and superior weaponry.

"For two hours we travelled west to our next line of defence—Wetenburg-Steer-Ockerzell. It was very cold at 0200 hours on the morning of May 16th. We halted and were permitted four hours' sleep, lying beside our vehicles. This was for most of us the first experience of going without sleep for three days. Added to the fatigue of the battle, having not washed or shaved, we must have appeared a pretty dishevelled bunch. During these four hours we did manage to put this right, clean our guns, and receive a replenishment of ammunition. Hot drink and food was a welcome bonus at dawn.

"For me, this was the time when I realised we had 'withdrawn'. The thought of meeting the enemy and withdrawing had not previously occurred to any one of us. We had expected to hold our ground and then advance, not retire. We rushed from bridge to bridge giving the infantry as much support as we could, only leaving the position when we were sure that all our troops were safely across.

"It was a near thing at times. The whole operation being handicapped by masses of refugees moving west. It was a dreadful sight: the tears and terror in the faces of children and the elderly who had experienced this 25 years before. There was strafing from the air, too: many thousands of those poor wretched refugees were machine-gunned as they fled.

"The 15/19th Hussars were cut off on one occasion when a bridge behind them was blown prematurely. We managed to keep another bridge open for them but they suffered heavy casualties. Michael Maude was knocked out on one of these crossings. We thought that he and his crew had been killed but I was to meet him later as a prisoner of war. He had lost a leg. We were to be together for the next three and a half years.

"TSM Ted Imms was hit by a bullet which passed through his helmet, causing a graze. After medical attention he carried on. Ted was a worthy recipient of the DCM for the action he led here. For the Regiment's involvement in this withdrawal, Tom Williamson received a DSO; Alex Scott an MC, and Gilbert Monckton an MC for a later action.

"It is difficult to remember which events occurred on specific nights but I remember the wonderful feeling of comradeship in the troop. The horrific experience in which we had all shared had brought us very close to each other. We longed for a rest and a bath, but both were unlikely! We now saw the scenes we had read about: dead, stinking animals; dead soldiers; refugees without hope; fires and destruction. This was no dream but reality.

"We were through Brussels now. My driver was too tired to drive and I drove our carrier through the city. A well-dressed man spoke to me in perfect English and asked if I would accept a pair of Holland and Holland shot guns: 'mustn't be found with these,' he said. He pushed them on to my ammunition boxes but they were pushed off by Trooper Angel and run over by the vehicle following.

The crowds seemed to be moving in all directions, presumably trying to locate relatives and friends to face yet another occupation.

"West of Brussels we were able to halt in an orchard, now in leaf and giving some protection from the air. Food and rations appeared miraculously, but we were soon on our way to Mouvaux, just across the French frontier. It was a delight to find billets and, above all, a bath! During those 24 hours chickens were caught and plucked. There was no shortage of wine but the news grew worse. Arras and Amiens, battlegrounds of the Great War, had fallen. The Germans were pouring through a gap in the French lines on a 60-mile front. They had reached Calais and we were surrounded.

"The Colonel gathered the Regiment together in an open park and spoke to us all. He congratulated us on our achievements in Belgium, thanked us for our loyalty and unquestioning trust in his command, and paid tribute to those who had fallen during the retreat. He explained the gravity of the situation and expressed his complete confidence in our ability to meet whatever was to come with the spirit and determination to overcome all difficulties.

"How delighted I was that I still had all my Michelin maps of the area. All issue maps were hopelessly out-of-date, Great War editions!"

* * * * *

At the time of the initial attack upon our sector the Commanding Officer, having been told by Major-General Montgomery that it might be necessary for our C Squadron to assist the Coldstreams re-establish their position, made his way forward with Lieutenant Blacker to confer with Brigadier Whitaker, who was in command of the 7th Guards Brigade.

*Lieutenant Blacker* wrote this account of that meeting and subsequent action.

"The Brigade headquarters was situated on some high ground overlooking Louvain. The car could not be brought closer than a mile because the track was too narrow so we had to walk along a sandy track, winding upwards between high banks. In the bushes on either side lay wounded and bandaged soldiers, while every hundred yards one came upon a group of civilians who had been arrested as fifth columnists. Their captors were enormous Guardsmen who had removed their shoes and tied gags in their mouths. Whenever the suspected spies annoyed their captors, the gag was given a sharp twist, the wretched men, who were nearly all very small and seedy, were almost wrenched off their feet.

"The Brigadier was concealed in a dug-out and it was difficult to find him. He explained the outline of a counter-attack, for which he required two of our tank troops. We were introduced to the commanding officer of the Royal Horse Artillery who would support the attack. We then drove to 'C' Squadron and warned

Lieutenants Monckton and Maude to bring their troops to the headquarters of the Coldstreams. The CO, Lieutenant-Colonel Cazenove, Colonel Jack Anstice, and I descended into a murky cellar in Herent, where we found that he had been working out details of the intended attack by the light of a candle.

"There were a lot of people in the cellar and I wondered how we would stand the awful atmosphere. Outside the sun blazed down, while an enormous column of smoke drifted up from burning Louvain. Colonel Cazenove decided that a personal reconnaissance was necessary. Maude and Monckton arrived. Colonel Cazenove announced his intention of sending each of their individual tanks down to the canal and to take a look at the ground. He himself proposed to travel with one of them.

"They eventually departed, Colonel Cazenove travelling with Monckton. They returned in about ten minutes having been shot at by anti-tank guns, though not before they had seen what they wanted. There followed a hectic half-hour's planning. Our two tank troops were to form the spearhead and were to keep the enemy's head down while the Coldstreams' carrier platoons got into position, after which one company was to make the final assault. The whole operation was to be preceded by a bombardment by the RHA.

"At last the Gunner CO gave the order for the bombardment to begin, and a tremendous barrage immediately commenced. Both banks of the Dyle were plastered for a quarter of an hour. As soon as it stopped, the two tank troops were off. This was the first deliberate attack we had made and one could feel the tension. At the last moment Colonel Cazenove got on to one of the tanks to accompany them. In a quarter of an hour they cleared the enemy from the western bank of the canal. The artillery barrage had been so accurate that the Germans had retired at once and our counter attack had no difficulty in re-establishing the Coldstreams to their original line of defence."

* * * * *

*Lieutenant C H Terrot* added his account of his troop's withdrawal from the Dyle on May 16th and 17th:

"Neville Ussher's report on the wireless stating that he had been attacked was a warning that trouble was brewing for all of us. The Coldstreams were making their heroic stand against enormous odds which will ever be remembered as one of the bravest defensive actions during the period between May 10th and June 1st. We could hear the battle raging as the Germans attempted to cross by pontoon bridges and little boats, though each successive wave was driven back leaving some 75 per cent of their troops dead or wounded. Their bodies piled up in mounds to provide the German machine-gunners and their mortar detachments with a certain amount of cover.

"The Coldstreams had been ordered to fight to the last round and the last man, and they did exactly that. We were ordered to move to a position nearer to Neville Ussher and were in turn relieved by a troop of the 15/19th Hussars. We drew fire as we approached the new position and the offside track of one of my carriers was damaged. The driver heroically repaired it. Then came orders to withdraw to Erps-Querps.

"Just before we left, a raft was pushed across the canal carrying six enormous dogs. There had been reports that patrols had been using such dogs, trained to sniff out and indicate troop positions. They were great brutes, but nevertheless it wasn't pleasant to turn our guns on them as they trotted towards us. They were innocent victims of war.

"We were a little upset when a Belgian anti-tank gunner fired on us as we left. Fortunately the shot was very wide. By this time, the Belgians were firing at anything that moved, whether friend or foe.

"On May 19th the Regiment planned to arrive at new positions on the River Dendre and to take up position during darkness. Due to congestion on the roads, they arrived at 0530 hours. They were covering a front from Ninove on the right (but excluding the village itself) to Iddergem. The whole front was some three miles in width for one squadron alone. The infantry commenced their withdrawal at 0700 hours and were completely away by 0900 hours. The division on the right flank withdrew at 1000 hours leaving no defence there at all. At 1100 hours we also withdrew, leaving one troop watching the exits from Ninove. The whole operation was a success but regrettably, as one of the troops withdrew, they were shot up by a party of the enemy who had made a crossing in the Ninove area. Trooper Tingle was killed during this action.

"I took up my position on the river and walked to the other positions with my three section leaders. I had a difficult area of some 600 yards to cover with my three vehicles and twelve men. It had been defended by at least a hundred men before I took over. The uneven ground sloped down to a street of ruined houses, between two factories. I could not actually see the river.

"The Northumberland Fusiliers' company commander, from whom I had taken the position, informed me that they had experienced a pretty sticky time on the river bank but, at the time of hand-over, only indirect mortar fire and some sniping was taking place. I positioned the three carriers behind a wall surrounding a football ground.

"The wall stretched some 200 yards along this sector. The two Bren guns and three anti-tank rifles were placed into good dug-in positions behind this wall and within the area of the football ground. I told them to knock holes in the wall and dodge about, firing from different positions, so that the enemy would think there were more troops than I had.

"I was in wireless contact with the 'B' Squadron carrier troop and with Neville Ussher, but the distance between us was too great to be covered with our limited weapons. I made use of a DR who was attached to the troop to watch the gap between us. Nothing serious happened during the first hour. The enemy was probably having a problem bridging the river. The artillery barrage described earlier came down and was most effective but was not long left unchallenged. The German counter-barrage was of equal ferocity. There was no further reply from our guns, either because they had been hit or had already withdrawn. I suspected the latter. We knew that trouble would soon follow.

"At 1018 hours we were harrassed by fire from the factory in front of our position. The troop on my left reported that they were engaging enemy on motor-cycles. It took the Germans about fifteen minutes to reach the railway line in front, but they did so at enormous cost. Our Bren gunners, well concealed, were able to cut them down, however, but they still came at us in swarms, making no attempt to take cover. We continued to fire over open sights as fast as we could change the magazines. The Germans gave the football ground a wide berth, believing I suppose that our main force was there and that they could outflank it. The action lasted sixteen minutes, but seemed a lifetime. Fortunately the well-prepared positions left by the Northumberlands gave excellent protection and there were no casualties.

"At 1058 hours two enemy armoured cars appeared on my right flank. Both were knocked out by the anti-tank rifles. The noise was tremendous. Contact by shouting became impossible, nor could whistle blasts be heard. Fortunately, I had made a pre-arrangement to signal our withdrawal by firing a Very light. As we sped down the road leading to our next position I felt that we had given a very good account of ourselves and had dealt the enemy a heavy blow. None of the vehicles was seriously damaged though an armour-piercing shot had penetrated one vehicle and destroyed a tin of soup!"

* * * * *

*Lieutenant Blacker:*

"The Regiment left Mouvaux on May 23rd and headed for Locon, a small hamlet some four miles north of Béthune. No further orders had been issued and none of us had any recent information as to the situation, though our Commanding Officer was at that time in conference at Pérenches. There was no road in the whole of France known better to all ranks than the route we took from Mouvaux to Locon that day.

"Wambrechies, Verlingham, Pérenches, Radingham, Fromelles, Aubers . . . each of these small villages held some kind of memory from the recent eight months spent in waiting. Still untouched by bombs or shell fire, the countryside looked very familiar as the tanks and carriers rattled over the cobbles as though bound for one of the usual regimental exercises.

"We soon joined the La Bassée Canal and within sight of Festubert and Givenchy. A red glow reflected on a column of smoke left, no doubt, as to the position of Béthune, in which the battle for possession was still continuing.

"To our left the familiar spire of La Bassée was surrounded by many fires. Already the defence line of the canal had been attacked. No sooner had 'A' Squadron, who were leading, arrived at Locon, than they were ordered to Le Hamel to support the infantry holding this canal line. At the same time 'B' Squadron was despatched at once to Morbecque, nearly 20 miles north, where the enemy had made a breakthrough near Aire. 'A' Squadron then received a change of orders and were ordered to join the remainder of the regiment at Sailly, near Estaires.

"The Regiment was now under command of Major-General Curtis of the 46th Division, a Territorial Army Division only recently landed in France. Nevertheless, they were to play a very gallant part in the latter stages of the retreat. The troops were chiefly from those early Militiamen, brought to France to dig support lines. They were very inadequately armed and were trying to hold a front of 70 miles. At the time of our arrival, the position on their front was extremely difficult, for Aire, a key point, and a section of the canal to the north had already been penetrated by enemy tanks backed up by motorised infantry.

"Our Regiment was virtually the only reserve General Curtis had under his command. The news from Aire, newly arrived at divisional headquarters, caused our orders to be changed yet again. We were now to proceed to Morbecque as fast as our vehicles would permit and endeavour either to thrust the enemy back over the canal or prevent any further advance.

" 'B' Squadron were at that time some miles ahead of the main body. They turned about and continued through Estaires and Merville and the Forest of Nieppe. As the main body entered the forest, three Dornier bombers flew very low over the column and up the main road leading between trees to Hazebrouck. We could see a large fire some two miles ahead. This proved to be a lorry, bombed by these aircraft.

"This was not the full extent of their attack, for one of the 'B' Squadron carriers had been blown off the road and wrecked. The crew were badly burned and Lieutenant Turner in the following carrier had been wounded. Our haste was too great to permit any vehicle but the ambulance to halt and assist. Morbecque was but two miles distant. On arrival, all three squadrons spread out, 'A' on the right, 'B' centre and 'C' on the left.

"General Curtis had already made a personal reconnaissance in a 'B' Squadron tank and declared that the Regiment should first determine the extent of the enemy breakthrough and then try to prevent deeper penetration. The three villages of Blaringhem, Boéseghem and Thiennes were the main strategic points on our front and one of these was included in each squadron's front. Dusk was falling when the leading troops advanced towards these objectives. Very soon information was coming in: 'A' Squadron had found Blaringhem to be strongly held by enemy heavy tanks and infantry; 'B' had been able to advance to Boéseghem, only to find that enemy infantry were occupying the woods on the near side of the canal. But 'C', on the left, reached Thiennes and the canal unopposed and were able to patrol for the whole night along the line of the road into the Forest of Nieppe.

"It had been noticed that the Germans offered little attention once dusk fell. They made no further attempt to advance after 1800 hours, obviously consolidating the gains of the day. As soon as darkness fell, it became normal practice to see white Very lights marking the forward positions, presumably to guide supply columns to replenish. German echelons responsible for the main supply seemed to be very close behind the fighting troops. The night invariably allowed sufficient time for the armoured and motorised formations to recommence their advance by about 0800 the following day.

"At no time during the whole campaign did we experience any serious night attack. On this occasion, however, the Germans were not going to permit any of our troops to approach their recently gained territory too closely. Attempts by 'A' Squadron tanks to enter Blaringhem were repulsed with heavy fire. It was obvious that the village was very strongly held by a force which included an array of anti-tank weapons. It was also obvious that it was part of a force quite capable of breaking through our defences should it make a determined attempt.

" 'A' Squadron, now in a precarious position and out of touch with 'B' Squadron on their left, decided on a policy of bluff. Under cover of darkness, the tanks of TSM Ted Imms's troop rattled up and down the lanes along the 'A' Squadron front. Whether the enemy were deceived or not, they certainly made no attempt to move that night, for which we were all extremely thankful.

"May 24th dawned into yet another brilliantly sunny day, but the early morning was suspiciously quiet. Until 1000 hours we had no inkling that this day was to be perhaps the most critical we were to experience. It was at this time that some 30 enemy tanks advanced out of Lynde and advanced across country in the direction of Morbecque and Hazebrouk. With our rear communication and our regimental headquarters so threatened, 'B' Squadron was rapidly withdrawn to the rear of Morbecque to protect brigade headquarters and the main Hazebrouck road from this expected flank attack.

" 'A' Squadron holding the position in the area, were vainly trying to stem the rapid advance of these tanks, which were of a medium type, armed with a cannon and several automatic weapons and were quite impervious to our own armour-piercing weapons. Despite a brave resistance, 'A' Squadron was forced by the onslaught to the outskirts of Morbecque, having suffered the loss of several vehicles and their crews.

" 'C' Squadron also withdrew to Morbecque to form a concentrated square around brigade and regimental headquarters. Our only anti-tank weapons were some rather doubtful French anti-tank guns and our own Boyes rifles which were arranged as a battery pointing down the main road. We knew they would be of little value against the enemy mediums, unless one could hit a track. It was a very critical position to be in.

"There was no doubt that, had these German tanks chosen to continue their advance on Morbecque, it would have been impossible to protect the brigade headquarters. There was no apparent reason why they did not do so: they knew their superiority and could have ploughed straight through our position to Hazebrouck. But Morbecque, now surrounded by waiting men, remained quiet for an hour and a half. Then we realised that the Germans had never planned to allow their tank columns to batter their heads against resistance. Their task was to find and exploit the gaps on the flanks. Having found any number of armoured vehicles defending an area, they were diverted elsewhere to find a better hunting ground. 'A' and 'C' Squadrons again advanced to the line La Belle-Hôtesse-Steebecque, while 'B' Squadron remained in reserve.

"At about 1300 hours, brigade headquarters reported that the greater part of a battalion of Northumberland Fusiliers were surrounded by German medium tanks at Boéseghem, on the Morbecque-Aire road and just in front of 'C' Squadron's position. We were ordered to counter attack and extricate them. 'C' Squadron, with a squadron of 13/18th Hussars, were ordered to advance under cover given by the artillery. They were to advance to Boéseghem and somehow keep the Germans occupied so as to permit the infantry to slip away. The attack was successful and had the effect of releasing a large number of German tanks from Boèseghem. These tanks advanced across our front towards Hazebrouck and again 'A' and 'C' Squadrons became engaged with them."

* * * * *

*Lieutenant Ussher* recalls this action:

"About midday we were approaching the Forêt de Nieppe and the Aire canal to the south west of Hazebrouck. There were many canals and deep ditches which were tank obstacles. At Morbecque, the small village on the top of a hill, we halted and I had orders to proceed to a canal to the south and deny the crossing to the enemy. When I got there I found I had a mile-wide front and so we got busy trying to set up a camouflaged position using flower pots, sticks etc to pretend we were there in force. How crazy this seems now! We were there all night but not attacked.

"The battle seemed to be on my right flank. At dawn I was withdrawn and almost at once sent off again down the main road into the Forêt de Nieppe, where it was reported that the enemy were advancing with infantry and anti-tank guns. German tanks had not then been seen.

"On entering the Forêt de Nieppe it soon became obvious that the enemy were moving up through the trees and we opened fire on all we saw and advanced quite a long way into the wood. My Boyes rifle came into play—almost for the first time. This .5 anti-tank rifle was supposed to penetrate armour plate, but it was good for shooting at the enemy crossing the road from one side of the wood to the other. Like shooting rabbits crossing a ride! We made several sorties but were not hit. There were other remains left there from earlier encounters.

"The German shelling and mortar fire became more accurate and we were pulled back, only to be sent out almost at once west of Morbecque to Steenbecque to report whether or not the enemy had penetrated with armour to that point. I was to fight my way through the woods on either side of the road, which were in German hands, and I would have a tank troop of the 13/18th Hussars (actually Bobby Neave—a great friend), in support. There was a company of Northumberland Fusiliers in support, too.

"There was a lot of shelling and mortar fire. There was an enormous explosion under my carrier and I thought we had been blown up but, no, all was well and we went on. We kept up our fire into the woods on either side, and held the German infantry down for a time, but they had intense mortar fire laid down in front of their advance.

"I reached the crossroads at Steenbecque at about 1400 hours and found no enemy armour in sight. If there had been armour there I was to do my best to engage and to prevent their further advance so as to protect the retiring infantry to the east. If I found nothing, I was to take up a defensive position and await further orders.

"This was open country and the only cover was a straw stack at the crossroads. I put Sergeant Wall's carrier to one side of the stack and he was to cover the carrier with straw. My second vehicle was sent to the south, where a small bush offered some cover. I was about to seek the cover of a big ditch to my rear when, suddenly, about 1000 yards in front of me, I saw several tanks, their great grey hulks coming slowly over the brow of the hill. Through my glasses I could see they were German tanks and in a flash I saw a tracer shell coming straight towards us. I remember I had time to say to my driver: 'God', if that hits us we're done for. It did.

"The explosion was terrific. The armour-piercing shell passed through the front of my carrier, splitting the armour plating like matchwood, and seemed to explode in the radiator behind me. There was hot water and oil everywhere and I felt as if I had been struck by a heavy plank all down my right side. It was more shock than pain. The obvious thing was to get out before being hit a second time. I think my driver had got out, but the smoke was too thick to see. I fell down into the ditch at the side of the road and, at that moment, the ammunition on the carrier started to explode in all directions.

"I heard the other two carriers roar past me. I suppose they thought we had been blown to bits and that there was nothing else to be done. If they had halted they would have been an easy target. The smell of gunpowder, burning oil and the steam was frightful. The only thing to do was to stay in the bottom of the ditch until the carrier had burnt itself out.

"It seemed to be very wet, but there had been no rain for days so I could not imagine why there was water in the ditch. Then I realised it was blood—my blood—which seemed to be seeping through my battledress. But I could not feel anything: I could move my legs and arms.

"It could not have been more than ten minutes when I heard the hum of engines above me and there, standing at the edge of the ditch, stood three or four German tank crew in their goggles, black uniform and field boots, looking as if they came from another world. Would they finish me off? One of them, obviously an officer, came forward and, with others picked me up and carried me to the other side of his tank. It looked enormous and was, compared with our Mark VIB! He took my pistol, emptied my pockets. There was an I D card. 'Oh', said the officer, 'Neville'. 'Where is your Neville Chamberlain and his umbrella now? You are an officer: I will radio for an ambulance: Take your things and good luck!' How astonished I was!"

* * * * *

*Lieutenant Blacker* continues:

"While this action was followed on the wireless and reported by the survivors of Lieutenant Ussher's troop, the Regiment's situation was almost a repetition of the morning position. Again Morbecque was manned by the whole Regiment in preparation for a final stand but on this occasion, fortunately, there were also some British 18-pounders which could be used most effectively as anti-tank guns. German tanks attempted to enter Morbecque from the north and via the road held by 'B' Squadron. Our 18-pounders, firing at point blank range, put two out of action and the remainder withdrew. This enabled Lieutenant Robert Crockett to take his troop forward to mop up some German infantry occupying the woods to the north. His attack was most successful.

"By dusk, the situation was more confused than before. We had no orders to leave Morbecque and brigade headquarters had moved away after the afternoon crisis to La Motte in the Forêt de Nieppe. They were to be followed by the Artillery. The French anti-tank gunners were also restive and it seemed that we were to be left without anti-tank defence.

"Exhausted infantry came down the road towards Hazebrouck. They were men utterly spent. Some had not eaten for three days. It was obvious that this particular brigade would be quite unable to fight for a day or more. We heard that there were fresh troops in Hazebrouck. It seemed likely that we would be withdrawn after the infantry.

"Our CO went to brigade headquarters to discuss the situation but the meeting lasted so long, by the time he returned, darkness had fallen and it seemed better to remain in position for another night, even though without anti-tank defence. Patrols were left out and the remainder bivouaced in Morbecque together with the Northumberland Fusiliers whom we had extricated from Boéseghem. They were far too exhausted to do anything but sleep, though the enemy gave us a fairly severe shelling during that night.

"Morning broke without enemy activity and our position was quieter than it had been 48 hours earlier. We were able to leave Morbecque at our leisure and did so with great relief. Later we heard that the German radio had reported that, owing to large numbers of enemy tanks in the Saint Omer area, their tank columns had made a northward sweep instead of advancing through Hazebrouck. It was some consolation to know that our anxious hours had paid off. We moved to another sector of the front and towards Estaires and billetted in the small town of Steenwerck, not far from Armentières, which was under attack from dive bombers as we arrived. The Second Division was heavily involved on the La Bassée Canal and we were to form their reserve and remain ready to move forward at a moment's notice.

"The armoured troops within the Second Division now comprised the 4/7th Dragoon Guards, what remained of the 15/19th Hussars, and ourselves. Although the 4/7th had suffered comparatively light casualties in men, their vehicle casualties had been heavier and they could only muster one complete squadron. The 15/19th were reduced to one very weak squadron which had been attached to us for a number of days. We could put two strong squadrons in the field. General Irwin, our GOC, therefore decided that the three regiments would operate better as one amalgamated force.

"Our 'C' Squadron was absorbed between 'A' and 'B' and the place of 'C' Squadron was now to be taken by the remainder of the 4/7th DG and to be under the command of Major Frink, with Captain Williams as his second-in-command. The spare men who were without vehicles were formed into a dismounted party and placed under command of Major Mullens, of the 4/7th Dragoon Guards. Our own Commanding Officer, Lieutenant Colonel Anstice, was to command the amalgamated force.

"May 25th was spent fitting the amalgamated Regiment into the new environs of Steenwerck and in discussing the new amalgamation. German planes were continually overhead but did not attack us that day. TSM Crawley, who had been missing with his carrier crew since the engagement at Morbecque, rejoined that afternoon. We were unaware of the imminent fall of Calais and the Belgian surrender was unthought of. We were quite unaware of the seriousness of our position and were sincerely thankful for an undisturbed night.

"We had been warned that we were unlikely to have such a peaceful day on the 26th or the following night, which will ever be remembered for the systematic destruction of Estaires and Bailleul by German dive bombers. The Regiment moved into positions on the River Lys at 1430 hours on 27th to permit the infantry to withdraw. We were not to cross the Lys until 2000 hours. Major Frink's squadron was to send out patrols to Aubers and Fromelles, but to remain in reserve. Regimental headquarters was in Laventie.

"Although we were still ignorant of it, the Cameron Highlanders and Dorsets who we were to assist were already entirely cut off. We only realised this when medium German tanks came up the Estaires road and were engaged by our patrols. Our tank troops, hopelessly outgunned and out-armoured, suffered severely."

* * * * *

*Lieutenant J R Crockett* had led his troop forward to cover an important bridge and did so most effectively. Sadly, two of his troop tanks were destroyed. *Sergeant Charlie Bevan* gave this account of the action which could in itself be the making of a book:

"It was May 27th and I was covering the withdrawal of the rear elements of infantry in the area of Neuve-Chapelle. With my tank I was instructed to proceed to the crossroads and cover the Queen's Regiment in their withdrawal. After I had seen the last man out I decided it was time to move back but, alas, I was too late: my tank received a direct hit and started to 'brew up', I scrambled out through the hatch and saw that I was wounded in both legs. I looked at the gunner's turret which was belching forth black, choking fumes, and saw the gunner's head look out and disappear again. I grabbed him by his equipment and hauled him up and out, clear of the burning tank.

"Eventually we were both conveyed to the 29th Field Ambulance, where we were told we would be in 'Blighty' the following day if sufficient ambulances could be mustered. The following morning I was lifted into an ambulance with as many other wounded as was possible to crowd in. It was about 1800 hours on May 28th when the convoy started on its way to Dunkirk. After about an hour's run the convoy stopped and I heard an order: 'Get your rifle, the enemy is down the road'. What, I asked myself, was I to do: a helpless stretcher case, both boots had been removed and legs bandaged from knees to ankles. Should I get moving now, before it was too late. I had always had a premonition that I would come safely through the war, but could see now that I was going to be a prisoner for the duration. What a hopeless situation.

"The enemy opened up with everything they had, and I saw a sheet of flame silhouette across the ambulance. 'This is it', I thought, 'I am going to be burnt alive'. I forgot that I was a stretcher case, and opened the ambulance doors and got out, only to be greeted by two German tanks 50 yards away. I waved to the commander to hold his fire, and he waved back in such a way as to tell me to get the hell out of it. With the assistance of a slightly wounded soldier I got all the wounded out of the ambulance, and managed to get them to a farm building to the rear of the German tanks. What should I do?"

Meanwhile the Regiment fought on. It was now obvious that the majority of the Camerons and Dorsets must be doomed. Small parties of these gallant battalions managed to escape back across the Lys, but the remainder were seen no more. The Regiment moved back to within two miles of Estaires and made contact with a French tank unit which they had failed to locate that afternoon. They had very smart looking tanks and were generally more effective than the French infantry. To the last, these tank troops fought bravely and well. They then moved off to our left and we did not see them again.

The road to Estaires was now filled with retreating members of the French Army. The road was choked with men, carts and heavy lorries coming from the direction of Lille. When the congestion was at its highest, German planes became active over Estaires. The road blockage became complete as every man abandoned his vehicle and plunged into a ditch. It was with great difficulty that they were persuaded to drive on. Finally, in darkness, the Regiment crossed back over the bridge at Estaires manned by the men from our own dismounted party. We were ordered to return to our original billets near Steenwerck. Major Tom Williamson, now liaison officer at 2 Division Headquarters, was our only means of communication with our commander.

* * * * *

Here we bring in a story of one of our fitters, *Harold Platt,* who had only joined the Regiment a few weeks earlier. Remember that, at this time, there were no REME soldiers, our LAD was a mixture of RAOC tradesmen and our own regimental fitters under command of an enormous man known as Tiny Wright. Lieutenant Mick Muirland was the technical officer. Constant calls for recovery and repair often left the fitters in very difficult positions, but let Harold tell his story:

"Short of rations and leaving Mouvaux, we halted. A beautiful young bull had been slaughtered, but before it could be properly carved there was an order to move and we left the carcass hanging from a tree. The cooks stewed some of it the following day but it had not hung long enough and it was so tough that it couldn't be eaten. We watched Bailleul being bombed. There were 72 aircraft circling the town in three groups of 24. One aircraft suddenly detached itself and spotted the party. We could see the bombs leave the plane and there was a lapse of several seconds when nothing was said.

"Perhaps they would fall short, or overshoot? Then the whole party, as one man, realised they might fall on us and we were flat on our faces. They fell very close, but caused no casualties. The padre arrived and decided to hold communion! I distinctly remember wondering whether after years of sin I would have a clean sheet in the next life! The padre left and I found a map, the first I had seen during the operation. It was in the form of a leaflet which had floated down from an aircraft, probably with bombs. It showed our position completely surrounded by swastikas and invited us to surrender. The message said 'It is a lie and nonsense that we kill our prisoners. Come and see for yourselves!' 'Not bloody likely', I thought. Finally we left for an unknown destination. Roads were full of refugees and French horsedrawn artillery. I could not understand why they were all white horses. (Of course, had Harold been a proper cavalryman he would have referred to them as 'Greys'. There are no *white* horses!)

"Near Bailleul, the convoy came under attack from the air again. I thought we were being machine-gunned but then discovered that a Frenchman a few yards further on was firing at the planes with a Hotchkiss mounted on a truck. We sat in the vehicle gazing back at the road we had travelled and wondering why the driver was continually revving the vehicle up then slipping the clutch. I leaned out of the back to peer forward and saw a shell land in a garden only a few hundred yards ahead.

"Beyond that was a crossroads manned by one solitary military policeman standing on a box in the middle of the road trying to control the traffic. Just a short distance away was a group of Redcaps ready to replace the one on duty should he be blown off the box. Military policemen are never popular with the peacetime soldier but, in war, provide a marvellous service at such control points and their casualty lists are high."

Harold forgave them for the inconvenience they had caused him during his sinful past and has ever held them in high respect.

"Beyond the crossroads there was a church on fire. There is an eerie feeling about burning churches which makes one wonder about the values of life and the stupidity of war.

"Bomb craters and refugees eventually made progress by vehicle impossible. There were some horses in a field, crazy with fear and galloping madly round the field as soon as the sound of an aircraft was heard. There were lumps under their hides, undoubtedly where shrapnel had lodged. Orders were given to destroy the vehicles and the men started to march."

Harold saw a German spotter plane hedge-hopping just a short distance away. He dropped into a ditch intending to fire his rifle at it but he couldn't keep his eyes open long enough. Burning oil tanks in Dunkirk were beacons for their final destination. He eventually arrived, fell asleep on the sea wall, and woke the following morning unable to find any other member of the Regiment.

Rounded up by the Navy, he was put into a group of 20 and told to run like hell along the mole and over planks and ladders covering a large hole which had been caused by bombs the previous day which had made a direct hit upon embarking troops. He narrowly missed being put aboard some Thames sailing barges before being put aboard the SS Scotia, a railway boat from Dover. He met a friend from the workshop he had left before joining the Regiment and learned that all 200 of his old section had been taken prisoner.

* * * * *

*Lieutenant Blacker* now returns to the Regiment stuck in that traffic jam of all traffic jams.

"It took nearly an hour to persuade the French artillery to get their horses to the side of the road. Finally the column was extricated from this mess. Steenwerck was then discovered to be full of refugees and French troops and there was no room for us. Eventually the squadrons, separated during this harassing drive, found areas to spend what was left of the night. Our spirits were very low. We realised that it was too late to hope for a successful drive south, that the Lys was the last river defence before the coast, and that even that was to be given up the following day. We realised that, for reasons over which we had no control, our army was being gradually forced into the sea. To add to our depression the rain continued to pour down on us. May 27th had been a very bad day.

"On the 28th, as day broke on a cloudy day, Major Tom Williamson arrived with new orders and told us that the 2nd Division was retreating towards Poperinghe and that we were to form a flank guard south-west of the town between Watou and L'Abeele. We decided to avoid main roads and towns as far as possible. The squadrons reached their destination and new positions intact but with one unfortunate incident.

"The German Air Force continued to attack the retreating columns and concentrated on all main crossroads and the larger towns. Bailleul was almost continually surrounded by dive bombers. By some mischance, TSM Crawley found that his only route led through this battered town. While he was making his way through it, a new wave of bombers arrived and, in this raid, he and half his troop perished.

"That afternoon the Commanding Officer returned from a conference at divisional headquarters and gave the news that we were to retire to Dunkirk and embark with the remains of the British Expeditionary Force. We were to destroy all our soft vehicles, keeping only sufficient to carry those men not in tank or carrier crews.

"We were to take up positions at Bergues, south of Dunkirk but, by dawn, we still had eight miles to go. The road ahead was completely blocked by abandoned vehicles, so there was nothing for it but to push them into ditches. We arrived at 0900 hours. We did

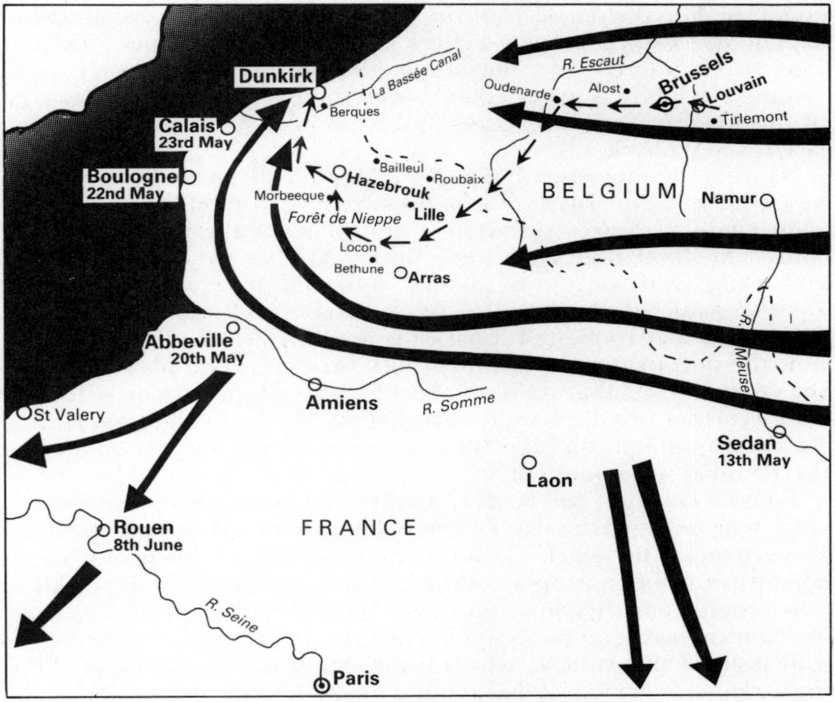


not destroy our vehicles at Bergues as ordered but drove towards Dunkirk. On both sides of the road there were vehicles crammed with ammunition, clothing and expensive technical equipment, worth millions of pounds.

"Dunkirk was a battered and deserted town, overhung with black smoke. It was midday before the various stragglers were brought into the little brick-yard at Rosenfael. Major Williamson visited us from divisional HQ and said that we would not be embarking that night and he had doubts about the following day. Stragglers from a number of regiments were continuing to arrive, disrupting the evacuation of those bodies who were in controlled groups.

"Those three days between May 29th and 31st were days of

continuous raids by the German Air Force who were making a determined attack upon the harbour and vessels waiting to take troops off. On the first day they did considerable damage without loss to themselves, but on the second day our anti-aircraft guns and those of the Royal Navy were able to put up a very effective barrage. The RAF, though heavily outnumbered, were also seen fighting above us in thrilling dog fights. It was to everyone's intense pleasure that the German casualties began to increase.

"From June 1st onwards, the attacks eased. As the Regiment was established on the outskirts of the town, we suffered no casualties at all. On May 29th, there was a check on casualties and about 20 souls were unaccounted for, including the medical officer. It was assumed—rightly as it turned out—that some of these were unaware of the Regiment's whereabouts and would eventually arrive at the beach and embark.

"During the morning of May 29th, Major Williamson brought the news that the 2nd Division would embark that night. Preparations were made to destroy our vehicle and plan for the journey to the shore. At 1600 hours we were informed that we would not be embarking with our own division: our old friends of the 46th Division had been ordered to hold the line right of the Bergues Canal and had requested a back-up force of armour. As we were now the only armoured regiment left, we were to be placed under the command of that division. All thoughts of embarkation for at least a further two days could be forgotten. We again had a job to do. At about midnight on May 30th there was a message that an attack on the canal was imminent.

"Majors Harding and Scott roused their squadrons and moved to their new headquarters at Tiegerveld and Notre-Dame-des-Neiges, respectively. The attack did not materialise but our men remained on the canal line in support of the infantry. On the morning of May 31st, regimental headquarters also moved to Tiegerveld. Major Williamson had acquired a small blue Fiat, and we grew to dread the approach of this vehicle, which invariably brought bad news. The embarkation seemed to be going slowly and the troops we were supporting were the poorly-equipped and inexperienced Territorials. It was doubtful that we could hold out against a heavy attack. A supply of petrol had been removed from the numerous abandoned vehicles and we received half-rations of food. These were supplemented by food procured from a systematic comb-out of the town. Bread was the one commodity in short supply though bully and biscuits were plentiful.

"On May 31st the embarkation proceeded in a more orderly manner. The wrecks of many ships lay in the harbour and off the shore. At midday the canal line was attacked by infantry. The heavily flooded countryside seemed to have prevented the Panzer Divisions from any further advance. There was shelling from shorter-range guns, too, whilst the longer-range guns concentrated upon the beaches and Dunkirk itself. Our own artillery replied and, from then on, a duel continued for 36 hours. It was believed that if the enemy attacks could be held for a further 24 hours and the embarkation could continue, there was a chance that the whole of the BEF could be evacuated.

"At 2300 hours, Major Tom Williamson appeared yet again and informed us that 1st Division on our left was being heavily attacked and had requested armoured support. 'A' Squadron was to be detached and placed under command of that division. The 4/7th Squadron were also despatched to support 50th Division on the extreme left and holding the Furnes and Ostend road. As 'A' Squadron was now under command of 50 Division, our own headquarters was left with nothing to command. The CO could only listen to reports transmitted over the radios.

" 'A' Squadron were able to hold their sector but suffered one casualty. 'B' Squadron's front had been heavily attacked and they were ordered to counter-attack. There was a sharp engagement which caused more casualties but was successful. The position by midday seemed more stable. The shelling became more severe but the air attacks less frequent. At 1300 hours, the CO attended a conference at Leffringkoucke. This village had been singled out by the German artillery and the conference was conducted with extreme difficulty.

"News from the conference was that the remainder of the BEF was to embark that night, June 1st. 'B' Squadron was to cover the infantry withdrawal to the town and then embark at once. As the CO had no direct command, RHQ moved back into the little brickyard. It was thought that all troops would be withdrawn to the beaches by 2230 hours and that the whole force would defend itself while embarkation continued. Evacuation was expected to be complete by morning.

"There were wounded men and horses to be dealt with and the withdrawal was still going on as dawn broke. The darkness and shelling made this move difficult and there was now no communication between RHQ and the squadrons. The beaches were crowded with British and French troops. At 0100 hours on June 2nd, RHQ tanks and carriers drove on to the beach, the guns were spiked, and the engines made useless. Everyone waded into the sea and waited to be picked up. The squadrons were less fortunate. They arrived too late for embarkation that night and were forced to spend an unpleasant day on the beaches. Fortunately, for no apparent reason, the ground and air attacks had slackened and by nightfall the boats returned and took off those troops remaining."

* * * * *

Every man in that evacuation has a tale to tell. Bob Price, a young wireless operator in a Mk VIB tank commanded by Captain Arthur Carr, was left outside a headquarters while his commander was conferring inside. A senior officer, whom he believed to be a general, came out, popped his head into the turret, and told him to transmit a signal in morse on as many frequencies as possible. Bob, uncertain of the officer's rank and authority, told him that he could not leave his regimental net. The officer, no doubt accepting the correctness of Bob's reply and refusal, returned to the building and emerged with Captain Carr. Bob was then told to take the tank to a point about a mile away and transmit a signal to All Stations BEF. "Use VERMOUTH ruthlessly", was the signal to be transmitted on as many frequencies as he could in a period of an hour. He never knew the meaning of it but accepted that it was one of those small details in which life and death could be in the balance.

For a young man, the sight of mutilated horses amidst blood, bandages and screams were memories for life. Bob had come from country folk in Gloucestershire and had an ambition to become a gamekeeper. He had expected to be a cavalryman but was now more than content to be in an insensitive tank. He made his way to the beaches in the darkness. "We lined the tanks up in nice straight lines just to show the enemy that we had not left in panic." They were destroyed and Bob awaited evacuation.

The *Shikari* took him off with a number of French cavalrymen. His last memory as he was rowed away from the shore was of the boat being followed by the horse of one of the Frenchmen in pursuit of its master. What could have been going through its mind? What agony was the owner in? How far would it swim? Would it turn back?

# Sand in my Shoes

*Corporal 'Slim' Ingley* recalls his experiences:

"It was Wednesday, May 29th, 1940 and the Regiment, now a composite force comprising the 15/19th, 13/18th Hussars and the 4/7th Dragoon Guards, arrived at Rasendael, Dunkirk. The headquarters was in the brickyards, which we shared with the French. The harbour was not a haven, for it was heavily shelled for the whole of the night. The morale of the French troops was low, and they were depressed and argumentative. We, who were trying to escape the country, have since realised what a disaster it was for them. How would we have felt if, fighting on English soil, we were forced to flee to France?

"In the brickyards the men, tired, dirty and hungry, slept the sleep of the exhausted in the stench of gunpowder, black smoke, and the whistle and crunch of falling shells. Huddled in corners, we tried to ignore the gnawing hunger pains, our heads balanced on gas masks which were substitute pillows. But we were bound for Blighty, and due to embark at Dawn. Hip, hip, hooray! Little did we know.

"The memories of the long, wretched retreat were still vivid; the misery of the animals; the rolling eyes of hysterical dogs with their white, foaming mouths; the distressed cattle overflowing with milk as the movement of back legs on the overloaded milk bags caused the milk to drip.

"The stench of death from the bloated bodies as they swelled to bursting point. Refugees, in abject misery, pulled and pushed barrows, handcarts and prams loaded with blankets and pots and pans. The crackle of flames from burning houses. The knowledge of a lost battle.

"The beaches on that day were packed with massed formations of silent men, queuing amid the racket of falling bombs, the scream of shells, the machine-gunning and the roar of planes. Troops flooded into the perimeter: Belgians, the First French Army, and the remnants of the BEF.

"The weather was bad and the smoke dense. Two of our destroyers were sunk in the early hours. And there was a change of plans: we were turned to join the perimeter forces for the final defence of Dunkirk.

"My new squadron leader was Major Perry Harding and his second-in-command was Captain Teddy Swetenham. I was his operator. The weather was good now. Overhead, massed formations of bombers with fighter escorts that darted, gnat-like, in the unguarded skies.

"I always thought a week went by before we were evacuated, but much was packed into the next couple of days. It was repetitious: moving from one position to another. And always there were the darting Stukas. What a sight that was! How deep can one dig? Answer: very deep.

"I picked up a message: a very calm English voice announcing that the enemy had broken through—an estimated strength of 2,000 men, motorised infantry, tanks and artillery. I wasn't surprised that the squadron was on the move in minutes.

"I do not remember eating or drinking, but I do remember nodding off to sleep, banging my head on the base of a .303 machine-gun with each nod. Everything was noise, movement and misery, but no-one doubted that we would escape and live to fight another day.

"On Saturday, June 1st we moved back to Dunkirk. We struck across country and on the minor roads to avoid the crush of refugees. The PBI hitched rides on the backs of tanks, and some even climbed on to plodding disconsolate dray horses. The riders, bootless, dangled bleeding feet.

"We arrived sometime in the evening, though I don't know the actual time. A thick pall of black smoke hung over the town, flames shooting skywards from burning oil. The debris-strewn beach was potholed from shelling. Bodies were tarpaulin-covered. Shelling was heavy but indiscriminate. It was shattering to the soul to hear piercing screams.

"Orders came to smash all equipment and the No.11 set—which, completely outmoded, had served us well—came under the hammer. Trucks were broken. Then we dug under the derelict tanks for protective cover until it was time to go to the water's edge.

"Attempts were made to board a small, bobbing boat. Someone, terror-stricken, dived in; the boat rolled, and we dived out. Syd Shepherd was one who came up—but this time not blowing his trumpet!

"It was approaching four o'clock, dawn shelling was heavy, and there was a lot of scrambling and screaming. I tried to help an unknown soldier who was completely dazed by what was happening. I fished him from the water twice but, in the confusion, lost him. I have often asked myself 'Did I try hard enough?'

"Eventually, we sheltered in some houses along the front. Now it was light, the planes came roaring in. The house doors were open and we found coffee and a working stove, but no water. I set off with a couple of water bottles. Flames silhouetted the skyline. Debris—human and machines—littered the roadway. My footsteps echoed in the eerie silence. I thought I could feel eyes boring into my back and broke into a run, but there was no movement. No troops. No sound. I found a tap, filled the bottles in double quick time, and sprinted. Three days short of my 19th birthday I drank my own health in Dunkirk water. My mates in the cellar were Jack Gould and Syd Drinkwater.

"We found a seven-pound jam tin with a smattering left in the bottom. Miraculously, hard tack biscuits appeared. It all went down well. Filthy, in sea-salted clothes beginning to dry, we stretched out and slept. Bombs were our alarm clocks, and I saw I had slept on a heap of bricks.

"Scouting for information, we gathered in Bren guns and cleaned them for use. We were told we might need them. At about 0900 hours, we formed in pairs on the beach. Men armed with rifles and bayonettes and wearing white arm-bands were in staggered formation. They served a dual purpose: guards and guides. 'Don't break ranks, boys', they ordered.

"It was light enough for enemy aircraft to give us a buzz, and bombs fell further along the column. But, for the first time, we saw the RAF Three fighters swooped in and drove the bombers away. Shells were still falling.

"Gradually we neared the mole. It appeared to be two miles long and about twenty feet above the sea. Numerous gaps were evident but matelots had strung gangplanks across the gaps.

"We stood aside to give priority to walking wounded. Each man was heavily bandaged around the eyes. A sighted man led the way; the unsighted followed, each man with his hands on the shoulders of the one in front. A sympathetic but subdued cheer went up. A few bodies were entangled, and hung from the supporting woodwork of the mole.

"The smoke was thick, stinking and black. Edging forward along the mole, we saw the ships bumping alongside. Patiently we waited our turn. Our ship pulled in: it was French but had our matelots on board. Shells were whining overhead, splashing and crunching into the sea. A naval officer was yelling instructions into a megaphone. It was deafening.

"I jumped, up and over the rail on to the deck as the ship nosed in. What a thrill to feel the deck. A matelot steadied me, grinned, took the Bren gun and dropped it overboard. 'No room for that, mate' he said. 'Too many passengers.' Down below we went and buckets of tea were passed around. A pint enamel mug and hot, sweet tea: nectar of the Tommy. Engines roared, and we swung away as the last shells whistled into the sea. Homeward bound! At last!

"I sat in the corner and slept until we landed. I think it was at Folkestone. The Red Cross provided tea and we boarded a train for a destination unknown. A miracle ride across the beautiful—and green, green—English countryside brought us to Aldershot: three Skins together—Jock Gould, Syd Drinkwater and me.

"Back in Dunkirk, which we left behind at 2355 on June 2nd, we left the Germans an inheritance of blackened ruins; dead men floating in the water; grave yards of smashed vehicles. But thanks to the Navy and RAF and hundreds of small boats, 186,558 British troops had been saved, plus 123,095 French."

Our faithful DR, Syd Shepherd, had had a close shave during the retreat. He had left his bike leaning against a barn and taken a few hours' essential rest. During the early hours of the morning there was a shout: "Mount up and move. The Germans are only just down the road." He grabbed his machine but it wouldn't start. The plugs were too wet, he guessed. The last of the carriers was pulling out so he left it and climbed aboard.

Many years later his old friend, Tiny Hill, attended one of our reunions and completed the story. Tiny had also tried to start the machine but without success. He was fired at and wounded and then made prisoner of war. Syd believes that it was Tiny who brought the message to move in the first place. He was given another motorcycle, which he left outside a headquarters in Dunkirk. "It was nicked," said Syd.

He had taken a message to the HQ and delivered it to the General. The Divisional Commander was sympathetic and immediately realised how tired he was. "Take a lie down," said the General. "It could have been his bed for all I know," Syd relates. When he received the reply to take back and found his bike had been stolen, he had to await the arrival of Bill Maltby, a fellow DR, who gave him a very bumpy pillion ride back to RHQ.

He made for the beach with the remnants of the squadrons. His height now paid off and he was able to wade out to meet a small boat. About ten men tried to climb aboard and it sank. After righting it, the sailor who had brought it said that he could only take six. 'Boggie' Whelan, one of the many jockeys serving in the Regiment, climbed on Syd's back and vaulted over the top. Syd didn't get in. There was nothing for it but to return to the shore and wait. He eventually arrived in Dover on June 3rd.

Sam Hayward was a tank driver in 'A' Squadron and in the crew of Captain Teddy Swetenham who was destined to play a major role as CO in the return to France in 1944. Sam's tank broke down in Brussels and was recovered on a trailer. On arrival in Dunkirk and seeing what he calls "an army scrap yard" he was given another tank in full working order. He was now detached from the Regiment and his commander was an infantry sergeant. They were ordered to proceed to the village of Soew some eight miles south of Dunkirk. A unit of mixed troops was holding this village and they were to give what assistance they could.

The troops were thin on the ground and they had no other armour. They knocked holes in the tank's exhaust pipe to create the impression that the tank was larger than it was. They moved forward to probe the positions ahead, soon discovering that the noise they made served only to attract much more attention than they had bargained for.

During one of these missions they nosed slowly around a bend under cover of a hedge and found themselves looking at a much larger German tank. The speed and manoeuvability of the smaller tank saved the day as they swung round and made off in a hurry. They lost that tank in Bergues one night whilst resting in a building. It was buried under rubble.

Sam now attached himself to a party of Welsh Guardsmen and headed for Dunkirk again. The walk, which had to be via the fields to avoid strafing from the air, was a nightmare. His young gunner was with him but could not stay awake. Every time they dived into a hole, the gunner went to sleep. The boat which took him off was holed by a German shore battery. He never met the members of the mock-up crew again.

* * * * *

Lieutenant Colonel Mike Ansell, an officer to become famous for his subsequent fight against blindness and captivity, had been posted from the Regiment. In the preceding March he had been given an order to take over command of the Lothian and Border Yeomanry. He tells his own story of the bravery of these Territorials under his command in his own book *Soldier On*. It is a story of their fight against impossible odds and subsequent retreat, not to Dunkirk but to St-Valéry.

After destroying their remaining vehicles they were to make for the beach in small parties. They were already surrounded and faced a hopeless task. From the top of the hill they went down to this small fishing village to find the remains of the Highland Division and hordes of French soldiers there. There was no ship awaiting them and it looked unlikely that there would be. It rained for the first time in weeks.

*Colonel Ansell* recalls:

"We moved about trying to find our own men and encourage them to escape but they were spent and utterly exhausted. I dreaded the thought of being taken prisoner. I teamed up with Harry Youngman and Charlie Hopetoun (later the Marquess of Linlithgow). We also had another stalwart from the regiment, SSM Duff Waymark.

"We decided to move south and away from the coast. We set off in pouring rain, keeping to the hedges and trees looking for a place to lie up. We climbed into the loft of a farm house, took off our rain-sodden clothing and slept. Some time later another party of Englishmen, also looking for somewhere to sleep, entered the farm. The French occupants of the farm had heard our party enter the loft and thought that we were Germans. The new arrivals fired upwards and through the floor and the trap door as they burst in. We took the full blast of a Tommy-gun from a range of ten feet. There was a lot of shouting . . . the firing stopped . . . and voices in French and English were heard below. I knew that I had been hit in the head and hands and realised that I was blind. Harry Youngman was dead and Charlie Hopetoun had been hit in the leg.

"I believed that I had had it. I asked Charlie to let my wife know what had happened and to tell her that I loved her! I was convinced that I would die. (This message was received by her after three months). Waymark said that he would stay with me. Charlie agreed to take the others and still try to escape. Waymark tied up my hands and after a while I felt better. We then decided that I must give myself up. I had no alternative. I was blind, both my hands were in a sorry state, and my head a mass of blood.

"I cannot recall much about the long and tedious journey: numbness was the primary sensation. I thought endlessly of my wife Victoria, and by now was determined to live. We even wondered whether we might still get away. We crossed fields till we came to a railway cutting, through wire fencing, down an embankment, over and up the other side. Still vivid the effort of climbing in my newfound darkness. I don't know how far we walked—perhaps four or five miles. How Waymark got me there I shall never know. I must have been very fit because I had lost an immense amount of blood from my left hand. We hit a road and, by chance, a French dressing station. Waymark took me in, and I was given morphia and dressed. A couple of hours later I was aroused by the shouts of Germans. An armoured patrol had arrived. Waymark came to my help. We were ordered to walk again—this time back to St Valéry, some seven or eight miles. After two or three miles a German truck picked us up and took us into the town."

* * * * *

Those who eventually rejoined the Regiment in Bovington were the lucky ones. They had gained invaluable battle experience and were to pass that information on to the new armoured regiments to be formed and to the new recruits to re-form the Regiment. Above all, they had a burning desire to return to France with better weapons and much improved know-how. But what had befallen those men now left behind enemy lines? What of Lieutenant Neville Ussher, lying wounded in a ditch and destined to become a prisoner of war, and Sergeant Charlie Bevan, desperately trying to avoid the inevitable.

*Lieutenant Ussher* completes his story:

"It seemed no time before I was being lifted by ambulancemen into their grey ambulance and laid on a stretcher and away . . . to God knows where. It never occurred to me that I had been taken POW and it was not for ages that it dawned on me. For all of us, the thought of being taken prisoner had just never been considered. Killed or wounded, maybe, but not POW.

"We had not gone far before the ambulance halted. I was very numb and I thought I was no longer bleeding, but my torn battledress had stuck to me. I was carried into a large château. There were many white-coated people around, large Red Cross flags everywhere, and many ambulances coming and going. I was carried into the building and into a big room and put on a table. A big man, with shaven head and metal-framed glasses, came forward, obviously a doctor. He cut away my blood-soaked battledress, shirt and pants so that I was naked except for my boots. He wiped my side and tied a large label around my neck and said the word 'Operation'. He gave me an enormous injection—obviously anti-tetanus—and I was carried out and put back into an ambulance. An efficient casualty clearing station.

"Off we went and continued for about half an hour with lots of stops, eventually arriving somewhere. I was carted out of the ambulance and dumped on the ground in the forecourt of a large building which I assumed to be a hospital. It was not long before I was carried into the building and put into a long room with thirty or so beds. The mess was dreadful: bandages around everywhere, smell of hospital, and foul smells, too. I was put on a bed.

"I just lay there, exhausted. Where was I? And a new thought. What ever had happened to the rest of my crew, my troop, the squadron and the Regiment? I thought of those thirty tanks going on and was Sergeant Wall able to get back to warn everyone?

"It was still only four or five hours after I had been hit, but a lot had happened. In the evening a French doctor came round, looked me over and suddenly, with his scalpel, cut a large piece of metal out of my back. That hurt! But it was the best way to do it. I was not hungry, and there was no food anyway, though I got a drink of water later.

"My schoolboy French was now needed because it seemed everyone here—wounded and staff—was French. I found I was in St-Pol Hospital. I was here for nearly a week, on a straw mattress, and I do not remember being re-bandaged. The smell was getting bad, from me and others. I got the end of a shoe box and, on its cardboard end, wrote to my mother to say I was wounded but OK and a POW. It somehow got itself posted through the Kriegsgefängenpost and arrived in England in August. I still have it.

"By this time I had got a bright blue French hospital coat and trousers but I had not walked yet. All the things so carefully strapped to my leg with sticking plaster by the German doctor at the casualty clearing station had long been stolen. I had kept my boots on all this time or they would have gone, too. On May 31st, in the morning, there were shouts in French and German 'All out'.

"Now we were moved back into ambulances, but destined for where? After lots of stops and starts, we came to a halt! 'All out' again. I crawled out into the road. And there we were all laid down in the gutter with water rushing around us, as we lay there in the stream! After a few minutes I realised we were in danger of being squashed any moment by heavy German tanks and lorries. We were, I discovered in Doullens. Having got this far, to be run over by a tank in a gutter in Doullens would be a poor way to end it.

"I suddenly saw a Salvation Army flag flying from a building on the opposite side of the road. Here, perhaps, was help. I risked a lull in the traffic and crawled across and into the building. It was a mess. The floor was covered with straw and bodies which, to judge from the smell, had been there a while. But there was help, and I found straw in a corner on which to lie down and think again.

"It was always said that the further you get behind the lines, particularly as a POW, the worse it is. There was no doubt about that now. The few Salvation Army staff were doing their best for the dying, but I began to feel there was no hope. I was not going to get to a hospital but just lie here like the others.

"At about 6 pm I heard lots of noise outside and there were about 20 French ambulances. Now they must be going somewhere better than this, so I crawled across the road towards the nearest of them. 'Stretcher cases only' shouted the driver in French. But he seemed worth talking to, in my best French, so I told him I did not want a stretcher but would lie on the floor. 'I have no time to discuss it. Do as you like, but don't get on a stretcher,' he ordered. I crawled in underneath and out of sight. It was a hard floor, but hope was rising.

We waited a long time and it was dark when I heard the engines start up and we moved off. Where to now? Some other French wounded above me on the stretchers said we were going to Le Touquet. This was wonderful news because I knew the French had their enormous base hospital there.

"It was the early morning of June 1st when we arrived at the Hermitage, one of the best pre-war hospitals. At last, some hope of help. There were nurses and doctors. First a lift, then a room, a bed and sheets. I was washed and examined by a doctor. I still had those original bandages of May 24th and it was now June 1st. But still I seemed to be all right. Was it only the superficial wounds from the carrier radiator exploding into my back? I was tidied up. There was little food except old macaroni and a piece of French army-issue hard, black chocolate. And ersatz coffee.

"I slept and slept. On the third day, when I thought I was much better and using the bed bottle, I just passed blood, so much of it that it filled the bottle, which overflowed on the bed and on to the floor. It would not stop and the pain was dreadful. God, what had happened? The nurses did their best but I was suddenly in a poor way. This went on every two days until the end of June. I got thinner and thinner and could not drink without blood pouring out again.

"A very dear French lady, Madame Lucy Labbaye, came daily to help change bandages and sheets. She was a volunteer French Red Cross nurse and had been so 20 years before, in the 1st World War. She was wonderful. She was a very tiny person but was able to carry me, now less than 7 stone, down to 'another' room—nearer the mortuary. So perhaps, this time, it was the end. There was no more morphine and the pain was still dreadful.

"On July 1st—a Monday, I remember, because I kept a card to

mark off the days—I was seen by Capitaine Le Fèvre, a surgeon, who was also a POW. There was an X-ray and a massive blood transfusion. Four waiters from the White Star Hotel in Le Touquet came and I was transfused with about a litre of blood from each of them, person-to-person. Then to the operating theatre.

"I knew no more until I woke up in the presence of the surgeon, nurses, Madame Labbaye and others. I was alive! They told me I had had my right kidney removed. A piece of shrapnel had become embedded therein, and that had been the problem. There were many other bits of metal there but it was better that they remain where they were, and they are still there now! I felt an enormous bulge of bandage and cotton wool on my right hand side and protruding, the finger holes of several metal clamps. It was explained that the Germans had not provided any ligature thread and supplies had run out, so clamps had been left in! Later I had a drink and no stream of blood resulted. There was no pain, either, so sleep was possible. Life had returned. But I had so many bed sores I could not move and there was little with which I could be treated.

"With wonderful attention and an increasing amount of food each day (some smuggled in by Lucy Labbaye) I gained a bit of weight. I lay and listened to the contrasting sounds of the off-duty medical staff playing tennis on the courts outside and the German bombers collecting over the town of Le Touquet to bomb England.

"On July 7th a group of German officers charged into my room 'Why is he here? He should be on the list. No excuse. No lingering of POWs. German soldiers move out of hospital after operation at once.' What a turmoil. But the Oberstabsart meant what he said.

"In the afternoon I was put on a stretcher and carried down to the front hall of the Hermitage, five weeks after I had entered there from Doullens on that dark night. I still had these six or eight pairs of clamps in my side but, by lying on my left and holding on for grim death, I managed to be all right until we reached Lille about five hours later. I did not know so then, but I was carried into a small, low building and up into a little room where there were two beds. One was already occupied. 'Welcome to the Maternity Wing of the 17/21st British Hospital at Lille'. This was Captain Michael Fleming, Oxfordshire & Buckinghamshire Light Infantry. His leg had been amputated high up at the thigh. He looked dreadful, yellow and thin. We were of a kind, and it was wonderful to talk.

"Next day I was seen by the senior surgeon, Lieutenant-Colonel T H Wilson, RAMC. He came over from the enormous Faculté Catholique opposite, which was full of 'walking wounded', all British POWs. He opened me up and removed the clamps while I held on to the Nun who was there to help. He exposed a large hole. 'You could get a football in that, but it's clean. It will heal.' Poor Michael Fleming was worse. The gangrene was spreading. There was no more leg to cut off. He died there. We had been the greatest of friends for those ten days. He was the elder brother of Ian, famous author of the James Bond novels.

"I was helped to get on my feet and, as soon as I could walk a bit, was moved over to the main building and into a room where I found Alastair Robertson, 7th Argyll and Sutherland Highlanders. He had a leg wound from serving with the 51st Highland Division at St-Valéry. We became friends at once. Also there was Jimmy Langley of the Coldstreams, who had had his arm off, and Oswald Normanby and several others with whom we spent the next three-and-a-half years.

"Alastair and Jimmy were planning to escape and hoped I could join the party. Alastair was walking quite well but I was nowhere near fit enough to join and would have been a dreadful handicap to them. I would have to remain a POW. Now these notes are not intended to become a Prisoner of War diary, so I will relate only briefly the story of those three-and-a-half years.

"I got better and better all the time. POW food was in very short supply, and we were hungry all the time. When, eventually, Red Cross parcels came through, our lives were saved. None of us could have got through without them.

"After Alastair and Jimmy had left, (they both got back home by way of Spain and Gibraltar) we were moved to a large school building at Enghien in Belgium. We were now subjected to the full treatment: guards with bayonets, barbed wire, searches, overcrowding, bad-tempered German officers, smelly and dirty places, and poorer and poorer food. The glorious weather did mean we could be out in the exercise yard a lot. Still no news from home, nor did we know if they at home knew about us and our fate. We thought of nothing else but news of home—and food.

"In the late autumn we were moved again, now into Germany: on to the train, hard arse, eight to a compartment, Germans shouting, bayonets flashing. We travelled a very long time, through Holland and on down the Ruhr, through Wuppertal, Cologne, Essen, Dortmund, Krefeld and Bochum. Eventually we went up into the mountains and the snow to a German hospital at Sallfeld. From here to Obermassfeld to meet up with more friends. I had a relapse here for two weeks, but got over it. The first Christmas of three as a POW was spent here. One extra potato for supper was our treat from the Germans. But we did get a small consignment of the first Red Cross parcels here. Manna from Heaven!

"From here, at last, to Spangenberg—an organised POW camp. Oflag 1X A/E 'Unterlager'. At Obermassfeld the International Medical Commission Red Cross visited the hospital and saw all the British wounded who thought they had a chance of being repatriated as passing 'unfit' for further military service'. I was lucky to get my name on the list although, by now, I was getting quite fit again. At 1X A/H I met up with Michael Maude, and we remained together for the rest of the time.

"Those of us who had qualified for repatriation were sent in the autumn of 1941 from Spangenberg to Rouen and on to Dieppe, with the hope of being exchanged across the Channel with wounded German POWs from England. It never came off and, although Mike Ansell and I tried to fix up an escape from our camp at Rouen racecourse, we never made it.

"When it became clear that Hitler was not going to be a party to exchanging 47 Germans for 1,200 British, we were suddenly moved to Poland! We spent four days and nights in the train without boots and with very little food and drink. We arrived at Schildberg—Oflag 21—and it was cold. But, in the building where we were put, it was warm and infested with bed bugs and we were very overcrowded. We spent the winter there. Miserable it was. In the spring back to Spangenberg.

"I remember doing two weeks in the 'cooler' here. One was for swapping beds with Lance Pope to enable him to be nearer the wire for a night escape attempt. A cat ran in front of him after he had got through the wire and the sentry-box flood light went on—directly on to Lance. He would have been shot if he had moved. So, a failed attempt. And I was found occupying his bed! The second week was for putting a nail into the fuse box so we could go on playing bridge into the night!

"In 1943 we went to Oflag IX A/Z at Rotenberg-am-Fulda, formerly the Jacob Grimm Schule turned into a POW camp. By October the International Red Cross had, at last, arranged repatriation of those on 'the list'. My name was still on it, as also were those of Michael Maude and Mike Ansell. We came back through Sweden. I was invalided out of the Army for a while but rejoined when I was appointed ADC to the Earl of Athlone, Governor-General of Canada, and I was there for the last eighteen months of the War."

* * * * *

Sergeant Charlie Bevan had been reported missing and believed killed. He was subsequently awarded a posthumous Distinguished Conduct Medal which was, of course, presented to Mrs Bevan. The citation read:

*"On 27th May, 1940, Sergeant Bevan was ordered with his tank to cover the withdrawal of the rear elements of infantry in his sector, near Neuve-Chapelle. He remained in position in the face of heavy anti-tank gun fire until the infantry had passed to safety and his ammunition was exhausted. Then, when he and the remainder of his crew were wounded and their vehicle in flames, he withdrew."* (London Gazette, December 20th, 1940.)

Sergeant Bevan had indeed been wounded but was far from dead and was not thinking of becoming a POW. His own story told some 38 years later, covers his escape which had earned him the further award of a Military Medal. Both awards were well deserved.

*Sergeant Bevan's* story:

"It was then that I remembered the lectures I had attended, way back in the early 1930s, on 'Escapes' by Major Harrison. Why wait to get inside a cage before trying to escape? Now was the time, I told myself. So I crawled away, hoping that I could get back by semi-circling in the rear of the German tanks and on to the road which we had travelled down. I had about half completed my task when I almost exposed myself to a German half-track vehicle which caused me to hide myself in the hedge. This vehicle parked itself near me and was responsible for my lying in the hedge for three days.

"By the end of this time I was very thirsty so I crept out, crawled down the hedge-side, saw an abandoned British vehicle, and found canvas shoes which must have been made for me. I also found a half-full water bottle and had my first drink for three days. I spoiled the rest of the water by adding whisky which I also found, along with a jar of cauliflower. After eating the cauliflower, I soon found that whisky and vinegar together are not good for a thirsty man.

"Found bandages, so attended to wounds and bound legs with puttees made from army blankets. With army blanket round my shoulders on the third night, and as soon as it was dark, I started to walk. After some distance I decided to rest in a farm building, hoping to find civilian clothes the following morning. When I heard the farmer moving I cautiously crept out and went over to the cowshed where he was milking the cows. As soon as he saw me he was badly frightened, and tried to tell me the Germans would shoot him if I was caught in his yard. I begged some milk from him and decided to move on.

"After walking across two fields I came to a small house and found a Frenchman standing outside the door. I spoke to him, and he called me inside. Without asking, he prepared me some food and met my requirements by way of civilian clothes. I ascertained the direction of Dunkirk and started on my way. After walking about a mile I came across some German soldiers and my heart-beat began to quicken. As I got closer to them I felt like retracing my steps but, just then, two refugees came along and I followed close behind. I got the impression that the Germans were not taking much notice of the refugees, and my heart began to resume its normal beat.

"More refugees came and I decided to follow them until I could find my bearings. They turned down a road to the right, but after half a mile the Germans stopped anyone going along that road as some British soldiers were still fighting it out, although by now it was May 31st and Dunkirk was many miles away. I turned back and followed the refugees. When anyone spoke to me I pointed to my ear, trying to indicate that I was deaf. This I deemed to be the best policy, having little knowledge of the French language. Not knowing that our troops were evacuating from Dunkirk I assumed that by following the refugees I should be going away from the Germans and it would only be a matter of time before I came to my own lines.

I was soon to find out that my assumption was quite wrong. The first British soldiers I met were prisoners.

"Continuing on my way I entered Ypres. It was then I knew I was going in the wrong direction. A German band was playing in the square and an officer was standing on a window ledge taking photographs. I listened to the refugees asking directions, and I heard them mention 'Menin', which I knew to be on the Franco-Belgian frontier. I carried on but kept asking myself 'Why am I walking this way, when I know it is just opposite to the way I should go? But a hidden voice inside me kept saying 'Keep on', so I kept on.

"I spent the night in a cowshed after asking the farmer if I could. The following morning he came in with a drink of coffee, then I rejoined the stream of refugees, passed through Menin, and heard the refugees asking the way to 'Courtrai'. This was still farther away from Dunkirk, but again that hidden voice kept saying 'Keep on'. I rested, fed on some young peas from a field and put a few potatoes in my pocket for my next meal. By the time I eventually entered the outskirts of Courtrai, my wounds were playing me up and I was finding the going very heavy. In the main street I noticed some British soldiers who were prisoners. I was about all in and decided to give myself up when I noticed a white flag with a Red Cross on it on the opposite side of the street.

"I walked inside and saw a number of exhausted people sitting on the floor. The man in charge came to me and, without speaking, I pointed to my legs. He took off the old bandages and gasped. He left me for a few minutes and soon returned with an official who took a good look at them and asked me about them. I pointed to my ear without speaking. He got his mouth close to my ear and shouted. What he said I did not know, but I replied 'Oui'. To this his assistant said 'Je ne comprends pas'. My legs were dressed and I left the building.

"I walked on, passing over a bridge which the Germans were re-building, and left the town behind. I approached a farmer in his yard, and in the best French I could think of, told him I was very tired and asked if I could sleep in his building. He accused me of being a German, but on being told I was English he led me into a building. I had found a real friend. Food was brought to me and afterwards I asked for a towel, soap and razor.

"It was now five days since I had been wounded, in which time I had neither washed nor shaved. I settled down for the night, but my legs were too painful to allow me much rest. The following morning the farmer came in with some breakfast and advised me to rest for the day as it was Sunday. It was a lovely sunny day so I washed my socks and put them in the sun to dry. I sat out and watched the German bombers going over.

"The farmer fed me well—a lovely dinner of chicken and peas at noon, and supper in the evening. The following morning he again came with my breakfast. As I sat wondering what to do next the farmer returned and told me it was OK for me to go to Roubaix. 'Get a sack', he advised, 'and put some straw in it. Sling it over your shoulder. The Germans will think you are a workman.' He gave me a loaf and a bottle of coffee, a five-franc French piece which I knew to be obsolete, and four Belgian francs. The Belgian francs were to buy me a drink at Moucron and the five francs for one in France.

"With a struggle I moved on, clinging to a refugee cart until it stopped outside a café. I went in behind two men who asked for a drink. The landlord then asked me if I wanted a beer, to which I replied 'Oui'. He took three of my four francs, and I learned later that I had been charged for the drinks of the other two as well. Refreshed, the two men went out and I followed. They and the cart went in a different direction, so I plodded on alone.

"I entered a town which I was told was Tourcoing. I had been billeted here for a fortnight in November, 1939, when we had our first flap. Recognising a café that I had frequented a couple of times, with the sack over my shoulder I went in and sat down. The Garçon came over and asked if I wanted a beer. I replied 'Oui', and he brought me a glass of beer, for which I gave him the obsolete five-franc piece. He looked at it, hesitated, went to converse with his father, and returned with four-and-a-half francs' change.

"I beckoned to the landlord and asked him if he remembered Kennedy (one of my tank drivers and a pal of his). 'Willie Kennedy'? he asked. 'Oui' I said. 'I am a comrade of his and wounded'. On hearing this he held a conference with the rest of the men in the café, who all gathered round and asked if I had an identity card. I said 'No'. They asked me if I could speak French. Again I said 'No'. So how had I managed with the language problem? When I told them I had been acting deaf and dumb, they replied 'Bravo'.

"Two of the men left the café and I learned later that they had gone to try to get me an identity card, but had failed. I was then taken across the road to the house of one of the men. I was made to get out of the clothes I was wearing and given a fresh suit which had been sent over by the landlord of the café. My wounds were dressed and I was given a good meal. They told me I could rest and then move on when it suited me.

"Towards evening I was taken back into the café to say thank you for the suit. I was given a glass of beer each time a round was paid for, but each one seemed to make me thirstier and I began to shiver. My legs were very painful. At nine o'clock there was a curfew, and the Germans started to patrol the streets on motor-cycles. It was time to move. I stood up with the 'Patron' but I was all in. I just managed to get across the road to his house.

"We sat down to supper but I was so thirsty I asked for water. The 'Patron' and his wife looked at me and could see I was not well. I was put to bed and given aspirin and awoke next morning feeling better, but was unable to stand. The 'Patron' whose name was Monsieur Demarque, introduced me to his married daughter, and between them they dressed my wounds twice a day. There I lay for two weeks, with nothing to read but one sheet of the Daily Mirror which I read over and over again.

"On Monday of the third week, I had just had breakfast in bed when I heard footsteps on the stairs. I was disturbed and wondered whether to jump through the window. But I stayed put, and in walked two men wearing armbands, followed by a woman and the 'Patron'. In good English, the woman asked if I was an English soldier. I did not speak until I had been assured by Papa Demarque that it was OK. I told her I was. She looked at my wounds and said 'Follow me'. I dressed and walked downstairs still uncertain of what it was all about. An ambulance was outside. I was told to get in and it moved off. When I got out about fifteen minutes later, I found German soldiers on duty outside a building, which was the Hôtel de Ville. I was taken down into the basement, which had been turned into an emergency first-aid station, and put on a bed where two nurses silently started dressing my wounds. This happened every half hour until, finally, one of the nurses spoke. 'What a coincidence', she said. 'The English radio last night broadcast that one of our local boys had been admitted to a hospital in London, and here you are!'

"Negotiations were apparently going on to get me into hospital, but by lunchtime I was told it was too difficult. I was then taken to a big, fine house by the nurse, her husband, and the woman who had fetched me in the ambulance. There I was given wine and cigarettes, and the wireless was switched on to hear the news from London. I then sat down to a good dinner, after which I was taken back to Papa Demarque's house. They explained to Papa that I was to visit the first-aid station twice a day, 9 am and 4 pm. This I did for a week and, on the following Monday, I was told that I was going to the hospital to see a doctor.

"I was told to carry on as I had been doing, speaking to no one. A car flying a Red Cross flag took me to the hospital. On arrival there I was received by a nun, who pressed a bell for a male orderly. He took me into a ward occupied by Frenchmen, pointed to a bed, and gave me a white shirt and two towels. When one of the Frenchmen spoke to me, I made signs to indicate I was deaf and dumb, and got into bed. Word went round that I was deaf and dumb.

"Later that day the nun came with the director of the hospital, who told me I would see the doctor the following morning. It was 11 o'clock on June 27th when I was wheeled into the X-ray room and emerged with seven crosses marking the places where shrapnel was to be removed. The following day I was again wheeled into the same room where the nun—Sister Marie, as I now know her—indicated that she was going to administer the anaesthetic. In my deaf and dumb language I asked her if I had to inhale the stuff. She nodded.

"I awoke at 3 o'clock in the afternoon back in the ward. As the days went by, I learned quite a few words of French by trying to grasp the conversation that went on around me, and by the wireless, which was switched on each time there was a news broadcast from London. I had a job to restrain myself from joining in the conversation when various subjects of interest arose, such as types of British tanks that were being used.

"One day Albert, the ambulance driver, came into the ward. From his actions I could tell that he knew I was English. During the next few days he came in quite often, and gave me tobacco, cigarette papers and chocolate. The other patients asked him if he knew me, to which he replied, 'No, I just feel sorry for him'. When I improved, I was allowed to walk in the hospital grounds. During one of these walks Albert approached me and took me into his quarters in the grounds, where he and his wife were living. I asked him how he knew I was English. His uncle, he explained, was in the café on the first day that I had arrived in the town.

"He switched on the wireless and we listened to Sandy Macpherson playing request records, the first of which was 'I'll remember you, my darling, though I'm far across the sea'. I was lost in a world of dreams until Albert asked me what was the matter. The sweat was running down my face.

"The barber used to come round the hospital twice a week to shave the patients, and it was on one of these occasions that he tried to explain to me that I had a comrade coming into the ward. Another British soldier, I thought. I had heard them discussing what I thought was a plane crash, and guessed it might be one of the crew. But the newcomer on a stretcher turned out to be a real deaf and dumb man, not an Englishman as I had hoped.

"My wounds took a turn for the worse and I was again confined to bed. I tried to avoid looking towards the deaf and dumb man but, alas, one afternoon he wanted something which the orderly could not understand. Could I interpret in the deaf and dumb language? By various signs I managed to make the orderly understand that I did not know the deaf and dumb signs.

"This, apparently, did not satisfy the deaf and dumb man, he made signs that he wanted paper and pencil and wrote a note which the orderly read and brought over to me. This, I thought, was where I fade out. But it was evidently not intended for my eyes because he had written, in words I could understand: 'I think this man could be an English spy'. I passed it to one of the patients, at the same time making signs that I thought the deaf and dumb man was crackers. He passed it off as a joke.

"The following morning I managed to show Sister Marie the note. When she had completed her round of the ward she paused at the door and said 'This ward is overcrowded. We must make room for any new patients by moving these three into the small ward. I was one of the first to go.

"Sister Marie warned me to be very careful and not to speak to anyone. Eventually I began to get about again and would often walk in the grounds. On one occasion Sister Marie came hurrying out to tell me the Germans were visiting the ward and to stay out until she gave me the 'all clear'. Many amusing incidents happened during the weeks that followed.

"I was taught to play cards by one of the patients whom I had summed up as being very pro-British. I made him understand that I could tell what he was saying by watching his lips, and he proved to be a good pal. Several patients were rather curious about my identity and he told me I had been called every nationality except British! To save my skin I had to speak to him. So, after four months of being 'deaf and dumb', I told him I was an English soldier. On hearing this he went to his locker and gave me half of its contents which consisted of cigarettes, wine, chocolates and fruit. He also arranged for me to live with him when I left the hospital. He left himself a week later, but his wife and sister visited me regularly, each time bringing a flask of tea which was welcome after weeks of coffee.

"One day Albert came and told me that Winston Churchill was going to broadcast a speech in English and then in French. Would I like to hear it! With the agreement of Sister Marie, he took me to his room on the top floor of the hospital, where we listened to the speech. When the French version was followed by the Marseillaise, Albert turned the volume full on and there were tears in his eyes when it finished.

"There was a change of doctor while I was on my own in the little ward. The first morning he came round I was trying to read a French paper. He looked at my wounds and asked Sister Marie who I was. When she told him she did not know, he replied: 'He's reading the paper, so it should be easy to find out.' He insisted that I be given a piece of paper and a pencil. This was too much for Sister Marie and she left the ward, the doctor following. Later that day she came in with an English book lent to me by the doctor, and said another would be available when I had finished it. I was to remain in this hospital until early autumn.

"On the first Saturday in November Sister Marie came rushing in to say I was going out. I was told to walk in the grounds, where the director joined me and led me off to his own house situated at the main entrance to the hospital. There I was introduced to his wife and we drank to victory and kissed each other. I was then taken into the garage and put into the back of a van in which was a Frenchman who said his name was Paul Bricout. The van moved off and when it stopped some time later I found myself at the home of Paul Bricout.

"Another English soldier was already there, and I learned that Paul was a member of the Resistance. A route was to be found to get us back to England, the idea being that if we got to Marseilles we could get on an American ship which was bringing in supplies of Red Cross flour. Paul Bricout, a tram conductor, and his wife, were true patriots like Sister Marie. After the war I heard that the whole family was arrested in 1942 and imprisoned at Loos. The children were released but Paul Bricout was taken to Sonnenburg concentration camp where he died in June, 1944. Madame Bricout was sent to Ravensbruck concentration camp and on to Belsen. She was never seen again.

"Towards the end of January, 1941, Paul Bricout took us to the station where we met our guide and another English soldier. The four of us bid farewell to Paul and set off for the south of France, breaking our journey at Béthune, Abbeville, Paris, Tours and Bordeaux before crossing on foot into the Unoccupied Zone where we caught another train to Marseilles.

"We reported to an address given to us by our guide, whom we left behind when we crossed into the Unoccupied Zone. The address was that of a Seamen's Mission under the care of the Rev. Don Caskie, a Scottish minister. There was no question of getting on a flour boat. The only possible escape route was through Spain to Gibraltar where I arrived in May, 1941. Ten days later I was on an aircraft carrier bound for England. I arrived home in July and found that I had been reported killed and my wife had been supposed a widow."

Summary of Events and Escape Route

Left hospital first Saturday in November, 1940, to live with family of Paul Bricout on outskirts of Tourcoing. Rumours circulated about returning to England by air. Later it was suggested that American ships were coming into Marseilles with supplies of Red Cross flour. Rumour again prevailed that they were in fact British ships. An escape route had to be found to Marseilles. At the end of January, 1941, Paul Bricout took an English soldier and myself to Lille to meet the Resistance movement guide. We found him waiting with another soldier and a Frenchman who was on the Gestapo's wanted list.

*Stage 1:* Lille to Abbeville by train where the journey had to be broken. The Germans searched the train before allowing it to cross the Somme. A special permit signed by them was required. This problem was overcome by a friendly Frenchman who had the necessary documents and loaned them to us, removing his photograph and substituting ours.

*Stage 2:* Abbeville to Tours by train where we hoped to cross the demarcation line. Here again the Germans had made it necessary to have a special permit. The guide carried a revolver and was prepared to use it but, after enquiries, we left on the next stage by a different route.

*Stage 3:* Tours to Bordeaux by train.

*Stage 4:* Bordeaux to Langon where we had to break the journey again, the train being searched before crossing the demarcation line into the Unoccupied Zone.

*Stage 5:* Langon by car to Bazas, where we were treated very well. The guide, who was at first suspected of being a member of the Gestapo, finally convinced contacts and fixed for another guide to take us over the demarcation line. Funds were low and, after giving us the fare to Marseilles, he returned home. Darkness saw us walking down the road and, at a given point, we left the road to cross 500 metres of 'No Man's Land', and a 12-kilometre walk to reach Marmande.

*Stage 6:* Marmande to Marseilles by main-line train. A relief to be in Unnocupied France, but heard we would still be arrested by French police. Ex-Belgian officers on the train told us that identity cards were checked at Marseilles. Mine was a Belgian card and I required an additional paper from the Belgian Consul. One of the Belgian officers lent me his identity card wallet, so that I could fold my identity card in such a way that only the page containing the photo was revealed.

On arrival at the station we found all exits policed. Covering my identity card as much as possible with my hand I took my chance and approached the busiest policeman. I had passed before he realised that something was not quite right with it, but I was soon lost in the crowd.

We arrived at the Mediterranean Seamen's Mission in the care of the Rev. Don Caskie. This seemed to be the end of the escape route as planned by the Resistance. French detectives visited the mission every morning looking not only for British Servicemen but also for Frenchmen who, they alleged, were using it to try to join General de Gaulle in England. Although it was known as Unoccupied France, there was a German Commissioner who insisted that no British subject would be allowed to leave the country unless outside military age—under 17 or over 40 years old.

The American ships bringing in Red Cross flour really were American, not British. It was not possible to get near them, so escape that way was out. After many enquiries I settled for a medical board which sat every month. My chance came in April, 1941, when three doctors of different nationalities declared me unfit. It was then necessary to get three visas: one to leave France, one to enter Spain, and the other to leave and proceed to the nearest British territory, which was Gibraltar. Four of us from the mission, all Servicemen, had to join up with others at an internment camp at St-Hippolyte, quite a distance from Marseilles.

A few days later, a party of 25 of us, set off for Perpignan for the journey through Spain. The first stop was Barcelona, where the British Consul installed us in the best hotel for the night. The following morning we caught a train for Madrid, where the British Ambassador placed us in another very good hotel and then gave us a talk on how the war was going. We rested for the remainder of that day and set off for Gibraltar at night, arriving at Malaga the next afternoon.

We then made our way by bus, through customs at St-Rocque, and on to British territory. After an interview with the Governor, Lord Gort, and questioning by intelligence, we waited for an aircraft-carrier which delivered planes to Gibraltar and returned to England with damaged ones. Eventually we found ourselves on board the carrier *Argus*, and set off one night after dark. We travelled all night and found ourselves back at Gibraltar just as the sun was rising. Our escort of destroyers—*Fearless, Fortune* and *Foxhound*—dashed off down the Mediterranean.

After a few days' wait and a 12-day voyage, we arrived on the Clyde. A sight to remember . . . A night train took us to London where we were taken to a hotel for questioning by M16. Then it was a train to our nearest depot, mine being the Tank Depot at Farnborough. The following morning I was on the way home for a month's leave. The same day my wife had received information that I had arrived at Gibraltar.

* * * * *

*Lance Sergeant Henry Suggitt* was yet another to survive escape attempts. Near Waterloo, south of Brussels and where the Regiment had fought with the Union Brigade in 1815, Henry was fighting a rearguard action as a member of a Bren carrier crew. He was wounded by an anti-tank gun while trying to get through a German convoy proceeding in the same direction as himself. His driver and gunner were killed, the operator managed to escape. He was picked up by the Germans and loaded into a vehicle with German wounded, then conveyed to hospital.

After six months in hospital he was sent to a POW camp and to work in coal mines in Silesia and later joined working parties on other tasks. This he thought, would be the easiest way to escape. Henry specialised in forgery and twice managed to walk out of the camp in German uniform. His first escape attempt was recorded in one of three newsletters sent to members of the Regimental Association. As in the Charlie Bevan story, the reader is left to use his own imagination to assess the stress and danger of such a mission:

"On Monday, August 25th, 1941, Henry left with a Arbeitskommando (working party) 18 strong from Stalag VIIIB at Lamsdorf and was taken by train from Annahof, en route for Triebitz, Sudentenland. After seven hours' travel through some very pretty country, they arrived at Triebitz and were given soup at the station. They were marched to a billet, washed and were permitted to swim in the lake, knock apples from trees and generally settle down. They worked for two days. During the third night they escaped through a window by tying blankets together.

"The party of three walked for half an hour before arriving at a railway workers' hut where they stole clothing. Finding the trains impossible to jump they decided it would be safer to walk and set off for Brunn. During the following day they rested in a small wood while civilians worked in the fields only yards away. Navigating by the Plough, which indicated the North Star, the party headed south-east. There was no shortage of water but they stuck to the rules of health and only drank running water. After three days of walking, hiding places were becoming difficult to find. One member of the party was attacked by a swarm of bees.

"They decided to walk by day and sleep by night. A party of walking men, if spotted at night, would raise suspicions. There was a rapid escape from an empty house. They slept in what appeared to be a building under construction, but roused by the sound of heavy hammering downstairs. After hastily dressing they descended but were caught by a workman. They found the workmen to be Czechs who kindly gave them the remains of their breakfast.

"After this welcome feed they were shown how to follow the correct routes through the forest by means of colours marked on trees. After a few hours they arrived at the first of five villages which they were told would lead to Brunn. They slept for a while in a small park. Henry saw a small shop and risked recapture when he went to purchase two kilos of tomatoes, three jellies and six matches. He was served by an old lady and her semi-blind son. The old lady's pity was aroused when Henry told his story and she gave him a slice from her own precious ration. They were now having to rest in the woods by both day and night, according to circumstances. They came upon another railway line and, by the lights from low signals, were able to read the destination on waggon tallies. None indicated destinations which they considered suitable, so they continued on foot but kept to the line. While prowling round a small station yard they had to hide suddenly when a number of passengers arrived.

"They mistook the second village for Brunn because of modern buildings and a splendid motorway. They crossed a stream by the rail bridge and made for higher ground where they could observe the trains passing 50 feet below them. They slept in a copse of fir trees and the following day, made good progress and were well into a mountain area. The railway was still visible below but, about 200 yards ahead, it disappeared into a tunnel. It was guarded by special tunnel guards which meant they would have to find the exit to pick up the trail. There was a mountain stream of fresh water and they chose to have a good clean up. After two more days' travel through the forest area they emerged at a point where they could see Brunn.

"Suddenly coming upon a small refreshment kiosk, they bought beer and some macaroons. The proprietor was suspicious and asked many questions. Henry, being the only member of the party who could converse in German, did his best to answer the questions while his companions thought it prudent to leave. They moved on to the outskirts of the town and Henry left his pack with his friends to go on alone and investigate. The plan was to find a gradient where the trains would slow sufficiently to permit them to mount a truck. It seemed that all weekend trains carried passengers, so they decided to wait and watch.

"The following day, armed with a ration card, Henry entered the town again and queued for a ration of cigarettes and anything else he could get. He walked round the local church and again risked entry to a Gasthaus. Just as he was about to speak to two men who were obviously Czechs, a third arrived and Henry changed his mind quickly. He looked at the clock on the wall and as though late for an appointment, left hurriedly. He stopped and glanced into a shoe shop to ensure that he was not being followed, then returned to his friends, who were not impressed with his purchase of just two cigarettes.

"Boarding a train became very risky and they decided to move west of Brunn. They stole carrots from a field but were caught by an old man who raved at them in Czech but refused payment. It was now 2.30 in the morning as they moved through Brunn. A dark shape appeared, shone his lamp on them and challenged them in Czech. Henry replied saying that they were German workers about to go on shift in a local factory. Their packs were examined but when they were found to contain only a little fruit and a towel, they were allowed to proceed. The lack of good food was having an effect upon them and they risked another Gasthaus to exchange a 20 mark note. The owner refused to sell bread without a card but she did give them a slice from her own loaf and they ate it with blackberries.

"Taking shelter from rain in an orchard, the group supplied themselves with plums and apples then moved on to seek better cover for a dry out and a 24-hour rest period. There were many shrines in the forests of Bohemia and Moravia and they were able to make the most of these.

"The following day they came upon a small factory with its own small rail link and by following it, they found the main line again and boarded an Italian coal truck. They spent many hours in a truck but were eventually discovered by railway employees. Chained together they were marched through the silent streets to the police station, where they were questioned before being thrown into separate cells. During that six-day stay, Henry was able to exchange his Czech money for German Marks again. A German military guard duly arrived and they were escorted to a French POW camp where they were issued with French clothing. This was followed by a period of 13 days in isolation before being conducted back to their own camp. it had been ten days' of worthy liberty."

The second attempt came in April, 1944. Henry walked out of the camp dressed in a German sergeant's uniform. His Australian companion was suitably clothed as a German corporal. Unfortunately, his companion's poor German led to a speedy recapture and further punishment. In April, 1945, as the Allies moved closer to their camp, they were moved further east but Henry escaped with 18 others and made it to our own lines.

# Who was to blame for our defeat?

The defeat of the Western Allies in 1940 was a direct result of our unpreparedness. It is difficult to believe that the intelligence services of Britain, France, Belgium and Holland were not aware of the build up of forces by Germany and unforgiveable that our forces were obliged to face such odds. The years prior to the outbreak could have been better spent in rearming, but it was too late. Even in 1937, the Army Council was debating upon the use of cavalry and the Regiment, together with the Royal Dragoons and Royal Scots Greys, were to remain as cavalry. Only in October of that year was it decided that only the Greys should remain horsed.

Our nation is renowned for fighting against superior odds, but at what a cost this had been. We are left to ponder what would have been the outcome if Neville Chamberlain had not resigned and we had not found a leader such as Winston Churchill.

The humiliation of Dunkirk roused the country to its finest hour, and to a new belief that it was everybody's war and not just the battle of the armed forces. No expense was too great. Industry, women and children had to be brought into the planning to rearm, retrain and return to Europe. Initially, of course, it was still expected that the Germans would invade, and we were still on the defensive. Signposts, railway station names, and any shop front which gave away the location, had to be removed. Anyone asking the way was immediately suspect and likely to find himself at the sharp end of a farmer's pitch-fork.

Was Hitler the initiator of the flight by Rudolph Hess to seek an armistice with Britain? Whatever prevented the invasion gave us the breathing space so dearly needed. New regiments were raised and special forces trained for individual tasks—to fight in the desert, up mountains and in a variety of special roles. There was hard work to be done under new leaders with new ideas.

We had lost a number of good men but, because of the brilliant leadership and the discipline of the Regiment, casualties were comparatively low considering the extent of its involvement in the fighting. It was soon realised that the Regiment could provide the cadres for the formation of other regiments: officers, non-commissioned officers and men were promoted or volunteered for other arms. Of those shown in the command structure on September 23rd, 15 officers were to be promoted and posted. Within three years seven would be in command of other regiments and three would soldier on to become Generals.

A final plea on behalf of the Belgians, who were adversely

criticised by those who gave accounts of the withdrawal. Soldiers are unaware of the intrigues which brought about their plight. Lord Keyes, who wrote a biography of King Leopold of the Belgians, gave great credit to the Belgian Army for holding and gaining vital days which permitted so many of our troops to get away at Dunkirk.

The King was faced with impossible odds and knew that his country would suffer the same fate as Rotterdam and other cities. We know now that he made the right decision, but it cost him his crown. The Regiment remained loyal to him and he continued to serve as our Colonel-in-Chief until his death in 1983. Those who were privileged to meet him also know the anguish he suffered during those years.

# PART II

# Reforming, Rearming and Returning

The move of the cavalry regiments to France in 1939 brought into being the formation of new Armoured Training Regiments, two of which were to be set up in the Tidworth area, one at Farnborough and another at Bovington. The 54th Training Regiment RAC was to become my home for the next two years. Having joined the 10th Royal Hussars in March, 1939, I was one of eight band boys to be warned at 2130 hrs to be ready to move at 2200 hrs on November 8th.

We were not told at that time where we were being taken. But it was a cold night to travel in an open GS wagon, and we were relieved that it was only two miles up the road to Perham Down. The boys of other regiments, including 5th Royal Inniskilling Dragoon Guards, had already arrived, and there were about 100 of us in all.

A band was readily available to the senior bandmaster, Mr Norman Richardson, from the Skins. Some boys were already proficient instrumentalists and there were many senior bandsmen who were too old to be retrained to fight with their regiments. I was neither trained nor interested in music and was delighted to carry out other tasks, even though they were sometimes very hard duties. There was coal to be moved, the cookhouse ever requiring assistants, and the stores and offices too absorbed a few more of us.

I was fortunate in falling for a plum job in one of the squadron offices and becoming a runner for the sergeant major and orderly sergeant. There was a surplus of Army education warrant officers at Perham and this permitted us to attend school in the mornings. I had left school on my 14th birthday, so the additional and professional tuition gave me the opportunity to obtain Army Certificates of Education which would otherwise have taken years.

My post in the office progressed to 'leave clerk' and I filled in pass forms, warrants and ration cards. There was also a certificate to be signed by every man proceeding on leave. It read: 'This is to certify that I have been warned to proceed overseas and that if I am absent I am liable for trial by courts martial as a deserter.' I learned to type this certificate at great speed, but it was the limit of my typing capabilties.

The bandmasters had the right to recall any boys they required, so I found myself reduced to the cymbals which required little practice. This suited me fine: I could wear gloves, which I could not when playing the clarinet, and I could make myself heard. I was also excused the long, boring, note-blowing and scale practice during the evenings. We were recalled for several parades, including funerals and long, cold marches in slow time; once or twice we had to escort a draft from Perham Down to Tidworth station at the unholy hour of 0400.

Those of us serving King and Country on the home front heard of the attack on Belgium and the use of paratroopers. This was something very new but we still had the utmost confidence in the ability of our army to hold and defeat the Germans. The French Maginot Line would teach them a thing or two.

The scale of the tank assaults were also reported in the press and acts of gallantry were already being recognised. It was a great and rude awakening when, about June 2nd, there was great activity in our washrooms and showers during the night. We were up at reveille to find that not only was the camp full of men from every regiment in the British Army but Frenchmen and Belgians, too.

I was sent to help to receive the train loads which were still pouring in and, working at tables set up on the side of the main road through Perham, I spent four days recording the number, rank, name and regiment of each arrival. Other boys led the bedraggled men to a tank hanger and issued each of them with a straw filled palliasse and three blankets. It was fortunate that the weather was so warm.

The cookhouse was running a 24-hour service and all ranks dined together. The men's stories of their escape from Dunkirk and the savage attacks they had endured from dive bombers were frightening. For the first time, we began to wonder whether we were as good as we thought. There were a few Skins among the gathering, but I had already met the Palestinian Squadron when they had arrived in January. They had marched from Andover station, a distance of eight miles in the most dreadful weather conditions. They had left Palestine in the 80's and facing these conditions had not pleased them.

They were soon off to rejoin the Regiment, then in France. There were also a number of senior ranks holding key positions at Perham, among them SSM Webster and SSM Godman. Green trousers were becoming a common sight. During my duty on the reception tables, many men gave me French francs as souvenirs and, on June 4th, the NAAFI agreed to accept this currency. Never had band boys had so much money or stuffed themselves with so much cake.

The presence of a hundred young boys paid a shilling a day, of which they were permitted to draw two shillings a week (tenpence in decimal money), full of energy and with little constructive employment, led to a few problems. NCOs avoided the task of supervising them and many were reduced in rank because of misdemeanours committed by this devilish lot.

There was a liberal period of daily PT and at least an hour's drill added to the daily routine, but this led to more discontent. Our drill was second to none and we resented being used as a squad to train young NCOs who frequently gave the wrong order or gave it on the wrong foot. This training was probably devised to absorb the abundance of energy otherwise employed in raiding the cookhouse, NAAFI and other establishments.

The RSM was fed up with the constant police searches and having his guard room full of delinquents. We still wore our service dress and were very proud to have this distinction, showing that we were pre-war soldiers. During one of the drill sessions there was an event which was to bring about a great change for most of us. We had already been drilling for about an hour in the sun and thought we were about to be dismissed when the dreaded tick of the RSM's pace-stick was heard behind us. We knew that trouble was not very far away.

There was a bull-like roar from the edge of the square. At first this was directed towards the performance of the NCO who was drilling us, but it gave the RSM the opportunity to vent his wrath upon this squad of sinners. RSM Voller, who had been posted in from one of the Royal Tank Corps battalions, was a very smart man but had developed a strong dislike for boys. The NCO was ordered to get us into quick time and get our hands above our heads. His weak, pathetic voice ordered various turns, but the squad was getting further and further away from him and we were having to listen very carefully for the next command. As we headed for the edge of the square, RSM Voller took control and ordered "About turn," to which somebody in the rear replied audibly: "**** him," or words to that effect. Nobody turned about, and we were off the edge of the square. The order was repeated several times but we kept going like stampeding cattle, jumped over slit trenches, then up and over the mound of chalk removed from them, and on down the slope.

After trotting on for about a mile, still with our hands above our heads, we stopped and sat down. What was to be done now? There was clearly nothing for it but to return. But how? We agreed to stick to the story that we didn't hear any order to about turn, and that we understood a good soldier kept going even if it meant going over a cliff. I don't think we expected it to work, but it was the best we could think of. Since my office duties included marching recruits to the dentist in the next camp, I was elected to march the squad back. My associates probably thought I would be held responsible, but I reasoned that I might be seen to have shown some initiative.

I insisted that if I was to take this upon myself, we should march back in fine style, head up and arms swinging, so that the squad came up the Ludgershall road in a manner that could not have been faulted in a Guards depot. RSM Voller, was standing waiting on the edge of the square, he ordered me to halt squad. It was a most impressive halt and worthy of a little praise. Mr. V. walked round the squad, glaring at each one, then told me: "March them to the bottom guard room and put six in each cell. March the remainder to the top guard room and put the rest in there." As an afterthought, he shouted, "And put yourself in with them." After half an hour we were released and given two extra pack drills with marching at 180 paces to the minute.

This was a comparatively light punishment for such an act of defiance. We must have had a friend somewhere, for we were each sent for individually and told that, if we wished, we could join an intake of recruits and complete a proper course of training. The thought of wireless, driving and gunnery, less physical exercise, appealed to us all. The greatest bonus was to be able to retire to bed later, and to swear and smoke! But, disappointingly, our pay would not be increased.

I joined a squad of "Geordies" who immediately christened me "Jim". This was an improvement on my nickname "Snatch", inherited from my father, and saved me the embarrassment of revealing that my proper name was Clarence. How could I survive a military career with a name like that? The experience I had already gained in drill, and the fact that I was very tall, qualified me for the coveted post of "right-hand man". The training included all the trades of the tank crewman and I was to become a wireless operator. There was still live firing to do and, in October 1941, I set off to fire a two-week course on Castlemartin tank ranges. As this was the time of the invasion scare, the tanks were kept fully loaded with ammunition and crews slept in them at night, one member being placed forward with a Bren gun to act as a listening watch.

I spent a terrifying night alone, believing that the defence of the country was dependent on me. My fears were not lightened by the frequent scurrying of rats and the moan of the foghorn down on the cliff front. Every object I could see through the mist seemed to move, and I was very tempted to fire a burst from my Bren. Daybreak took on a new dimension for me from that night onwards.

I might have been more relaxed had I studied a map and noted that any invasion force would have to travel round Land's End and that they would be unlikely to scale the cliffs. The incident did pay off in later years when, fed up with other war stories, I could throw in my bit and challenge: "I bet none of you were on active service in a tank at the age of sixteen." It was a trump card, but usually treated with some suspicion.

The following day I was to fire my first round from a Valentine tank. The flag was down and I was given the necessary order to get on to a target. I pressed the trigger, but there was only a click. "Misfire", I called out. There was immediate action by those on or near the tank, because a mis-fire could lead to a premature explosion in the breech. Only the instructor remained in the turret with me, and we moved forward up the range while all other firing stopped. Nothing happened, and now we were faced with opening the breech, extracting the round, and throwing it out of the tank.

Still no detonation. As I was in the gunner's seat, it fell to the instructor to stick a red flag into the ground for future demolition. It was unfortunate, to say the least, to have a misfire on the first ever round to be fired. I don't think I ever experienced another.

# Reformation

The Regiment had gathered at Bovington Camp for refitting and rekitting and had been granted a week's leave. Moving north to Keele Hall, in Staffordshire, they had no vehicles and were still equipped with Lee Enfield rifles left over from the Great War. During the invasion scare in September they were moved for a five-week stay in Builth Wells.

Hitler's planned invasion, codenamed "Operation Sea Lion", had been thwarted by attacks on the barges he intended to use. We in England, however, were unaware of this and defence systems were set up. Pillboxes were built at key points and in the areas where aircraft might land, and large poles were set into the ground. Those who had been wounded during the retreat to Dunkirk reappeared and new drafts were posted in.

In November the Regiment moved to Northampton, where proper billets were commandeered and individual training could begin. During an 18-month stay there, many friendships were formed and marriages contracted. The locals accepted the disruption of their lives, and the strong branch of the Regimental Association in that town today is evidence of the strong ties fostered then.

Despite the heavy air attacks upon our cities and airfields, our factories were able to maintain production. The RAF was more than holding its own and, in that wonderful month, September 1940, shot down 212 German aircraft. Hitler was beginning to realise that the war was far from over.

New regiments and specialist units were being formed, causing large drafts of men to be posted out, and the Regiment was given the option of reverting to its constituent regiments, the 5th Dragoon Guards and the 6th Inniskilling Dragoons. But the amalgamation was now well and truly consummated, and new honours had been won under the present title. Besides, there would be property and funds to divide; and how would the prefix "Royal" be used by two separate regiments? The dress had been so arranged that buttons and badges were a complete representation of both regiments. The offer was therefore rejected.

They were then asked to form two regiments carrying the same title—the 1st and 2nd/5th Royal Inniskilling Dragoon Guards. There would still be a problem with funds, and it was agreed that it would be preferable to form new armoured regiments which could be disbanded after the war. Accordingly, the 22nd Dragoons, 23rd and 26th Hussars, and 24th and 27th Lancers were raised. Each regular regiment was paired with a new one to provide a cadre of officers, NCOs and men. In all, seven officers and 63 men were transferred from the 5th Royal Inniskilling Dragoon Guards, mostly to the 22nd Dragoons. Pride of place, however, went to Major Perry Harding and Captain Monkey Blacker, who became CO and Adjutant, respectively, to the 23rd Hussars.

The Regiment now became the senior regiment in the newly formed 28th Armoured Brigade under the leadership of their old Commanding Officer, Brigadier Ugly Martin. They were reunited with their old friends, the 15/19th Hussars, and joined by the Fife and Forfar Yeomanry. The Brigade was part of the 9th Armoured Division whose GOC was Major-General M D Burrows, DSO, MC, late of the 5th Dragoon Guards. Many internal promotions took place, including that of Lieutenant-Colonel Jack Anstice, the much revered Commanding Officer who had led the Regiment so courageously through France. He, more than any other man, was responsible for the success of the retreat to Dunkirk, and richly deserved his promotion to Brigadier in a newly-formed Brigade.

Colonel Jack had followed a line of the Anstice family reaching back to the Boer War. In his place came a hard-hitting, no nonsense CO—Lieutenant-Colonel "Hook" Sangster, who had a reputation as a hard-riding cavalry officer. He resembled, both in appearance and manner, that old war-horse, General Yorke-Scarlett, a past commanding officer of the 5th Dragoon Guards and leader of the famous charge of the Heavy Brigade at Balaclava. Colonel Hook, was undoubtedly a man's man, a Churchill type who quickly won affection and respect by out-smarting most old soldiers with his vocabulary of swear words and lively defence of his regiment against all comers. His cavalry-type instruction to accelerate was "kick it in the belly", and his signal sergeant kept a good supply of headsets to replace the ones he broke on the turret when using the microphone as a whip. Women were now being heard over the network and our Colonel frequently told them to get off our so-and-so net. Apologies were occasionally necessary, for we still respected our ladies. He had, it seemed, often been ordered to apologise to the ladies by the umpires at polo matches, too. He would do so by galloping up, reining to a halt, announcing "Sorry ladies", then galloping away muttering "Shouldn't bloody well be here, anyway."

In the ranks, too, characters were emerging. Mention of "Ginger" Livingstone is guaranteed to inspire discussion of his many misdemeanours. Ginger was no academic, but he was no fool either. He could not be faulted in his unenviable job as Regimental Sanitaryman (old soldiers will know it by a less polite title!) but was frequently in trouble for over-reaction. The toilets were often a long row of self-made wooden seats over buckets, which could be removed via a trap door at the rear. Anyone unfortunate enough to be meditating within when Ginger was doing his rounds could be rudely awakened. He was quite likely to remove the bucket and slap a liberal amount of whitewash over the occupant's private parts as well as the woodwork.

The SSM at this time rated a batman—a role to which Ginger was appointed. One dark and windy night Ginger was taking advantage of the comforts of the SSM's quarters and using his shaving kit and after-shave when the air raid warden called out that he was showing a light—an unpardonable sin. When Ginger rudely told him to go away, the warden demanded to know his name. "Rushton", replied Ginger. The first the SSM knew of this was when he was summoned to appear in court.

On another occasion, when some stores had been misplaced, receipts were checked and one was found to have been signed "J Livingstone, RSM". Asked to account for the stores and for the appelation "RSM", Ginger replied: "Regimental Sanitary Man".

At about this time Rudolph Hess, Deputy Fuhrer of the Third Reich, had made a spectacular flight to Scotland and parachuted into captivity. A strange story was told about this to the sergeants' mess in 1960. I was by that time, the Regimental Sergeant Major, and I received a call from a Captain Larcombe, who told me he was serving in REME near our camp in Germany and that his father was visiting him from America. Arthur Larcombe had been RSM before Maurice Peters and had handed over in 1938. Hitherto he had been no more than a name on a board in the orderly room corridor, listing all past RSMs since 1938. I invited him to lunch.

His story should encourage any soldier who believes it is important to be in the right place at the right time. Arthur certainly was. He admitted that in pre-war years, he had great difficulty in obtaining his Army first class certificate of education which would qualify him for promotion to Warrant Officer, Class 1. So he paid another man ten shillings to sit it for him and was duly promoted.

In 1938 he was commissioned to serve as a quartermaster with a territorial regiment, a post which he did not enjoy. He resigned. After only six months, war was declared and he was recalled, transferred to the Pioneer Corps, and sent to France to set up a prisoner of war camp. Few prisoners were taken and he narrowly avoided becoming one himself. Back in the UK he was appointed second-in-command of a POW camp and more prisoners were brought in. He was now a captain and, as the camps filled up, another was built in Wales with Arthur appointed commandant, now in the rank of major.

When Hess arrived, he was placed in Arthur's care. He had a very friendly relationship with this high-ranking prisoner, whom he respected, and the men corresponded until Arthur died in about 1978. Hess made a fuss and claimed a number of privileges, one being that he ought to be guarded by someone of higher rank than a major. Arthur was promoted Colonel!

# Action on the Home Front

The greatest disruption to life was being caused by air raids. Travel through London was not permitted and journeys were long and tedious. We boys still battling on Salisbury Plain were allowed a week's leave in the spring of 1941. My father had moved to Bromley, Kent, to take up an appointment as recruiting officer. I travelled up to London and saw for the first time the chaos and destruction. Londoners were claiming their places on the platforms of the Underground for the night, quite oblivious to trains and passengers passing through.

Nightly attacks had been the way of life since August, 1940, and when I arrived at Bromley North station at about 1800 hours the outer barrage in the South-east had already started. I quickened my pace, hoping to reach home before any attack commenced, and broke into a trot when a lump of shrapnel struck an iron gate beside me. Although I was accustomed to nights in a shelter or slit trench and had watched the attacks upon Southampton and a heavy raid on the night fighter RAF station at Middle Wallop, it was a new experience for me to be among civilians.

I arrived home to find the family already in the cellar which they shared with another family already homeless. My father stood in the doorway watching the flares overhead. He had an area to patrol as a fire watcher. I was carrying my steel helmet, as required to, and resented his suggestion that I ought to be wearing it. Wearing a helmet on leave was not in my scheme of things and would, in my view, have been an act of fear. Father said: "If you're not going to wear it, I will," and put it on immediately.

The night of April 16, 1941, saw one of the heaviest attacks upon the South-east and proved to be a night to remember. I was half-way down the cellar steps when two bombs struck the house simultaneously at front and rear, reducing it to a heap of rubble. I was still sitting on the stairs in a cloud of dust, but the stairs were at an angle. The cellar was in total darkness, with coal dust everywhere. Nothing was said for a few seconds, then everybody seemed to shout at once.

Miraculously my father, who was no more than five yards from the edge of one of the craters, suffered only a cut head, though my steel helmet had a gouged side and a broken chinstrap. Shouts from outside directed the family out through the coal chute while I joined my father over the rubble. A boy was shouting from the house next door that he couldn't find his grandfather. I went to help but it was hopeless and I returned to my father.

The family had made off to an air raid shelter and we made for a small church. Incendiary and high-explosive bombs seemed to be falling all around. We obtained a jar of water from somewhere and I bathed my father's head, then applied my field dressing which we carried at all times. When I opened a rear door to check the escape route from the room in which we were sheltering, I was caught in a blast of flame. The room was already well alight. We left hurriedly through the door we came in by.

Not knowing Bromley, I had no idea where air-raid shelters were located. The lane we entered was a mass of incendiaries, but all we could do was move them cautiously to the middle of the track to prevent their setting things alight. Five women were screaming in a surface Anderson shelter, outside the door of which an incendiary had embedded itself in the ground. My helmet came in handy as a scoop to cover it with earth and allow the occupants to get out for some air.

One woman begged me to go back to her house to recover some documents. We dashed up the stairs to find the bedroom alight. She scrambled under the bed to recover her treasures. There was a surface shelter in a timber yard, not the sort of thing to offer much protection from bombs but at least a place where I might have a proper look at my father's wounds. I was still in uniform but minus my side hat and was hoping the MPs would not see me. I also kept thinking of my best boots and wondering how they would ever be fit for parade again. It all seems so stupid now but relevant to life at that time.

A boy of about ten was trying to operate a stirrup pump from a bucket. I took over the pump while he climbed up tree trunks to direct the jet of water on to an incendiary lodged between the trunks. A bomb fell about 100 yards away and the trunks moved. We both ran out of the yard as the lot slipped and demolished the fence behind us. The water mains had been fractured, depriving the firemen of water from the hydrants, and burning gas gushed from broken mains. I thought Bromley would be totally destroyed.

The raid lasted until 0400 hours, and when I walked back to look at the ruins I realised I no longer had a home. There was neither gunfire (probably out of ammunition) nor fighter cover, and it seemed that we were at the mercy of the enemy. It was a hopeless mess but had to be endured. On the way back I saw my younger sister standing at the entrance to a shelter. She reassured me that my mother, brother and other sister were quite well, and I told her that father was all right but still bleeding. We later discovered that she had relayed this message as "Father's all right but still breathing." It did nothing to reassure anybody!

A young girl, who had been visiting one of my sisters, was desperate to return home at the other end of town and I agreed to go with her. The streets were covered in debris, bomb holes full of water, and every pane of glass in the shops was broken. We rounded the corner of her street only to find that she, too, had lost her home.

She left after being assured by someone that her family were safe, I never saw her again.

There was a further raid on the following Wednesday but it was directed towards Woolwich Docks, the intended target of the first raid, and very few bombs fell in Bromley. I spent the nights in a shelter and the days salvaging items from the house. It is depressing to find half burnt photographs, cherished belongings destroyed and above all, to wonder where the family would live from now on. That was solved by a 'phone call to an old aunt in Cheshire with whom they went to live.

After seven days I returned to the comparative peace of Salisbury Plain. There was no sympathy when I reported to the SQMS that I had lost my cap, that my steel helmet was useless, and, that I had used my field-dressing on my father's head. He replaced my helmet, said there was nothing he could do about my coloured side-hat, and charged me ninepence (3.75p) for a new field dressing. That hurt a bit and of course, if I had made a fuss, I would have been given a free replacement.

The SQMS, not a person to upset, informed me that field dressings were for an emergency and, even then, not for use on civilians. I had only been back a few days when three German fighters swept across the camp at low level, shooting up everything in sight. They caught a squad of recruits in the nearby officer cadet training unit, killing a total of 18 including the commanding officer. Our Lewis guns, manned 24 hours a day, were caught completely unawares and remained silent. But when a Wellington bomber flew low over on the same route a few minutes later, everything in the area opened up at it! How they failed to shoot it down is a mystery. The crew probably had something to say about it on landing.

While these events were going on in England, on other fronts members of the Regiment were serving in almost every theatre of war. The story of one indicates the sort of action they encountered. Farrier Major "Gus" Newport had served with the Regiment since 1920 and was a much respected authority on the horse. Already 40 when mechanisation came, and having no wish to retrain for the short time he thought he had left to serve, he transferred to the Royal Dragoons, still equipped with horses. When they too, were forced to mechanise, he transferred to units still using horses and mules in Greece and Crete. The mule was, and still is, excellent transport in this type of terrain. Gus was commissioned into the General Service Corps and sent to Greece. Aged almost 90 in 1988, he vividly recalled his experiences:

*Major Gus Newport:*

"At about 1900 hours on April 11th, 1941, I was supervising the unloading of mules and horses from a ship called the *Quiloa.* We had unloaded about 300 when we were attacked by German aircraft. The off-loading had to cease when a bomb exploded in the engine room and there was total darkness below. The remainder were safely off-loaded the following day. On the 14th I received a sudden order to proceed with six soldiers by train to Larissa, to set up an advanced remount depot. I could expect to receive a hundred mules the following day.

"The train had to make frequent halts to avoid air attack and it was 0100 hours on April 16th when we finally arrived. Failing to find anyone to report to on the deserted station, the officer in charge of the train decided that we should back up the line to a place where the men could safely stretch their legs and rest. It was a wise decision because, when we moved back to the station at daybreak, we found it had been heavily bombed. We moved out and slept in slit trenches on Larrissa aerodrome. It, too, came under heavy attack before dawn. I made yet another attempt to find Headquarters, 81 Base Sub Depot, and eventually found where they had been. I learned that all troops had been evacuated and that the town was about to be. Later that morning I found No 1 Company of the Royal Army Service Corps and attached my small army to them for the remainder of the day.

"We joined a convoy which left for Athens that night and, on arrival, I was detailed to take command of 120 mixed ranks, 300 mules and 27 horses. Two lorries were attached for supplies and we were directed to march to Argos, a town some 80 miles distant. My orders were to do the journey in 48 hours. I pointed out that 40 miles a day could not be maintained over that sort of mountain terrain, but I agreed to make all possible hast.

"Departing at 1830 hours, we marched throughout the night. But the harnesses were intended for horses and fitted badly; packs slipped and had to be recovered in the dark; some mules broke loose and were lost. Each man rode a horse and led two mules, each loaded with two packs. It was a strenuous journey. We marched continuously until April 23rd when I rested the men and animals for four hours. At 1330 hours, on a mountain track overlooking the sea, we were attacked by fighters. It was beautiful country, but no place to be caught in an air raid. There was no escape. Six Stukas dive-bombed and machine-gunned us continuously. We had nothing to retaliate with and our casualities were heavy. Forty animals killed and 60 injured. Seventy stampeded and were probably killed in falls. We cleared the road, destroyed the injured animals, and set the remainder free to fend for themselves.

"The main question now was to get the wounded men to a hospital. We made our way to the nearest road and were fortunate in stopping a lorry which took the worst cases on to Argos. I reported to the officer responsible for evacuation on April 24th and was advised to take my survivors up into the hills to await further orders. None came, so I set off to find the senior offiçer who, I was told was located some 12 miles away. The best advice he could offer was that we should remain in the hills. On April 26th, we were ordered to evacuate to Kalamata, but the lorries in which we travelled were constantly under attack and we suffered more casualties.

"The following day I was ordered to hold my party in readiness for embarkation that night. We marched to the beach but there was no ship, we saw we had no choice but to return to the hills and hide. There was no hope of any ship getting men off by day, but perhaps something would come in during darkness. Nothing did and there were still more casualties. We made our way down to the beach the following night but were informed that the Germans now occupied the town and the quayside. We were about to return to the hills when a Colonel Godwin, from the 81 Base Sub Area, asked for men to try to retake the town. It was our only hope.

"I still had several men but they were tired and most were Pioneers and non-combatants. I rounded up about 70 and linked up with some New Zealanders and there were a few 'odds and sods' from other units. Our desperate attack forced the Germans to withdraw but, besides killing about 140, we added to our problems by taking prisoner two officers and about 100 other ranks. We were in no fit state to look after ourselves.

"The Colonel and I reported to the Brigade Headquarters that the town was again clear and being held. The Brigadier thanked us for our effort but pointed out that we were in a hopeless position. Half the men available to him were non-combatants and those who still had arms had little or no ammunition, so he saw no alternative but to surrender. He added, 'If any officer or man wishes to try to get away, they should do so'.

"The garrison still comprised of some 8,000 troops and my men had scattered. I searched for them but, by dawn, gave it up and joined a mixed party of 25 officers and men. Our only hope now was to move down the coast and away from the occupied area, though we were not at all sure which areas were occupied. We managed to move about 25 miles down the coast and commandeered a small boat which the Greeks call a 'Caique'. We put to sea, with no navigating instruments other than a pocket compass, but came under immediate attack from an aircraft which bombed and straffed us with machine-guns. The boat caught fire. We were some 300 hundred yards out to sea when we abandoned it and started to swim for the shore. More men were wounded, making the swim even more difficult, and two were drowned in the attempt. We dressed the wounded with the limited dressing we had and moved on, leaving them in the care of an Australian Major who was himself wounded and unable to walk.

"We were a bedraggled and diminished party. Some had no clothes or shoes, and those of us who had were very wet. Greek peasants came to the rescue with trousers and some footwear, but there seemed nowhere to go, hope was beginning to fade, and we rested for a day and a night. I never knew how contact was made with the Royal Navy from the village of Trikale, but in some way it was and a British destroyer came and took us off. We were in Cairo the following day, into beds, being cared for and fed".

The story leaves much of the emotional and physical stress to the reader's imagination. We were being forced back on all fronts and there were few places to hide. Shipping was heavily attacked and much was lost. Loved ones had no address to write to, and those letters which were sent home took months. Added to this was the concern created by daily reports of air attacks on home towns, which did nothing to lighten the anguish.

# 'Work and Play'

The Regiment continued to re-train. The main problem was the many different types of vehicle held. Fitters needed to have a wide knowledge of the many types, and the technical stores had to stock many different spares to keep them in service. There was still a mixture of Covenanters, Humberettes, and Dutch light tanks. The first big test came in May, 1941, when they were sent to Linney Head in South Wales to fire on the ranges. They received an excellent gunnery report despite the many hold-ups caused by shipping which clung to the shoreline. This situation still persists on the Castlemartin ranges.

By autumn, the whole Regiment was equipped with the Covenanter, giving the ability to move across country fast and crash through obstacles which would have halted the Mk VIB. The 30-ton Covenanter, equipped with a two-pounder gun and one BESA machine-gun, was the forerunner of the new range of Cruiser tanks to be introduced. The Valentine was also brought into service with other regiments, Valentine being an abbreviation of "Vickers Armstrong Limited of Newcastle-upon-Tyne". BESA was taken from "British Enfield Small Arms". Confidence was building; farmers accepted the damage caused to their crops and the land, though the crews repaired fences whenever possible. Hope was further raised by the news of the German attack on Russia, which would further drain German manpower, and the Japanese attack upon Pearl Harbour, which brought America into the war.

Individual training continued over a seven-day period but sport, which included boxing contests, could be included. During one of the early contests, Lieutenant Terrot, who had made a Beau Geste defence on the football pitch in Belgium, was matched against Lieutenant "Monkey" Blacker which resulted in a terrific contest. The Thompson brothers and SSM Bob Ruston still played a very professional game of football, strongly supported by the pre-war Cavalry Cup-winning team and by talented players from civilian clubs, some of them ex-professionals. Major Perry Harding, who had been an outstanding steeplechaser, had recruited a number of professional jockeys, among them Cyril Mitchell, Bryan Marshall (who was to win the Grand National two years in succession after the war), Jack Bissell, George Archibald, Boggy Wheelan (already mentioned in the Dunkirk evacuation) and Brian Hollis. A trip to Newmarket races was a "must" whenever it was permitted. The "Smokers" continued, small dance bands were formed, and life was made as tolerable as possible.

*Major Tony Leavey,* who was the adjutant during the Northampton stay, tells of an incident which requires little imagination and may enlighten one poor bus driver:

"Regimental headquarters was established at Thorplands, just outside Northampton. Divisional headquarters was at Cottesbrooke, where Major Percy Legard was serving as a staff officer. Percy, a talented and somewhat flamboyant officer and a great party man held the ski-jump record for Britain which stood for many years. He invited the officers to a fancy dress party. The theme of which was 'Heavenly Bodies'—liberally interpreted.

"I chose to impersonate that well embellished film star, Mae West. In a large picture hat and more than ample busts, a long flowing dress and very scarlet lips, I was told I was irresistible. Major the Marquess of Kildare, as the God of Light, wore a very close-fitting and all revealing sequinned garment. Lieutenant Basil Fleury-Teulon decided to be Mars, God of War; dressed in a helmet and armed with a sword, he fitted the part well. Lieutenant Maurice Williams, who chose to be the Devil, gave an impersonation such as to make any sinner repent instantly. His dress included horns, a jet-black outfit and a forked tail.

"Although it was a turning point in the war, 1942 was a grim year. Among the many restrictions was the absolute necessity to have hooded lights on all vehicles. On a typically foggy and frosty November night, we set off in my small car, eking out the rationed petrol. I fear that the crew was better fettled than the car and, alas, we ran into a sheep lying in the road. She was gravely wounded, and we decided to put her out of pain. Unarmed as we were on such missions, the only weapon to hand was the starting handle and it fell on me to deliver the coup de grâce, advised if not assisted by my companions.

"Regrettably one blow was not enough. As further blows were rained upon the unfortunate creature a glimmer of light heralded the approach of a vehicle which turned out to be the bus from Harborough to Northampton. Sliding back his misted window, the driver peered out at us, paused for perhaps five seconds, slammed it closed again, let in the clutch and, with a jolt, sped into the night. It was a wonder to us then, and has been ever since, what that driver thought he had seen and what if anything, he said about it. Perhaps there is a bus driver now long retired who long, long ago suffered a horrible experience quite beyond explanation."

* * * * *

Meanwhile, back at Perham Down, I was accepted as a tradesman but too young to be paid as one. There was, however a bonus when the War Office made a ruling that boys might enter man's service at the age of 17½ and be paid at men's rates. I had been employed as a driver on the Wireless Wing for some months and was keenly looking forward to rejoining either my own regiment or going to another. In February, 1942, we were told that although we could not rejoin our own regiments as they were serving abroad, we could join an armoured regiment in the UK. The 10th Hussars were now serving the Desert campaign and I was offered the opportunity to join the 5th Royal Inniskilling Dragoon Guards. On March 6th I entrained with nine others to join the Regiment in Northampton.

It was late afternoon when we arrived at Headquarters Squadron office in the Drill Hall. Sergeant Charlie Bevan, already wearing the DCM and MM ribbons, was appointed to see us into a billet and, the following day, to arrange interviews to decide our future. The story of Charlie's escape through France soon spread to we new arrivals. We were told that he was still far from a fit man and that he was not to be questioned about it. Other escaped POWs were still in the pipeline and any disclosure of information could jeopardise their lives.

He was a quiet, kindly man, and I would have loved to discuss his exploits. I might have contained myself if I could have foreseen that, 40 years later, he would be staying at my home as a personal friend. I was back on a wireless operator's course and I found it different from the wireless world I had left in Perham in that it included the elements of electricity, Ohm's law, and many subjects previously untaught. The regimental signals sergeant, "Mac" McMahon, knew his stuff and was a military psychologist as well as a professional and demanding instructor.

I had only been with the Regiment two weeks when an appeal was made for volunteers for the Airborne Forces. I volunteered. The excuse given for my non-acceptance was that I was in training and still under 18. The Regiment moved to Narford near Kings Lynn. The wireless course joined the Gloucester Hussars at West Tofts Camp, Suffolk, to enable us to complete it under better conditions than could be offered under canvas. The training I had already completed, and the experience gained from taking out recruits operating on Morse, enabled me to gain a high pass mark and promotion to the hallowed rank of lance corporal. This qualified me for an instructor's course at Bovington.

Although I was a Provisional, Unpaid, Acting Lance Corporal, it was progress unforeseen a month earlier. Bovington, too, had much to offer, not only the more intricate workings of a wireless set but also in the accurate map-reading demanded by the daily exercises out into the country in two-man teams. There were no sign posts to assist. We made long trips into the West Country and, soon found the many tea and cake shops that had set up in each village. I paired up with another NCO from the Regiment, George Elliott, a very nice man who had been a jeweller before the war.

Having had no previous experience as an instructor, I found the teaching practices difficult and calling for much study before each lesson. At the end of the course I was by no means certain I would qualify as an instructor. For the final summing-up we were paraded outside the chief instructor's hut and called forward, one at a time. Since I was the last in line I was able, before entering, to hear the chairman of the board discussing my performance in complimentary terms. I was very young, he said, and given more time would doubtless become a very sound instructor. What he actually told me, however, was quite different. I had much to learn, and would require a lot of hard work to make an instructor. Had I not heard the previous discussion, I would have expected a fail report, and would have returned to the Regiment feeling depressed. I did not agree with this sort of criticism and never applied it in later years.

There were a few weeks to complete at Narford before the whole Regiment moved to West Tofts. My sergeant major "Tosh" Baker, was a rough diamond and at first I didn't understand him. He often called men by their nicknames and names of his invention, but he endeared himself to me when, on my first exercise, I found him sitting by the cook's wagon peeling potatoes. His large stick was frequently brought down on the backside of some sleeping individual, but he protected his men against all other SSMs. In one early-morning fracas a very nice chap, Charlie Rae, was emerging from the guard tent after a night duty. He carried his blankets under his arm and had to walk past 'B' Squadron reveille roll-call. SSM Jack Robinson pounced on him. "Who are you Corporal?" he demanded. "Lance Corporal Rae of Headquarters Squadron," Charlie replied. "Well hurry up and get out of my lines," replied JR. "You are a nasty smell in this area." Charlie was hurt and, as Headquarters Squadron were also on parade only a few yards away, he made for our Sergeant Major. "Excuse me, Sergeant Major", said Charlie, in his grammar-school accent. "Sergeant Major Robinson has just referred to me as a nasty smell and I resent that very much." "Did he kid?" replied Tosh, and immediately stormed across the open space between the two squadrons. "The only nasty smell around this area is you" he retorted. "If any of my men are considered nasty smells I will be the first to deal with it." Cheering broke out in the ranks of both squadrons at this public confrontation. It was not good discipline, but relieved some of the routine boredom of our tented existence.

SSM Jack Robinson, DCM, was the scourge of the idle in 'B' Squadron. His own turn-out, speech and punctuality were beyond reproach. He would bounce up and down on the balls of his feet and address an assembly in scorching tones. "I will descend upon you from a monumental height," was a favourite threat. His perfection was such, indeed, it became a challenge to put one over on JR. A few tried it and even fewer succeeded. Lance Corporal "Poggy" Cooper nearly did.

Few of us owned a watch at that time and those who did were relied upon to inform the others. Crew commanders were issued with a very accurate pocket watch. As 'B' Squadron assembled at

0830 hours, Jack Robinson eyed the latecomers sneeking into the rear rank. He studied his watch and at exactly 0830 hrs called the squadron to attention and handed over to the Squadron Leader. Poggy Cooper who had placed himself in a position where JR could observe him, shook his head in disagreement with the time. Eventually the sergeant major consulted Poggy. "What time do you make it, Corporal Cooper?" Noting that a few stragglers were still trying to get on parade, Poggy pulled out his watch from his field-dressing pocket and announced: "Twenty nine minutes past." This procedure became routine and saved many a latecomer from a blistering. But someone must have tipped JR off because, one day, he ordered the luckless Poggy to the front of the squadron to show his watch. What Poggy withdrew was a foot of string and then a boot polish tin, from which the paint had been scraped off. There was no watch!

On another occasion at West Tofts the CO decided that, as we had not been together in one camp for some months, it might be a good time to hold a regimental parade—a dignified affair with a band. There were still a few bandsmen about and some chaps in the ranks who could play something. The NAAFI piano was duly mounted on a three-ton truck, and a set of dance band drums added. There was also an accordianist, a saxophonist, and a chap on a cornet. This assembly could not march and was therefore driven ahead of the parade and parked beside the saluting base for the march-past.

One of the more memorable "Smokers" was also held here. MQMS "Danny" Spridell sang "Trees" with great emotion; "Danny" Daniels offered his party piece, "With the end of me old cigar"; and the RSM gave his impersonation of an Italian goalkeeper, diving all over the stage after an imaginary ball. Suddenly a local farmer burst in and forced his way on to the stage, from where he waved his stick at the CO and berated the audience for the damage we were causing to his crops. The old chap, complete with side whiskers, stick and cap, gave everybody a good roasting in that lovely Suffolk accent. Then a whisker fell off and the farmer was revealed to be Captain John Ward-Harrison.

Ginger Livingstone's act was off-stage. The Regiment had acquired a proper sentry box from somewhere and placed it at the main gate. On a wild and wintry night the guard commander heard a loud crash, followed by much shouting. The guard turned out, only to discover that Ginger was flat on his back in the box with his bayonet stuck in the roof, preventing him from getting up. He explained to the guard commander that "I was just singing 'Lilly of Laguna', Corporal, and I got the box rocking. It fell over."

A major dress change came about in West Tofts. For years we had trampled the poor girls' feet at dances with our big army boots, but now we were permitted to wear civvy shoes. Our head dress had been the khaki side cap for work and a coloured Regimental one (irreverently called a "Dogging Hat") for walking out. We were allowed to wear the beret, a much more sensible form of head dress which kept its shape and would not fall off. The green backing long worn behind the cap badge, was changed to red to show up the badge against the black background.

Apart from the poachers, who enjoyed rich pickings at West Tofts, we were not sorry to leave Suffolk for Northumberland in December. There was a night stop on Doncaster racecourse, where the stables made excellent sleeping places. Arriving north of Newcastle, the Sabre Squadrons made for Felton and Swarlands, while Headquarters Squadron and the LAD established themselves in Longframlington. We were welcomed in this very pleasant village where the village hall became the mess room and old Mrs Elliott opened up her house as a canteen. There was no set charge: she just kept the table stocked with home made cakes and provided pots of tea. You told her what had been consumed and paid her on the way out. It was so nice just to sit in an ordinary house. 'B' and 'C' Squadrons in Swarland also occupied the village hall and a large house which had been the home of Lady Hamilton during her affair with Lord Nelson. It became the stores. It was reported that Her Ladyship haunted the house and was often seen walking the grounds. Lonely-hearts hoped she would. Swarland was still noted for the famous Swarland blanket. The mill was still in use and, on two days a week, the Regiment used the large dying vats as communal baths.

*Alan Merson* remembers it:

"The building, full of steam on bath days, offered some warmth on a cold Northumbrian day. The vats, about six feet square and five feet deep, were cleaned out for our use but were never quite free of the pink dye used for the blankets. It was a luxury to sink into that steaming hot water with about six others, but woe betide the poor soul who got his nether-ends over the steam pipe because there was always a joker who would open the steam valve. You never came out with the whiter-than-white look. That tinge of orange turned you into a redskin."

* * * * *

Nights out were important. Ashington was to be our stamping ground on this occasion, and "Passion Wagons" were to take us there and bring us back. (The official title, "Liberty Wagon", did not quite fit the intent!) The venue could be too far distant because, if you missed the return wagon at 2300 hours, one was in for a night's walk. But who wanted to leave a dance at that time, perhaps just when negotiating a walk home with some unsuspecting maiden. Some had to be forcibly loaded aboard for the return enlivened by "She'll be coming round the mountain", "My bonny lies over the ocean" and "Kiss me goodnight, sergeant major". There was no reprieve from reveille roll call the following morning, either.

Ashington was a hospitable town and almost every soldier had a private home to visit. It was here that I met my future wife Joan, a relationship nurtured because her mother fed me and my friends so well! Many men were in trouble for accepting an invitation to lunch and then failing to turn up. They would be diverted by one of the many clubs in the town where, after sampling Newcastle Brown Ale and McEwans Special Bitter, they would accept a different invitation for lunch. An order was published. "Discipline—Sunday Lunches", it read. "Anyone who accepts an invitation for Sunday lunch and fails to attend will be severely dealt with by the Commanding Officer".

A brigade Driving and Maintenance School and a Gunnery wing were established in Gateshead whilst the regimental wireless courses were held in Swarland. There were additional courses in mine-laying, mine-lifting, demolition, armoured recovery and convoy driving exercises; and aircraft recognition was given high priority. There was still the drain upon trained men to reinforce other regiments and, worse, whole regiments were being moved to other divisions.

There was new hope for a few of us when it was announced that a reconnaissance troop was to be formed to provide first-hand information direct to the commanding officer. It would be a sort of commando troop which would probe up to 20 miles ahead of the Regiment and destroy supplies. I was chosen as a wireless operator because of my morse capability. The troop was issued with Bren carriers and Daimler scout cars and placed under the command of two Irishmen, Lieutenant James Ussher (not related to Neville) and Sergeant Bill "Ginty" Gilliland, who had just returned from an attachment to the No. 4 Commando.

Ginty had seen service with the Commandos in Madagascar and been a reinforcement for the Dieppe raid which had gone very wrong. The two men soon established a friendly, effective relationship and we felt that we had a role in life. Detachments on troop training and concentration on map-reading were an enjoyable change from the normal tank trade training.

We soon found out, however, that although we were sent on ahead, our vehicles could not keep up with the tanks. Colonel Hook urged us forward but we had a poor cross-country performance. I was the rear link operator, responsible for maintaining the link with higher formation. When the CO asked for information about a particular situation the procedure laid down was to tell him to "Wait Out!", then switch to another frequency to ask the troop leader for the information required and relay it back to the CO. I was frequently blasted off the air with "Don't tell me to bloody well wait, I want to know." Eventually, to keep him happy, I would invent an answer and then inform the troop leader what I had passed back. The whole thing was working back to front, but no-one had the courage to tell Colonel Hook why I couldn't give him instant information.

John Pilborough was also a founder member of "Recce" and later wrote a separate account of our adventures in a small book entitled *First In. Last Out.* It was much referred to in the writings of Major-General Roger Evans when he wrote the Regimental History in post-war years. In the "Foreword" John said:

"For the soldiers of 1943, England was a land of mock warfare, canteens, short passes and blanco. That year saw the Germans driven out of Africa, Allied troops across the Mediterranean and firmly established in Italy. England had become a confident country which was labelled the "springboard for the attack upon fortress Europe". The 9th Armoured Division almost despaired of ever going to war. Nevertheless, they prepared for it with instructional courses, manoeuvres and drill parades. We disliked them all, for they never seemed to lead anywhere. The older soldiers had been doing them since their return from Dunkirk. The younger ones saw the same routine stretching ahead for many years to come.

* * * * *

The giant exercise "Spartan", which was held in Oxfordshire, became a testing ground for the whole Regiment and brought about many changes. We in the Recce Troop began to feel that we had a wonderful part to play and new tactics and skills to develop. After the exercise we withdrew north again, this time to Yorkshire and to accommodation in the wooded area of Duncombe Park, Helmsley. The "Passion Wagons" rolled for Scarborough and York, and a verse or two of "When this bloody war is over, no more soldiering for me" was frequently added to the repertoire of songs. New exercises were devised to test the postal services, bath units, rations, petrol and ammunition distribution, and there was distance-judging and a variety of initiative tests.

A new type of training was, TEWTS (Tactical Exercises Without Troops). It was during one of these exercises, which assembled on a hillside on the Yorkshire Wolds, that I first came face to face with Colonel Hook who arrayed himself before us and, pointing to a long slope ahead, said: "I want you to imagine that you are commanding officers and that, at the disposal of the brigade commander, there are three regiments of armour and a battery of artillery, and that you are to attack that hill. Think about it. I shall ask you about it in a minute." I was the one to be asked. Knowing that this was all about tactics, I used every tactical description I could remember from my sand table exercises at Bovington. "I would send one squadron to the left and advance up the hill in a two-up formation. The centre squadron would send two troops up the track in front in a one-up formation and take up a hull-down position and the other troops would remain in reserve. My third squadron . . . " The Colonel was turning from red to blue and beginning to jump about. I started to continue about snake formations and line abreast, when he blew up. "Balls, balls, balls!" he bellowed. "I said that I had three regiments of armour and a battery of artillery. That's sufficient to charge the bloody thing, I've done it on a horse and I'm bloody sure I can do it in a tank. I don't ever wish to hear about 'one-ups, two-ups' or any other ups. Do you understand me." "Yes, Colonel", I replied. The message was very loud . . . and very clear!

"God help us," muttered one of the senior NCO's. "If old Hook takes us into action we'll be in Berlin a month before anyone else but there won't be many of us left to celebrate." Even so, his type of aggressiveness appealed to most of us and we much respected him.

On May 1st in any year, God issues a special order that the Army Summer has begun. Irrespective of the weather, we were ordered into shirt sleeve order, fuel issues ceased, and we handed in one blanket. On May 1st 1943, it snowed and we commenced an exercise on the Wolds. For the Recce it was quite pleasant. We motored all over the area fixing four-gallon petrol tins to posts to mark the location of pits and quarries, which were plentiful. Many tanks had charged through hedges only to discover a nasty drop on the other side. A turret lid would frequently come over and strike the crew commander or operator on the head, causing very nasty injuries. When we were not employed doing that we were searching out remote farms and scrounging eggs.

After the exercise we moved from East to West Yorkshire. The squadrons were accommodated in Skipton while Headquarters Squadron and the Recce took over an old school in Cross Hills, a cotton town in lovely country on the edge of Ilkley Moor. The Recce Troops of the three regiments in the brigade were able to train together under some very professional instructors. Our next move was to Kirkby Stephen, then in Westmorland and now Cumbria. Having lost the toss, we were detailed to act as permanent fatigue regiment for the other two regiments, who used our tanks to fire on the nearby Warcop ranges. These were weeks of hell, resulting not so much from the duties as from the weather. It rained continuously and the tents were awash. Small ditches were dug and trenches were gradually enlarged until each tent was on an island. Our clothing was as wet when we dressed as when we took it off. Two rations of rum a day failed to keep out the cold and wet. Half the Regiment slept by day to work at night, debogging tanks left on the range in order that firing could commence at first light. If you had enough dry clothing to go out at night, someone had to walk to the road to carry your boots back. The mud was ankle deep and shoes were useless.

Wireless operators were asked to volunteer for a special mission the preparation for which, we were told, entailed three training parachute drops. I made my way to the squadron office to register but withdrew my name after receiving a letter from home which told me that my mother's health was giving cause for concern and it was hoped I might get home soon. After the war I discovered from "Ginger" Hyde who did go, that the mission was to serve with Tito's forces in Yugoslavia. The timing of that letter certainly changed my life and probably extended it.

On average, the Regiment moved every three months. As soon as we arrived in one place there was a rumour about the next. We were never told where we were moving to and took very careful notice of the route taken by the tank trains. At every halt, the crews would make for the 24-hour canteens while one went forward with some cigarettes and squared the driver up to find out where he was taking us. Any move could have been part of the move towards an invasion. The journey from Kirkby Stephen took us south and, once again, back to Suffolk, this time to a camp just outside Bury St Edmunds. That poor town was trying to cope with American airmen, the RAF and the Polish Armoured Division, as well as our Division. Saturday night at the Corn Exchange usually turned into a riot, and to be NCO in charge of the town patrol was an unenviable task. I was detached to Brigade Headquarters at Newmarket to attend a high-speed Morse course. Someone told me that there was now an appeal for volunteers for the Glider Pilot Regiment. I was very keen to have a go but regretted I was not with the Regiment to submit my application, for which there was a deadline. On returning to camp on a Sunday afternoon I was summoned to see the Squadron Leader, who told me my application could go ahead. "I've already submitted your name," said Major Paget. I wasn't sure whether he was trying to do me a favour or was just fed up with me. We were to parade outside the CO's office at 0900 hours the next day. When I arrived, I thought it was a squadron parade: 61 applicants were there, mostly for the Palestine Police. I learned later that Colonel Hook had informed the War Office that, if so many applicants went, they would succeed in breaking up a Regiment. Only Captain Knox Chapman went.

# We Become the Aggressors

In the Livermere Woods, we settled down to watch the 1,000-bomber formations assembling overhead—Americans by day, RAF by night. The war stories told in pubs and dances all added to the impatience we all felt. To make matters worse, the additional pay the Yanks received ruled out any hope for us with the local girls. Our "Dogging Hats" could be discarded. The crunch came when we were allocated to the local farmers to harvest the sugar beet and potatoes.

There was then a further exercise and a move to Brandon, a few miles away, where we paraded for an address by Colonel Hook. He had just returned from a conference at Divisional Headquarters and "the news was not good", he said. The Division was to be broken up and units would reinforce other Divisions. Those regiments not selected as reinforcements would form part of the home defence system. We feared that we would be in the latter group.

The Colonel could not hide his own disappointment. We knew that we were efficient and would give a good account of ourselves if given the chance. We were very proud of the 9th Armoured Division, too. We had all trained together, knew men in the supporting artillery and divisional support units, and had a sound working arrangement with the 15/19th Hussars and the Fife and Forfars. "I have tried to get you to the sports," he said. "I have failed you now, but will continue to badger my superiors. I hope something will turn up."

This news did nothing for our morale. The Italians pleaded for a separate armistice causing the Germans to occupy Italy. The Japanese were being driven back in Burma and the South Pacific Islands. The massive bombing raids round the clock had been giving the Germans a headache. Surely the invasion would commence soon!

The pre-war Old Comrades' Association was given a booster by Major-General Roger Evans. A new committee, chaired by Colonel Mike Ansell, was set up to keep relatives informed of our activity. He had only recently returned, blind from the POW camps, and was intent on overcoming this handicap.

In January, 1944, there was a move North-east to Whitby. The weather was very cold, the shores were an entanglement of wire and metal obstacles, and the beaches were heavily mined. Most of us shared accommodation with civilians. After three weeks we again made for the Northumbrian moors, but to different locations: RHQ with 'A' and 'C' Squadrons in huts within the grounds of Linden Hall, Longhorsely, whilst 'B' Squadron and the Recce (now at

Squadron status) moved to the outlying village of Netherwitton. The moors provided a good training area and a gunnery range was set up at Forestburn. We practised indirect fire with the six-pounder and here one of the most unfortunate accidents occurred.

There were three tanks on the firing point when a Spitfire flew low overhead and obviously thought it was a marvellous practice target. He made several very low-level runs. A young gunner waiting his turn to fire was heard to remark that if he had been up one of the trees, he could have touched the plane as it came over. On its next run, the plane took the top off the tree and killed him. The young sergeant pilot flew back to his base a few miles away and found Trooper Peter Maher's head embedded in the wing. Few people will ever witness an aircraft striking a tree, and the chances that a man would be up it are millions to one.

Many changes were being made in the supporting Arm. Our cooks had been transferred to the newly-formed Army Catering Corps, while the Royal Army Ordnance NCOs and men attached to our fitter sections were now to become Royal Electrical and Mechanical Engineers (REME). Our own regimental fitters continued to service our vehicles but under the management of a new professional officer, Captain Charles Maple. We were always suspicious of these professionals. *Charles Maple* recalls his initiation into the Regiment:

"On reporting to the Commanding Officer, I was told that the Regimental fitters would deal with the tanks, and we could look after the motor-cycles and Bedford three-tonners. From this I deduced that he had no faith in this gang of specialists. The first blow came when I personally drove a Cromwell down from 'A' Squadron tank park to the LAD (Light Aid Detachment) area, situated near RHQ which was in Linden Hall itself. It was worth seeing the RSM's outraged visage. He was demanding to know what so and so idiot was driving the bloody thing. I appeared from the driver's hatch and apologies followed, but with some reluctance, I am sure. I was properly informed that tanks were not permitted near the hallowed ground of RHQ.

"Slowly but surely, as our values became appreciated, we were allowed to touch tanks! The accommodation allocated to the LAD was a muddy stable yard and very difficult to find. I had a large flag made and hoisted it over the stable. Colonel Hook Sangster came round and enquired, 'who I thought was attached to whom!' My arrival became more apparent when I borrowed Maurice Peters's second-best green trousers to act as a second during the Brigade Boxing Championships in Morpeth."

Captain Maple may rightly claim to be the first officer to join the "Green Mafia". In 1983 he returned to Linden Hall as sales director of British Leyland, when a press conference was being held there to launch a new car. The hall is now a very up-market hotel and the old stable provides lunches. You may still find a horseshoe nailed to the door of his old office. The BBC also attended the lunch on this occasion to launch a new book about the hall. Walking into what had been the officers' mess ante-room, Charles looked up at the lintel over the door, made famous by Captain Desmond Sarson, regimental signals officer, who had made a death defying leap from it on to a sofa, which he missed. He broke a leg. "I was enjoying the nostalgia of these memories," recalled Charles, and related some of them to the manager of the BBC team, who immediately switched his programme to include an interview with me for Tyne Tees TV that night.

There was yet another course for young NCO's; the unit intelligence course. This month-long course was particularly attractive because it was held at Eastern Command Intelligence Centre, Welwyn Garden City, and each student had to take a motorcycle. Morever, each student had to be at least a temporary sergeant. Now quite a senior corporal, I was selected to attend and stitched sergeant's stripes over my two chevrons, drew a motorcycle and set off. I did not wish to become the regimental intelligence NCO, but from the beginning, enjoyed the very professional instruction which delved deeply into German tactics and into uniforms, which could yield much information and help us in the Recce Squadron if we were ever to meet an angry German.

Each week we had to study aerial photographs of an unidentified but defended strip of coastline on which there were progressive signs of activity. During one of these sessions, I became very excited when I discovered that one of my fields now had faint white dots in a regular pattern. The instructor initially shared my enthusiasm but after further study, discovered that the light dots were caused by heaps of manure which had turned the grass a lighter shade. My minefield had been nothing more than a muck-spreading operation!

During another exercise we created a situation similar to that which had frightened the bus driver in Northampton. Our exercise required half the students to dress in German uniform while the other half observed and logged what went on. If you were laying barbed wire and burying mines, it could be reasoned that you were intending to defend rather than attack, birds suddenly flying off in alarm was a clear indication that someone had disturbed them. I paired off with a very tall sergeant from the Grenadier Guards who, because he could not fit into one of the uniforms provided, remained in his own while I masqueraded in the uniform of a German Luftwaffe officer. Our plan was to dig a trench and create the impression of a defence position. Having myself dug to some depth, I handed over the shovel to the Grenadier and stood over him holding my rifle. A truck driver drew to a sudden halt and watched with some disbelief as a German officer stood over a British sergeant. He drove off muttering "Where the hell am I?"

The Regiment, now fully equipped with the Cromwell tank with 75mm gun, entrained for Kirkcudbright ranges. Recce Squadron had been issued with a similar tank but with a different engine which was called a Centaur. We could more than hold our own across country and, with a six-pounder gun, wondered what the other squadrons would be required to do! The Polish Armoured Division, who shared the range and proved themselves to be very efficient, had even more reason to get back to Europe. Those Poles now serving as pilots with the RAF had already shown magnificent courage, fuelled by hate and revenge.

We were called to the fireing point and Colonel "Hook" was beaming. Standing on a tank in the pleasant sunlight on that memorable May 29th, he told us that we were to mobilise at once and prepare to proceed overseas. It is difficult now to understand how we felt, and those who have not endured years of training and destruction to our country, loss of homes, friends and relatives, might think we were suffering from some form of sickness. Perhaps we were. But we could not have been given a better booster and packed our kit to return to Northumberland.

New tanks and vehicles arrived immediately, The large white star painted on each of them gave us a new pride. We were to join the famous 7th Armoured Division (the Desert Rats). Divisional signs had to be sewn on as we changed our 'Panda' for the Jerboa, the Desert Rat. We all grew ten feet. The squadrons were issued with a Sherman 17-pounder to each troop but the Recce suffered a setback: Our Centaurs were replaced by American Stuarts (Honeys). They were small, with a three-man crew and carried a 37mm gun with two Browning machine-guns. But they had automatic transmissions and were fast.

We were out on the moors, giving the LAD recovery crews some training in recovery from a bog, when Colonel "Hook" appeared with Major Teddy Swettenham. Our beloved old fireball was a broken man and could not hide his deep depression and disappointment as he told us, in faltering words, that having got us to the sports, he was not being allowed to accompany us. We shared his feelings. He turned about and walked away, calling back: "Best of Luck. Colonel Teddy Swettenham will lead you." We admired Colonel Hook as a strong man, but he was handing over to a battle-experienced officer, for Colonel Teddy a thinking man and tactician, had served in the desert and had just returned from staff college. Colonel Hook had rebuilt the Regiment into a professional fighting force, given us confidence, and passed on some of his aggression. It was sad to see him go, and we felt for him.

There now followed a programme of innoculations. vaccinations, dental checks and first aid lectures. We learned from the BBC on June 6th that we had missed the assault stage of the Normandy landings, but were not surprised. We had neither waterproofed our vehicles nor taken part in the numerous sea trials. So we continued with the conversion courses and waited patiently. A week later came the order to load our tanks on to tank transporters, and we were off.

It was a bit confusing to find ourselves heading back to the Kirkcudbrightshire ranges on the west coast of Scotland. Where were we going to embark? The 15/19th Hussars had gone off to carry out some special mission, so perhaps we would open up another front in Norway or Denmark. Nothing of the sort. We were there to fire yet another course on the ranges. Two more weeks of ammunition fatigues and beach-combing.

Hardly had we arrived back in Northumberland than things began to happen. We again loaded our tanks—but this time onto railway war flats in Alnwick—and headed south, thinking of those we had left behind and to whom we had not been able to say our goodbyes because we had been confined to camp. Colonel Swettenham, permanently attending conferences, had hardly been seen. His rear party was still in Kirkcudbright, the advance party in Bury St Edmonds, and the main party on a train or travelling by road with the echelons.

Fornham Park, Bury St Edmunds, was a hive of activity. We were told that we would not be taking our own tanks and that we would have to carry our own kit. A kitbag with a spare battledress and other items would travel in one of five soft vehicles, but much kit had to be discarded. Civvy shoes and other personal items were placed in a pile in the huts for someone to collect. We were paid 200 French francs and taken on a route march to see how we would perform on foot. An overcoat and one blanket was the only permitted protection against the night cold. We were also given water purification kit: one bottle contained white tablets to kill bugs in water while the other was intended, but failed, to remove the taste of chlorine.

We were now on 24 hours' notice to move, and those who could get home and back in that time were allowed to. Few could. Charles Maple, EME was one who made a close-run dash for nearby Newmarket. He shanghaied a water cart to return and leaped from it at Bury station just as the train was pulling out. "Cut it a bit fine, Charles," observed Colonel Teddy. Charles explained that he had been delayed "for domestic reasons".

The train ride gave time for thought. Would we be as good as we thought we were? Who would come back? What about our relatives and girl friends who were not aware of our move? What were we going to do without our vehicles? The journey took us through the north London suburbs and on to an embankment where the line via Addison Road (now London Olympia) joins the Southern Railway (now the Southern Region) at Clapham Junction. The damage caused by a flying bomb to the end of a terrace of houses was still visible. Rescuers were frantically digging in the rubble as we halted above them. "Give the bastards hell." We hoped we would. Some troops threw what English money they had left to the children. This scene strengthened our determination for the conflict to come. As we sped towards Portsmouth, Red Cross ambulance trains passed in the opposite direction. Clearly, there was plenty to do yet.

No man can know how he will react under active service conditions. Driving up a road or across a field and being told by an umpire with a white flag that you have just been knocked out by a tank or gun had been something of a pleasure, to be followed by a brew of tea or a quick nap. It would be different to push through hedges, search buildings, and have real mines to encounter. Some of our noisier members, who had boasted of what they would do given the chance were already quieter. It was a time for thought and hope.

Although the Regiment had missed the initial assault, many of its members who had trained with us were there. Captain Knox Chapman, who had trained as a glider pilot, made a successful landing at night on D minus 1. Lieutenant-Colonel D'Arcy Anderson, who served on the Staff during the retreat to Dunkirk and had been awarded a DSO for rescuing a member of his crew from a blazing tank, now commanded the Sherwood Rangers in an assault landing at Arromanches and was wounded during the initial assault. Lieutenant-Colonel "Tich" Harding commanded the 23rd Hussars and, with Major "Monkey" Blacker as second-in-command, led that regiment in some very tough fighting. Major Arthur Carr was second-in-command of the 4th County of London Yeomanry, the Regiment we would eventually relieve. He was in the first push south towards Villers-Bocage, but after only a week, his tank was knocked out and he and his crew taken prisoner.

Many of our friends had reinforced the 1st and 5th Royal Tank Regiments and were in at the very beginning. A party of 20 officers and men including Lieutenant "Gavin" Murray and Lieutenant "Barney" Cowdy had volunteered for service with the Commandos to crew assault tanks.

*Allan Merson* who wrote of his experiences in the Swarland blanket factory baths, was one of that élite party who quietly slipped away in February, 1944, to commence training. He tells his own story:

"We were sent to Corsham in Wiltshire to join a Combined Operations armoured assault group. We were equipped with 'Centaur' tanks, but with the six-pounder gun replaced by a 95mm howitzer. We learned that we would be giving close support during the much talked-of forthcoming invasion. We were a very mixed bunch, predominantly Royal Marines in the turret, with Royal Naval and a few RAF personnel. I was to be a driver. Royal Artillery personnel, Royal Signals and REME filled specialist posts. Firing exercises would be carried out near Calne, wading training at Instow, Devon, and most night exercises started in The Hare and Hounds local pub!

"In mid-May, 1944, we moved to a Hampshire village, Rowlands Castle. Here our vehicles were waterproofed and more practical landing exercises carried out from landing craft. The pace hotted up. Then without warning the camp was sealed: In early June we embarked at Gosport to form part of the great invasion. Our task was quickly over and, for most of us, was fairly uneventful. In small groups we returned to Corsham, leaving our vehicles behind. We thought we would qualify for embarkation and disembarkation leave but, alas, a signal arrived ordering all 5th Royal Inniskilling Dragoon Guards to return to their own Regiment. I was back in Northumberland, up to Kirkcudbright, and then south to Bury St Edmunds and now heading for Portsmouth and Normandy again."

## REGIMENTAL COMMAND JULY – OCTOBER 1944

| | |
|---|---|
| Lieutenant Colonel J E Swetenham | Commanding Officer |
| Major P A C Bridgewater | Second in Command |
| Major J M D Ward-Harrison | 'A' Squadron |
| Major the Marquess of Kildare (wounded August 1944) | 'B' Squadron |
| Major J A Leavey | |
| Major A C Gibson | 'C' Squadron |
| Major E C Paget | HQ Squadron |
| Major J R Crockett | Recce Squadron |
| Captain G A Glover | |
| Captain J N B Ussher | |
| Captain M D Williams (K.I.A.) | Adjutants |
| Captain R P Kettle | |
| Captain G T Blundell-Brown | |
| Captain F H Robson | Quartermasters |
| Lieutenant J R Robinson, DCM | |
| RSM J Burrows | Regimental Sergeant Major |

# PART III

# Into Battle

The Regiment detrained at Fareham and was quickly taken by TCVs (Troop-Carrying Vehicles) to a tented camp north of Portsmouth. A meal was awaiting us and we soon settled down, much relieved to shed the equipment we had carried. The camp, was clean, dry, and well organised, with a cobbler's shop for instant boot repairs, facilities to wash clothing, and a Quartermaster's store where worn clothing could be exchanged. Most of us managed to obtain at least a nice new pair of socks. There was a barber's shop to crop our already short hair. A few ventured to have all-off haircuts whilst other adopted the tonsured "monk" style. One man went too far and ordered that a 'V' should be cut out. This called for a halt as we were informed that we looked too "un-British".

Our burden was increased by the issue of two 24-hour emergency ration packs. A compressed cube of sugar, milk powder and tea formed a liquid resembling tea when immersed in hot water. A compressed meat cube and some dehydrated vegetables swelled to quite a meal when immersed. The breakfast course included an oatmeal cube. The whole was adequate for a few days but would have become very boring over a longer period. A further gimmick, new to us, was the "Tommy Cooker"—a small folding frame which supported a methylated tablet and was capable of heating a mess tin or mug of water. The most attractive inclusion was a tin of self-heating soup. This was a can of normal size with a fuse running through the centre which, when lit, burned down and heated the contents. To complete our needs there was a pack of three sheets of toilet paper and a strong vomit bag for what could be a rough crossing. A large NAAFI was open all day and staffed by the prettiest girls we had ever seen in that employ. A large certificate hung at the back of the counter informing the customers that they had just won the first prize for being the best looking team in the south of England. If we were to die, what memories we would take with us!

The stay was not intended to be long and we were embarking on to TCVs the following morning. This time it was to a naval barracks in Portsmouth. There was no furniture in the rooms and we lounged about for most the day awaiting the final call. It came about three that afternoon. July 17th was a glorious day, a little too warm for marching with full kit. We assembled and marched out of the barracks and followed a well-trodden route along the harbour front. Groups of civilians were enjoying the afternoon sunshine and reading their newspapers. Few bothered to look up. Some responded to the feeble wolf whistles, but the majority were indifferent. Had the war already ceased to be a concern now that the battle had passed to the other side of the Channel?

The harbour was busy and ships of all sizes moved about the dock area. Those already loaded had moved away from the quay and dropped anchor again, awaiting the completion of the convoy. We boarded LCIs (Landing Craft Infantry) which were tied up to specially constructed piers. The conditions were cramped and there was a strong stench of diesel oil to contend with. In the holds, the bunks were in tiers of three, very close together, and left hardly any room for our equipment.

We were free to move about on the small deck and to take in the scenery. The woop, woop, woop of the various ships and clear calls over intercom systems were unfamiliar to most of us. Bustling calls of "Now hear this", which preceded every instruction, competed with conversations conducted over loudspeaker system between naval officers, and the summoning of crews to harbour stations. The hoisting of balloons from some of the vessels reminded us that we did not yet have complete command of the air. We moved away from the quay to a short distance from Southsea.

There was great excitement and for some, I have no doubt, sorrow at leaving loved ones. It was for most of us the first experience of leaving the shores of England. We were all mature enough to realise that we might be seeing our country for the last time, but these thoughts receded in the bustle of preparation. The absence of the tanks, the tools of our trade, left us feeling somehow naked and useless without them. How much nicer if we had been on a Tank Landing Craft.

At 1800 hours we moved out into the Channel in strict line ahead, at intervals of about 100 yards.

Once clear of the harbour the small craft dipped and rolled and most of us looked for a piece of rail on which to get a secure grip. The shoreline of Portsmouth and the South coast faded under a blanket of smoke from the chimneys of the town and the black, oily fumes from the ships. The size of the convoy gave us that animal instinct of security in numbers and after being instructed how to evacuate the vessel in emergency, most settled down on a bunk bed for the night.

We were in a sort of no-man's land at the mercy of the elements and our Naval friends, who had doubtless made this journey so often during the past five weeks that it had become routine. The convoy maintained a steady 12 knots to permit the slowest ship to keep position. Our course was cleared of mines and marked by buoys. The smell of diesel below decks was now aggravated by a few who couldn't wait to try out the "Tommy Cooker". For anyone without a cast-iron stomach it was all too much. What food we had consumed soon fed the sea gulls! Waves occasionally came over the bows, but this was preferable to the smell below. I was fortunate in finding a coil of rope to curl up in and try to sleep.

Each vessel carried only sufficient light to render it visible to the leading and following craft. The only noise was the steady turning of the engines. We had settled down, content that there was nothing else to see, when two motor gunboats raced up the side of the convoy. Immediately, and from every boat, came the shattering din of twin Oerlikon cannons as they fired at a target being towed astern of the boats. This brought every man up from below decks. As the action was over before most of them emerged, there was explanation to be passed to each before they returned to their bunks. German E-boats were still very active from the Channel ports and had caused some casualties to earlier convoys. It was this thought which had been the concern of us all.

The timing of our arrival off the French coast coincided perfectly with the coming of dawn. Our first sight was of hundreds of other ships lying at anchor and we moved between them and in towards the long, sandy shores of Normandy. Overhead, wave after wave of our own Halifax and Lancaster bombers were returning from a mission, some bearing the scars of the action fought only minutes before over Caen. We now saw what an enormous undertaking the invasion had been: the prefrabricated Mulberry harbour created by floating large concrete blocks out from England and sinking them with old coasters to form a protection against the seas for unloading ships. The number of ships at anchor indicated the quantity of stores and reinforcements needed to maintain our flimsy foothold, still only a bridge-head.

We aimed at a point on the coast east of the harbour and between two large warships, one of them the *Warspite*, firing heavy broadsides at targets inland. We were concerned about our disembarkation: our type of craft could not be beached like a tank landing craft, and we were likely to be in 12 feet of water when the anchor dropped.

The weather was gorgeous: a clear blue sky above the thin coastline of sand dunes. What had that first wave of invaders felt as they approached? We at least would not encounter mines or wire and were assured that the enemy had been cleared from our landing area. The front was now some 12 miles inland and stretched from the mouth of the Orne river and west to the Cherbourg Peninsula.

The craft slowed and stopped as we prepared to disembark down ropes hanging over the side. We were still some 200 yards from the shore but there was no danger of a wetting. Large rafts, 12 feet square and powered by two outboard motors, were on their way to ferry us ashore. Our landing area cleared of mines and marked out with white tape, turned out to be "Juno" beach, just to the west of Graye-sur-Mer.

The village had been very badly damaged during the initial

assault, and on either side of the track through the dunes still sported German signs warning of the presence of mines. A guide led us through the dunes in single file and to a track a few hundred yards inland, where we joined a road. In line ahead we plodded on, some weakened by the night's loss of sleep and vomiting. It was now some time since we had enjoyed a cooked meal. Added to this was the weight of our equipment and the heat of the morning sun. Some

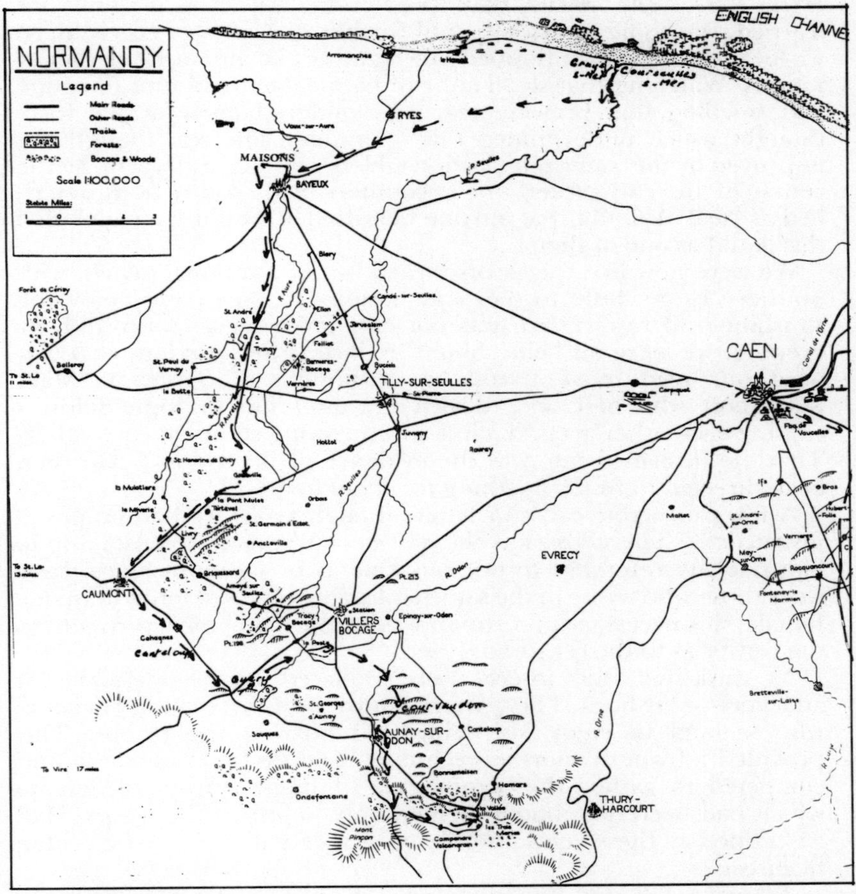


tried to get a song going but most preferred to conserve their breath and to plod on, grumbling about being like the PBI (Poor Bloody Infantry). Those who had been infanteers tried to make light of it all and boasted of having marched 20 miles a day under worse conditions.

The attack on Caen was at its height. Gunfire from the battleships behind us and the shorter-range weapons in front made a fearful din and gave us food for thought as we marched in single file through the dust. The few civilians about treated us with the same indifference as had the civilians in Portsmouth. Old ladies moved about among tethered cows, milking them before moving them to new grazing. After about three miles we came to a tin hut erected beside the road and signposted "The Ritz". Beneath the hut were about six containers full of tea and a box containing biscuits. No Hyde Park "Ritz" could have been more appreciated. This, we learned, was to be our home until further orders were received, so we lowered our packs, flopped down and broke into our emergency rations. Watching that small cube of oatmeal expand into porridge and smelling that brewing tea, we wondered anew at the forethought which underpinned this operation. The tea, though not improved by the water purification tablets, was wet and warm. In the course of an army career, one encounters many concoctions described as "tea". I doubt that anyone blindfolded would have included this liquid as one of them.

We were now like spectators locked out of a football match, with nowhere to go, little to see, and nothing to do except enjoy the sunshine and rest. There was not enough water to wash and, by evening, we were all being bitten by insects and anxious to know what our next move would be. I thought of Sergeant "Mac" MaMahon who had once drawn my attention to some soldiers chasing each other around a hut and throwing stones at each other. That, he informed me, was the evidence of boredom. I had then been directed to find something for them to do.

A few now wrote cards or letters though as yet we had no postal instructions. There also was the new encumbrance of censorship to blot out any reference to our movements or location. Since there were those who wrote in the same endearing terms to more than one female, this necessary precaution was as much an embarrassment to the censor as to the censored.

As dusk fell, the insects were replaced by a new wave of attackers—May bugs. There were hundreds of these clumsy aviators who seemed to enjoy low-flying and buzzing the troops. This provided a form of sport as each man used his beret as a swat and competed to gather the biggest pile of bugs. Anti-midge cream which had been distributed seemed only to attract the wasps. Had we trained all these years and travelled such a distance to be beaten by insects?

As night fell and the guns ceased their bombardment, men wrapped themselves in their blankets and tried to get comfortable. There were distant sounds of mortar and some small arms fire, but our fields remained quiet until, suddenly two aircraft swooped down the beach and drew fire from a hundred weapons mounted on the ships at anchor and the anti-aircraft units on the shoreline. For five minutes we were treated to a firework display second to none. The slow tracers from pom-pom guns climbed and were lost as the trace burned out. The aircraft, probably on a mine-laying or photographic mission, were soon away and drawing fire from other sectors. We could not help admiring the courage of the pilots even though they were the enemy.

There were no further incidents that night. Dawn brought another ideal day for sun-bathing which unfortunately, we could not strip off to enjoy. Those who complained of the inactivity and the seeming lack of urgency might not have done so had they known what our Commanding Officer was trying to achieve and the reception he had received.

The day prior to our departure he had left with a small staff—including the adjutant, quartermaster and intelligence officer—with the intention of ensuring the smooth arrival of the Regiment and arranging for the immediate issue of vehicles. He was thwarted from the moment of departure. Because his ship was fogbound and arrived four hours after the main party, none of us knew what we were expected to do on disembarkation.

The message received in England spoke of an urgent need to relieve one of the regiments in the 7th Armoured Division, so the Colonel had borrowed a car and set off to find the rear headquarters of the Division. After a difficult and frustrating journey, his reception at Divisional HQ was, to say the least, disillusioning. Expecting that we would relieve the "Sharpshooters" (4th County of London Yeomanry) who had suffered heavy casualties, he was now told that they were heavily committed to "Operation Goodwood" in the Caen sector and that, despite their heavy casualties, were in excellent spirit and performing magnificently. They were quite unaware of any relief and it was considered to be of the utmost importance that they should not find out. Our CO doubtless felt that it was of equal importance that his Regiment should not discover that they had no role to play in this decisive battle for Normandy.

From the daily news-sheet which was distributed to keep us informed of progress on the front we learned that there had been an attempt on the life of Adolf Hitler at a conference in Berlin and that the Germans seemed about to buckle. Our training had prepared us well for the waiting game, so without realising the full seriousness of the situation, we basked in the sun in a false belief that it was all part of a major, well thought out plan. On July 19th we were taken by TCVs to billets some four miles from Bayeux. RHQ and the Recce Squadron occupied a farm at Maisons, while the squadrons were distributed in other villages near by. Our standard of living was greatly improved when our own vehicles arrived with our spare kit bags and cooking equipment, which would allow us to come off the emergency ration packs and have a proper meal.

Beside a track leading from the farm towards a church I saw the first of the graves of our predecessors and of Germans. The Germans had placed notices warning the French that death was the penalty for assisting the invaders. Any act of sabotage would bring death by shooting. The beach was only a few miles away. What better occupation than to have a swim, rid ourselves of the fine powdery dust and wash our under-clothing? We set off in high spirits to a point a little west of Arromanches. A steep cliff path led down to the beach where some Canadians were already making the most of the sea. We quickly stripped and joined them in the water.

I have never been a strong swimmer and quickly realised that there was a strong undertow. After an hour or so Captain John Newson, our padre, who was in charge of the party, ordered those still in the water to come out and dress. It then became very obvious that some of them had been trying to get back to the shore for some time and were becoming very tired. The tide had turned and a nasty wind had suddenly blown up to add to their problem. We found a net lying on the beach which had corks tied to it, and this was thrown out as far as possible to enable about five men to reach safety. Some of the stronger swimmers went back into the water to assist others and the padre, an excellent sportsman himself, quickly assembled a lifeline of men by holding hands and wading into the water. But those who had re-entered the water were now themselves in trouble and drifting further from the shore. A happy afternoon was suddenly turning very sour.

Our life-line pulled in the men nearest the shore. Being tall, I was second in line to the padre, who constantly reached out to those in trouble. Sten guns were fired into the air to attract the attention of the many ships off-shore, but they no doubt thought we were having high jinks. The chain went out again. All those in it were fully clothed and wearing boots, and our clothing was becoming very heavy. A particularly high wave came in and, in pushing ourselves off the bottom to ride it, the line broke. I was cast on to the beach like a wet fish, but others were left floundering in the water. I saw the padre only feet away and reached out to him, but another wave came and he disappeared. It took some time to get everybody ashore and to hold a roll call. Three were still missing: The Rev. John Newson, Lieutenant Rawlins, and Trooper Bloom. It was a sad beginning. It seemed such a silly way to lose lives when a war was being waged only a few miles away.

It was quite late when we left the beach and marched inland. Our clothing was very wet, the sun was losing its warmth, and there was nowhere to dry out. Considering the number of men in the water, we consoled ourselves that we had been lucky to lose only three.

The following day we were to suffer yet another tragedy when Lieutenant Pat Leavey took a party of NCOs from 'A' Squadron to look at a knocked-out German tank and visit his old regiment. The vehicle was under observation and drew the attention of the enemy, who shelled it. Pat Leavey was killed and Sergeant Piper badly injured. If the Padre was our first casualty, we could dismiss any hope of assistance from the heavens, though I think most of us were mature enough to have discounted that already. Simple recreation in swimming had accounted for three lives and a seemingly sensible visit to examine a German Panther tank had caused another death. What would happen when we were actually in the front line? Major Gerald Kildare, Lieutenant Ben Tottenham and brother, Tony, collected Pat's body and buried him in the Bayeux cemetery. To add to our discomfort came one of the worst storms to hit the French coast in many years. Supply lines were damaged and the prefabricated harbour broke up and was put out of action. The waterlogged land also halted the break-out from Caen.

A week passed with still no plan for us, though we were given maps to study and details of the front were explained. One of my sergeants, Eric Roodhouse, suggested a walk to try to buy butter and during the expedition, amazed me by speaking perfect French. Eric, obviously very well read and better educated than me, explained that his father had sent him to school in France when he was 11 and he had spent some years in the country. His ear was good enough to detect that the first man we had spoken to was not of these parts. "He has a Marseilles accent" he informed me.

After a week's inactivity, the CO got permission to employ some of us in a nearby Armoured Replacement Group which was preparing new tanks and repairing damaged ones. This gave us valuable experience as well as something useful to do. When we did eventually take over a few vehicles from the 4th CLY they were in a pretty poor state and would require a lot of maintenance to make them battle-worthy. Our experience enabled us to select and prepare new tanks for our own use and return the damaged ones to the establishment.

The Sabre Squadrons were expecting to take over Shermans. This, we thought, was why we had spent those last days on the Kirkcudbright ranges. The Recce Squadron had retrained with Stuarts Mk V and VI. It was a nasty shock for the squadrons to find themselves back on to Cromwells and the Recce to be issued with very dilapidated Stuarts Mk III, a vastly inferior tank to the Mk VI. To boost each troop's firepower, and to give them a chance against the deadly Tiger tank armed with an 88mm gun, there was one 17-pounder Sherman per troop. The Recce Squadron had only one tank per troop and were completed with Daimler scout cars and Bren carriers. A new "Ack Ack" troop had been formed in late 1943 to deal with air attack and was equipped with the old Mk VIB tank carrying four machine-guns mounted in a box formation. The Luftwaffe had taken a beating and such air threat that remained could be dealt with by the Bren gun and turret-mounted machine guns which could be operated free of the turret traverse.

Those men who had been taken from the Recce Squadron now returned to us to boost our strength to three troops. The new vehicles had to be painted with the Jerboa (desert rat) to indicate the Divisional formation. The Armoured Brigade consisting of ourselves and the 1st and 5th Royal Tank Regiment carried the tactical signs 51, 52 and 53, in order of seniority. Since we had been formed in 1685 and the RTR (ex RTC) in 1916, there was no doubt about that! When the 4th CLY formed part of the Brigade they had, of course, carried the most junior Tac sign, 53. Our arrival in the Brigade now meant the two tank regiments taking the 52 and 53 title. This did nothing to endear us to these two battle-hardened regiments who had fought throughout the desert campaign and in the 7th Armoured Division with great distinction.

The Sabre Squadron crews were quite delighted to go back to the faster Cromwells, which we understood better. The Sherman had a nasty habit of catching fire and reports from the RTR indicated that they went up as soon as hit. The 7th Armoured Division had been in continuous battle since D + 3. Some of our old friends posted to them after their return from the desert now came to see us and tell of their experiences. The Division was commanded by a very experienced General, Major-General Erskine. The 22nd Armoured Brigade, which we had now joined, was commanded by Brigadier Hynde, who had been with the 15th/19th Hussars and closely associated with the Regiment during the withdrawal to Dunkirk. The other battleworn cavalry regiments, the 8th and 11th Hussars, provided divisional reconnaisance cover. The motorised infantry regiment in the Brigade, with whom we would have to work closely, was the 6th Battalion of the Rifle Brigade.

Against the experience of these very famous regiments, we were very much the new boys. Our new-found companions were quick to take advantage of this situation and told stories of 88mm armour piercing shells which went in one side and out the other. The dreaded 88mm mounted on the Tiger, which had outgunned our armour in the desert, could still dominate the battle here.

Our first encounter was to be "Operation Bluecoat", planned to expand the bridgehead south and capture the dominating Mont Pinçon. On July 29th the Regiment moved south to a harbour area and to join the other regiments in the Brigade. With our freshly-painted tanks as yet unblooded in battle we passed by a regiment which had pulled off the road to allow us to pass. There were cheers and some cat calls. One called out "Who are you lot?" "The Skins" someone replied. "Never 'eard of yer'."

We had a distinct advantage in having spent four long years training in close country of the type now to be encountered. A new word "bocage" entered our vocabulary. This is a Norman word to describe a geographical region where the fields and meadows are enclosed by high banks of earth along which hedges and rows of trees are planted and where human habitation is dispersed in small hamlets and isolated farms. This kind of terrain imposes severe limitations on tank deployment and is of great advantage to a defender who can make good use of the sunken lanes for protection.

*Sergeant Pat Whitmore,* a 'B' Squadron tank commander wrote this following description:

"The dense hedgrows on top of the earth banks were considerable obstacles and the smallness of the fields meant that a tactical bound would be from one hedge to the next. It was usually impossible to see from one field to another. An additional hazard was that, having crashed through a hedge, there would frequently be a deep gully which served as a very efficient tank trap. The risk of shedding a track was considerable!

"Following the advice of our experienced armoured friends, we dug trenches about a foot deep and piled the soil at the side. The tank was then driven over the trench and this gave excellent protection for sleeping. Colonel Swetenham added the 'Drake' touch by taking a bath in the centre of the field."

* * * * *

My own friends in the Recce Squadron were now a very mixed bunch despite the years of training together. Captain Robert Crockett, who had assumed command just before we departed from Bury St Edmunds, had left to command a branch of the echelon and Captain Guy Glover, who had been Squadron Leader in Northumberland, came back. The troops were organised to include a Mk III Stuart armed with a 37mm gun and two Browning machine guns, a Bren carrier with a crew of three, and a two-man Scout car. We had all trained on these vehicles and were very inter-changeable.

I was allocated to 3rd Troop, under the command of Lieutenant John Milligan and we were selected to lead the Regiment through Caumont and to our battle positions, where we were to support the 131 Infantry Brigade and I gained the distinct honour of being in command of the leading vehicle. The roads had already been pounded by the Germans and our own troops, and the air was full of fine, choking dust against which goggles and handkerchiefs over mouths offered little protection. Roadside notices warning that "Dust brings shells" seemed futile. We were all permanently in a dust cloud which must have risen many hundreds of feet.

The Regiment was concentrated in fields at Crauville, two miles north-east of Caumont. As we approached Caumont we could see that it had been almost destroyed and the infantry were searching the burning buildings. At the cross roads where we were to turn left and head for the battle area I saw a tired-looking sergeant who had been on the same intelligence course in Welwyn Garden City. Although we were both filthy, we recognised each other and exchanged a wave. I realised that his regiment was one of those we would be supporting and felt comforted in the knowledge that we had friends near.

My mission was to lead up to the crossroads in Cahagnes, turn right and assess a field as a possible area for the Regiment to harbour for the night. Cahagnes resembled scenes from the Somme during the first war: trees were stripped of all leaves and many were severed by shrapnel; cattle lay dead in the fields and were already smelling of rotting flesh; the whole area was pitted with shell holes. I thought of Captain Scott's comment on arriving at the South Pole: "God, this is an awful place." Looking at an almost intact crucifix—every village has at least one by the side of the road—and wondered if it was symbolic of this bloody sight. This was certainly no "Green Hill".

It was dusk as we arrived at the entrance to the field. I decided to get out and walk and let the tank follow me. I was not expecting to meet any enemy, but there could be a minefield or some other obstruction which would need marking. I knew there were infantry in the adjoining orchard but was still surprised to hear a very loud order to "Halt". I replied in terms that only an Englishman would know, and a young officer came out of the gloom with several men pointing rifles at me. They explained that a tank which had entered the field the previous evening had turned out to be a German Panther followed by a half-tracked vehicle. There had been a fight and I was invited to take a look at the bottom of the orchard. The dead crew in and beside the burned out vehicle presented a horrible sight. Although I had experienced air raids and been close to casualties in the past four years, I had not actually seen a dead body. The burning had reduced the bodies to about half their normal size. The driver was still in his seat but his arms had dropped from the shoulder sockets. The hands were still attached to the driving wheel. I felt quite sick and disgusted that nobody had bothered to bury them. The troops who looked upon this as a proud trophy had suffered much during the past five weeks and this scene was nothing new to them. I tried to pretend that I, too, was indifferent to it and conceal the fact that such sights were quite new to me. When the rest of the troop arrived I was delighted to learn that another field had been selected for our stay.

We moved in just as we had practiced so many times in the UK: the tanks in lines side by side, allowing for the expected echelon to pass through with daily supplies of fuel, rations and ammunition. We dug our trench and drove the tank over it. A brew was prepared. The echelon arrived and threw off our fuel requirements in Jerry cans, each containing four and a half gallons. The can had been copied from the Germans and was an excellent container. The driver stood on the engine deck trying to find the funnel. An aircraft which had been circling now released some flares which allowed the troops to see what they were doing.

I was standing at the rear of our vehicle when the whole area erupted with small, grenade-like explosions. We were being attacked by small anti-personnel bombs. I dived for the hole under the tank, closely followed by the other crew members. There was a flash in front of me as I dived and I knew that I had been hit above the eye.

I was pinned in the hole by someone else lying on top of me and could hardly move my arms. Lying there, wondering how badly I had been hurt, I tried moving my toes and fingers and found all to be well. I wasn't in any great pain anywhere, but my right arm was very warm and sticky. I came to the conclusion that whoever was lying on top of me was bleeding heavily. I was quite surprised when everybody got out of the trench and made no complaint about wounds. I had suffered no more than a graze, which could have been caused by somebody's boot. Refuelling was resumed and someone asked if anyone had seen his tea, which had been near the entrance to the trench. The mug was found in it and I learned what had been warm and sticky.

We still had not fired a shot in anger and were not doing very well, I thought. I could not help thinking of my father who had served in the cavalry during the Great War. His stories were beginning to be better understood, though I could not imagine how he had survived four years of it.

At daybreak we discovered that we had been showered with anti-personnel bombs which had been released from a basket to ensure wide cover over an impact area. A few had not detonated and still lay among the tanks. At least fifty of them had rained down, yet only one man was wounded and he only slightly.

My troop was now ordered to carry out a recce of the road leading south towards Quéry. It had become very difficult to operate over the radio because of the number of stations on or near the same frequency. We were told to use our "B" sets for inter-troop communications. These were short-range sets which would only operate if the aerials were within sight of each other and unobstructed by buildings, trees, hedges or other vehicles. We had long since ceased training operators to use them because of their limitations, and I was not surprised to find that my set did not work at all. Other tanks and vehicles had the same problem. Another troop, commanded by Lieutenant Jack Bissill, was despatched to complete the task orginally allocated to our troop and their story is told in *First In. Last Out.*

"About a mile down the road, the troop came upon a troop of 'Cherry Pickers', the 11th Hussars, referred to as our 'red-headed friends' when passing information over the air. This was the first encounter of many to follow. Often having advanced upon a cross-roads we found a patrol of the 11th approaching from another direction and friendly rivalry was to develop. Corporal 'Chick' Strickland commanded the leading vehicle and drove past them on this occasion. Lieutenant Bissill, however, stopped to have a word with the troop leader. He called the leading tank over the radio and told them to halt. The driver, Ted Hughes, promptly drove off the road to turn into a gateway and returned to join the troop leader. They found themselves almost on top of a German tank. It turned out to be a wooden one, but it looked real enough to give the crew some concern, to say the least.

"As the troop moved on towards Quéry crossroads, Jack Bissill noticed a number of German Teller mines (plate mines) directly in his path. He was on an open road leading towards Villers-Bocage and, to avoid being stranded in the open, ordered his tank to turn round. Stan Burns, the driver, was negotiating this turn when a 50mm shot passed between the heads of Jack and Trooper 'Ginger' Marley, the operator. The shot then passed in front of the following tank which had just nosed into the road.

"Chick Strickland fired his externally-mounted turret Browning. This had the desired effect of putting the German gunners' heads down whilst the troop leader's tank turned. A Stuart with a 37mm could not deal with a well-placed 50mm. The troop was ordered to withdraw to a position where a troop of 'A' Squadron tanks were moving forward. As mortar bombs rained down on Corporal Strickland's position, he pulled further back. Jack's tank pulled to the side of the road to avoid one of the 'A' Squadron Cromwells and struck a mine which had not been spotted from the turret. The explosion blew off the driver's foot and temporarily blinded the co-driver, Ronnie Ash. Jack Bissill and Ginger Marley were shaken but otherwise unhurt. So ended the first Recce patrol."

The 'A' Squadron troop ordered forward to deal with the hold-up was led by Lieutenant Derek Philo and Lieutenant Ray Irwin, with Corporal Archie Carr commanding the third tank.

*Lieutenant Derek Philo* relates his first encounter with the enemy:

"We were ordered to proceed to the road junction at Quéry. Ray Irwin commanding the leading tank was soon in trouble. A tank in the troop ran over a mine which did little damage to itself but flying shrapnel and stones struck Ray in the face and cut him badly. I moved past him to take up the lead. We heard the report coming over the radio from Jack Bissill's recce patrol. The report, although warning of being fired on, was uncertain of the gun position except that it was somewhere on the left of the road leading towards Villiers. If it were a 50mm gun, we considered we could deal with it.

"I approached the junction and found a farm building blocking my view to the left. I could not see down the road unless I moved forward on to the road. When one tank is forward like this, there is a very restricted vision. The crew commander can see all round but only has one pair of eyes. The operator can also see 360 degrees, which halves the task. The driver can only see what is exactly ahead of him, while the gunner has to watch forward or wherever the turret is pointed. Speech between the crew is limited to the intercom and the noise set up by a 500 horse-powered engine limits all sound to earphones.

"When two or more tanks operate side by side, the arc can be divided between them. I ordered the gunner to traverse left, in the general direction of the suspected opposition, and warned the crew that we were going to move forward as quickly as possible and go straight across the road. From there we could get into a good position to observe and fire. Trooper Eddie Booth, the driver, knew his job and was ready to move. I gave the order 'Driver advance to cover', and we set off with a surge of power which rocked me back against the turret ring. We were right in the middle of the road when we halted with a jolt. The driver, being closer to the ground and concentrating on the way ahead, had spotted mines right in the centre, where normally there would be a white line. We halted about two feet short of them.

"I ordered 'Driver reverse'. We then learned that the enemy gun was a very well positioned 88mm and firing at a devastating range of about a hundred yards. The shot entered the co-driver's hatch and went out through the driver's side, killing both men instantly. The turret was jammed. We couldn't move, nor could we use the gun. We had no alternative to bailing out. I had gained the distinction of being the first tank in the Regiment to be knocked out by an 88mm.

The two crew members, Eddie Booth and Billy Hodgson, had been killed before we had a chance to fire a shot. To further complicate our escape the turret hatch had come down very heavily on my head when we were hit and almost knocked me unconscious. I grabbed a smoke grenade and threw it out of the turret to cover our exit, but it fell on the engine deck and almost choked us. I was still unaware that the two forward crew members were dead and hoped to be able to get them out. Fortunately, the German gun crew must have thought we were on fire and did not fire again. The three turret crew almost fell out of the turret, half blind and choking with the thick smoke. The other tanks in the troop, now aware of the gun position, quickly deployed and dealt with it. The Germans who manned it were mere boys. I was able to report what had happened, but I knew that the first-class account of the damage done by an 88mm would do nothing to reassure the others. The medical officer's half-tracked ambulance came forward and we were taken back. 'Doc' Forrester gave me a drink of something and I went out like a light. I was to remain away from the Regiment until the following December."

During Derek Philo's action, my own troop in the Reconnaissance Squadron was sent to observe the southern side of the Villers Bocage road and we positioned ourselves in an orchard. Taking a walk up the hedge to see what was on my right flank, I found that there was an extensive view but no sign of our troops. I moved to the end of the orchard, from where I could observe both to the right and ahead. Pete Lees, an operator from one of the other tanks in the troop, also dismounted and went to look in the farm buildings to the left, possibly more to "liberate" a chicken than to find the enemy. He came running back reporting that he had been fired at from one of the out-houses. An infantry patrol went off to investigate and soon came back with four prisoners. One boasted that he was a Pole and evidently expected some special reception. I was proud to be given the duty of taking the prisoners back to our 'Tac' Headquarters. Since I did not have to listen to the Regimental net for a few minutes I returned to 6.2 megacycles where incongruously, I picked up Victor Sylvester giving one of his BBC dancing lessons. "slow, slow, quick, quick, slow," seemed quite out of keeping with our crazy and dangerous situation.

*Corporal Syd Swift,* a 17-pounder 'Firefly' commander in 'B' Squadron relates his initiation to armoured warfare. Active service was nothing new to him for he had served as an infantryman in the Duke of Wellington's Regiment on the North-west Frontier of India from 1930 until early 1938, and after discharge had been recalled to the colours to again experience action in the 1939-1940 campaign in France where he was seriously wounded and brought home. After recovery, he was retrained as an armoured crewman and now specialised in gunnery, hence his position as crew commander of the Firefly. He recalls:

"While preparing Cromwells at the Armoured Reinforcement Group Depot, we received the news that the tanks we were now preparing for action were not for another regiment but for our own use. 'Make a special job of them' requested Major the Lord Kildare, my squadron leader. Four of us were called over to his vehicle and informed that we were to proceed to Carpiquet Airfield near Caen and collect "Fireflies". My crew was to be Smith 33 (driver), Smith 10 (operator) and Jack Riggs (gunner). Jack was already in his thirties and, compared to the two Smiths, quite an old man. Smith 10 had been a student until called to the colours and intended to return to study after the war. I was also over thirty and considered to be 'getting on a bit'.

"We were greeted by shelling on arrival at the airfield, some falling quite close to our vehicle. The Fireflies were all lined up and we were soon to understand why the soldiers manning them looked a pretty gloomy lot. They were men of the 4th CLY who, having just given a good account of themselves, had been told that their regiment was to be broken up. We were one of the knives to be twisted in their backs and felt sorry for them. The crew required to hand over their tank to us were completely heart-broken, having become almost attached to this steel monster as a cavalryman becomes attached to his horse. A vehicle, like a horse, will serve you well so long as it is properly maintained and treated. 'Don't fill her right to the top of the dip stick', cautioned the driver as we drove off, leaving four very sad and uncertain soldiers. They would probably be sent to reinforce another regiment, but it would never be the same for them.

"We were not permitted to use the coast road because of the congestion and fear of breaking the surface more than it already was. The air to the engine is sucked down through the turret and, since the crew commander and operator were wedged into the circular hatch, much of it travels down through the neck and out at the trouser bottoms. This is very cooling and acceptable in summer but devastating in winter. The fine, talc-like dust swirled in with the air and we were soon encrusted in the stuff, which choked the nostrils, filled the mouth, and covered the goggles.

"Returning to the point from which we had set off, we found that the Regiment had already moved. We found them dispersed in a field, where a space had been left in each troop for the 17-pounders. Digging in for the night, we noticed a nasty smell. We struck hard bone and realised that we were uncovering a dead cow. It was too late to start again so we decided to sleep in the tank. It was uncomfortable, but preferable to that vile smell. We soon established a procedure for cooking and brewing tea. At first light, and sometimes before, one man got the water on to the stove while others rolled up the bed rolls, stowed the blankets, sorted out the ration and selected the breakfast meal. Men from all walks of life were thrown together in this bloody affair. Smith 33, the driver, had been a Yorkshire miner; Smith 10, the younger, was fathered by Jack Riggs. All Smith's are 'Smudgers' in the army, so we had to establish that Smith the driver would be 'Smudger' whilst Smith 10, the operator, would be 'Dick'.

"Jack Riggs was a quiet Dorset man with a delightful twinkle in his eye to match his sense of humour. We worked furiously the following day to prepare the tank for action, stowing the ammunition, rations and water and checking and adjusting the firing mechanism. There were a few false alarms whilst we worked. The Squadron Leader was continuously being called to attend conferences and we watched anxiously each time he returned. 'Not this time' he would call, as he passed the row of tanks. We found a new place to park, dug a hole, and this time settled for a more comfortable night's sleep. The following morning, wave after wave of bombers passed over at about 500 feet. They had hardly passed overhead when they released their bombs and we could hear the crump, crump, crump of the bursting cargoes they decanted on to the suburbs of Caen. The German anti-aircraft shells also burst in the sky only a little way ahead of us."

I interrupt Syd's story here to add that, although I didn't know it until some time later, my future wife's brother was a member of one of those crews. He never returned from that raid.

*Syd* continues:

"The squadron leader came into the field once more and, this time, told us to get packed up. All troop leaders were to report to his vehicle for instructions. My troop leader, Lieutenant Bryan Marshall, was one of those jockeys who, with Jack Bissill, had been recruited into the Regiment by Perry Harding. He came running back and told us that we would move in ten minutes. The roar of 20 Rolls-Royce Merlin engines and Wright Cyclone engines replaced the noise of the bombing raid. The leading tank set a fast and furious pace which our Shermans could not maintain. Only a few miles up the road we passed one which belonged to another troop, upside down in the ditch. The crew were out but looking a bit shaken. Such a mad drive in vehicles which were strange to us was bound to result in such an accident.

"Life began to revolve around whether the next halt would be long enough for a brew. Many times the water was about to boil when we were told to move on. The stove was proving to be well worn and frequently the cooking had to be done on a fire made by soaking sand with petrol. It did nothing to improve the taste of compo tea but was warm and restored energy.

"We were passing through burning villages now and knew we were nearing the forward positions. We had passed batteries of artillery with their well trained crews firing 25-pounders and the smell of burnt cordite now mingled with the smell of dead cattle. I noticed a house which had been destroyed by gunfire except for one wall from which protruded a bedroom floor, still supporting a bed which seemed untouched. In other ruins there were stairways leading to nowhere. Chimneys remained intact where the houses had crumbled around them. The innermost secrets of each house, hidden from human eye since construction, were being revealed to the world.

"While halted in one of these villages, a unit of the Guards Armoured Division came through and there was quite a mix-up until we finally pulled off the road. We climbed on to the piles of rubble which had once been shops and houses. As the light began to fail we moved on into open country where, in addition to the dead cattle, there were now also burned-out vehicles, guns and equipment. The dust already covered the bodies of men who, only a few hours earlier, were still fighting. In a few days, a telegram would arrive at a house and inform the next-of-kin, bringing sorrow to a family.

"We harboured in open country for the night. The road we had just left was now attracting shell-fire. Our flaming exhausts and the noise of such a concentration of tank engines could be heard five miles away and easily detected and located. But no damage was done. The echelon arrived with supplies and engine noise was replaced by the clatter of off-loading Jerry-cans of fuel. The empties were collected and the echelon withdrew to their own sanctuary for the night.

"Not far away could be heard the quick burst of the Spandau machine-gun used by the Germans and then the reply from some infantry outpost with the slower thud, thud of their Brens. Periodically, a shell passed overhead, aimed at a particular crossroad in hope that it would catch someone out. The troop sergeant arranged

*Christmas card, 1939. Mk VI B Tank left, Bren Carrier right.*

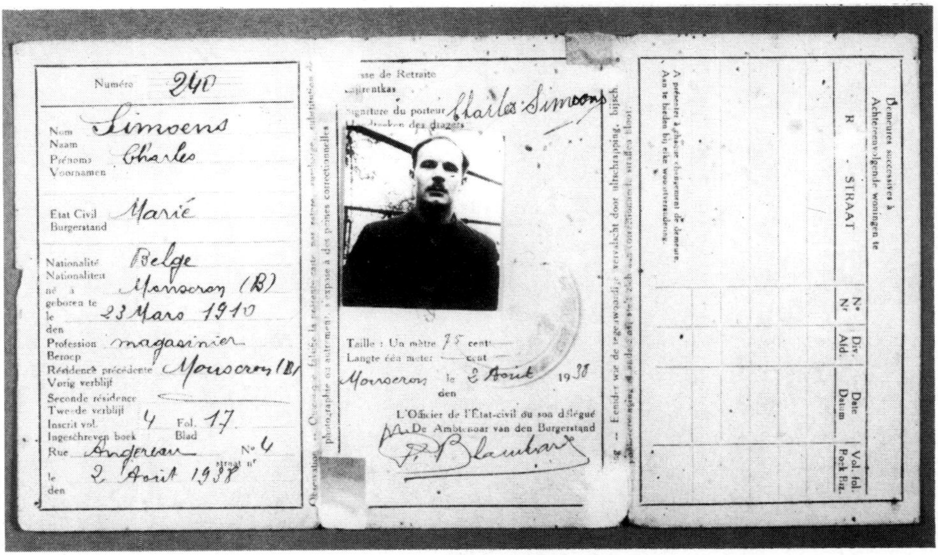


*False ID card issued to Sgt Bevan by the French Resistance.*

*Sister Marie after the war.*

*Paul Bricout and M Bricout. Arrested in 1942 and sent to Sonneburg Concentration Camp. Madam Bricout was sent to Ravensbruck and Belsen. She was never seen again.*

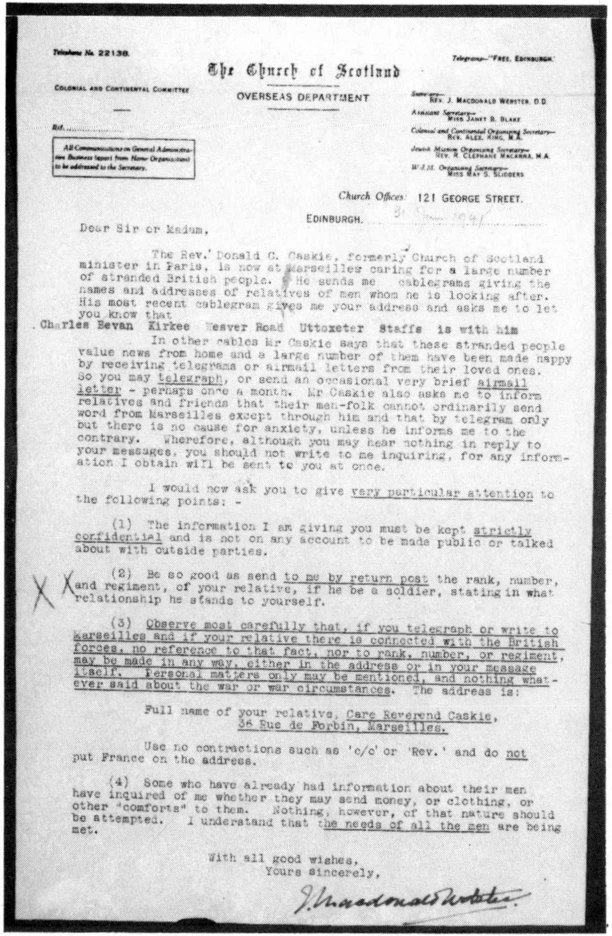
Telephone No. 22138.

Telegrams—"Free, Edinburgh."

The Church of Scotland

COLONIAL AND CONTINENTAL COMMITTEE

OVERSEAS DEPARTMENT

Secretary—Rev. J. Macdonald Webster, D.D.
Assistant Secretary—Miss Janet B. Blake
Colonial and Continental Organising Secretary—Rev. Alex. King, M.A.
Jewish Mission Organising Secretary—Rev. R. Clephane Macanna, M.A.
W.J.M. Organising Secretary—Miss May S. Sliders

Ref.............

All Communications on General Administration Business (apart from Home Organisation) to be addressed to the Secretary.

Church Offices: 121 GEORGE STREET,
EDINBURGH. 3 June 1941

Dear Sir or Madam,

The Rev. Donald C. Caskie, formerly Church of Scotland minister in Paris, is now at Marseilles caring for a large number of stranded British people. He sends me cablegrams giving the names and addresses of relatives of men whom he is looking after. His most recent cablegram gives me your address and asks me to let you know that

Charles Bevan Kirkee Weaver Road Uttoxeter Staffs is with him

In other cables Mr Caskie says that these stranded people value news from home and a large number of them have been made happy by receiving telegrams or airmail letters from their loved ones. So you may telegraph, or send an occasional very brief airmail letter - perhaps once a month. Mr Caskie also asks me to inform relatives and friends that their men-folk cannot ordinarily send word from Marseilles except through him and that by telegram only but there is no cause for anxiety, unless he informs me to the contrary. Wherefore, although you may hear nothing in reply to your messages, you should not write to me inquiring, for any information I obtain will be sent to you at once.

I would now ask you to give very particular attention to the following points: -

(1) The information I am giving you must be kept strictly confidential and is not on any account to be made public or talked about with outside parties.

X X (2) Be so good as send to me by return post the rank, number, and regiment, of your relative, if he be a soldier, stating in what relationship he stands to yourself.

(3) Observe most carefully that, if you telegraph or write to Marseilles and if your relative there is connected with the British forces, no reference to that fact, nor to rank, number, or regiment, may be made in any way, either in the address or in your message itself. Personal matters only may be mentioned, and nothing whatever said about the war or war circumstances. The address is:

Full name of your relative, Care Reverend Caskie,
36 Rue de Forbin, Marseilles.

Use no contractions such as 'c/o' or 'Rev.' and do not put France on the address.

(4) Some who have already had information about their men have inquired of me whether they may send money, or clothing, or other "comforts" to them. Nothing, however, of that nature should be attempted. I understand that the needs of all the men are being met.

With all good wishes,
Yours sincerely,

J. Macdonald Webster

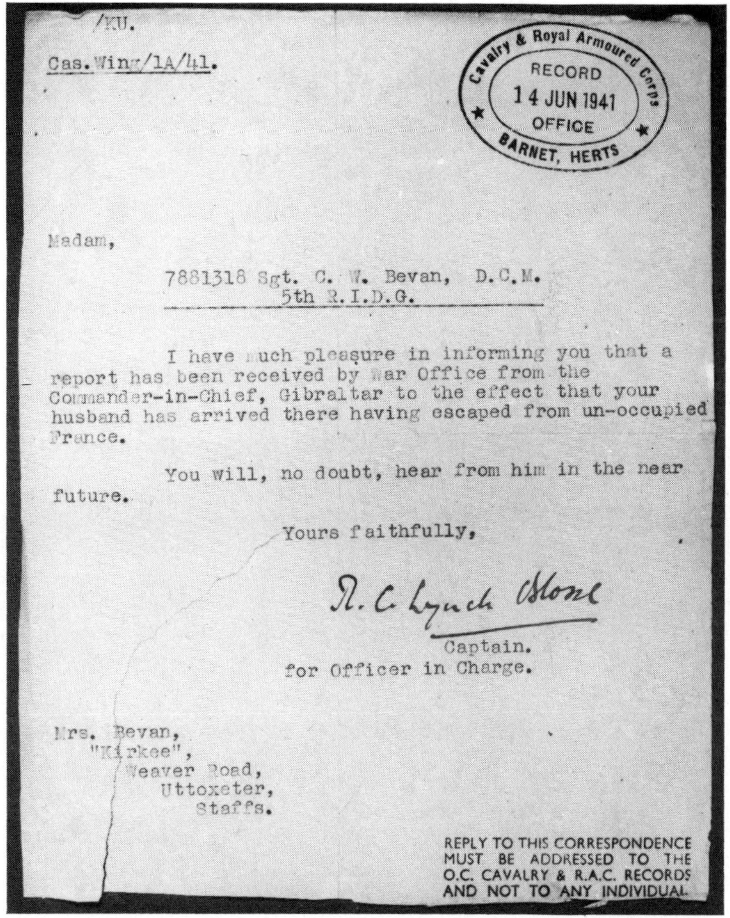
/KU.

Cas.Wing/1A/41.

Cavalry & Royal Armoured Corps
RECORD
14 JUN 1941
OFFICE
BARNET, HERTS

Madam,

7881318 Sgt. C. W. Bevan, D.C.M.
5th R.I.D.G.

I have much pleasure in informing you that a report has been received by War Office from the Commander-in-Chief, Gibraltar to the effect that your husband has arrived there having escaped from un-occupied France.

You will, no doubt, hear from him in the near future.

Yours faithfully,

R. C. Lynch Blosse

Captain.
for Officer in Charge.

Mrs. Bevan,
"Kirkee",
Weaver Road,
Uttoxeter,
Staffs.

REPLY TO THIS CORRESPONDENCE MUST BE ADDRESSED TO THE O.C. CAVALRY & R.A.C. RECORDS AND NOT TO ANY INDIVIDUAL

*Until these letters arrived, Mrs Bevan believed she was a widow.*

*Dunkirk 1940*

*Officers and NCOs of 'A' Squadron, 1943.*

*Juno beach, Normandy, July 1944.*

*Harbour in daylight. Ferret Scout Car and Cromwell Tank.*

*Lieutenant Colonel 'Perry' Harding and Major 'Monkey' Blacker visit Major Creagh Gibson during a lull.*

*'B' Squadron in battle at Couvedour prior to the advance to Hamers.*

*Moving into position at the base of Mt Pinçon*

*Aunay-sur-Oden from the south.*

*Crossing the Seine*

*The road to the Basilica, Lisieux, 40 years after the advance shown on the dust cover.*

*Sergeant Archie Carr, DCM with Sergeant Ted Glynn, DCM, MM, revisit Hamburg, 1987.*

*Alan Merson, Bob Nunn, Jack Clayton, MM, and Syd Swift revisit Wetteren.*

*The final surrender of German troops at Meldorf, May 1945.*

*Left: the General smartens up his army.*

*Below: talking to Tpr Dobson.*

*The final parade before captivity.*

*The Officers, Itzehoe, June 1945.*

*Warrant Officers and Sergeants, 1945.*

for each crew to do a guard stint for the night. I patrolled with Jack Riggs and made a check up a hedgerow. Another sentry further up the line shot a patrolling German, reminding everybody of his responsibility to protect his sleeping comrades. Dawn broke and after the usual radio check, the crews then prepared breakfast. The aroma of frying tinned bacon filled the air making a pleasant contrast to the other revolting smells. I thought of a poem written by Robert Service and recalled how the smell of everyday things brought back memories of home:

Crisp bacon on the blaze to fry,
And old ale in tankard foaming high;
Aroma sweet of baking bread,
And rich onion soup for supper spread;
Roast beans of coffee newly ground;
And a morning kipper, buttered brown.

"We remained in that field until noon and took advantage of the stay by preparing a better-than-usual lunch. Normally, it would have been biscuits; but today we opened a tin of stewed steak. When we moved on, we again found it difficult to keep up with the faster Cromwells. Each corner had to be negotiated by a reversing and forward movement while the Cromwells, with their ability to do a neutral turn, could slide round by turning one track forward while the other reversed. Each twist and turn lost us ground. A few miles more and we found the squadron fanned out on each side of the road and occupying the yellow, ripe cornfields. I spotted the tanks of our troop and joined them, further damaging the crop in the process. Over the radio we could hear a graphic description from a Recce tank which had struck a mine, while another Recce tank near by was trying to effect a recovery and having a rough time. I remember thinking 'we are in action'. I had no idea what day it was, but it was after three o'clock. The battle had not long passed this place. There was little dust on the foliage and the corn which had not been flattened by our tanks waved gently. The birds still managed to sing, too.

"My troop leader was called to the squadron leader's tank. Bryan was a Southern Irishman and sometimes quite difficult to understand. We had learned that 'trees' meant 'threes' and 'tort' meant 'thought' and most of us could do a good impersonation of him. This time he was excited as he ran back towards us. He shouted something as he passed me but, what with his accent and the engine noise, I had no idea what he said. He drove off and I followed.

"We passed out of the cornfield, into an orchard—small apples poured into the turret as we brushed under the leaves—and then into a lane between high banks and hedges. This kind of defile, in which a gun cannot be traversed, is a death trap for tanks and I felt some comfort in being the last tank in the toop. I was to learn later that this was a false comfort.

"We came to a cluster of farm buildings which appeared to be deserted. The banks became even higher and the lane was so narrow that we could only move forward or reverse. The troop leader was leading, followed by the troop sergeant, the second sergeant, and myself in the rear. From my high position in the turret of the 'Firefly' I could see that the lane was leading into an open field, beyond which was a wood. As Bryan's tank nosed into the field, I saw the flash of the gun that fired at him. He stopped. The tank in front of me began to reverse, forcing my driver to do likewise. Over the radio came Bryan's Irish accent: 'Oy've been hit, oy've been hit' he repeated. The squadron leader ignored him in an attempt to calm the situation and find out what had hit him and from where. The second tank moved forward and into the field and then made a complete circular movement. Bryan was quite calm now and reporting that he had been hit in the neck but that his tank was undamaged. An armour-piercing shell had damaged the steering of the second tank and it could only turn to the right.

"Bryan was told to make his way to the rear on foot and to bring the crew of the damaged tank with him. The second sergeant and I were to move forward and take up a position at the end of the lane. Another troop would be brought forward to assist. We moved forward and spotted five Germans crossing through a gap in the hedge and heading towards us carrying a white cloth. I proudly reported over the radio that I had five prisoners but immediateliy realised I could not move forward into a good position and take them with me. Nor was there anyone to hand them to.

"Smith 33 tried his school German but they didn't understand him. He said that they claimed to be the only Germans in the area, having been left behind to demolish tanks. A Scout car came forward and took them away. We moved forward to the end of the lane to find a better position. Our present position was not ideal: my back was to the hedge and in front was an area of dead ground which could not be observed. Failing to make radio contact with the sergeant commanding the other tank, I dismounted and went over to him. All appeared to be quiet but I was not happy about the ridge in front of us. We decided to advance about two hundred yards and across some open ground to a line of scrubby trees, covering each other as we went.

"In this new position, with all-round vision and some cover, I felt much happier. Three hundred yards to my left there was a small farmhouse surrounded by the familiar orchard, a potentially good enemy position which I decided to rake with machine-gun fire. Though there was no reply to our fire, I was not at all certain that the area was clear. Taking a closer look through my binoculars I noticed movement, a German was crawling along the hedge bottom. Another appeared, then more of them. I could not be certain of the number concealed there. Occasionally I saw a head, then an elbow, as they inched nearer.

"I gave the gunner orders: 'Two hundred, hedge bottom, fire

when on'. Dick raked the hedge but the enemy instantly went to ground. I was about to tell the gunner to fire again when the Germans decided to call it a day and stood up. One by one, their hands held high. There were four of them, each carrying a rifle and with two 'Bazookas' between them. I reported our capture to a relieving troop which took the prisoners away.

"It was now I realised we had been on the ridge alone. The other tank, which I thought had covered me forward, had discovered a firing mechanism fault and returned to SHQ. The farm was found to be clear and we were able to move forward unchallenged.

"As dusk fell and we returned to the ridge, I took a look at the damaged tank which had been abandoned. I thought we could recover it with our vehicle and was told to try. We switched off our engine, attached tow ropes to it and one of my crew climbed into the driver's seat of the casualty. But when my driver tried to start up in readiness for the tow, we found our batteries were completely flat. I radioed that I now needed recovery as well.

"We discovered that although the damaged tank would start, its gears were jammed and it could only be moved in reverse. And we could not reverse down the lane because it would impede the approach of the recovery vehicle on its way to rescue me. It was a slow return to the squadron location in reverse and across country. My own tank was recovered but it was 0200 hours when we settled down for the nightly routine. A long and eventful day was still not quite over, for the echelon arrived with fuel and rations. This time I required some ammunition and the two new batteries. There were only a few hours to go before dawn and, as it was too late to dig trenches, we slept in the tank.

"The morning brought me a new, fresh-faced troop leader, Lieutenant Bill Bradfield, whom I liked instantly. The damaged tank had been repaired during the night and we were again ready to move as a complete troop. We were beginning to understand the French maps, much larger in scale than those we had previously used, and already were developing instincts about likely enemy positions which were proving to be more right than wrong. But the long days, continual movement, and guard stints at night, were having their effect, and we were given pills to help us keep awake. Days passed without opportunity to wash. Often the only food we had time to eat was the army dry biscuit munched with accompaniments from open tins perched around the turret—jam, bully-beef, chocolate, sardines, anything. Some nights the echelon could not get up to our positons and we had to walk some distance in darkness to carry the 50lb tins of fuel and water, plus ammunition. All this, in darkness and then the stowing of supplies before morning, added to the fatigue. It was small wonder that nerves became ragged and tempers flared. But that wonderful brew of tea and a joke always did the trick.

"At the daily O-Groups, we learned of the mounting casualties.

Each person brought back a special memory and, in particular, one thought of the families. Each day became a day to be grateful for, an achievement to be proud of. There was a new day ahead and plenty to take the mind off such things. This dependence on one another for survival brought us all together in a new-found friendship."

* * * * *

The greatest deception of the war was now being played out and working in our favour. Hitler, unheeding of his generals, believed that the Normandy landing was intended to draw his Panzer divisions down from the Calais area and that once committed, a new assault would be made across the Channel at the narrowest point between Dover and Calais. He did not believe that we could maintain supplies over the distance between Southampton, Portsmouth and the Normandy beachhead. He did move some armour from the south of France to reinforce his army in the Normandy area and this permitted the Americans to move south and then east very quickly. He ordered his army to stand, fight and hold the line in Normandy. Denying us the use of the Channel ports was of upmost importance, he thought, but he had not known of the Mulberry harbour, nor of the direct fuel pipeline (Pluto) that would be laid across the Channel.

*Sergeant Pat Whitmore* wrote this report in *"Caen Grande-Bretagne"* 20 years later:

"As we moved forward to our positions, there was the unforgettable stench of Normandy in one's nostrils. Those who had fought in the desert always said that it was clean and almost antiseptic—man against man; but here in Normandy lay bloated corpses of the cattle, the finest breeds in the world, rotting. Many had been killed in the initial air raids, others were caught by shell fire as the battle rolled east. There were horses, too; the Germans, desperately short of petrol, had requisitioned every horse they could find and there were many in this country before the tractor became the domestic toy. They had been driven until they dropped or were caught in the rocket and machine gun fire from aircraft which harried all roads. The ditches and cross roads were littered with them and their bodies had become the breeding ground for flies. Many wounded horses had stampeded in terror and had wandered with the cows. The poor animals had not been milked for days and were in agony, pitiful victims of war. Tank crews often risked their lives to try to milk them but most animals were already wounded and too frightened to be touched.

"For the tank crew moving into action for the first time, the moment was propitious. The line was beginning to crack although forward movement in the Caen area was still impossible. Away in this bocage country there was the first stirring of what was to become a rout. That this was possible was scarcely our doing; all credit must be given to those who held the pivot and continued to hold the line at Caen, later accepted as 'The Anvil of Victory'. Somewhere during that approach move, we halted momentarily by a grave hastily dug beside the road. The simple wooden cross bore the name Lieutenant D. Grahamme-Parker, RAC. We had been at school together and I remembered him winning the cross-country on Hampstead Heath—of such are the memories of war.

"When, after a terrific artillery bombardment, Villers-Bocage fell, the way to the south lay open for a few miles. We had edged slowly towards the town, but always in bounds of a few hundred yards, from one hedgerow to the next, our view forever obscured by apple trees. The green, unripe fruit fell as we brushed under them. The tanks became vast, peripatetic cider presses. Added to the stench of dead cattle was the smell of roasting apples jammed between the hot exhaust pipes. Some blocked the air louvres causing engines to overheat. Shelling became a constant ordeal. We rapidly became accustomed to the whine of an approaching shell and judging where it would fall. There was perhaps a three second warning. Those passing over or to the left or right were ignored, but one coming close to your area caused a dive for cover. Many of our early casualties were caused by shrapnel. Wearing a headset prevented the advantage of hearing the shells approach. The first indication was the concussion of the exploding round. Our own artillery barrages were enormous and continuous. One had to give credit to the Germans for holding their positions against such harrassing fire, frequently backed by attacks from the air.

"All that our Army had endured during the retreat to Dunkirk was being returned with a ferocity seldom seen since the battle of the Somme in 1916. Suddenly, with the fall of Villers-Bocage, we were free to move without the hedgerow fights. In one day we covered the countryside between Villers and Aunay-sur-Odon. We harboured for the night on the ridge at Hamars, much exposed to German fire. The early dawn broke into a beautiful day; Mont Pinçon to our right, rising out of the early mist; in front a valley, calm, untouched by the battle. The gunfire had ceased. It soon began again; the innocent valley was held by the enemy and we were harrassed as we moved forward. All day we remained on the ridge while on our right, and in every increasing intensity, the sound of battle swelled to a full diapason.

"A West Country division was working its way up Mont Pinçon after an air raid had reduced Aunay to rubble. A solitary church spire stood out to mark the centre of what had once been a town. The devastation was so great that the infantry could not get through the streets. Armoured bulldozers were brought forward to clear a path through the rubble and to construct a by-pass east of the town. As the troops worked their way through the orchards and sunken tracks which made all campaigning in Normandy so hazardous, they met systematic defence works prepared to delay the advance. When that battle was at its height, it seemed to us that hell itself was breaking out away to our left and in the Thury-Harcourt area on the east bank of the Orne, which was now suffering the same fate as Aunay. The shelling of our position died down and finally stopped. We were ordered forward late in the afternoon and made our way up the slopes of Mount Pinçon. The broken trees and shattered farms were evidence of the battle's course. We harboured almost on the summit and were launched in pursuit at dawn the following day."

* * * * *

*Sergeant Bob Price* (who had sent that signal from Dunkirk, "Use Vermouth ruthlessly", and then witnessed the sad farewell between a French cavalryman and his horse), was now a Troop Sergeant in 'C' Squadron. For him the Battle Honour, 'Mount Pinçon', has a special memory: he played a part in that assault and takes up the story:

"Lieutenant Peter Martel was my troop leader. We stood to an hour before dawn on August 12th. There was always the threat of a counter attack between 0400 and 0500 hours each morning. We had enjoyed the usual four hours of intermittent sleep. We were all very tired after two weeks of continuous fighting and movement, long days and short nights affecting most of us. Added to the tiredness was the extreme and continuous stress. The troop leaders returned from the squadron leaders' order group and told us to we were to support the infantry of the Wessex Division and clear the way for an evening and night operation to follow. During the day's fighting we had lost the 'Firefly' in the troop. The enemy had also lost three tanks, a Mk IV and two Panthers plus two 50mm guns which were credited to the squadron."

The Regimental Diary read: "*August 12th 1944.* Supporting 5 Wilts; 'C' Squadron moved forward to capture the high ground at Le Jardin-la-Vardière. This was done without much difficulty but no sooner was the squadron in position than they were subjected to heavy and continuous shelling. Major Ward-Harrison was able to deploy his whole squadron into fire positions, including his own squadron headquarters. The feature presented an ideal hull-down position. In the early stages, only two troops were deployed but as soon as enemy tanks were reported, the whole squadron moved into position. Three enemy tanks were knocked out at about 1600 yards range. There was 1 Mk IV and 2 Panthers. Two 50mm anti-tank guns were also sighted and knocked out. The shooting was excellent and many German infantry were killed. Our own casualities were light, only Trooper Verrell being wounded in the wrist and Captain Blundell-Brown wounded in the arm. During this action Corporal Carr's tank was brewed up. The crew baled out successfully but were attacked by German infantry as they dismounted. Corporal Carr was able to get hold of his Sten gun which was kept on the outside of the tank for such purpose. He shot three enemy at close range, enabling the rest of his crew to get back safely."

Major J. M. D. Ward-Harrison was awarded the DSO for this action.

* * * * *

*Sergeant Bob Price* continues:

"2 Troop was to be part of the preliminary attack on the lower slopes of the hill. I, as troop sergeant, was to lead. A way had been discovered to get tanks on to the apparently impossible hillside, and, it was hoped, out of sight of the enemy. This would enable the troop to give close support to the infantry. They would then move through the orchards below us. Our presence would prevent any counter-attack on them from above.

"Late in the afternoon, having managed some food and replenished with ammunition and with a fourth tank loaned from another troop, we set off with the usual butterflies in our stomachs. The infantry, waiting under cover as we passed to take up position to their right and well above them, looked as though they were spending their last day on earth. We swung east and reported 'On the start line'. The attack began perfectly, at the time previously arranged. Elsewhere along the front could be heard the sound of battle to free the beachhead. The sun was setting behind us now, which would be to our advantage if the enemy were observing us through sights. We had been briefed to keep just a little ahead of the infantrymen below. If the slope was to be defended, it could hardly have been expected that any tanks would take part in the attack. We fired our machine-guns at any likely obstruction whether enemy was seen or not. The other tanks in the troop, slightly above me, could also bring fire to bear on any target.

We advanced round the open hillside. A few hundred yards ahead of us was a hedgerow, with open ground between it and the orchards below. I made for an opening in the hedge so as to outflank any troops intending to hold that line and not a shot was fired at us during this move. But what lay beyond the hedge? Germans. A quick burst from the turret BESA caused the rows of helmeted heads to disappear. A second burst persuaded two officers to leap out with hands aloft. A third burst along the hedgerow, where we suspected others were taking cover, brought the two officers to their knees in supplication. Our part in the action was almost over, and the infantry came forward to handle the mass of prisoners.

"Trouble came as the infantry consolidated and we awaited orders in the gloom to get off the hill and rejoin the Squadron. One of the tanks in the rear had shed a track and called for assistance. While the troop leader made his way down the hillside, I returned to help. It was only 'summer dark' and quite possible to see. Repairing a shed track is normally no great problem, but the procedure could not be carried out on a hillside. As we started to pull the tank and its broken track down the hill, the enemy holding the ground above us brought down some very accurate mortar fire. Unlike a shell, there is no warning whistle from a mortar fired from close range, it is only the firing of the bomb which is heard and one is not aware of its direction until it arrives.

"I was pinned down but thought I would stand a better chance if I made a run for it. I leaped into the turret, helped by Lance-Corporal Armitage. Whether the Germans ran out of ammunition or thought we had moved, I know not. But the track was fixed and we moved back to squadron headquarters. The echelon had arrived and the usual fuel and ration drawing took place. This time I required quite a lot of ammunition.

"Someone had relieved a prisoner of his musical box and its notes softly played 'Liebestraum'. It was a balm to my wearied soul. I was suffering the first stabbing pains of a migraine and was asleep quickly. The following morning, Peter Martel was transferred to another troop and I was given command of 2 Troop."

*　*　*　*　*

The Regiment's move south was hampered by abandoned equipment, some of it booby-trapped. Mines were laid, bridges blown. The state of the prisoners was a clear indication of an army in retreat. The Germans were in no state to fight a rearguard action. A tragic accident in Tac HQ caused the death of the adjutant, Captain Maurice Williams (one of the four who set out for the fancy dress party in Northampton). Tiredness and fatigue was affecting efficiency and the gunner of the tank following Maurice's accidentally put his foot on the firing switch of the turret gun, firing a burst into the forward vehicle killing Maurice instantly. It was the second death in Tac HQ. Corporal Charlie Ray, who had caused the confrontation in the woods at Narford when he walked through Jack Robinson's morning parade, had been killed by shrapnel. Both were respected men and would be a great loss.

*　*　*　*　*

The Reconnaissance Squadron had been very active during the approach to Mont Pinçon and, now that the heavies were engaged, had a chance to regroup and carry out some necessary modifications. Our vehicles, in a poor state when we took them over, had been made more unreliable in their subsequent battering. The batteries were badly affected by constant use and heavily drained by the electrical power traverse system. A tank with a flat battery was as good as useless: no gun, no radio, and no engine. The "Honey", as we called it, was fast. It had five forward and reverse gears and a hydromatic transmission which would today be called an automatic gearbox. But it had too high a profile, was slightly top heavy, and prone to topple over when on a slope or the edge of a ditch. The crew commander and operator could hardly move in the turret. The driver and co-driver had quite a lot of room but usually became casualties if the tank struck a mine.

Many lessons had been learned. At first an attack on a target brought retaliations and casualties. The 37mm gun, though effective against soft targets, would not penetrate armour of any thickness. And it emerged that all men are not equal: some accepted the necessary risks while others were beginning to step back at every opportunity. And there were men—officers, senior ranks and juniors—who had been quiet and self-effacing in training but proved themselves to be leaders in this situation. No-one was pressing for promotion: a leader is inevitably more exposed to danger, and extra pay was little inducement on the battlefield. Despite this, leaders were forthcoming, often from unexpected quarters. Men who had often been in trouble for untidy dress or for flouting the rules were now proving to be the better soldiers. The assumption in training that all men are equal and prepared to die proved to be unjustified. Every man has his breaking point, and some had reached it long before they were faced with a front-line task. These realities had to be recognised and reflected in our tactics if we were to gain the most from all ranks.

One reality was the vulnerability of the leading vehicle in a troop. It was decided that the main rôle of the troop leader, in the second vehicle, should be to recover the crew of the leader if hit or mined. The two vehicles therefore kept very close together and, if the leader was pinned down by opposition, the second vehicle would fire smoke over the top and try to effect a rescue. In tactics, the leader would proceed some hundreds of yards while covered by the second vehicle which, in turn, would be covered by the third as it moved forward. This tactic, known in the Recce Squadron as a "snake patrol", was also employed by the sabre squadrons.

My own driver became an early nerve casualty. He was a nice, unboastful man but was jittery, queried my decisions, stayed in the tank when there was an opportunity to get out and, worst of all, wore his steel helmet whenever he was out of the vehicle. These were the tell-tale signs of a man who was going or had gone "bomb happy". The final breakdown came after a move through a cornfield. As we passed through a gate I was horrified to see a Tiger tank only 30 yards to my right. The driver could not see it and, if I had said anything, I was certain he would have stopped. I waved to the two vehicles behind me and told the driver to speed to the other side of the field. "What for?" he asked. I tried to tell him, as calmly as I could that we must cross the field quickly and to get on with it. It turned out it had been shot up by aircraft and abandoned by its crew. This episode, which the rest of us tried to make light of, did nothing for my driver, who began to query every order I gave.

Later that day, when leading over a crest and in full view from the opposite ridge, he stopped. We were a sitting target, but he refused to move another inch. I told him to get out of the tank and threatened to shoot him if he refused, but he was incapable of even understanding our situation. The gunner kicked him. Voices over the radio were asking why I had stopped. Evenually he was pulled out of the driver's seat and the operator took over. I left him sitting by the side of the road, a broken, weeping wreck. I never knew what happened to him.

Captain Guy Glover, our Squadron Leader, was slightly injured by shrapnel and had to go off for treatment. Captain Robert Crockett, who had assumed command at Bury St Edmunds, now came back to lead us. Robert had been Charlie Bevan's troop leader in France in 1940 and knew how to get the most from his men. He was sparing with his praise and very critical of failures, but had sound judgment and a dry sense of humour which endeared him to us. After listening to our tales of woe and reasons why we were held up, he would reply: "Well, just push on, will you?"

Sergeant Eric Roodhouse had been posted from us before we set off from the farm in Maisons to command a new and monstrous tank known as the Challenger which was quickly scrapped because its enormous turret and 17-pounder gun proved to be too heavy for the engine. Eric now returned to the reconnaissance task to which he was well suited. His perfect French and outstanding courage gave us the boost which we badly needed.

Since observation was of prime importance it was decided to remove the turrets of some of the Stuarts. This left an enormous hole which allowed plenty of movement for the two-man turret crew. Two additional Browning machine-guns were fitted, one each side, and a Bren-gun and smoke-discharger mounted on the front. Brownings could, if necessary, be aimed into ditches at the side of the road, and the crew were comforted to know that, if they had to bale out, they could do so very quickly. The "sawn off" vehicle, as it was now known, was not very elegant but was faster and more stable. It presented a smaller target and was a very much improved reconnaissance vehicle.

Our objective for "Operation Bluecoat". which was to capture the high ground and Mont Pinçon, was now complete and we headed south towards Condé-sur-Noireau but were recalled to support the Canadians about to break out to the east from the Caen sector. The move was brilliantly arranged and admirably executed. We drove back a few miles to a field and found sufficient tank transporters lined up to take each tank. Traffic controllers guided us to a vehicle each and we drove straight on. There was no immediate move and this gave us a much needed opportunity to have a good meal, wash and then sleep, bedding down on the backs of the transporters. By dawn the following morning we were moving through the devastated streets of Caen.

*Pat Whitmore* gives a moving account of that journey through this once beautiful city and to the flat Caen Plain to the south:

"We passed the airfield at Carpiquet where only a few weeks before we had been looking at a knocked-out German Panther tank. Caen was a miracle of which the French have the prerogative: life was beginning again. We had not seen any civilians at all during our move south to Mont Pinçon but here was life. I can still vividly remember seeing a girl on that August morning. We had entered Caen by the road which leads down to the centre from Carpiquet. In the remains of the street the column had made one of its innumerable halts. A few houses and shops remained. The girl emerged from one of the shops. She had, I remember, a scarf round her head and wore a blue skirt. On her arm was a shopping basket. She was coming out of a grocer's shop which still had a few meagre wares for sale behind the shuttered window. Life had begun again for her and, in a direct way, I felt involved. For weeks, obstinately and tenaciously the inhabitants of Caen and the Faubourg Vaucelles had lived in the very centre of the battle, sheltered as best they could in the cellars. These people were as much the victors as the troops who had sallied forth to battle.

"André Gide in the remarkable preface to Saint-Exupéry's *'Vol de Nuit'*, quotes from a letter about the nature of courage which suggests that mere bravery when one has something active to do is not a particularly laudable virtue. I doubt if I would have agreed with Gide and Saint-Exupéry then, on my way to join in the pursuit of the routed German army. On more mature reflection, I am convinced that they were right. I agree that there is an *élément vulgaire et sportif* in being in action which takes one's mind off anything but the immediate practical problem, thereby diminishing contemplation and, subsequently, courage in its deeper significance. The real heroes and heroines of the war were epitomised by the girl I had seen coming out of the shop.

"Even more did I admire the untold heroism of the Resistance who, carrying on the deadliest of warfare, had to do so in their own country, often in their own town or village. We had come from across the Channel and there was, perforce, an impersonal element in everything we did.

"We took our tanks off the transporters and moved south on to the vast Caen plain to the south of the city where we witnessed a sad sight. A regiment of Sherman tanks stood motionless, almost in perfect battle formation. A Polish armoured regiment had been caught in the open by six well-sited Tiger tanks. The Shermans, too slow to reach cover, had caught fire, and many of the crews were still in the badly burnt vehicles.

"This was good country, where tanks could be deployed as they were intended to be, and the enemy armour had been the first to take advantage of it. We moved through the knocked-out formation and south towards Troarn, Cagny, Frenouville, Vimont and beyond to Airan, Vieux-Fumé and Saint-Pierre-sur-Dives. Each village bore the scars of war and some were destroyed completely. We entered Livarot cautiously after a night in harbour near Mittoi and Boisey. It was, if I remember correctly, untouched, though we fought a sharp skirmish on its eastern boundary. We turned north towards Lisieux to find that a screen of German troops had remained to cover the withdrawal of their divisions remaining on the coast, whose only escape was towards Rouen.

"Somewhere between Livarot and Lisieux we were halted on the outer fringe of the enemy positions and, with some difficulty, established ourselves on a crossroads which we held during the night. Edging gingerly into an orchard at first light in order to take up a fire position, I ordered the driver to switch off the engine. Shortly, in the silence of the morning I heard, 'M'sieu Tommy'. Out of a building, which was part of a small farm, came a young man. Once he established that we were British, the rest of the family emerged bringing with them a bottle of calvados, hidden since the fall of France in 1940. Glasses were fetched and we drank to la France, de Gaulle, Churchill and the Allies.

"We learned from the farmer that this family had sheltered the French-speaking crew of a crashed Canadian bomber. As the battle drew near and a German headquarters was set up in the farm, everybody—French, Canadian and German—had taken shelter in the cellar under the cow sheds! The previous day the Canadians had judged it safe to escape to our lines.

"This brave family now gave us fresh meat, milk and bread and, more important, information about enemy positions around Lisieux. The farmer was an important member of the Resistance and his farm became a clearing-house for information. While we were there, the curé of one of the villages came through enemy lines and, at untold risk, brought us up-dated information of gun positions. Fortified with this information and more calvados, we advanced. It was a wild and deadly fire that the enemy encountered a mile or so down the road."

# Pursuit to the Seine

The 7th Armoured Division, with the Regiment leading, headed south-east from Caen towards Livarot and then swung north to assist the 51st Highland Division to capture Lisieux, a strategically important rail junction. Dominating the skyline for many miles to the west was the impressive Catholic Basilica, a beautiful building with a dome not unlike that of St Paul's Cathedral. Pockets of German troops were left to harrass us on the advance but, in this kind of terrain, we could deploy as soon as contact was made with any defences, just as the Germans had done in their advance through France in 1940. There was no point in sustaining casualties in head-on attack when an out-flanking movement could cut the enemy off. Villagers came out and gave us an ecstatic welcome but we had no time to stay and join in their celebrations. One village, which greeted us with flowers and bottles of wine, started ringing its bell as well. Reluctantly, we had to stop it. Our positions were already vulnerable enough. But it was wonderful to meet such jubilation after the weeks in the bocage.

The Americans were moving rapidly to our south and threatening the Germans. If they could reach the Seine, turn north, then hold the crossings, a vast army would be cut off.

At one point during the advance to Lisieux, the Regiment was attacked by both German and British aircraft. Three Spitfires straffed during the day and, that same evening, the enemy dropped more scatter bombs. Fortunately, the only damage was a petrol lorry which caught fire, though one crew commander had his nose damaged by his own operator as they dived into their tank.

These long daily moves now placed a severe strain upon our supply lines and the tired echelon drivers were having to cover at least four times the distance of our advance in a continous forward and backward movement. The water carts were separated from the other vehicles in the echelon and their drivers had to use their own initiative to obtain water and then find their own squadrons. The two-wheel drive vehicle itself was not particularly efficient and, when full, weighed well over a ton.

*Corporal Cyril Blanchard,* in charge of a squadron water cart, describes the problem:

"Keeping a squadron of tanks and the echelon supplied with water was a difficult and continuous chore but a very necessary one. Initially each water-cart operator found his own supply and moved up the line to join the main supplies at night. During the dry, dusty months of July and August, 1944, the demand was constant. As the

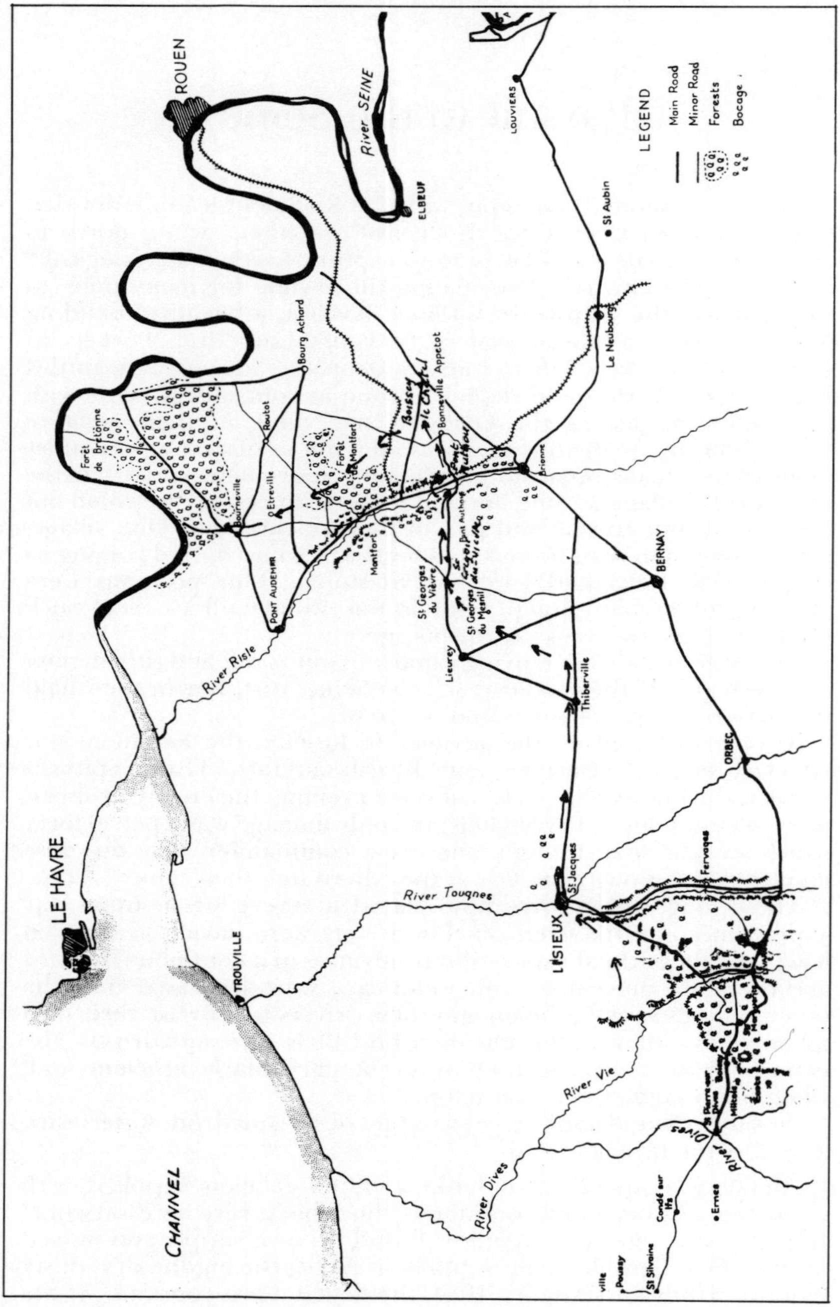
ROUEN
River SEINE
ELBEUF
LOUVIERS
LEGEND
Main Road
Minor Road
Forests
Bocage
St Aubin
Le Neubourg
Bourg Achard
Routot
Bonneville Appetot
Forêt de Bretonne
Forêt de Montfort
Etreville
Bourneville
Montfort
Pont Authou
Brionne
PONT AUDEMER
St Georges du Vièvre
St Georges du Mesnil
BERNAY
Lieurey
River Risle
Thiberville
ORBEC
LE HAVRE
St Jacques
Fervaques
River Tougnes
TROUVILLE
LISIEUX
River Vie
River Dives
CHANNEL
Condé sur Ifs
Ernes
St Silvaine

troops moved forward, the problem became more difficult until eventually the Royal Engineers set up water points and we were free to draw water which had been tested by experts. I had attended no fewer than five water courses before moving to Normandy so I could claim to be quite expert. The golden rule was to always 'drag' water from rivers and canals, never from wells or ponds. Running water cleans itself to some degree, while wells and ponds are static and easily polluted.

"We could never keep up with the troops. There was no radio fitted to a water cart, so there was no choice but to follow the main signs of our own divisions until we found our brigade, and then the regiment and squadron. Maps were in short supply and, in any case, we had no idea where our next delivery would be. It paid to note any river or canal crossed and to follow it through to the nearest point to the front line. A full cart was essential at the start of the day.

"My driver was a chap named Bill Jones and we were together from Normandy to Itzehoe. That was a lot of water under many bridges. A Mono pump attached to the engine of the truck dragged the water and passed it through filters. The complete load of 200 gallons, weighing 2,000lbs was then treated with four scoops of chlorine powder and four taste-removing tablets. After 20 minutes, the water was fit to drink. It was during a long, thirsty day that I was introduced to calvados. We were travelling up a narrow road when a young French boy jumped on the running board and offered me a drink from his bottle. I took a deep swig and thought my throat was on fire. I had never experienced anything like it. We harboured in an orchard where we were given a bottle of it by the boy's father. It was eventually consumed on VE day, some nine months later.

"Our slow moves up the line were tedious. Unbeknown to Bill and I, the other drivers in the convoy were filching our water from the taps at the rear. Infantrymen, too, obviously thought this oasis was too good to miss. We arrived at the tank harbour area and the crews came down to fill their usual two Jerrycans of water only to find we were dry! The squadron leader was not amused and sent us off to refill. I could not remember passing any river or canal and thought the prospect of doing so in the dark very remote. After driving for miles in search of a stream, we decided to stop at the next village in the hope of finding a well or some other supply. I did not need Bill's reminders of the dangers of well water: but I had to take a chance. We persuaded an old man to show us the village well and pumped it dry. After treating our tank with the usual chlorine and taste tablets and waiting the requisite 20 minutes, I offered the old man a mugful of the water. He would have none of it, so I brandished my revolver in desperation. The sight of it, and the offer of cigarettes and chocolate persuaded him to drink. We waited another half hour to see what it would do to the poor chap. He appeared to be unaffected and, by the time we left, the well was filling again. Everybody was happy. Ever after that incident, which cost us a night's sleep, we kept a good watch on our taps during moves. Later, during the advance, there was an incident at Oudenarde.

" 'Oudenarde' is a battle honour proudly displayed on our Regimental Standard. Our forebears in 1708, and during the Marlborough campaign against the French, could not have known that 236 years later, the regimental water-cart would once again liberate that town. I used my initiative and went to the local brewery for water. Yes, they could supply us, but they only had a one-inch pipe, so it was going to be a long job. Halfway through the operation, the manager came rushing up and gave us to understand, in his tenuous English, that we were ahead of our troops and the Boche had returned. On his advice, we pulled down the roller doors to hide the truck, and he kept watch while we continued to fill. After a few hours we decided to make a run for it and, when we eventually found our troops and our centre-line signs, I was given a right ticking off for being so late. When I explained that we had been cut off in Oudenarde, the squadron leader told us that the Germans had been chased out some hours earlier. The fact that we had hidden in a brewery did little to prove our innocence!"

* * * * *

Life in general was now settling down to a regular routine of daily patrols mixed with the sadness of casualty reports. The postal service was magnificent, and letters were reaching us in about five days. We in turn could send as many letters as we wished, though opportunities for writing them were limited. We were issued with small buff cards which only required filling in and amending according to circumstances. The messages offered for permutation were:

*I am fit and well.*

*I have been wounded and have been evacuated to base hospital.*

*I have received your letter/postcard/parcel.*

We were not allowed to write anything else on these cards, but they served a purpose. We had the greatest admiration for the Salvation Army, too. Their mobile canteen arrived in the most unlikely places and under very dangerous conditions. The vans, run by two men, carried luxuries such as handkerchiefs and green envelopes which could be used to enclose three short letters which were not censored by regimental officers but were attended to at some base depot. This meant that some private thoughts could be expressed without troop officers learning about them. I am sure those 'Sally Ann' trucks liberated a few places without knowing it.

During the five weeks we had been in action we had matured, acquired a different outlook towards death, and become very dependent on each other. There was no more idle boasting; no financial rewards for anything we did. Money now played no part in our life at all, since there was nothing to buy and nowhere to buy it. I have, since then, often met the men I served with in the war, and the relationships forged in those days still endure. I could not tell them anything about myself that they would not already know: one's soul was bared. Tough men have broken down and wept over the loss of a comrade. War brings out the truth in a man—different truths in different people with different values. I am ever reminded of a dead German soldier lying in the middle of a road and on a corner where the tanks were turning at some speed. As the first and second vehicles ran over him, the crew commanders looked back and then ignored the scene. By the time we rounded the bend, the remains were hardly recognisable as human and I, like the others, looked back with no feeling of remorse. Now I avoid dead birds and cats on the road as the memory of that poor soul flattened on the road returns to me. I understood the feelings of the infantry in that orchard on my first day of action.

The oil seals on my Stuart tank failed completely and we had to be recovered to our REME workshops located with 'B' echelon. The turret was removed and left in a ditch for someone else to pick up as scrap. Jack Robinson, once the scourge of 'B' Squadron, was now the Regimental Quartermaster Sergeant and second-in-command of the echelon to the Quartermaster, Captain Fred Robson. All were to become very close friends of mine after the war but, at that time, the relationship between a corporal, the RQMS and the Quartermaster was remote. I handed over the tank to the LAD early in the morning and, since we were very tired and looking forward to a few days' rest, we found ourselves a spot at the edge of the field and the crew were soon asleep. I was about to join them when I heard the dreaded parade-ground command to "Fall in". I looked up from my prone position in disbelief. Surely, I thought, parades were not still being held when just ten miles up the road there was a war going on. As JR looked at my crew and did his heel-rocking act, I thought for a moment he was going to tell me to get them on parade. But then he ignored us. He almost certainly sensed how I felt. He had, after all, been awarded the DCM during the retreat to Dunkirk and knew what action was all about. He informed the gathered parade that he had found a small quarry down the road and that every man in the echelon would that day fire at least one magazine of Sten ammunition. One of my crew, Jeff Ward, a saucy character at the best of times, could not control his mirth when he heard this. I warned him to keep quiet, but his outburst had been heard by JR, who now directed his order to us: "That goes for you big tankmen". After the parade I politely approached Mr Robinson. "Excuse me, sir," I said. "My crew are very tired and we have a number of more important things to do than fire our Sten guns in a quarry." Ward, who had followed behind me, added: "That's right, sir." "Be quiet you", replied JR. "I'm talking to the engine driver, not the oil rag." I pushed Ward away before more things could be said.

"So what have you to do?" enquired JR. "Sew buttons on our trousers, clean our weapons, have a wash," I replied. This brought me a lecture on what a soldier must first do when coming out of the line and I was reminded that cleaning of personal weapons should have been our first act. I agreed and said it would be done. We had no sooner completed our personal chores and again drifted into sleep than Jack was back again. "I have a duty for you, corporal," he announced. "When we move tonight, you will command that Sherman on the other side of the field. It's a reinforcement tank and has to move with us. You'll find a chap named Sawtell somewhere over there and he's the driver." I walked over and met Bob Sawtell who was also to become a lifelong friend. "Does it run?" I enquired. He assured me it did, so I collected my bedding and washing kit and stowed it on my new charger. Since the others in my crew had no particular place to ride in the echelon, I told them to do likewise.

It suddenly occurred to me that I ought to know where the echelon was going and that I had no maps forward of this position. I thought it imprudent to wake JR, who was asleep under a truck, so I found Fred Robson, the Quartermaster, and said I would like some details of our new location in case we broke down. "Go and ask the RQMS," replied Fred. "He's asleep," I answered. "Well wake him up," ordered Fred. So I returned to JR, who had obviously overheard the comment and responded loudly enough for the QM to hear: "The next time I want to * * * * * * sleep, I will go three fields away." I began to wish I was back with the squadron.

The night move went very slowly. I had been ordered to remain at the back and stay with any vehicle that broke down. One had to be repaired by the fitters several times, but on each occasion we caught up with the convoy very quickly. It was dawn as the column pulled into a field. A hundred yards short of the gate, the vehicle broke down again. As it could be seen from the field, I pulled past it and found a space near a hedge, where the crew set about digging a hole to drive the tank over for our sleeping quarters. JR appeared. "Now big tankmen," he said, "somewhere on this journey I have lost one three-ton four-by-four truck. Have you seen it?" I told him it was just outside the gate and was being repaired. "I told you quite clearly to remain with any vehicle that broke down," he insisted. He was obviously not impressed by my explanation that the vehicle was visible from the field and that I would have caused an obstruction by remaining with it. Jack's military world was made up of blacks and whites, and what he said was what he meant.

He now diverted his attack towards the crew who were digging the slit trench. "What are those people doing?" he demanded. Told they were making a safe place to sleep, he replied: "It's not necessary here and in the morning and before we move again, you'll fill it in and I shall inspect it." Suddenly, with perfect timing, two aircraft roared across the field at hedge-top level firing wildly at anything in sight. Nobody actually saw them as we dived for cover. Ten men climbed into my tank and another ten went under it. "That's what the holes are for," I commented. Nobody knew whether it was an allied aircraft chasing a German, or vice versa, or two of one side or the other. Whoever they were, I was grateful for their intervention.

Captain Guy Glover arrived from hospital, having been patched up and asked what I was doing here and what was going on in the squadron. During a friendly chat I told him that things were not too pleasant in the echelon and that I could not get back soon enough. He went off to find Fred Robson and came back with a Jeep. "Put your kit on here," he said. I was saved . . .

The following day I paired up with a very nice young boy from Acklam, near Middlesbrough and we drew up a Scout car. Dennis Grieves, straight out of grammar school, had a smattering of French and was a good driver, and I knew we would get on well. He had been the operator in the tank during the early days in Normandy and had taken over after we had extracted the nerve-shattered driver, so I knew him a little. Our vehicle, a new Daimler with a useful turn of speed, had no radio but I was told that one would be sent up the following day.

Working past Livarot with the Rifle Brigade on August 20th, both Recce Troops found themselves forced to remain out in enemy territory. One of the RB vehicles was so badly ditched that it could not be recovered in the dark and under such conditions. The vehicles in front of it could not pass to return and nothing could get forward, so there was no choice but to spend a wakeful night in a defensive position. In the morning, it was found that the enemy had laid mines only 50 yards from the position, but there was no attack. The constant German moves and disturbances had made the men extremely tired, so men from the echelon were brought forward to give them a break. Everyone had to share these guard duties periodically, and Orderly Room Corporal *Steve Melhuish* describes one of those nights:

"It was raining hard and the rain dripped steadily through the apple trees on to our waterproof gas-capes. I paid periodic visits to the troops, who occupied slit trenches. We were guarding our tactical headquarters which consisted of three tanks, one of which maintained a radio watch. The off-duty crews and sentries shared a barn with a pig which grunted throughout the night. Bursts of spasmodic machine-gun fire could be heard as wandering German troops fell upon our sentries but, apart from that, all was quiet until about midnight when I heard a much louder boom from the east. It was followed by a high-pitched whistle and a burst of high explosive in the next field. All sleeping troops were instantly alert and looking for better cover. The barn was relatively dry but offered no defence against shells. The tank crews climbed into their vehicles while others joined the troops manning the slit trenches.

"I crouched against the wall of the barn as the salvo came down.

Fortunately, the German gunners had the range just wrong enough to cause the shells to drop into the next field, but they must have cleared the barn roof by only a few feet. Two miles away, from a village still in the hands of the enemy, came a constant spluttering of Spandau fire. The Tank BESAs and Bren guns were easily distinguishable as they returned the fire. A FOO (forward observation officer) of the Artillery with TAC HQ now opened up his radio and was calling his batteries and giving ranges for a counter - bombardment. In two minutes shells were travelling over us in the opposite direction and I heard them fall on the village. There was a glow in the sky as a house caught fire. The enemy fire eased and finally ceased. The 'stonking' certainly woke everybody up, but after a cigarette and talk about near misses, we all settled back to rest. I continued my sentry-posting duty, aided now by a full moon. No damage had been caused, but we had been lucky."

* * * * *

*Major Creagh Gibson*, Commanding 'A' Squadron, wrote home to his father giving a clear picture of the war as it had affected us up to mid-August:

"August 14th, 1944: We came out of the line last week after some weeks of battle. I will endeavour to give you an account of our daily life but it is difficult to be descriptive because of security. I cannot say which formation we are in, although it is probably quite clear to the Boche.

"The battle divides itself into two different types; one when we are working with a similar formation to ourselves and the other when supporting infantry. Armoured battling has been on a very small scale on our sector because of the very enclosed country. There is no doubt that the Boche has made good use of the terrain. He has proven himself to be clever, subtle and crafty. A few determined men, well sited and camouflaged and manning an anti-tank gun, can give an armoured regiment a very bloody nose in a very short time. They lie up in the ditches and hedgerows and cannot be seen. The first indication of their presence is when a leading tank is knocked out. Even when this happens, you cannot tell from whence the shot came. They seem to use some smokeless powder and there is no flash. They also employ many snipers who have very accurate rifles with telescopic sights. They play havoc with the crew commanders who frequently have to have their heads out of the turret to observe. These snipers are very brave and continue shooting for a long period after the forward troops have passed. Many are caught but it is certain that some get back through our lines to fight again. The general method of advance in this sort of country is to attach a squadron of tanks to a battalion of infantry. The infantry try to ensure that there are no nasty people manning anti-tank guns or carrying 'bazookas'. The tanks deal with machine-gun posts to protect the infantry. The co-operation between the two arms is difficult but we are getting better at it.

"On a typical day we get out of our protective trenches at about 0430 hours and 'stand to' till just after first-light, which is between 0530 and 0600 hours. We are usually only a field away from the infantry who hold the line at night. As soon as it is light enough each vehicle crew cooks breakfast which may consist of anything from tinned soya sausage to tinned bacon and beans with bread or biscuits and tea. It makes a very good meal and everyone is quite ready for it. It is often the only cooked meal of the day. There may already be one or two troops of tanks in support of the infantry and these have to be relieved. The advance begins through the thick countryside until a strong point is met.

"During the past week, prisoners have been coming readily but not before they have been soundly shelled. Each pocket of resistance has to be dealt with. Artillery fire is called down and tanks deploy to get in a shot from a flank. We have excellent artillery support which can be called down on to targets only a hundred yards ahead. The enemy dig very narrow slit trenches which give them excellent protection, but their casualties are very high. They also dig in their tanks and these a devil to deal with. They can only be dealt with by an armour-piercing shot and when a tank is brought into position where it can observe, so can it be observed. Rocket-firing Typhoon aircraft are often called for to deal with them. Provided the target can be identified, they can usually destroy a tank. The aircraft comes down in a steep dive. The combined roar of the engine and the rocket has a devastating effect upon the morale of the defenders.

"I have spoken about 'being in the line'; in fact there is no line. Pockets of resistance are left behind which have to be cleared. This pushing, probing and clearing up goes on throughout the day and until dusk when we form what we call a 'loose laager', i.e. groups of tanks dotted about. Our casualities have really been very light. Those we have suffered have nearly all been caused by mines, shelling or mortar-fire. We are perfectly protected inside our vehicles but you have to get out sometimes and it is then that chaps get caught."

## An Early Breakfast

"Would you like a Mk IV for breakfast?" This was partly a question and partly a request made by a company commander of the 1/5th Queen's near Livarot. It was addressed to *Lieutenant Henry Woods,* commanding 2nd Troop, 'C' Squadron. On August 21st Lieutenant Woods was informed by radio of a contact made with German infantry and tanks. The 'Queens' were deployed astride a track running parallel to the main centre-line and on the spine of a ridge. The troop moved forward to assist. As it arrived, the company commander of the Queen's climbed on to the troop leader's tank and asked the question. Both officers dismounted and passed through a gap and into an orchard. Looking across the valley below and on to the next ridge which was about 800 yards away, a German Mk IV tank was moving cautiously eastwards and along an open field below the crest. In this fluid battle, the Germans had little idea of the whereabouts of their enemy. Henry Woods remounted his tank and moved through the orchard to find a fire position. It was difficult to find a place where both the gunner and the commander could observe together. They manoeuvred between the trees. Once into position, the gunner was given the estimated range and fired. The first round seemed to strike the Mk IV very low and without much effect. After the second round, the crew baled out. There followed a few wisps of smoke from the turret of the enemy tank before it burst into flames. The infantry moved ahead and soon rounded up 70 bewildered and tired enemy infantrymen. The troop rejoined the squadron. The problem caused by close country, thick orchards and hedgerows, and small fields, left both sides vulnerable to surprise. The attacker was more likely to be so than the defender. On this occasion, it had been the defender, but only because of the fluid nature of the battle.

## Lisieux

Just as Mont Pinçon, Quéry, Courvaudon and Hamars hold personal memories for Bob Price, Syd Swift, Derek Philo and Pat Whitmore, so I have a special memory of Lisieux, and in particular the magnificent Catholic Basilica which dominates the city from a hill above the railway station.

As we drove into Lisieux, the road was packed with infantrymen waiting to move forward. The Germans were showing that, although outmanoeuvred and short of equipment, they could still put up a fight. The 51st Highland Division was having to fight house by house and street by street and had to capture the Basilica which dominated the area. The city had suffered extensive damage during a heavy bombing raid in June, 1944. It was a very important rail junction and commanded the countryside to the east, into which we had to advance. It had been a beautiful city and an example of medieval French architecture, but its fine timber-framed houses had no resistance against high explosive bombs and soon collapsed and caught fire.

The bombing which had certainly caused some problems for the Germans, now caused the Allies much delay. The rubble concealed German infantry who had prepared good escape routes as we approached. A leading tank of the 1st Royal Tank Regiment had become an early casualty and was blocking one of the main approach roads. As we approached the forward position, the constant stream of stretcher-bearing Jeeps with badly injured troops from both sides was indication of the resistance being encountered. As our troop of three vehicles came up to the leading infantrymen of the Queen's Regiment, the young officer commanding the platoon indicated the enemy positions. There is a sort of mutual respect between infantrymen and tank crews, neither liking each other's job. The tankmen see the PBI as having to depend upon rations brought forward for them, usually getting very wet, sleeping with one blanket, and having a thankless task. The infantrymen sees a tank as a fire trap, noisy and attracting fire, sometimes on themselves. They do not enjoy working closely with them. The platoon was in a single file and keeping close against a wall. I cannot remember ever feeling more pity for them than I did on that occasion. As the Bren crew went forward they became instant casualties. The Piat crew took up the leading position and joined the Bren crew. The platoon was soon either dead or wounded. Before we could assist with our machine guns, we had first to get across the road and then up towards the Basilica. Fortunately for us, this move coincided with the enemy's withdrawal to the area of the Basilica. We followed up with our vehicles. The side of the road leading up the slope was potted with bomb and shell craters and in one of them I noticed a corporal of the Queen's who had been shot through the head. His steel helmet had not moved an inch. Some days earlier my own Sten gun had been run over by a vehicle and the butt was badly bent. This was the chance to replace it, I thought. I jumped into the crater and carefully rolled the corporal over. His Sten, immediately below him, had dug into the soil as he fell. As I eased it out of his hands it fired a burst which narrowly missed my head. It could so easily have prevented this account from being written!

As we arrived at the base of the Basilica, we quickly realised what a wonderful point of domination and observation it offered. From our position to the north-east of the building, however, we could only see back over the countryside which we had just passed through. Shells were passing over us and landing on the rail centre below, where our 'B' Squadron was trying to find a new route up to our position. Lieutenant Jack Bissill reported over the radio that we were in the grounds of the Basilica and described the view. Whether he was instructed to find out whether the dome (which resembled that of St Paul's) was being used by the enemy, or decided to do so on his own account, I never knew. Sergeant Eric Roodhouse arrived and organised the troop into an assault force to search the grounds. Jack Bissill told me to get a Bren gun and some magazines and try to find a way up to the dome. As I looked up at it with admiration, a Frenchman appeared from the vaults and told us that there were some 2,000 civilians taking shelter there. He also directed us to the base of a circular stone staircase which would lead up to the dome.

I set off in a perpetual upward and circular climb in a clockwise direction. Being right handed, I carried the Bren under my left arm to get a better arc of fire round the corner should we encounter opposition. Jack supported me from behind. The climb seemed endless, and I have never tackled a circular stairway since then without being instantly reminded of that ascent. For some inexplicable reason, I counted the steps. I thought it was 262 but, forty years later when I climbed them with my son, David, we counted 268. Considering the stressful situation, I was not far out! Below, all hell was breaking out. We could hear Eric Roodhouse and Chick Strickland shouting instructions. There were calls of 'Kamarade' and other unprintable advice. I saw a party of Germans run almost beneath my position and fired after them. There was even more shouting from below, and I remember that Jack was telling me to give him the gun. I was unlikely ever to enjoy such a dominating fire position and I was not going to give up such an opportunity. I fired magazine after magazine. All the built-up stress I had felt during the past weeks, and particularly the climb to the dome, was being released in those long bursts of fire. They only stopped when all my ammunition was exhausted. An agitated Frenchman came up and begged us to cease for fear of attracting counter fire. There were sick children and adults in the vaults who had been there for three days, he informed us. We made our way down. A party of Germans had been rounded up and were being searched. The position was quickly consolidated and an OP officer arrived. We pointed him towards the stairs and off he set with a short-range radio.

Beyond the Basilica, the rearguard action was still being fought out; stretcher cases were still coming down the steep slope to the east of the Basilica. It started to rain and we were wet. After handing over as many spare rations as we could to the French civilians we harboured in an orchard for the night. It was too wet to dig, so we made do with what sleep we could manage in a sitting position in our vehicles.

# The Break-Out

We hoped that the dogged defence shown by the Germans was a final show of defiance and that, having gained the high ground to the east and above Lisieux, we would have a fast run to the east. It was comparatively easy going but caution was still called for.

Captain Robert Crockett, Recce Squadron leader, decided to deploy two troops to the left and right of the centre-line and to lead the Regiment on the main route. The advance was down the N13 and towards St-Georges-du-Vièvre, via Thiberville. Robert had become well known for understatement and treating major issues lightly. "The Lord has been on the other bugger's side today" was a greeting which would open an "Order Group" gathering in the evening.

On this occasion, the Lord was quite definitely on Robert's side! Sergeant Reg Worman, his driver and operator who kept control of the outlying troops, was sitting low in the Ferret scout car, and Robert was perched on the turret lid, as they made a steady 10 mph down the road. Reg noticed a column of vehicles approaching but thought little of it because some Canadians had crossed our front earlier. Nobody was quite certain of other troop positions. The leading vehicle passed and the officer, who was obviously a German, gave Robert a wave as he passed. Robert replied by saluting. Reg noticed that there was no escort with the convoy and yelled to Robert over the intercom: "They are bloody Germans, Sir." "What did you say, Worman?" asked Robert, as the second vehicle passed. "They are bloody Germans" repeated Reg. Robert reached inside the turret for a hand grenade, pulled out the pin and tossed it at the third vehicle in the convoy. Reg stopped and the grenade almost fell on to the back of the scout car. He relayed a message. "Enemy column has just passed me and is heading down the road towards you."

Sergeant Ginty Gilliland, who was commanding the vehicle behind, also stopped and his driver, Busty Woolley, fired his Bren gun. The Germans left the road and headed into a wood followed by Sergeant Eric Roodhouse, who disconnected his Browning from its mounting and gave chase across country. Eight enemy, two motor-cycle combinations, and a Volkswagen car, were in the bag. My troop, out on the left flank, listened to this engagement with much interest and some amusement. Now that our leader had encountered the enemy personally, perhaps he would be less critical of us. We knew he was suspicious every time we reported an enemy position, thinking we were just playing for time to make a brew. His standard reply to one of our reports was "Just push on and don't bugger about." And it can be admitted now that he was, as usual, absolutely correct!

We were now advancing along a very narrow road, flanked by thick woodland: beautiful countryside for an afternoon drive. I was despatched down a side road to check a small bridge over a stream. Still having no radio and unable to go very far from the troop, I observed the bridge through my binoculars and thought it looked secure and untouched. We drove towards it and Denis Grieves halted about 50 yards short and covered me as I walked down the road towards the bridge and a dense bank of wood which lay beyond. I was aware that such a wood could conceal an army, but a chance had to be taken. I looked under the bridge, found no wires or signs of explosive, and was about to retire to the scout car when there was a mad stampede from the woods.

It was too far to run back, so I jumped into a ditch. From the woods came, first, a Frenchman, then another, then followed by what might be termed 'a crowd' of them', women, babies and children running towards me with their hands out and shouting "Tommy, Tommy"; "Les Anglais". The first man almost threw himself upon me. I was hugged and kissed—by men and women—and shook everybody's hand several times. I asked Denis, who now joined the party, to use his French to find out when the Germans had left. "Les Allemands sont partis" they repeated several times. "What's that?" I asked. "The Germans have gone," he replied. They had it seemed, withdrawn up the hill some hours before. The war was definitely becoming more interesting.

As we approached St-Georges-du-Vièvre, two troops united under the leadership of Eric Roodhouse. We had not all joined together like this since the beginning of the advance in Normandy, and Sergeants Eric Roodhouse, Tom Broad and 'Ginty' made a strong trio of leaders. We halted some half a mile short of the village. One of the Bren carriers had a petrol blockage, so we decided to leave the vehicles with the drivers to clear the blockage while we went on foot to investigate woodland which lay between us and the village. It was getting dark and, to add to our concern, an American Thunderbolt fighter was circling our position. We watched anxiously, not wanting to give away our position and were ready to throw out tins of yellow recognition smoke if need be. The plane made about three circuits and then flew off.

About a dozen of us set off in single file, Eric leading, some watching the woods to the left while others covered the right of the road. As the track began to climb up towards the village, Eric signalled us to stop while he and Ginty crept forward. They returned after about five minutes saying there was a German vehicle in an orchard. Since it was too dark to see, we thought it better to leave well alone, especially as we were some way from our own vehicle, and one of which was a doubtful starter. So we rejoined our drivers and, since we had not eaten since early morning, settled down to prepare a meal, using the cookers under tarpaulins so as not to show a light. Then we went off to rest—all except poor Sergeant Tom Broad, who had to take a party of infantrymen back up the track to observe the German vehicle we had located.

* * * * *

*Corporal Ken Wheeldon and Trooper Spink* were members of Lieutenant Henry Wood's troop who ate Mk IVs for breakfast. Ken tells a nice little story of one of their guard stints which emphasises the chaos in the forward areas:

" 'D'ye mind if I get my head down, Ken?' 'I suppose you can,' I replied, not relishing the thought of spending the next two hours alone. 'Spinky' was like that—a bit of an ostrich. He reckoned that if he had his head down he wouldn't know about the one with his number on it until it was too late! He lay down under the hedgerow, rested his head in his steel helmet and was asleep.

"I walked quietly up and down the lane where we were supposedly 'on guard'. We'd drawn the midnight till 2 a.m. turn and I felt like joining my slumbering friend. I slung my Sten over my shoulder and, to help while away the hours, I re-bandaged my right hand which I had injured the previous day, when I scuttled into my tank during a sudden mortar attack. This reminded me that I still had to face a charge for disobeying my troop leader's order to go to the medical orderly to have a proper dressing put on it. But there had still been a mortar or two falling, so I had chosen to treat myself rather than be caught in another attack.

"My mind wandered to other things. I could even imagine this lovely countryside under peacetime conditions. The weather was warm and there was no moon, but plenty of stars. The silhouettes of the tanks, which I could just make out beyond the hedgerow, did not fit in with my peaceful thoughts. When our two-hour stint was up I roused Spinky and told him to go and wake up the two who were to relieve us. We walked together to the gap in the hedge which was nearest our tank. 'Tell them not to bother looking for their Stens. They can use ours' I said, hoping to speed up the handover. Tired men sometimes took ages to gather their wits and even had to have a smoke before their brains would function. He reported back, confirming that he had given them a good shaking, and after about five minutes I saw a figure moving away from the tanks and towards the gap. I unslung my Sten and stepped forward into the field.

"I must have moved very quietly because the leading figure stepped on my foot, then stopped instantly. I was about to swear when he turned his head sideways and I noticed that he was wearing one of those helmets which dipped very low at the back of the neck. 'It's a bloody German,' I thought, jumping backwards, I collided with Spinky who was sleepily about to hand over his gun. I noticed that there were at least four more figures behind the one who had stepped on my foot. The leader didn't move, so I said the first thing that came into my head: 'Hands up'. A split second passed before a little Jerry at the rear of the party raised his hands. To convince me of his friendship, he repeated my words in his best English. Spinky, still not quite with us, dropped his gun and started to raise his hands. 'Not you, you silly b . . . . .' I yelled. I stuck the muzzle of my gun into the toe-treader's ribs and repeated my warning. This time he raised his hands, as a well-disciplined German should. I took the revolver from his right hand, and the others were disarmed. Lieutenant Woods and Sergeant 'Shorty' Irons then appeared with a torch and we noted that the prisoners were an officer and four senior non-commissioned officers. I didn't expect a VC but I thought it might stand me in good stead as far as the threatened charge was concerned. I was told to take them to Squadron Headquarters.

"They were marched across the field to where I knew SHQ to be and roused the first person I found, who turned out to be the Squadron Leader, Major John Ward-Harrison. 'It's Wheeldon sir, I've got five prisoners,' I said, beaming in the gloom. My dreams of mitigation were shattered. 'What the hell do you expect me to do with them? Take them up to RHQ and hand them over to the RSM—and close the flaps as you go out!' I consulted with Spinky who informed me that RHQ was at least three miles up the road. When we eventually found the RSM he was as displeased with our capture as was my Squadron Leader. We were told to guard them for the rest of the night. When I rebelled and told the RSM that I would shoot them first, he relented and woke someone else up. We managed to get our heads down at about half five, an hour before 'Stand to'."

* * * * *

Before daybreak on August 25th both Recce troops were out on patrol. The First Troop, led by Eric Roodhouse, followed the same route as the previous night and soon reached the infantry at the far end of the woods. Dawn was breaking and a better view of the enemy would soon be possible. Following the infantry's confirmation that there was definitely something in front of the position. Eric decided on a direct approach and set off down the road. A troop of 'A' Squadron tanks, which had moved up noisily, were just out of sight as Eric rounded the bend just short of the village. He was greeted by a burst of Spandau and dived into a ditch, expecting the tanks to come forward and deal with the attacker. It was the vehicle he had observed the previous evening and which he now identified as a camouflaged Mk IV. He waited a few minutes before beginning to crawl back but Corporal Strickland's tank, leading the remainder of the troop drew fire from the Mk IV's 75mm gun. It fell very short, but shrapnel from the shot wounded Eric deeply in the hand as he made a dash for it. He was furious to be put out of action in this way and particularly berated the tank crews of 'A' Squadron troop for not coming forward. Sadly, the wound was to keep him out of action for some months. When he did recover, he was posted to Italy and did not rejoin the Regiment until after the war. The German tank crew must have been a pretty poor lot: they had fired at almost point-blank range and caused little damage. The tank was knocked out and the position consolidated.

On that morning, while Eric led his party toward St-Georges, I again joined a troop, now called 2nd Troop under command of Jack Bissill. We frequently changed troop to replace casualties. With me leading the way in the scout car, we were to recce a route to the south of St-Georges and try to join the main centre-line some two miles east at a place called St-Grégoire-du-Vièvre. After only a mile we found the road blocked by a felled tree, through the branches of which I could see the reflectors of an upturned trailer. The only way around this suspect object was a track which led into a wood and which could be easily mined. Approaching cautiously for a closer look, we found a drain running under the road and below the fallen tree. We were about to examine this more closely when a Frenchman appeared from a cottage nearby and warned us that there were demolition charges both up the drain and in the trailer.

Our troop leader reported the situation over the radio and requested 'Holdfast' (code name for the Engineers) to come forward and deal with it. Jack, who spoke good French, asked the Frenchman about the track through the woods which led to St. Grégoire. He thought it would be all right but seemed less than certain. The CO told Jack to check the route on foot and I was ordered to accompany him. We set off for what promised to be a very long walk through the woods, taking with us the Frenchman who told us he was a member of the Resistance movement, the Maquis, and knew the countryside well. We had not travelled very far before Jack had misgivings and decided to return for a vehicle to serve as a back-up and to speed our return. That left me and our Maquis friend who, after trying unsuccessfully to converse, now had to content ourselves with smiles and shrugs of shoulders. Even if my companion grasped what I wanted to say, I could not understand his answer.

The track, leading down a slope towards a stream, brought us to a single-track railway line which came out of the wood on my right and continued at an angle to my left. The track, which was not particularly level, was probably used to convey cider apples or logs, I thought: I had seen similar tracks used in East Anglia for sugar beet. After crossing the stream and a dry ditch, the track, bounded by a few houses back in the fields, climbed away towards the village. There was no sign of life and I felt decidedly uncomfortable.

Nobody appeared as we approached Saint-Grégoire-du-Vièvre, a small village consisting of perhaps ten houses round an open space beside a church. But, when my friend shouted, a wooden shutter in an upstairs window was thrown open and, soon, everybody came out. It was still only about 0730 hours, and they were unprepared for liberation, but we were persuaded to go into the schoolroom where clean white table-cloths and glasses soon appeared for a toast. The dreaded calvados came out and I had to show willing and managed about three toasts which included 'Vive la France' and 'Vive L'Angleterre'.

I learned from a local who spoke very good English that the enemy had pulled out during the night and had never in any case, been in any great strength here. This was a relief and explained why my French friend had been so relaxed during our approach. I explained that I had to leave. "Where are your friends?" I was asked. Wondering about the answer and whether my troop leader was going to arrive and find me paralytic, I could only reply that "They are just down the road".

Such power! The whole British Army was waiting for me to tell them that they, too, could come and enjoy the fruits of liberation.

Taking a short-cut across the fields, we returned to our original position. I was in high spirits and I remember Jack Bissill saying: "I didn't think you would ever come back."

I was now feeling very important and more than willing to lead the troop and regimental headquarters to the village. The track was very narrow in places and I just hoped that one of the vehicles would not break down. On returning to the village, where the other members of the troop had taken advantage of my absence to have breakfast, we now got our cooker going and brought out some food. The sight of white bread, which they had not seen since before the war, produced a greater effect on the admiring French civilians than had my earlier arrival. Sharing it was like trying to feed the five thousand. My moment of glory was soon over and I was ordered to report on the state of the road to St-Georges-du-Vièvre. It was clear, and I arrived in St-Georges just as our tanks were emerging.

When we returned to this place almost 40 years later, Pat Whitmore, Max Cooke, Bob Sawtell and I measured the track, which now has a tarred surface, and found it to be a mile and one tenth in length. Assuming I had walked at four miles an hour, I must have been away from the troop for at least 40 minutes. The stump of the tree which had been blown was still to be found, though very rotten. The cottage from which my French friend had emerged was no more but there was another further back in an orchard, where a woman was picking apples.

Pat told her the story. Though she had been born in 1951 she knew of the incident and was able to tell us that the Frenchman, whose name was Robert Stourdon, had died some three years earlier, though his mother was still alive. We also learned that St-Georges had been the centre of the Resistance in that area, who owed much of their success to a telephone communication line which ran under the centre of the railway track, where the Germans had never thought of looking. In June, 1944, the Maquis, led by a lady doctor, had thought they were strong enough to liberate the village themselves and hold it until the arrival of the Allies. Sadly, they had to wait a further ten weeks, during which time they were overpowered and shot. The doctor, chief of police and head of the fire brigade were among those who died.

There was a reception and ceremony at the village cenotaph when a party of old comrades, together with serving members of the Regiment, re-visited St-Georges in 1984. The head of the Maquis, leading his old comrades, told me of a meeting near Lisieux between a member of the Resistance and our CO, Colonel 'Teddy' Swetenham. The Resistance, still smarting from the atrocities, asked our CO not to attack St-Georges, saying they preferred to liberate it themselves. We had not been aware of this request but it may account for the 'softly, softly' approach made on the morning of August 25th. We will never know whether the French were also unaware of our presence in the woods to the west of the village, but an attack upon the Mk IV would certainly have saved Eric Roodhouse from being wounded. No shots were fired into the village, which has retained its rural look to this day. I have now returned to the area on three occasions, the last in April, 1987, with my wife Joan, and Pat Whitmore. We retraced the route of 1944, feeling once again the sense of insecurity and fear that every bush might conceal an enemy, even though the scene was now of spring wild flowers in bloom. That track will ever remain my personal 'Track in Europe'.

Corporal Ginger Proudlove was leading his troop, which included a Bren carrier down towards the crossings over the Risle at Pont - Authou. The river was divided into parallel courses in the village, each about 20 feet wide. As the troop arrived surreptitiously on the western bank they found the nearest bridge already destroyed and a party of Germans preparing to demolish the second bridge. This seemed a splendid opportunity to turn the carrier's four-inch mortar on the enemy and so save the bridge. An HE mortar-bomb was duly loaded but unfortunately, both the bomb and the barrel had been subjected to much rain and there was still water in the barrel as it was fired. The bomb fell only a few feet in front of the carrier. A second bomb did better and flew over the heads of the Germans. But this only served to alert them and they returned a much more professional mortar attack which compelled the troop to withdraw. Soon after this, and before any heavier assistance could arrive, the second bridge was destroyed.

A troop of 'A' Squadron tanks, commanded by Sergeant Archie Carr, moved along the western bank of the Risle to seek a crossing point and, some half a mile upstream, came to a Mill with a wooden bridge. It spanned the river over a width of some 20 yards and, though supported in the centre by wooden pillars was clearly not intended for anything heavier than a horse and cart. A Frenchman came out of the Mill waving a Swastika flag. Fortunately for him, he realised his moment of liberation had arrived and ran back inside the Mill re-emerging with the French Tricolour. Realising that he would never know the strength of the bridge unless he tried it, Archie cautiously edged his tank forward to the centre and over to the other bank. It had not budged an inch. The remainder of the troop moved over and headed quickly down the parallel road towards Pont-Authou. That bridge was to carry all the tanks and echelon of the Regiment and the whole of the 7th Armoured Division.

The Germans withdrew from the village leaving the way clear up through woodlands and on to the flat ridge to the east. It was getting dusk now, and a halt was called to consolidate. A lot of ground had been covered and most vehicles were running low on fuel. The whole Regiment moved into an open field and prepared a much-needed meal. Some of the wheeled vehicles had difficulty in entering the field because of a nasty ditch beside the road. Ronny Ash and Ginger Marley, the crew of a scout car, collided with a Cromwell and were injured A haystack on the edge of the field caught fire and lit the field up. A German aircraft came over but failed to take advantage of the situation, the pilot probably being uncertain of the forward position of his own troops. The usual ritual of guard duty was divided between the troops and we all settled down just as the echelon arrived. There was more work, refuelling, drawing rations and distributing mail. Everything except my sorely-needed radio without which I felt very out of touch and limited in performance by the inability to report. The Squadron Leader expressed his displeasure to the echelon commander, who promised to bring one the following day.

We slept soundly—too soundly. Whoever was meant to be keeping watch had himself fallen asleep, and so committing the unforgivable sin which usually earned the poor victim a six-month jail sentence by court martial. There was no time to establish who the culprit was: we had to get out of the field and under cover in an orchard. Radios were opened up and the squadrons already moving out. Water was almost boiling on stoves when my troop was ordered to search a farm on the main road between Rouen and Brionne and a mile to the north of Boissey-le-Châtel where 'A' Squadron was already in action. Jack Bissill led in his Stuart—one of the few still with its turret and carrying a 37mm—and we found the farm and halted some 100 yards short of it. Seeing what looked suspiciously like a German staff car silouetted through a hedge to the left of the farm and having no radio to report it, I drove over to Jack's tank just as he traversed his gun on to the position. Leaning over the side of his turret he shouted to me to go up the road to the right and find out what was going on in Boissey-le-Châtel, where there was already a lot of firing. I was quite delighted: I loathed searching buildings.

We had made a bad start to the day. The sleeping guard had let us down badly. We had missed the morning brew and now felt uncertainty because we had had too little time to discuss a proper plan for this move. I was delighted to go off and do my own thing. We headed south at about 50 mph along a road which, though it was straight and hedgeless, was bounded by a low bank. 'A' Squadron was approaching from my right and the crew commander of one tank, which had halted about 100 yards away in the field was waving frantically and indicating that I should go over to his position. I did not much fancy crossing road verges which were frequently mined, but his signals were urgent. We took a chance and I pulled in behind Corporal Bill Peat's tank. He shouted to me from the turret that I had just passed an 88mm gun on the left of the road as I had approached. The gun which could only just be seen from my comparatively low position, was dug in behind the low bank and its long barrel protruding through the mound of earth beside the road, was pointing in the opposite direction to my approach. I told Bill Peat that I would have to return that way so he agreed to give the gun a burst, even though it seemed to be unmanned.

Back on the road again, we sped past the gun position and on towards the farm from where a black column of smoke was rising. I thought of the suspicious object I thought I had seen before I left. As we got close, I could see that the smoke was coming from the Bren Carrier commanded by Ginger Proudlove, which now lay on its side in the road. Its ammunition was exploding as it burned and there seemed to be a body lying in the road. I told Dennis to keep as close to it as he could, reasoning that if they had been mined, any other mines would have been detonated. "Keep your head down" I shouted as I lined the Bren up on the way ahead.

As we drew level with the burning vehicle we were enveloped in an enormous explosion. Being in the centre of an explosion is a difficult thing to describe. There is blackness, dirt and the noise. I remember thinking that we had struck another mine. Recovering from the shock I remember shouting to Dennis that we would have to get out—a task rendered easier by the fact that the front wheels of the scout car had been blown off. But Dennis, deathly white and slumped in his seat, only fell towards me as I shook him. As more ammunition exploded around us I tried to lift Dennis from the burning vehicle but his feet were trapped under the accelerator and brake pedals. The seam of his trousers was split from top to bottom and blood was pouring down the front of my tunic, though I was not conscious of any pain. I stood up, pulled Dennis on to my seat, grabbed my Sten gun from behind me, and stepped out on to the road. My boot fell off. All the stitches had burst in the impact and my foot would not take any weight. I hopped towards the farm buildings, into the short driveway to find myself confronted by a party of five or six Germans. I pointed my Sten and pulled the trigger, but there was no magazine on it. It must have become detached in the explosion. My initial experience was a feeling of hopelessness—I could not run and there was nowhere to run to—this gave way to a sense of relaxation, possibly acceptance of the fact that the end had come. I was not the least bit frightened. In a way, it was a relief to know what my end would be. I had thought about it many times and had accepted that, by the law of averages, the end would come as surely as it had for many friends already. It was probably the same acceptance that we see in those suffering a terminal illness.

Throwing my Sten into the hedge in disgust, I could think of no plan other than to turn my back on the enemy and hop away to the centre of the road. I must have been almost at the end of the driveway before it occurred to me that I had a chance. There had been no shots, nothing. I did not dare look back, but saw a ditch at the end of the drive, made for it and dived in. Peering out from my place of safety, I could see no Germans. I have thought about it since and believe that they were probably trying to give themselves up. It was fortunate for them that I had no magazine on my Sten. Realising that I had to get myself away from the knocked out vehicles, I did a check on myself. I found that my teeth had cut the inside of my mouth, my nose was very sore and at an angle, and I had cuts about the face—all probably caused by the butt of the Bren gun which I had been clutching. My foot had swollen to an enormous size and was also a bit out of shape. To my relief I first heard and then saw Jack Bissill's tank approaching. Pedro Sharpe, our Argentinian friend who acted as his operator, ran towards me with a first-aid box. I told them that Dennis was still in the scout car, but they found he was dead and would have to be cut out. Len Elson, the operator was also lying dead, though I had not seen him. What I had thought to be a body as we approached was a tarpaulin. The tank had returned with Ginger Proudlove, and Frank Hume, who had been badly burned. This was a sad start to a day and elaborates on the comments in the War Diary and in my 'Introduction' which record the event as follows:

> *"During the day the Regiment suffered some casualties, particularly in the Reconnaissance Squadron, in getting forward towards Bourneville and Montfort."*

There was no sign of any Germans at the farm and nobody was very keen to find any at that time. I travelled back on the deck of the Stuart. Pedro was itching to inject me with a shot of morphine but I was in no great pain. At Tac HQ, Robert Crockett came across to the half-tracked ambulance and asked what had happened. I thought I might qualify for some sympathy, but his conclusion was: "You'll have to look where you're going in future. It looks as though you've sprained your ankle and you'll need a few days rest."

The ambulance rattled back over 'Archie's Bridge' to a forward clearing station where I was given an anti-tetanus shot, labelled, and reloaded into a better ambulance along with a German soldier who was in terrible pain. The orderly thought he had appendicitis. I felt sorry for him. What a time to have appendicitis, I thought. The orderly checked that I still had my pistol and told me to keep an eye on him. We moved off and I offered him a cigarette, which he accepted gratefully. I felt no hatred for this representative of the enemy. We were very much in the same boat and I felt that his situation was worse than mine. Yet an hour earlier we had been trying to kill each other.

Corporal Bill Peat, to whom I had spoken on the outskirts of Boissey-le-Châtel, was also to have an eventful day. His troop, led by Lieutenant Gillett and Sergeant Bill Daglish, had moved forward from the field where I had met them. A report later submitted by OC 'A' Squadron reads as follows:

"It was thought that Boissey-le-Châtel was clear of the enemy. On reaching the outskirts of the village, the troop leader dismounted and made a personal reconnaissance. Approaching from a side road, his attention was attracted by a woman waving from a window. From her signals, he understood that some enemy positions were just around the corner. His move must have been watched by the enemy, who withheld their fire for fear of drawing the attention of the tanks. In order to determine the strength of the enemy, Sergeant Daglish was covered by the Troop Leader's tank as he edged forward. He was able to destroy two machine-gun positions near the main crossroads. He continued his advance towards the church but was struck by an armour-piercing round which jammed the turret traversing gear. Lieutenant Gillett ordered him to withdraw and, at the same time, put down smoke to cover him. Bill Daglish managed to reverse almost 100 yards to a position nearly level with the troop leader's tank when a second missile struck his tank. It was probably a bazooka. The petrol tank exploded and enveloped the tank in flames. Bill Daglish managed to scramble out, but his hands were very badly burned and he was unable to assist the other members of his crew. Bill Peat, in the tank behind, dismounted and, assisted by Lieutenant Gillett, tried to release Trooper Wheeler, the driver, whose hatch was jammed. He shouted to Wheeler to cross to the other side and try the co-driver's hatch. In this way he was brought out.

"The whole troop now came under attack from a party of Germans who had moved closer to them. Corporal Peat remained very calm during this attack and continued to assist Trooper Wheeler. Trooper Wright, the driver of Peat's tank, saw the situation and ordered his co-driver to take over. He dismounted and ran to the side of the road where he was able to engage the enemy who had taken cover in the thick hedges. He most successfully wiped out a small party who were trying to reach the burning tank. After the withdrawal, the troop manoeuvred on to open ground and brought fire to bear upon the remaining enemy. Sergeant Daglish and Trooper Wheeler were the only survivors of the five-man crew.

Troopers Makepiece, Huntington and Paige died in the impact of the missile attack and subsequent fire."

It was this early-morning action which partly motivated me to write this personal account. The 'A' Squadron action was very fully reported because an officer survived to give his account. Corporal Peat and Trooper Wright were each later awarded a well-deserved MM.

With every casualty, there had to be the official signal despatched to inform the relatives. The personal call of the postman, vicar or policeman was dreaded by every family. (In the case of my wife's brother, killed during the raid south of Caen, the police sergeant knew her family well and withheld the information until the morning. The original signal read, 'Missing, believed killed.' Later one member of the crew was found in the sea and it was presumed that the whole crew had perished in that way.) In the Regiment, friends searched personal belongings for letters and themselves wrote to girl-friends and other friends who might not be known to the parents and would not otherwise be informed. The squadron leaders had to find time to write though they had plenty to occupy their time. Major Creagh Gibson retained copies of all the letters he wrote to the next-of-kin, both of the killed and injured. In many cases there had to be follow-up letters to parents who wanted fuller details of their sons' deaths. The sad case of Trooper Makepiece and his mother's anguish indicate the difficult and sad decisions which had to be made. Creagh Gibson's first letter, written three days after the trooper's death, tried to conceal the fact that he had died from the result of the fire. Indeed, nobody knew whether or not he had been killed instantly, but he had been seen to be half out of the turret before being enveloped in flame. Major Gibson informed the parents that he had been killed when the missile struck the tank.

Trooper Makepiece's mother replied: "The recent tragic death of my boy has left a heart wound which will probably never heal, but your letter has consoled me and I feel comforted. You tell me that my son died bravely when in direct contact with the enemy, and I am sure he would not have wished it to have been in any other way. Naturally I have thought long and often since the sad news was broken to me. I feel that I am reliving his last moments. To you, Sir, and all under your command, I return my grateful thanks for such a sweet letter. I ask you in my son's name to carry on as bravely as hitherto. God bless and you and my son's comrades and may you all return safely. My son would have wished this as I do."

There followed a second letter from the parents after they had received the War Office notification. This read:

"Once again I am writing to you about my son, Trooper Makepiece. I received a letter from the War Office telling me that my son lost his life when his tank was set on fire and it stated that his body was never found. You gave me the impression that my son was killed instantly and did not suffer. I assumed that my son was killed instantly. At the same time I could not help having doubts and have made continuous enquiries until information has reached me that my son was seen half hanging out of the tank but could not be saved owing to the enemy attacking from that side of the tank.

"Surely, Sir, as my son was only half in the tank, there must have been some remains and at least an identity disc to identify him. Is it possible that he is still living somewhere? Perhaps after you moved, the enemy got him. I know I have no idea what it was like there but there must have been confusion. I cannot convince myself that nothing remains of him. This is causing me great anxiety and until I receive definite proof, I will have no peace of mind. Will you please write and tell me the full facts, no matter how painful they may seem."

The Regimental Association took up the case and tried to pacify the mother. Creagh Gibson also wrote and explained that a tank loaded with 200 gallons of petrol and carrying over 50 rounds of ammunition which exploded, leaves absolutely nothing to identify. When it was possible for the fitters to approach the tank after it had cooled down, they had carried out a thorough search.

The mother attended séances and was told that her son had not arrived on the other side. She wrote again and asked for a full search to be made of the hospitals. The medium had informed her that her son was heavily bandaged and burned down his left side and could not talk. These distressing letters and their equally difficult replies added to the anguish suffered by both the parents and the officers who had to deal with them.

Notification of a wounding was just as distressing as that of death, since the message simply said: "We regret to inform you that- . . . serving in the 5th Royal Inniskilling Dragoon Guards has been been wounded and is being returned to base." Being wounded could mean the loss of limbs, sight, or some other terrible injury from which a man might never recover, and parents naturally tended to fear the worst. Anyone who was taken from the line as a casualty, even for only a minor injury, was reported on in this way. So for the next of kin, there was a long wait until contact could be made with the injured person. Understandably, the War Office sent out thousands of such messages each day and were themselves unaware of the details.

The Regiment now moved north-west, away from this heavily mined area and towards Bourneville. The heavily wooded country-side was not good for tanks and the Germans, although in full retreat, still put up a fight. Each time we overran their defences, they gave an excellent account of themselves.

The Recce Squadron re-formed yet again and put two troops forward. On the outskirts of Bourneville, they met a patrol of the 11th Hussars who informed them that there was an anti-tank gun a little way ahead—news which drew an enigmatic response from Robert Crockett to "Push on". Fortunately, the Germans withdrew.

Both troops fanned out into very wooded countryside which runs north and parallel with the river Risle. Reading a map was difficult because of the many tracks available. During one of these moves, a wrong route brought the troop to a village where they were accorded a riotous welcome. They were given eggs and milk, and the inevitable bottles came out. Amid cries of "Vive les Anglais", there were kisses for even the dirtiest and most bearded soldiers. Robert Crockett, quickly realising that his men were not where they ought to have been, recalled them to the centre-line.

It was getting dark when, as they moved through the woods, they saw figures among the trees and opened fire. It was soon discovered that the troops were part of 'C' Squadron who, equally unaware of their attackers identity, returned the fire. Then the two factions recognised the type of fire and broke off the "engagement". A lone Frenchman crawling up a ditch in a grey suit was the only casualty. Robert Crockett delivered one of his most disapproving addresses to the troop and went off yet again to apologise to another squadron, whose leader referred to the troop as a "load of bandits".

The troop was despatched once more, now keeping to the right track, and arrived at their objective which they searched by torch-light. The area seemed to be deserted until a Frenchman, whose curiosity overcame his fear, eventually emerged to inform them that the enemy had left the village an hour earlier, taking a gun with them. The other troop had a similar experience. Reports from villages indicated that the Germans were avoiding main roads and using the woods to get to the Seine crossings. There was yet another sleepless night. Prisoners had to be escorted back to collecting points and others had to remain on watch all night. Early the following morning, 1st Troop set off in the same direction as they had the previous night. This time the French were ready for them in a big way and had arranged a party—cognac, cider and, of course, calvados. The troop, feeling that they were still under the shadow of the previous night's fiasco, proferred their apologies and moved on. Sergeant Tom Broad, in the leading Stuart, came upon some sleeping Germans and gave them a rude awakening. Troopers Paddy Boyle and Paddy Byrne, two Irish step-brothers, were in separate vehicles. They tried their French: "Avez-vous vu les Boches?" "Pas vu", replied the Frenchman, but even as he spoke the leading tank was fired on by a machine gun. The track was too narrow to turn in, so they raced forward into the village. A bazooka flew past the front of the carrier. Paddy Boyle stopped his scout car and shot the man who had fired it. A German armed with a Spandau leaned over the bank and sprayed the carrier at point-blank range, adding a burst of fire into Paddy Boyle's bedding roll for good measure.

The troop had now manoeuvred behind the enemy, whose turn it was to make a run for it. Chick Strickland saw two of them racing across a field and gave chase, firing while being thrown about in the carrier. The two made it to the side of a wood, from where they returned the fire. The troop gathered on the other side of the field to decide a course of action and sensibly decided to call for some heavier tanks, then checked the damage to their own vehicles. Tom Broad's water cans had been punctured: the scout car had gathered some lengths of wire which had to be cut off, but the carrier's external bins had been riddled, and its aerial shot off, and all the Thermos flasks broken. Chick Strickland's pistol, which hung at his side, now had no trigger guard, while John Pilborough had a furrow across his back where a bullet had grazed it.

It was still only midday but they had seen plenty of action. The other troop discovered eight sleeping Germans in a barn. There was the customary problem: what to do with them? They moved back to the main centre-line and found SQMS "Nipper" Daley there with his 15cwt truck. He took the Germans over with reluctance, and spent an uncomfortable two hours guarding them with an empty pistol and no ammunition.

'A' Squadron put a few well-placed rounds of HE into the woods and were rewarded when a further 150 Germans gave themselves up, smiling as though it were the end of a game. Many were Poles and Czechs who had been given a choice of fighting for the Germans or a worse fate in a POW camp. There were also four very unhappy Russians, who had towed a 75mm Howitzer all the way from the Eastern front. They claimed they had only fired four shots with it!

The squadrons were heavily involved in these mopping-up operations. 'A' Squadron were having a difficult time in the woods. 'B' and 'C' were operating together. 'B' managed to pass through 'C' and on through the town of Bourneville, then struck out north and north-westerly. The leading tank soon met resistance. The ground fell gradually away towards the Seine, which was not yet in sight, and the leader of Lieutenant Bill Bradfield's troop came under fire from an 88mm as he led the way out of the village and crossed over the crest of a hill. The troop deployed for a defensive position near a farm. 1st Troop, 'C' Squadron, was ordered forward to assist but there was a communication problem. All three Sabre Squadrons were operating on different frequencies and were therefore not in communication with each other. As 'C' Squadron drove through, they were unaware of the situation and deployed astride the road. The two leading tanks passed over the ridge and were fired upon. The two following tanks immediately took a hull-down position with an excellent view of the farms and woodlands 1,000 yards ahead.

The leading tank, now over the ridge, was fired upon and its turret jammed. The other tank in the lead, realising it was vulnerable and no match for an 88mm, headed back towards the ridge. The second tank was also hit and, when it caught fire, the crew baled out and took shelter beside a wayside crucifix.

That well-placed 88mm had bought just a little more time for the Germans to withdraw across the Seine. For them, just as during our retreat to Dunkirk, every minute counted. The Germans had twice foiled the Allies' attempt to cut off their army. Troops had escaped from the Falaise Gap. Of the 100,000 troops estimated to be almost cut off, 10,000 had been killed and 40,000 taken prisoner. The 50,000 who escaped might have been trapped on the west banks of the Seine if the Americans could have moved north up-river and held the crossings.

War is all about 'ifs'. The Germans still held Dunkirk and Calais and denied us short supply lines by sea. It was from this area that they were able to continue to launch the VI Rockets which were devastating London. We know now that Hitler pinned great hope on the production of an atom bomb. What would we have done if such a devastating weapon had been used against our cities? The ordinary soldier, knowing nothing of these threats, fought on.

The Germans were now retreating in the face of the Russians, in Italy and, on the Western Front, where we were fast heading for the Rhine, the last great obstacle. The Canadians moving along the northern coastline, by-passed the ports of Calais and Dunkirk. Dunkirk fell in September but Calais held out until the end of the war. No doubt the old brickyard provided shelter for them as it had for the Regiment in 1939. It would surely have been possible to clear this area completely but, with one of the ports open, it may have been considered more costly to the Germans to keep it supplied. A lot of mopping up had to be done west of the Seine but the Regiment had earned a rest. They were withdrawn to Graveron, eight kilometres north of Evereux. There would be trips to the mobile bath units, clean clothing, hair-cuts, and a lot of letter-writing to do.

Lieutenant Colonel Teddy Swetenham had to wait until Malines before writing to the Colonel of the Regiment, Major-General Roger Evans:

"Dear General, I feel most guilty, having not written to you before to let you know how we have been getting on, but ever since we joined the Division and started fighting on August 1st we have never had a let-up. Until the last three days we have only had two periods of rest, each lasting 24 hours.

"You have probably heard of our terribly unfortunate start when we lost Anthony Rawlins, Padre John Newson and Trooper Bloom drowned when trying to rescue others. Then Pat Leavey was killed by a stray shell when visiting his old regiment and looking at a knocked-out German tank. This before we had commenced battle.

"Maurice Williams, my Adjutant's death, was equally a terrible tragedy. He is an irreplaceable loss. He was killed by accident by the tank behind him and just as we were forming up for an attack. Rupert Kettle has been Adjutant since then and has done awfully well. Although very young he is extremely quick and imperturbable. He has been a great success and I am glad I chose him. Most of our casualties have been from shell and mortar fire when caught out of tanks. Shellfire is quite unpredictable and unexpected though some were as a result of being under observation from somewhere.

"Of the officers you would know, Brian Berry and Derek Sedgwick were killed that way and Gerald Kildare and Guy Glover were wounded. The latter is back again and quite all right. David Dickson was the latest officer to be wounded. I don't think he is bad though, wounded in the legs and arm, no bones broken and no long-term damage. Gerald Kildare was unlucky, he was hit in the back of the head and as you probably know, it has affected his sight and he will always have a hole in the back of his skull. I saw him immediately after it happened and didn't think he was too bad but the shrapnel must have gone deeper than was at first thought. He had done so well as 'B' Squadron Leader. Tony Leavey has now taken over and is doing extremely well.

"Of the senior ranks, Sergeants Knaggs, Daglish and Heaps and SSM Clayton have been excellent but are now wounded. They are a particular loss though I hope none are serious. Sergeant Chester lost a hand, we shall not see him back, I fear, but Creagh Gibson had a very cheerful letter from him.

"So far, this letter seems to be nothing but a casualty report and nothing of what we have done and how we have done it. The reputation of the Regiment is well established here now, certainly in the Division. It is difficult to know what outsiders do think but the odd remark, 'Oh, you're the Inniskillings, I've heard about you, your chaps are ready to go anywhere and do anything', usually from an unknown infantry officer, are frequent. The chaps have really done terribly well and are in tremendous heart and ready to have a real go at anything.

"It is difficult to pick out individuals either from among the officers or men—tney have all been really terrific. In John Ward-Harrison, Creagh Gibson and Tony Leavey I have three splendid Squadron Leaders. Troop leaders have also been quite excellent and in recent actions I would single out Barney Cowdy, Bill Aykroyd, Bill Bradfield and Martin Fitzgerald. Jack Bissill and Ben Tottenham have done particularly well in the Recce Squadron.

"We have already fought under three different Corps, mostly with our own Division but for a short time when the rest of this Division were resting we were fighting with Errol Prior-Palmer's Brigade. We have experienced every kind of battle except a real tank-v-tank battle. We have not met German armour in force. For the most part we have fought in very difficult country for armour and, when in good tank country, we have met little or no opposition. In the last fortnight we have had a tremendous gallop and though we met some opposition every day, we have had long advances to maintain supplies, the only delays being caused by delirious crowds in the towns. The ammunition being used against us being flowers and fruit, some of the latter rather unripe and almost armour piercing!

We have had a wonderful welcome all through north France and great assistance from the FFI (Resistance).

" 'Tadpole' Bridgewater's newsletter which was sent through official channels to you was returned by Public Relations Branch of the War Office because the fact that the Regiment is in France has not yet been released. As the letter was only for private circulation among next-of-kin who are well aware of the fact, I cannot see the point. Another letter is ready to go and we will try again.

"I heard from Mike Ansell and Edward Barron that the Inniskilling Society is working well. Yours ever Teddy."

* * * * *

My own journey back through a number of casualty clearing stations was tiring but I slept a lot during the rather rough rides. At each stop I was checked, my card was marked, and I was placed into another ambulance. A cup of tea or some other refreshments were very welcome. At about nine o'clock that same evening I arrived at the 89th British Hospital, Bayeux. It had taken me twelve hours to return to the start point and over ground which had taken six weeks on the outward trip.

I had thought all day of the casualties and what I would say to Denis Grieves' mother when I could obtain her address. I felt very responsible for his death because he had acted exactly as I had told him. I tried to console myself with the knowledge that we had not much choice in the events which had led to his death. I knew that he was an only child and would be badly missed.

On arrival at Bayeux, I really started to experience marvellous treatment but I had to learn to cope with it: Red Cross workers who insisted on putting their arm around me to sit up when I was quite capable of sitting unaided; a nurse who lit a cirgarette, placed it to my lips for a puff, and then sat holding it and my hand until the next puff. I was having to pretend to be worse than my injuries warranted.

I can just remember being put between those wonderful white sheets in a bed and under the cover of a large marquee. I was soon asleep. I was awakened in the morning by a rumpus at the foot of my bed: the doctor was giving the ward sister some stick for not cleaning me up the previous night. It was all action for ten minutes and I was given the treatment, then off to X-ray in another tent and back into the ward. In the bed to my left was a Pole who spoke little English but understood playing cards and insisted that we play gin rummy. "We heard what happened to you." he said. "Who told you," I asked. "You did," he replied. "You have been shouting out all night."

About midday, the doctor and an entourage of matron and nurses visited everybody but, on arrival at my bed, notes were consulted and the party passed. Feeling somewhat left out, I caught the eye of the trailer nurse. "What about me?" I asked quietly. "You're being sent home," she said. This unexpected prospect was one to savour. The nurse explained that a broken bone in my foot would take some weeks to set. Within an hour I was on a slab in the operating theatre. A Canadian was already undergoing an operation on a slab beside me and, though he was completely sedated, his language was atrocious. I was concerned that I might also disgrace myself: after all, I had not been in any female company for weeks and the language throughout this period had been very basic. I was relieved to learn that I was to have a plaster cast fitted and would not need an anaesthetic.

That afternoon I was put into an ambulance yet again and, after a short drive the door was opened and I found myself looking into the interior of a Dakota. But it was to be no more than a view. The ambulance doors closed and we drove for another half-hour, at the end of which I was loaded aboard a tank landing craft. The ship had brought out vehicles and was fitted with special stretcher racks for what turned out to be a very rough crossing. I felt sorry for those who had to have injections and transfusions. The doctor who administered them had to be pinned firmly against an upright by an orderly while he inserted the needle. There were some Germans on board and I learned that Wehrmacht troops, ordinary German soldiers, had attacked and broken the jaw of an SS officer.

A hospital train took us from Southampton to a Canadian hospital in Farnborough for a thorough examination. After two days I was off to Liverpool and by road to Ormskirk. It was now a matter of waiting for bones to heal. My parents, who had been evacuated to Alderley Edge in Cheshire, were not on the telephone but I was able to contact my sister who was at work. They were greatly relieved to know that my injuries were fairly trivial. What a delight it was to see my father that night. I felt nearer to him now that I had experienced active service and could swop stories.

# Seine—Rhine

The short rest and refit was soon at an end. Once more the tanks and echelons took to the road and headed east. It seemed only a matter of time before the Germans would crumble completely: they were tired, shell-shocked and disillusioned. Those who were left to fight a rearguard action, and who were subsequently captured, were of a poor quality. But we were wrong to assume that the German Army and the Luftwaffe were spent. The enemy, withdrawing to strategic positions, was far from beaten and there was a lot of hard fighting to come both before and after we entered Germany. We were also unaware of the faith pinned by Hitler on the creation of an atomic bomb. It is now easy to understand why the Germans fought so fanatically to play for time.

*Lieutenant Ben Tottenham,* troop leader in the Recce Squadron, wrote the following account of the new phase and the different tactics brought about by the long daily drives east:

"After the dust, stench and destruction in Normandy, the break-out came as a great uplift to the spirit. We set off on August 31st, Recce in the lead, in pitch darkness and pouring rain. The Regimental column shattered the silence in Louviers and we crossed the Seine at St-Pierre-du-Vauvray shortly after sunrise. At some point during the move, my operator passed me a biscuit loaded with marmalade. Unfortunately, in the half light, he failed to notice that the liberal coating was embedded with wasps. At least one, and I suspect more, gave me a nasty sting and I felt as though I had swallowed crushed glass.

"We covered over 70 miles during that first move. When the pace slowed down we were mobbed by villagers. Flowers, wine, butter and fruit were thrust forward as tokens of appreciation. Tanks were covered with zinnias, hydrangeas and chrysanthemums."

* * * * * *

*Lieutenant Henry Woods* recalled:

"The pace varied according to reports from Recce troops and the nature of the country. On open uplands, the squadrons halted only now and again when doubtful of a prominent feature like a large wood on a crest. Sometimes the rear squadrons remained halted on the road for up to an hour and had to be deployed to observe from a prominent feature on a flank, in battle formation, sometimes up to two or three hours. There were no pauses for rest or maintenance, though during any halt there was an attempt to eat or 'brew up' something hot to drink. Start time was from 0530 hours and the Regiment was never in harbour before last light. Mechanical troubles were fortunately few, though a few tanks had to drop out because of overheating. This was the result of months of battle running. Leaves, twigs and dust clogged up the radiators. The Regimental LAD (Light Aid Detachment) picked up and repaired them if repairable or towed them until the end of the move, when fitters could work on them."

* * * * *

The Somme countryside, through which the first part of the advance took place, requires no further description to those who have read of the fearful battles of the Great War. The many cemeteries told the story of a slaughter in this area only 28 years earlier. Every copse and wood carried a name familiar to those who studied that war. These hills and valleys had been the stage for the 1916 Somme offensive when 60,000 men had perished in a day. This flowing country of hills, valleys, copses and woods extends from the Seine till the high ground drops to the plains of Northern France and Belgium. A rich country, full of fine cattle and prosperous, happy farming communities, it was indeed a pleasant relief from the dust and carnage of Normandy. The inhabitants' welcome was touching to each and every one of us. There was a pathetic desire to do everything possible for us. The troops usually had only a three or four-hour rest each night, and sometimes even less when guard duties were called for. There were only occasional signs of the Germans. Abandoned lorries, guns and burned-out cars were evidence of their retreat, but many of the villages were quite untouched by the dreaded events of war.

Our Regimental History, *Change and Challenge* records:

"On September 2nd, the 8th Hussars, the leading regiment of the 7th Armoured Division, were held up by strong enemy resistance at St-Pol. The Regiment was ordered to carry out a night march round the right flank and to cut the roads leading east from the town. This manoeuvre was successfully accomplished and by daylight some 70 prisoners had been taken. The eastern flank was open but during the morning RHQ was suddenly and viciously shelled. Lieutenant Sedgewick was killed and 14 men wounded. Our medical officer, Captain 'Doc' Forrester, rose splendidly to the challenge as he always did. 'B' Squadron, who were protecting that flank, were immediately in action and during this action Corporal Poggy Cooper fought a lone action which deservedly earned him the award of the MM. Poggy dismounted from his tank and went into a wood, some believe to answer the call of nature! Whatever he intended was interrupted when he came upon a pocket of enemy. He destroyed a machine-gun post and captured 11 prisoners. Nobody recalls whether he completed his initial intention.

"The advance continued towards Lille and in the evening the Regiment was held up at Cambrin, where we had spent two nights in September, 1939, on the way to our concentration area behind the Belgian frontier. The 11th Hussars reported a semi-demolished bridge over the La Bassée canal, the very same bridge over which the Regiment had passed when leaving the village in 1939. Enemy small-arms fire prevented a close examination of the bridge which was partly burnt. 'C' Squadron forced a crossing with 2nd Troop, 'A' Squadron (Lieutenant David Dickson) but the bridge finally collapsed behind the last tank commanded by Sergeant Ted Glynn. The 1st Rifle Brigade formed a bridgehead supported by the troop of tanks.

"Work continued throughout the night and by morning the Royal Engineers using a Scissors Bridge (a structure carried by a tank and hydraulically lowered in front of it) had made it possible for the remaining 'C' Squadron tanks to cross. 'A' Squadron also crossed and the operation to enlarge the bridgehead was going well, though still against dogged opposition. After this painful reminder that there was still a sting in the enemy tail, the Regiment had a comparatively clear run to the Belgian border, which they crossed at Toufflers.

"The further the Allies had advanced from the Normandy bridgehead, the more enthusiastic and rapturous had become the welcome to 'Lés libérateurs'. Grading the inhabitants of Northern France as enthusiastic would upgrade the Belgians to ecstatic. Tank crews were enveloped in a wave of emotion, speeches, embraces, tears of joy, fruit, flowers, eggs, butter and cheese, and some managed to gain even greater favours! It was often difficult to keep the columns on the move. Orders were received to seize the bridges over the Schelde in the Wetteren area and to cut the roads leading eastward out of Ghent. 'B' Squadron and the Reconnaissance Squadron had now established communication with the 'White Brigade' who came into the open and were very active. SSM Jack Clayton and Sergeant Ted Glynn were each awarded the Military Medal for their part in holding off a German counter-attack on the Wetteren bridge."

Sergeant Glynn's citation reads:

*During the night of September 4th, Sergeant Glynn, who was temporarily attached to 1st Troop 'B' Squadron, was in position with elements of 'A' Company 1/6th Queen's, and established in a defensive position. Shortly after midnight, the position was subjected to a determined attack by enemy infantry, the focal point of which was directed against the position occupied by Sergeant Glynn. In the course of this attack, Sergeant Glynn was attacked with close-range anti-tank weapons and grenades from the vicinity of a cottage in close proximity. This attack he beat off with the greatest vigour. He would have at any time been able to destroy the cottage with his heavy armament and thus remove the menace, but he consistently refused to do so as he was aware that the cottage was occupied by a family of Belgian civilians which included several children. He preferred to engage the enemy at close quarters rather than cause casualties among the civilians. This fact and a further series of accurate reports on the situation were made by radio to the Squadron Leader. Sergeant Glynn acted with courage and coolness which was an inspiration to the remainder of the Troop. By his staunch defence, Sergeant Glynn was successful in preventing the penetration of the squadron position.*

Sergeant Bob Price had been in reserve with the echelon and awaiting a new tank; his driver, Trooper Swain, had been wounded and blinded during the action. Bob now came back as a reinforcement in 'C' Squadron. He recalls that it was well worth being there to see SSM Jack Clayton's temper when the enemy had the audacity to brew his tank with a 50mm shot at short range. *John Pilborough* recorded this encounter in *First In. Last Out.*:

"Recce troops were ordered to check the bridges at Melle and Wetteren which were some five and eight miles, respectively, south-east of Ghent. The Melle bridge had already been blown but the Recce patrol under the leadership of Lieutenant Ben Tottenham, found the Wetteren bridge intact.

It was a stout wooden bridge with sections which could be raised in drawbridge fashion to permit vessels to pass up the canal. This section was, at the time of arrival, raised and covered by small-arms fire from the opposite bank. The Belgian Underground, La Brigade Blanche or White Brigade, came to the rescue and assisted in lowering the section to permit 'B' Squadron to cross and clear the houses in support of our infantry. The Regiment was then able to cross and, against slight opposition, cut the roads running east to Calcken and Lockeren.

The German garrison was trapped as the 5th Royal Tank Regiment already held the western edge of Ghent and had cut the road leading north to the Scheldt estuary. That night, a strong counter-attack was made by a troop of SS to destroy the Wetteren bridge and prevent our tanks from advancing. Our A1 echelon was at that time ready with the daily supplies and occupying the station yard, only just clear of the bridge. The echelon drivers quickly joined forces with some Royal Engineers to hold the bridge until 'C' Squadron could be brought into action. Things were warm while it lasted and one of the only times our echelon had to show that they could fight as well as the Sabre Squadrons if called on to do so. The following day, Sergeant Andrews, who had only served with the Reconnaissance Squadron for a short while, brought back the CO of a German horsed transport section which had been captured intact with horses. Their Colonel rode on the 'Honey' while 200 prisoners followed behind."

*Lieutenant Ben Tottenham* wrote this account of the action:

"For my troop, the culmination of the 250-mile run came when we found that bridge at Wetteren across the Scheldt on the south-east side of Ghent intact. Whoever takes the credit for the subsequent events, we undoubtedly found the bridge. The 3rd RHA OP tank was close behind us in the dusk, and we used their shorter lines of communication to get the news back to our Sunray. We then set about lowering the centre section which was at the end of a timber causeway and held aloft by a system of chains; it had to be wound down. In all this the Brigade Blanche were involved. Having lowered the bridge, we patrolled on in the direction of Lokeren.

"Our Regimental Headquarters had set up for the night at the Château de Destelbergen, a few miles on. The rear link was in the front circular courtyard as the patrolling troops came in for the evening meal. The troop leaders were entertained by a rich family of Belgian bankers, Van Acker by name, and dined very well with champagne and brandy flowing. At some point Charles de Selliers made his first direct contact with the Regiment. Thirty years later, when I happened to be visiting Ghent for the anniversary celebrations of the liberation of that city, I visited the Château on the day the contents were laid out for sale. The tables were laid with china, glass and silver. It was as though I had been transported in a time capsule to 1944. Of course, the bridge at Wetteren had been replaced by a permanent four-lane bridge and was a little down-river from the original."

It was about this time that Lieutenant Tottenham made an important request of the CO. His elder sister had married a Frenchman before the war and had lived in Paris throughout the occupation. He and his family were anxiously awaiting news of her and Ben asked if he could be given a few days off to make a trip to Paris. The CO, though reluctant to allow one of his officers to be absent at this time, ruled that he could go if he could find a British or American plane and be back in four days. He continues his story:

"The first stage of my journey was to fly to Amiens; from there I hitched to Poix and again to Pontoise. In return for my fixing up billets for his Red Caps, a Military Police sergeant loaned me a despatch rider who took me 50 miles by pillion to the Gare du Nord. I was in Service dress by the way.

"As it was Sunday, the Métro was shut, but once again my luck held and a patrol of MPs, explaining kindly that Paris was out of bounds, took me to the Boulevard Jasmin in the 16th Arrondissement. Surprise was total when I finally reached the 6th floor (no lift) and my sister and brother-in-law were overwhelmed. Champagne flowed. Then we all bicycled off to the fashionable bars of L'Ascot and Fouquets and talked until the light failed. Getting back to Malines the following day was not quite so simple.

"My sister took me to Le Bourget by Métro but the cloud base was virtually zero. The pilot gave it up as a bad job after two attempts, one of which involved rapid evasive action to avoid hitting a coal slag heap at about 50 feet. On Tuesday, as the cloud continued, I had to hitch back up the Red Ball route, the American supply line. Just at the critical juncture when it was about to veer away from my centre-line, the fates were kind and a Regimental truck picked me up. It was only in the nick of time to save me from being absent without leave since the Regiment was back in action sooner than expected."

* * * * *

The German commandant of the Ghent garrison refused to surrender unconditionally but did withdraw his troops into the northern part of the city and away from the historic buildings which had accommodated the old 6th Inniskilling Dragoons before marching to the battle of Waterloo in 1815.

Part of the long citation for the well-deserved award of the Distinguished Conduct Medal to Sergeant Archie Carr contains a record of his bravery on the outskirts of Ghent:

> *At Ghent on September 8th, and in conjunction with a platoon of infantry of the Rifle Brigade, Sergeant Carr was ordered to watch the railway crossing and canal and the factory area on the far bank. The railway bridge was a swing bridge which was positioned amidstream and connected to the near bank by a rope. On the evening of September 8th, the Commanding Officer of the Queen's Regiment made a reconnaissance of the area with a view to the intended attack on the factory area the following morning. He was anxious to ascertain whether the bridge was usable or not. The only way to do this was to close the bridge by means of the rope. Sergeant Carr went up the canal bank in his tank knowing that 88mm guns had been reliably reported covering the waterfront and despite sniper and Spandau machine-gun fire which had been prevalent all day. On reaching the edge of the canal, Carr dismounted from his tank, attached the rope to his vehicle, and guided it whilst in reverse. As he carried out this operation, every weapon available to the enemy opened up from the far bank. With coolness and disregard and without hurrying, he continued this operation until the rope broke and the ends fell into the canal.*

Archie relates a previously unrecorded episode which he calls "Another funny event". While in the Ghent area, a relayed message from his Squadron Headquarters asked him to check out a report that there was a German regiment in a wood some two miles away. A local directed him up a lane, where he quickly came upon 150 Germans lined up to receive rations for the day. When they saw the troop of tanks, they dropped their mess tins and raised their hands.

Archie dismounted and gave orders to Sergeant 'Albert' Morris, his Number Two, to keep them covered. The senior German officer however, said that he would surrender only to an officer. Archie relayed this information to his Squadron Leader, Major Creagh Gibson who said: "Tell the officer that he has two minutes to decide. If he doesn't surrender, tell him you will shoot him, then swing the guns on to the rest of them." The Germans promptly obliged and the whole lot fell in and marched away escorted by the tanks for about a mile until a platoon of the Rifle Brigade took charge of them.

*   *   *   *   *

*Captain Charles Maple,* commanding our REME Detachment, was now well established and accepted as invaluable. He had battled through Normandy recovering tanks from difficult positions, including one which the Germans had ingeniously booby-trapped by inserting a charge into the starter solenoid. He had coped with the removal of turrets for the Recce boys and the ever-increasing demand to fit yet more Browning mountings to the hulls of tanks. Charles tells his own story:

"What marvels of logistics were performed by B and A2 Echelons to keep the Regiment moving. It is remembered as a blurred kaleidoscope of dust, night expeditions to steal spares, and the relics of a stricken army. At this time we acquired the 'boat'. Since the time elapsed now precludes me from court martial, I can write about it.

"Most tank crews loathed the outcome of a lost tank which resulted in relegation to the Forward Delivery Squadron, which was responsible for the issue of a replacement vehicle. There was also a very real threat that the crew would be posted to another regiment requiring reinforcements. No 'Skin' worth his salt was going to suffer that! Nor did they wish their tank to be scrapped if it could be repaired: there was some value in knowing a tried and tested vehicle.

"The silly rule was that if a tank required more than four hours' work by a fitter, it would be sent to the rear for repair. There was no rear in the fast, daily moves during the break-out, and a system had to be evolved to ensure that we could repair our own tanks and wheeled vehicles. Any tank which had to be temporarily abandoned was rendered thief-proof to the infantry by lightly welding its hatches. Later, and when time permitted, the tank was retrieved by a tow forward, breaking all rules.

"During this time, the crew was housed in what was termed 'the boat'. This was a German army engineers' pontoon bridge, some 40 feet long, mounted upside down on its modified trailer. The crew lived, slept and cooked in it while it was towed by a Ward-la-France tractor or Scammell. As soon as the tank was repaired, the crew took it over and rejoined the Squadrons.

"No-one needed a breather more than our echelons. The lines of communication still reached back to the Normandy beaches and the distance grew daily. Their journeys were not only extremely tiring but, on occasions, hazardous. So fluid was the military situation that there were no flanks in the accepted sense of military tactics. Enemy detachments and armoured vehicles, themselves lost and out of touch with their command, frequently and discourteously interrupted the flow of supply. Those who served in the echelons were certainly the heroes of this phase.

* * * * *

There was a light-hearted adventure in the Regimental newletter which recorded a lone operation carried out by RQMS Jack Robinson DCM and Sergeant 'Jock' Irvine. Jack was acting as 'Harbour Master' for B Echelon during the move over the borders of France and Belgium. They were given a six figure map reference on a quarter inch to the mile map to meet a Brigade representative. The instruction was to turn left at the given map reference and at that point to leave the main road. The pair set off ahead of the echelon in a Jeep driven by Jock.

At about midday they arrived at the crossroads at Kerkhove. They duly followed instructions and turned left and after about two miles arrived at the village of Tieghem. They were surprised to be met by wildly enthusiastic crowds and were unable to continue for fear of running over someone. Huge bouquets were presented and they were showered with fruit and wine. Concerned that they were obviously the first allied troops to arrive, they pressed on for another mile and met with a similar reception. Uncertain about the location of the representative from Brigade but enjoying the hero worship, they pressed on to Ooteghem. As soon as they arrived, the main street became crowded, flags appeared miraculously at the windows and again there was a series of presentations coupled with even more flowers and fruit. An English speaking inhabitant came forward and insisted that they should visit his house for a formal presentation from the Mayor. There was no way out of this but by this time they were convinced they were on the wrong road. The Jeep was parked outside the house and they were entertained to a full civic reception complete with champagne. They were on the point of leaving and trying to clear flowers to find the seats in the Jeep when there was a shout of 'Allemands'. The streets were cleared as though by magic. Jock Irvine saw a small camouflaged car coming up the street. He could not see the occupants but knowing that another regiment in the Brigade had been using such a vehicle for some time, he called to Jack Robinson, 'We're in the right place alright, here comes the Harbour Party'. As the car drew level, an SS officer stood up and looked at them, but passed on up the road. The car was followed by four armoured cars. Jock and Jack took up a defensive position behind the Jeep but only having a .38 pistol each, could hardly put up a fight. They decided that discretion was definitely the better part of valour and withdrew back into the house. As each armoured car passed, the back door opened and a sub machine-gun was pointed at the Jeep but no shots were fired. The enemy uncertain of the strength of our occupying force also

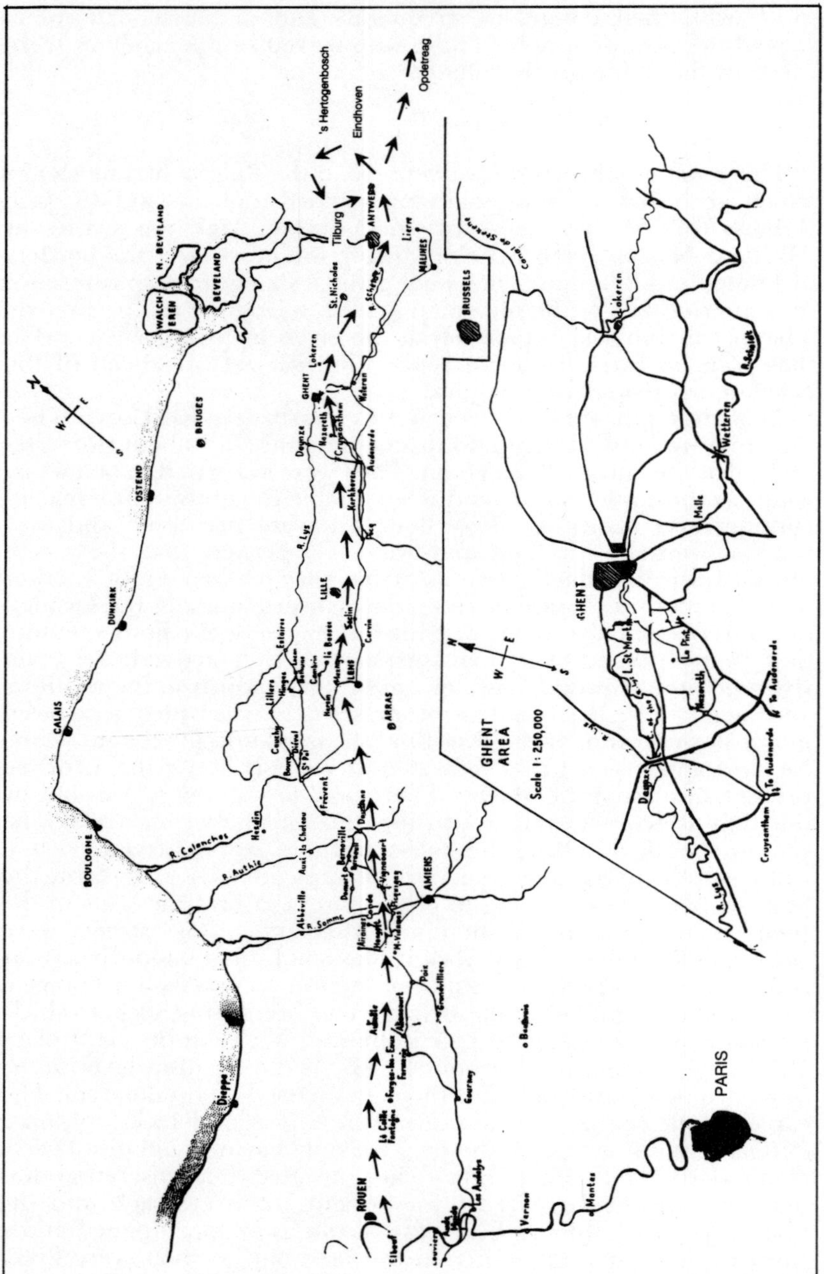
's Hertogenbosch
Eindhoven
Opdetreag
Tilburg
ANTWERP
WALCHEREN
N. BEVELAND
BEVELAND
BRUGES
OSTEND
DUNKIRK
CALAIS
BOULOGNE
Dieppe
ROUEN
AMIENS
LILLE
ARRAS
GHENT
BRUSSELS
GHENT AREA
Scale 1: 250,000
PARIS
Mantes
Vernon
Lokeren
Wetteren
Melle
Nazareth
Deynze
Cruysenthem
To Audenarde
R. Lys

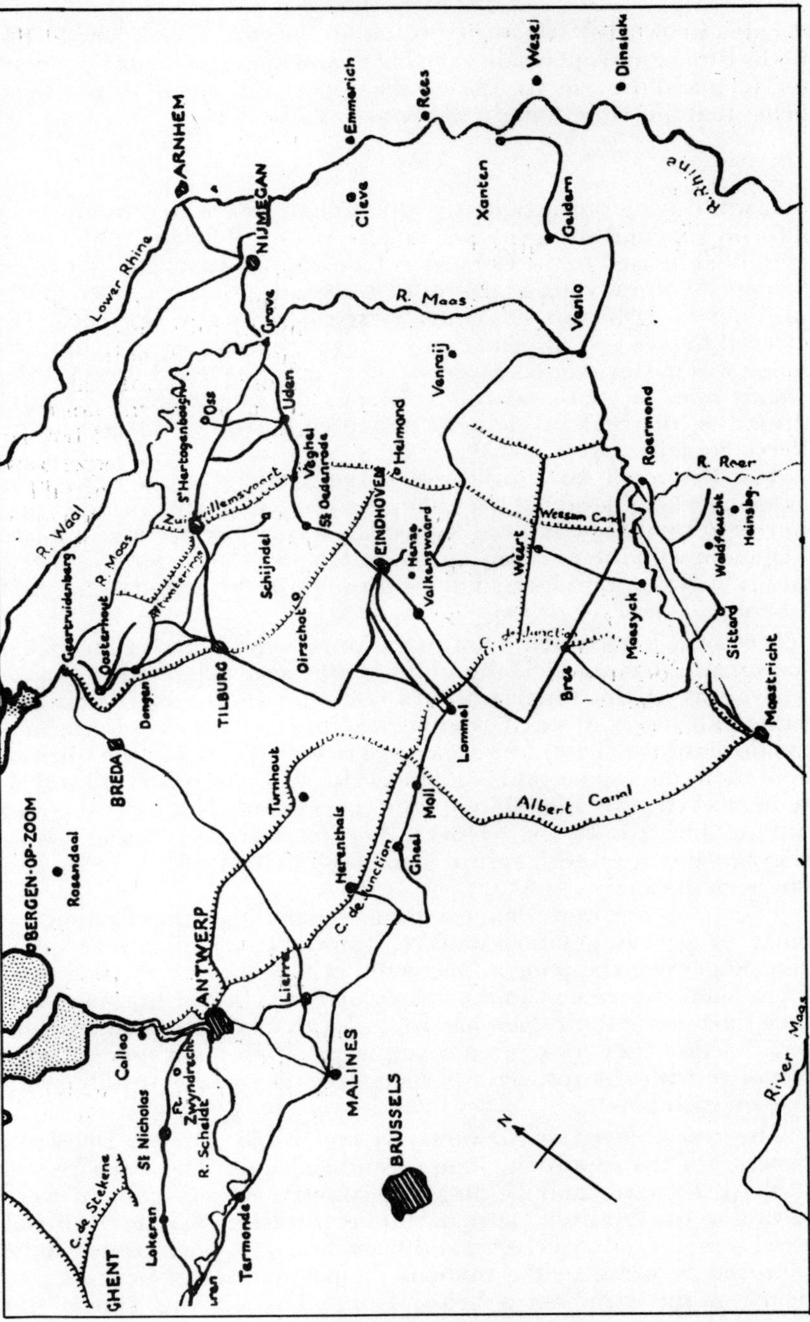
ARNHEM
NIJMEGAN
Emmerich
Rees
Wesel
Dinslaken
Cleve
Xanten
Geldern
R. Rhine
Lower Rhine
R. Waal
R. Maas
Grave
Venlo
Venraij
Uden
Oss
S^t Hertogenbosch
Zuid Willemsvaart
Veghel
Helmond
St Oedenrode
Schijndel
EINDHOVEN
Hense
Valkenswaard
Roermond
R. Roer
Wessem Canal
Weert
Waldfeucht
Heinsbg.
Maesyck
Sittard
Maastricht
Bree
C. de Junction
Oirschot
Tilburg
Dongen
Oosterhout
Geertruidenberg
Wilhelmina
BREDA
BERGEN-OP-ZOOM
Rosendaal
Turnhout
Lommel
Moll
Gheel
Herenthals
Albert Canal
ANTWERP
Lierre
Calloo
Zwyndrecht
St Nicholas
R. Scheldt
MALINES
BRUSSELS
Termonde
Lokeren
C. de Stekene
GHENT
River Maas
N

decided to back off and turned round in the road then headed back in the direction from whence they had appeared. Jock quickly ran to the Jeep and the pair sped off in the opposite direction. It was their belief that the Hun thought the Jeep was a hearse!

* * * * *

It was during our action at Wetteren and Ghent that there came into Regimental history the motor-cycling Belgian. The rider identified himself to the Colonel as Lieutenant Chevalier Charles de Selliers de Moranville, an officer of 1er Guides who had been taken prisoner in 1940 but subsequently released by the Germans. He offered to pass any information we might require. At first, his own home was in German-occupied territory and he passed through the enemy lines on many occasions. Eventually, he was given a battle-dress suit, the rank of Lieutenant, and command of a troop in the Recce Squadron.

The Regiment now withdrew to the Wetteren area which was enjoying a long period of liberation. No one will relate the individual stories of that stay but it only lasted a few days before the complete Regiment with the echelons moved to Malines (Mechelen) for a rest and refit. They were housed in the grounds of the Seminarium of St Joseph, a school for priests!

It was not a particularly holy occasion, for the whole of Mechelen was on an extended holiday and the troops were delighted to join in. There was hardly a man who did not enjoy the pleasure of a bed with clean sheets. It was a grand climax to three exciting weeks and the thrills of the chase. *John Pilborough* wrote: "Leave out the spirit of liberation, the cognac and mademoiselles, and Mechelen will still be remembered for something else—ice cream! Not cornets and wafers, nor two-by-four blocks, but masterpieces decked with cherries and laced with syrup. The 300-hundred mile journey had not been in vain!"

There was yet more letter-writing, repairs and modifications to tanks to permit greater comfort. Tank crews had a very great advantage over the poor infantrymen in that they always had with them blankets, shelter and a supply of food. In the first instance, both tank and infantrymen had to deal with medical casualties. The initial action they took often saved a life. Two good medical kits, complete with chloroform and morphine, were kept readily available on each tank.

The rest enjoyed at Malines was not wholly for the Division's benefit, for the supply situation was now serious. Those troops still pushing forward, and holding the country already gained, were having to eat captured German rations consisting mainly of tinned stew, tinned Limburg cheese and black bread. A port needed to be captured to bring in the millions of gallons of fuel necessary to maintain the army on a broad front. The obvious choice was

Antwerp, though the enemy would have to be cleared from the approaches on the River Scheldt (Escaut). If a crossing of the Maas and Rhine could be made at Arnhem, the operation would be over very quickly, and Montgomery's promise to have the war over by Christmas might still be feasible. The War Lords agreed that it was worth an attempt, and the operation was code-named 'Market Garden'.

The success of this bold move depended on the 1st Airborne Division holding the bridge at Arnhem while the ground forces moved forward quickly to relieve them. The ground was wet and had been flooded deliberately to prevent the deployment of tanks. The corridor would be narrow and vulnerable over such a distance. The 7th Armoured Division was allotted the defence of the left flank of XXX Corps, while the Guards Armoured Division would drive straight forward towards Arnhem. Operation Market Garden began on September 17th and on the following day the Regiment, now skilled in co-operation with infantry, was detached from the Division to support the 53rd (Welsh) Division in the area south of the Meuse/Escaut Canal.

It soon became obvious that the Germans had recovered from the defeat in Normandy and still had elite parachute and SS troops available. They made every use of the natural obstacles and fought hard to hold each village. On September 21st the Regiment crossed into Holland to the south-west of Eindhoven and joined the 71st Infantry Brigade of 51st Highland Division who were attempting to capture a large village called Middlebeers.

*Lieutenant Henry Woods* recalls:

" 'A' Squadron advanced north from the main road running south-west from Eindhoven. While the Squadron dealt with a large wood on the east side of the village, 'C' Squadron and the left-hand troop of 'A' under the command of Lieutenant Charles Snell moved slowly forward and into the village. 1st Troop of 'C' Squadron commanded by Sergeant Ralph Chalmers advanced to a slight bend in the road and found a road block. The infantry thought the road was clear up to the obstacle but, as Sergeant Chalmers came up to it, his tank was struck by two bazookas fired at close range by fanatical SS troops. One struck the turret and penetrated it, wounding the gunner and killing the operator.

"The tank slewed round and into a shop. In spite of this, Sergeant Chalmers moved the tank forward to the support position of the infantry. It became a house-to-house battle. On the right flank, Lieutenant Snell's troop did valuable work by screening the advance with smoke and machine-gun fire from the strongly-held wood to the east of the village. 'C' Squadron was so accurately shelled by heavy mortar fire, operating this time from the west, that a further troop was despatched. It was suspected that the accuracy of the mortar fire was attributable to an enemy observer located in a church spire, which the troop was able to destroy."

The SS are not noted for sympathetic concern but *Sergeant Bob Price* recalls a commendable incident at Middlebeers:

"While the fighting was at its height, a white flag was waved and an SS man came forward asking if a medical officer could assist with a difficult birth in the house which they were defending. All fighting ceased, and recommenced only when the child was born."

What a crazy activity war is! Both sides attempting to kill each other but happy to permit a child to be brought into the world.

The Arnhem drop was not going well. The Germans, now fighting on the west bank of the Rhine, were determined that relief troops would not get through and threw everything they had into denying the use of the Arnhem bridge. The epic stories of that action have been well recorded. The whole operation was costly in men and material both to the Airborne Force and those striving to get forward to relieve them on the narrow supply line. News came through that the enemy had cut the supply line to Nijmegen, just north of Odenrode. At 0200 hours on September 24th, the Regiment now under command of 131 Brigade received orders to move at 0600 hours and reopen the Axis. (code name for our centre-line)

The road was packed with vehicles nose to tail, unable to move forward or back, but the Military Police once again played a wonderful role in sorting it all out. By 0700 hours the Regiment reached the main square in Odenrode where they met a very angry Corps Commander, Lieutenant-General Brian Horrocks, who was desperately trying to get forward to join his own tactical headquarters. Sergeant Bob Price led the column in a north-westerly direction and soon came upon four brewed-up Sherman tanks of the Guards Division. Ahead was a long line of burning vehicles caught in the attack. 'C' Squadron deployed and advanced in a two-up formation for about three-quarters of a mile. They were then told to halt as elements of the US 101st Airborne Division were advancing south and there could be confusion and mistakes. Despite this, the Americans did fire on 'C' Squadron. Lieutenant Henry Woods advanced on foot whistling 'God Save the King' to make contact. The Americans whose own supplies had not reached them were very hungry and grateful for supplies handed over. The gamble had failed, and instead of a sudden end to hostilities, there would be a house-by-house fight until Germany was completely destroyed.

On September 27th the Regiment reverted to 22nd Armoured Brigade and moved north to Nistelrode and then, on October 1st, to the area of Heesh-Geffen, east of 's-Hertogenbosch. After assisting the 11th Hussars to clear up the area as far as Oss, the Division was deployed on a 14-mile front—facing west to cut off German forces still denying the use of Antwerp. V2 rockets were beginning to pound London from launching sites in this area. The country was very flat and drained by dykes which posed formidable tank obstacles. Tanks were forced to use the roads which could be mined and protected by anti-tank guns hidden in the fir-lined approach.

*Extract from First In. Last Out:*

"The Regiment came into reserve for 48 hours and Recce with TAC HQ were harboured at Nistelrode. Two new Honeys arrived—Mk VI models, a great improvement on the Mk III. We had trained on these prior to D-day. They were roomier and had an automatic gearbox. The Squadron again formed into three troops under the command of Lieutenant Crocker who had been transferred from a sabre squadron, Lieutenant Ben Tottenham, and Lieutenant Desmond O'Dowd, a British Guyanan. Lieutenant Crocker was the son of Lieutenant-General Sir John Crocker, Commander 1 British Corps.

"The enemy, unable to break across the corridor which was now just short of Nijmegen, were holding a line along the flank of the British advance and concentrated on defending the approaches to 's-Hertogenbosch, thus denying the use of Antwerp. It was good country to defend. For three weeks, the Regiment occupied the area around Heesch and covering the eastern approach roads to 's-Hertogenbosch. Two static armies, both on the defensive, called for daily reconnaissance patrols to report on any new positions—a tedious and unpopular task which involved going over the same ground repeatedly. Each day the patrols made their way forward cautiously until the enemy was sighted or gave himself away. At night, the positions were handed over to the infantry to hold and, at four-day intervals, the patrolling passed to the Recce Squadron of the 1st Royal Tank Regiment. The Sabre Squadrons were having a comparatively restful time, though ready to move quickly if required.

"In the morning, a troop drove into Geffen and were enthusiastically greeted by the civilian population, from whom they learned that the Germans had moved back to the next village of Nulands. The Dutch were more reserved in their welcome, less prone to flag-waving than the French or Belgians but better organised and more reliable on the practical assistance they offered. They had been worse-treated by the Germans and the Dutch Underground movement had suffered heavily both during the occupation and while actively trying to assist the liberators."

The report on patrol activity in *First In. Last Out.* goes on to indicate the dangers when covering the same area:

"Almost immediately after entering Geffen, the Regiment took up a defensive position and Recce was called upon to begin patrols. First Troop was directed along the main road from Oss to 's-Hertogenbosch. Third Troop moved along the railway which ran parallel with it to the north and Second Troop took the ground between the two. The first task was to discover the enemy positions and then stay under cover and watch. 'Keep them under observation' became the new order in place of Robert Crockett's 'Push on'. Patrols were covering the same ground for three weeks with a limited choice of route and this called for more careful planning. Towards the end of the stay in that area the continual watching and listening was fraying the steadiest of nerves. On the first day out the enemy was not expecting us and we had no difficulty in finding his outposts. First Troop drove up the tree-lined main road to the cross track which led into Nulands. A road block of felled trees prevented the troop from proceeding further but Lieutenant Crocker and Sergeant Strickland went forward on foot and found three Germans sitting half out of a trench. Sergeant Strickland shot one with a rifle but this brought an answering burst of Spandau fire from a concealed machine-gun pit which came too close for comfort. They withdrew down the ditch and the troop moved back to a point where the road block could be seen and all the likely approaches covered. Meanwhile, Second Troop had a very similar patrol but had found their Germans without any difficulty when still at some distance from them. Second Troop, working along the railway line, saw Germans dug into the embankment and the Honey, under command of Sergeant Tom Broad, fired on them. The troop had come into open ground before Nulands and, even as the Browning stopped firing, a heavy mortar stonk came down around them. As they hastily withdrew, the bombs followed them, one falling beside the Scout Car containing Corporal 'Maxi' Cooke and Trooper Tom Gardner. At last light, the patrols were called in and they harboured with Tac HQ in the open ground between Heesch and Geffen, where A Squadron and a Platoon of the Rifle Brigade had assumed control and in a defensive position. It was to be a very eventful night for that troop commanded by Lieutenant Martin Fitzgerald and with Lieutenant Peter Kiddle commanding one of the tanks in the troop."

*Lieutenent Peter Kiddle* recalls that night:

"3rd Troop was dispersed along a road of small, straggling houses about a mile from Geffen. Late that afternoon the customary background noise of far-distant shell fire was interrupted by a sharp, resonant explosion at close range. Too heavy for a mortar, I thought. I rightly concluded that we were about to be 'stonked'. A number of rounds which followed made it only too clear that an 88mm gun was firing air-burst HE on a variety of delay settings. It became a 'head-down' situation for turret personnel for a while. No harm was done and no attack followed.

"But why should the Germans range in on such a featureless patch of countryside? It became the subject of heated discussion. That evening, under new orders, Martin Fitzgerald rattled his troop into Geffen. This was quite a large village, unoccupied by day but held by a Platoon of the Rifle Brigade plus a troop of tanks at night. The layout of Geffen, as I recall it, was that of a reversed 'E' with the legs facing towards 's-Hertogenbosch. My tank on the central leg of the 'E' commanded the road running west. I was sited alongside a Café on the west side of the small square. Martin Fitzgerald's tank and the infantry half-tracks were not more than 30 yards behind me and nestling at the base of the quite disproportionately large church and tower. The tower had already been damaged, having suffered the attentions of both sides, each conscious of its merits as an observation post in this predominantly flat landscape. Its main fabric was still in being for the brickwork was well over a yard thick; it therefore constituted highly desirable military property. The other two tanks of the troop took positions facing west along the upper and lower legs of the 'E' each commanding narrow brick-surfaced roads.

"Dusk was nigh and the time for preparation short. The infantry selected positions some 30 to 40 yards ahead, covering approaches where tank guns could not be brought to bear, and then set about enlarging ditches and existing trenches. Tank commanders registered fixed lines which would not endanger the infantry positions. Firing on prearranged fixed lines could be blind and so arranged to cover the area of defence. There was no infra-red equipment available to us at that time.

"Martin held two 'O' Groups at the first of which the most extensive set of artillery DF (defensive fire) tasks I had ever encountered were issued and marked up together with their code names. The radio net to the Regiment was endlessly checked and retuned to perfection. Martin made a tour of inspection. Despite all this activity, we knew from previous troops that the only battle we were likely to be engaged in was warding off sleep during the quiet, warm October night.

"It seemed to be soon after last light that our expectations began to prove false by the chatter of the flank Rifle Brigade sections' LMGs, quickly joined by the unmistakable 'burp' of Spandaus. There was no sign of the enemy to our front and no call for supporting fire at this time, and anxiety arose as to whether the infantry in front of us had been quietly by-passed. Then, as if in response, Martin came on the 'blower' and ordered me somewhat tensely to commence firing on fixed lines and added that all DF tasks had been called down simultaneously, that RHQ was under fire from air-burst high explosive and that understandably, communications were suffering as a result. There was no time to reflect on this news for, simultaneously, the quiet of the night became a chattering, booming, flashing pandemonium, not merely due to my own tank's guns plus those of the Rifle Brigade, but particularly the undivided attentions of the batteries of 3 RHA 25-pounders, serving that array of DF tasks. My feeling of reassurance faded somewhat when I realised that one particular gun's rounds were dropping short. Alternate rounds were landing on the road to my left (showers of brick dust) and the café forecourt to my right (showers of earth)!

Happily the arrival of any destined for the engine covers was pre-empted by all the guns on the task being lifted 25 yards at the request of the infantry. The racket continued. The coaxially-mounted machine-gun in the turret was overheating. The church tower stood in the path of some of the DF rounds and the louvres and other wooden parts were burning fiercely. Small flames now flickered in the undergrowth ahead of us. I began to catch glimpses of German helmets milling about near the Rifle Brigade positions.

"I started to intersperse the bursts of the co-ax with 75mm rounds of HE wherever possible. A hand fell heavily on my shoulder and I spun round, expecting to face the worse, but there was Martin reaching over from behind the turret. He shouted to find out if we were all right. I told him that we were and asked if the Germans had got through anywhere. He replied, 'Not yet', and on that cheerful note slid away. I became unduly conscious of the café building on my right. On its wall, about five feet above the turret, was a single glassless window, beautifully placed for a gentle grenade lob into the turret.

"There was suddenly a loud explosion just to the left of the tank. The co-ax started off in earnest again despite the totally helmetless prospect ahead. A second, louder explosion rocked the tank back on its haunches and I thought we were hit. So did all the crew for they told me so—but everything and everybody was operating normally and we continued to fire, very conscious that we were the target apple of some German infantryman's eye. There was no repetition and the firing all round became spasmodic, then ceased, to be replaced by a tense silence broken only by the crackle of flames as we waited for dawn. Nobody had the least difficulty in staying awake. The explosions had been caused by two Panzerfaust (bazookas) which had hit the road, one damaging the tank track.

"In old age I am unable to recall how long this action lasted. My memory tells me that it was over a period of some hours, but common sense suggests otherwise. Nothing further happened until well after dawn when Martin, the Rifle Brigade Platoon Commander and I walked the perimeter of the infantry positions. Having only caught glimpses of our opponents until then, we were completely unprepared for the sight that met our eyes. The area was strewn with scores of German dead lying singly and in heaps just as they had fallen. Most of them appeared unmarked and intact but there was not one living man among them. The first glance told us that the numbers involved had been far greater than anything we had imagined and it passed comprehension how we had come through unscathed. It took some little time before it became clear that, whatever our own efforts might have achieved, the people to whom a massive debt of gratitude was owed were our splendid and ubiquitous gunners of 3 Royal Horse Artillery.

"The subsequent issue of 'Desert Rats', the divisional newspaper, briefly reported that Geffen had been attacked overnight by a

German infantry battalion with artillery in support and that the attack had been beaten off. A certain amount of verbal rumbling in the ranks implied that, on the next occasion, the editor would be invited to attend in person. (Note: The establishment of a German infantry battalion at that time was about 800 personnel).

"Martin Fitzgerald was subsequently awarded the Military Cross, attributed to this and other examples of his bravery and coolness under fire. Memories grow dim and I began to mistrust my seemingly clear-cut recollections of that night in Geffen. The Regimental Association has twice returned to the area and passed up that road. On the first occasion, in 1984, these fears were confirmed in that there were a number of things which I felt I should have remembered, yet in fact I did not. Then, in 1985, when attending a liberation ceremony in 's-Hertogenbosch we again passed that way and went into Geffen. None of the scenery we passed en route evoked a flicker of memory. Then, suddenly, there was the church with the great tower now restored to its full splendour and, opposite, the café itself. The coach halted and I walked over to where my tank had stood 40 years earlier. I looked up and there was the window. It looked a little different . . . more friendly and, ah! yes, the glass had been replaced."

* * * * *

*First In. Last Out.* continues:

"The following morning we patrolled at first light. This time, the intention was to discover what type of weapons the enemy were using in the sector. Since the only successful way to discover this was to drive out and act as a target, no-one much cared for the idea! It was off on to the same routes as the previous day. First Troop, unable to pass the road block, turned down the track towards Nulands and, while the carrier crew dismounted with a Bren gun and fired down past the felled trees, the tank shot up the houses on the outskirts of the village. This drew only a single burst of Spandau in return.

"The troop pulled back and prepared breakfast. It seemed that the enemy was not to be drawn. Second Troop, adopting the same procedure, received the treatment meted out to Third Troop the previous day and were heavily mortared. They, too, withdrew and made a meal. Third Troop who this time approached Nulands from the north side of the railway, blazed away at the buildings in the village and congratulated themselves when they saw the answering mortar fire falling on Second Troop's position. They also withdrew, deducing that the enemy defence was based upon normal infantry weapons with one piece of artillery, estimated at 120mm, which mixed occasionally with the mortar fire.

"While some kept watch, others manned the radio to keep contact with HQ and others searched buildings and found eggs and bottles of fruit. The civilians on the German side had been evacuated back into Nulands. In due course, those who lived on our side were permitted to return daily to attend to their livestock.

"On the third day, all three patrols were out. The orders were to work forward to check that the enemy was holding the same positions. Third Troop, who had the main road to patrol, were becoming a little chary. It seemed risky to travel the same route every morning since, after all, the Germans would be well aware of this and could easily lay mines or arrange an ambush. Some distance short of the crosstracks and road block, they turned off the main road and took a track leading towards Nulands and parallel with the main road. They had no sooner arrived at a point level with the cross tracks than that same mortar stonk which had greeted Second and Third Troop on the first two days came down once again. It arrived at just the place they would have been. This victory of the mind, chiefly due to Lieutenant Crocker, was spoiled by a German sniper who shot Sergeant Strickland through the shoulder. The Troop pulled out.

"Second Troop had sent a foot patrol towards the village. Sergeant Tom Wagstaff and Corporal Pete Lees, moving cautiously, found a group of Germans sitting on the church steps. They shot them up with their Sten guns but wisely did not stop to count the bag. Third Troop also had a foot patrol out—Lieutenant O'Dowd and Corporal Micky Ryan. Corporal Ryan, on ahead, came face to face with a German with only a hedge between them. Micky shot the German with a burst of Sten. By 1000 hours, all patrols were back and making breakfast.

"So it remained for the rest of the day and until the Rifle Brigade Platoon arrived in the evening. The following day, the Squadron moved out to the usual positions and were shortly relieved by the Recce Squadron of the 1st Royal Tank Regiment. They shared a brew of tea and the positions were explained to the relieving troops. The Tanks sent a patrol straight up the main road and lost two Honeys and a Cromwell. Bazooka men were waiting at the cross tracks. The patrolling continued like this with hardly a day when there was nothing to report. Charles de Selliers had now been attached to Recce and frequently joined the Dutch civilians when they returned to tend their stock and came back with valuable information.

"The time was not without some humour. Army vehicles which had ignored 'halt' signs further back would come up quite unconcerned and head for 's-Hertogenbosch, believing that it was the route for Brussels. The best way to bring them to a halt was to fire a burst of Browning across the front and then explain the danger they were heading for.

"Sergeant Tom Broad took his tank forward one morning and under cover of mist. As the mist cleared he saw some Germans talking outside a house. An officer went in through the front door and Jack Sell, Tom's gunner, put a 37mm shell in after him. The house obviously contained ammunition and blew up. Corporal Ryan, with Trooper 'Ginger' Ford as his driver, was motoring forward with Lieutenant O'Dowd sitting on the engine cover. They struck a mine which shook Ginger up and caused injury to Mickey's foot. Desmond was thrown off the back and collected a very large black eye from the engine cover."

*Trooper 'Geordie' Stoker* remembers a mission which was a mixture of comedy and danger:

"On a particular day during this period, all the recce troops were out but there was still one road unchecked and suspected of being mined. Lieutenant O'Dowd called me to prepare the Scout car for a simple mission to check this out. We came to a road block constructed from earth and timber and interlaced with wire. We suspected that it contained some very nasty high explosives. There was a large house on the left of the road block and, before any patrol on foot and beyond the obstruction, we would have to check the house. Desmond ordered me to go to the rear of the house while he made a front approach. He was armed with a German sporting rifle while I carried the Bren. I crept cautiously round the house and entered the yard. I was suddenly confronted by the biggest, drooling, snarling Alsatian I had ever seen. It leapt at me. I must have jumped back six feet myself before pulling the trigger and emptying the complete magazine into it (poor b . . . . .) This brought Mr O'Dowd to the rear of the house to investigate. He was naturally very apprehensive. Then he looked at the brute lying there motionless and pointed out that it was on a very thick chain—I was very pleased to note that!

"It was decided that, as I had made such a lot of noise, we had lost any chance of a quiet look up the road and the mission was never completely carried out, nor did we discover whether we would have cratered the road if we had tampered with the road block!"

* * * * *

A few managed to get a night out in Eindhoven and some were allowed a 24-hour pass. There was a dance organised in Oss. The local Resistance took upon itself the right to exclude any girls who had ever danced with a German. This to quote Robert Crockett, included all those who were not eighty, grandmothers or deformed. The Resistance order was overruled and the dance was a great success.

The patrolling continued and became more and more difficult. The route could not be varied very much and the times were usually from first light till dusk. Foot patrols were preferred because they had the benefit of stealth and good cover from the ditches. On one occasion, Corporal 'Jock' Wiseman, creeping up a ditch, met a German coming the other way. The Boche was dressed smartly enough for a church parade while Jock felt quite ashamed of his battle dress and rather dirty condition. Both retreated quickly without damage to each other.

On October 17th, the Troop were once more sent out for a final check on held positions before the final assault upon 's-Hertogenbosch. Lieutenant Crocker and Corporal Wiseman were out early and travelled up to the usual daytime position by Scout car. They set out to advance on foot. The rest of the troop was to join them later and arrive by daybreak. As they probed forward they found a German asleep in a trench but, with a view to returning the following day, did not disturb him. The following day they were out again at the same early hour. It was expected that they would return through another Troop position. The remainder of the Troop had just arrived in position at daybreak when the stillness was broken by two rifle shots and followed by a burst of machine-gun fire. Corporal Johnny Dixon looked up the road and, in the morning light, could see Wilfred Crocker lying some distance up the road. He at once ran forward, shouting to the others to follow. Wilfred was very badly wounded and the Scout car which had followed as a back-up, took everyone back. He was able to explain that about a dozen Germans armed with Spandaus and bazookas shot him and left him for dead. Corporal Wiseman had been wounded in the leg and taken prisoner. Wilfred died from loss of blood. Jock Wiseman was the only member of the Regiment taken prisoner during the 1944-45 campaign in Europe. After the war, Mrs Wiseman was told by a Dutch civilian that her husband had either died or been killed on a forced march. He was buried at Duirnbach war cemetery in Germany so must have suffered a terribly long march. The recorded date of death was March 12th 1945, so he had survived for almost five months. The loss of these two heroic men was a sad blow to Recce Squadron and the Regiment.

On the same morning, 3rd Troop of the Reconnaissance Squadron had a happier adventure. Arriving at the house which they used as their OP, they noticed fresh footprints which aroused their suspicion. Sergeant Tom Broad who organised a search, led the way up some steps to the loft where, in the dim light, he could see a pair of jackboots. Their owner lay still. The troop spread itself around the house while 'Pedro' Sharpe and Lieutenant O'Dowd went into the loft. 'Pedro' in the lead, poked his Sten in the direction of the boots and discovered that they were on the feet of a German sergeant major who was encouraged to get to his feet, still clutching a pistol. As he got up he merely said "Kamarad". Though he said he was alone, a thorough search was carried out and 'Pedro' was left to observe through a skylight. Jack Sell, who came to relieve him about half an hour later, noticed movement under the hay. He called Tom Broad and another German was uncovered, armed with a machine pistol. A more thorough search was carried out and yet another German, a corporal, was uncovered.

# The Battle for s'-Hertogenbosch

On October 21st, senior officers came to view the area over which they would have to advance. Supplies had been brought forward and the artillery was ready to support the troops forward. Men of the 53rd (Welch) Division were to bear the brunt of the attack, supported by ourselves and a regiment of flame-throwers. The sun set for the last time behind the distant towers of the magnificent 's-Hertogenbosch Cathedral. The town was full of civilians, desperately short of food, many of whom were to die in the softening up bombing by the RAF before our artillery barrage commenced in the early hours of October 22nd.

*Lieutenant Henry Woods*, of 'C' Squadron, recorded:

"4 Welch Regiment, supported by 'C' Squadron, attacked the northern part of Nulands, which was strongly held. The first phase was to get the Squadron's tanks close to the village and in a position to support the infantry assault with Crocodile flame throwers. 1st Troop on the right and the Crocodile troops were soon bogged in soft ground, from which they extracated themselves only to run into a minefield, breaking tank tracks. 3rd Troop on the left came under intense fire from mortar and machine-guns sited in the village and the woodlands to the left front. Two tanks became bogged and Lieutenant Aykroyd was wounded by mortar fragments. In the centre, 2nd Troop under command of Sergeant Bob Price, managed to advance by avoiding minefields and boggy ground. He forced his way into the outskirts of the village. 4th Troop, commanded by Sergeant Jim Tartt, came forward to relieve 3rd Troop on the left but quickly lost one tank knocked out by a 88mm anti-tank gun. Another tank in the troop became bogged. However, both troops were able to give good supporting fire which, with artillery fire, seemed to silence the 88mm guns.

"Once the village was secured, bogged tanks were extricated and the Squadron reorganised into three troops. Two destroyed 88mm guns were found on a slight crest, 1000 yards beyond the village. Heavy mortar and machine-gun fire was brought down upon our leading troops from the thick woodlands to the left of our advance. Our own heavy fire from the tank Besa's and 75mm forced the enemy back and gave protection to the 4th Welch plodding along behind. Company attacks were made upon pockets of resistance and some prisoners were taken. 4 Welch established an outpost just south of Kruitstraat."

*Major Creagh Gibson,* 'A' Squadron leader, added the following details into the citation which led to the award of the DCM to Sergeant Archie Carr:

"During the night October 23/24th, the East Lancashire Regiment advanced from Rosemalen to the suburbs of 's-Hertogenbosch and it was considered vital that a squadron of tanks should go to their support as quickly as possible. Reconnaissance reported that the ground in this area was completely open, entirely flat, and too marshy to bear the weight of a tank.

"South of the railway, 'B' Squadron and a battalion of infantry were fighting their way forward through an enclosed built-up area and were meeting considerable opposition from enemy 75mm's and two strong points containing two 88mm anti-tank guns. To the north of the railway, the open country was completely dominated by the high banks of the dyke which ran parallel to the railway at a distance ranging from 500 to 1,000 yards, and there was every reason to believe that the enemy was still in position along the banks.

"The only possible route for tanks was along the railway line which ran on an embankment some 15 feet above the level of the fields. The country was such that it was impossible for the remainder of the Squadron to give any fire support. Notwithstanding this, Sergeant Carr showed great determination and dash and led his troop some 1,500 yards along the embankment until it was able to make contact with the East Lancashire Regiment in the town."

*Sergeant Carr* and *Sergeant Albert Morris*, who commanded the tanks in the troop, gave their personal account:

"The long, straight railway line leading into 's-Hertogenbosch was raised and provided a perfect silhouette for any anti-tank gunners. Smoke was to be fired to prevent observation from the dyke where we expected any fire to come from. The Sherman, commanded by Albert Morris which was armed with a 17-pounder gun, led the troop. Progress was agonisingly slow and demanded expert driving to keep the tank straddled across the lines. Any deviation could have resulted in the loss of a track, which would have been fatal. The smoke soon thinned out and the right flank was completely naked. 'I urged the driver to speed up, but he assured me that he was already standing on the accelerator', recalled Albert. 'Our progress seemed painfully slow! I reported that we had reached our position and the rest of the squadron came forward'."

Forty years after this action we were to learn from the Dutch, who had carried out much research into this battle, that there were in fact eight anti-tank guns lined up on the troop but they had used all their ammunition.

The story of 'C' Squadron's action is continued by *Lieutenant Henry Woods:*

"We advanced from Rosemalen railway station and were just short of a forked road junction. First Troop on the left flank were very

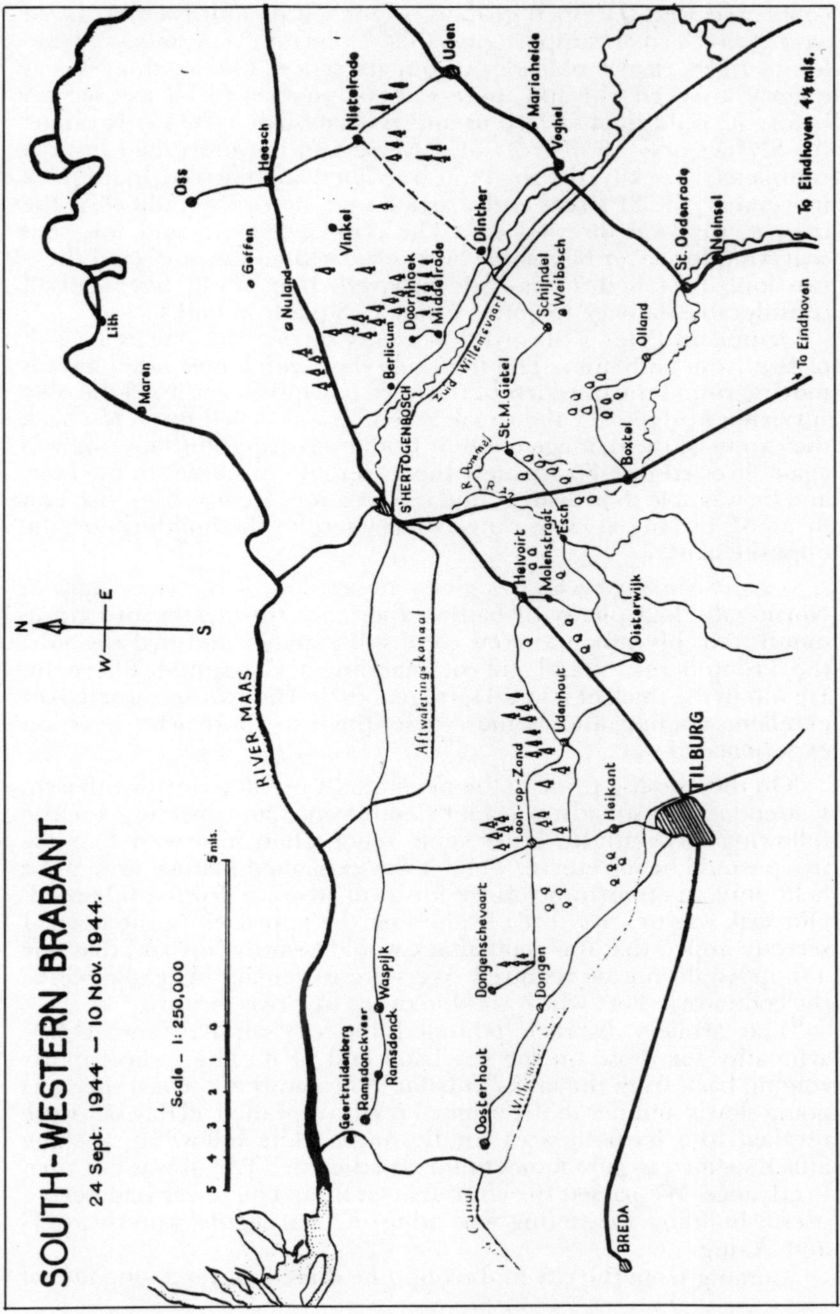
SOUTH-WESTERN BRABANT
24 Sept. 1944 – 10 Nov. 1944.
Scale – 1: 250,000
5 4 3 2 1 0
5 mls.
N
E
S
W
RIVER MAAS
Aftwaterings kanaal
Wilhelmina
Canal
Zuid Willemsvaart
R. Dommel
S'HERTOGENBOSCH
TILBURG
BREDA
Geertruidenberg
Ramsdonckveer
Ramsdonck
Waspijk
Oosterhout
Dongen
Dongenschevaart
Loon-op-Zand
Heikant
Udenhout
Oisterwijk
Helvoirt
Molenstraat
Esch
Boxtel
St. M. Gistel
Schijndel
Weibosch
Olland
St. Oedenrode
Neinsel
Dinther
Veghel
Mariaheide
Uden
Nistelrode
Vinkel
Doornhoek
Middelrode
Berlicum
Nuland
Geffen
Oss
Heesch
Lith
Maren
To Eindhoven
To Eindhoven 4½ mls.

concerned with the open ground on their left. Third Troop faced west. Two German support guns (SPs) came into view, moving from left to right, clearly oblivious of our presence. The leading SP was quickly knocked out and there was then a race to hit the second before it could turn to face us and retaliate from 400 yards range. An SP had only 16 degrees of traverse and therefore had to turn completely. Luckily, the road was tree-lined and narrow. In its quick movement, the SP's rear end struck a tree. Before it could clear the tree, it, too, was 'brewed up'. The crew baled out and was sent scurrying for cover by a short burst of machine-gun fire. Had these two long barrelled 75mm SPs survived, they could have caused considerable damage to both 'A' and 'C' Squadron tanks."

Lieutenant Peter Walworth lost a tank during this day as a result of fire from an 88mm. The following day, with a new tank, he was moving round the outskirts of the town to capture and hold the only surviving bridge over the canal, when he was called upon to check the extent of the damage to other bridges. During this move he was again 'brewed up'. Fortunately there were no casualties to the crew and he was able to provide sound information. He had been fired on by an SP lurking at close range somewhere in the buildings on the opposite bank.

*Sergeant Syd Swift* who has given an account of the early days in Normandy, had plenty of battle experience during the preceding months but his tank and crew were still together and Syd was now the Troop Sergeant and still commanding a 17-pounder Sherman. He was in the thick of it at 's-Hertogenbosch. His own account makes excellent reading and is most descriptive to those who have no experience of war:

"On the evening prior to the main attack upon 's-Hertogenbosch, I attended the squadron leader's conference and briefing for the following day's attack. I felt some relief when informed that my troop would be in reserve. Then it was explained that we were to be held until an opportunity arose for us to advance down a side road. Our task was to seize three bridges on the approach to the town. I secretly hoped that the main attack would be a success and that our Troop would not be required. We were to remain in readiness for the code word 'Pot', which was the order to move forward.

"The artillery barrage pounded the city all day and I had sympathy for those on the receiving end of it. The radio reports coming back from the tanks in front indicated that the advance was going slowly and not to the original plan. We waited all day but were recalled to a harbour area for the night. The following day, the attack seemed to gain momentum and then . . . 'Pot', it was our turn to advance. We passed the church at Geffen. The tower had been a useful building for testing and adjusting our sights, known as 'T' and 'A'-ing.

"Coming from the city in the opposite direction was a long line of refugees, bedraggled and dazed after the bombing and the barrage. We took a track beside the main road, past smouldering houses. What a contrast to the cheering crowds in Belgium. These people were sullen and dazed and must have wondered whose side we were on. The Squadron Leader's voice came over the air: 'Get a move on'. I looked at my watch and noted that it was almost 1600 hours. We had advanced about six miles. The country was flat and on each side was a deep dyke. We were restricted to the track. The first real hold-up came when we encountered some small mounds of earth on the road in front of us. It was assumed that the Germans had hastily laid mines there. The leading tank reported the obstruction. 'I think we can just squeeze past them', he reported. 'Hurry', came the reply. The tank pulled off the track and on to the verge separating the track and canal. As I watched anxiously, there was a blinding flash. The verge, and not the track, had been mined. The tank continued forward, gathering up its track as it went, then hurled it forward and off its rollers. Finally it stopped and the crew baled out. Fortunately none of them was hurt. They thought they had been hit by an 88mm shell. When they found the tank intact apart from the track, they climbed back in for comparative safety. Although prevented from movement, it was still a fighting machine and capable of doing a useful job.

"Mortars began to fall uncomfortably close. I searched the area with my binoculars and thought I could detect movement in one of the houses away from the road on my right. We fired a round at the house and out came a party of Germans with their hands held high. We were still being urged forward by our HQ. 'Keep moving' was the order of the day. A Flail tank fitted with chains to a roller to detonate mines ahead now joined us. Just as it edged past me, my tank received a direct hit. The shell landed on the engine covers at the rear. It shook us all up but did no great damage. The Flail continued to thrash a way up to the point where we knew the road was mined. The chains beat the road thoroughly but there was no explosion. We had been fooled by the mounds of earth. German anti-tank guns were brought to counter the Flail and struck it with two shots which did little damage. A tank behind me was also hit and caught fire. We decided to put down a barrier of smoke in front of us to cover our movements. As the Flail pulled to the rear and was passing me, I recognised the commander as an old friend whom I had last served with on the North-west Frontier of India. It was a strange meeting—both of us wearing different cap badges and playing a different role from the infantry days in the Duke of Wellington's Regiment. It was a short meeting but I was cheered to meet an old friend. It was getting dark; obviously we would not get into the city that day. We withdrew for replenishment and rest.

"In the early morning of the following day, we entered 's-Hertogenbosch without too much opposition. The terrific bombardment had caused terrible destruction. As a lover of old buildings, I was saddened. However, I had little time to dwell upon this destruction. We were still being urged forward. The tracks crunched over tiles and bricks as we sped towards our target, to take and hold the bridges. As we neared the first crossing, a loud explosion rocked the city and a huge column of smoke rose skyward, billowing above the the buildings, then lazily hanging in the still air. One of the bridges had been blown. 'Speed up' came the order. Now forsaking all normal caution we hastened through the unfamiliar streets. We reached the first bridge and were in sight of the second when that, too, was destroyed. The whole bridge lifted in a most spectacular way. A black, dirty cloud hid the destruction of a bridge which had been there for hundreds of years. When the smoke cleared we found that, although the main structure had been destroyed, the lock gates remained intact. I radioed back and described the damage. Fortunately, the infantry could still get across. As the infantry formed up to storm the crossing point, I moved away from the bridge. On the opposite bank there were a number of warehouses. To the left was flat open country. We gave covering fire by pounding away at the warehouses. A flame-thrower came forward and shot a stream of liquid fire across the canal. I saw a lamp post engulfed in flame. The flame was directed at another target but the lamp post remained burning fiercely. A German ran from a pill box, screaming. It was a ghastly sight as he became completely engulfed in flames. We kept up our fire while the infantry raced across the lock gate in single file. Only one man was wounded during this bold operation. They moved into the streets away from us and we were withdrawn.

"That night we leaguered in a farmyard which looked as though it had been a key distribution point for stores. Equipment lay everywhere. A haystack was burning in a glow of red ash. The embers were about 12ft in diameter and the heat from it was terrific. There was a large orchard to the rear of the yard but the light from the fire made it appear black and forbidding. I decided to ensure that no Germans had been left there. I stumbled over many, but they were all dead. I realised what an important point this must have been. There was clothing, equipment, ammunition, mines, picks and shovels, and a pile of boxes and crates. After a meal, we slept near the fire to absorb its warmth. The following day we were withdrawn to the Heesch area, our mission completed.

"The Division's next task was to clear Tilburg. The countryside was becoming very familiar, flat and covered with heather and gorse dotted with small trees. We advanced along a concrete road. There were reports coming over my radio informing us that the enemy was defending points ahead. Leading the Squadron, we left the road and drove along a track, through a small plantation and into open country. Ahead lay a thicker wood made up of deciduous and coniferous trees. I was suddenly aware that we were on fire. Smoke billowed from the engine covers. Fire is the fear of all tank crews:

with perhaps 150 gallons of fuel and a number of sensitive grenades and shells stowed below, the machine is a fire bomb itself. Normally, when a tank is hit in the engine, petrol flows under the turret and rapidly envelops the crew. 'Bale out', I ordered. We seemed to hit the ground together and ran for cover. The commander in the following tank sized up our plight and fired his smoke cannisters over our heads. Taking his tank in a wide sweep behind the smoke, he came back and picked us up. We drove to the cover of the nearest trees. We gazed at our beloved tank, now engulfed in flame. The blankets and rubber tracks burned fiercely and flames from the turret and engine were reaching heights of 30 feet. We had been the victim of a German SP. All we owned was what we stood in. A vehicle from the echelon came forward and took us to the rear, where we were quickly rekitted, given a meal and found a billet. We slept deeply with a feeling of safety.

"There was a family living in the house with six children, the youngest was a baby. I was horrified to see the mother feeding it on apples which she had mashed up in a frying pan. My fatherly instinct was to inform her that this was not good food for a child of such tender years, but she indicated that it was all she had. We decided to help. Since there were no individual rations to be had in the echelon, a central feeding point was arranged. We queued for a mess tin full of whatever was on offer, took it back to the house and emptied it into a container, then returned for a second helping. Though viewed with suspicion, we got away with it by saying that we were growing lads! As we had nothing to do, Dick and Smudger volunteered to help with the cooking. They always returned with extra rations. The reward was to see the child, now sucking its thumb, looking well and laughing like a normal child. Leave centres had opened up in Brussels. As we had no tank, we were the obvious choice. We were taken by army truck to the Hôtel des Colonies, near the main station, where we were given VIP treatment and slept in sheets again."

In 1986, Sergeants Pat Whitmore and Syd Swift returned to 's-Hertogenbosch for a ceremony to open a 'Welch' room where souvenirs are housed with the many gifts presented during the anniversary weekend in 1985. They had time to make a more detailed visit to Geffen. Through the endeavours of Agnes van Gent, wife of Luc van Gent, who has been the inspiration behind our renewed association with the city, they were able to trace two members of a family named Broeksteeg. Pat recalls:

"I can remember the name after all those years. Their farm, a few hundred metres south of Geffen, was in 'No-man's land' which we patrolled during the period October 1st to 21st 1944, preparatory to the battle. Mevrouw Broeksteeg, now 81, to whom we spoke through an interpreter. recalled the arrival of the Regiment and mentioned two people whom she called 'De Dikke' (The Fat One) i.e. Sergeant

'Tiny' Wootton, and 'De Lange' (The Thin One) which was me. Her daughter, Sjaan van Rhee, who had previously received us in her flat in Venlo, recalled sitting on the tank and being given compo chocolate and sweets. Mevrouw Broeksteeg now lives very close to the spot where Tiny Wootton shot a goat which, he alleges, replied in German when he challenged it one dark night while denying the enemy access to the tower of Geffen church."

Before leaving the story of the Battle for 's-Hertogenbosch, there were many glowing tributes paid to the Regiment by the numerous regiments in the 53rd (Welch) Division worthy of recording. The first was from Headquarters, 160th (SW) Infantry Brigade, and dated October 24th 1944. It was addressed to Major-General R. K. Ross, DSO, MC, the 53rd Division Commander:

"Dear General

"I wish to place on record my appreciation for the excellent support accorded the Brigade by the 5th Royal Inniskilling Dragoon Guards during Operation 'Alan'. The work of the Squadrons has been the admiration of every man of this Brigade and their assistance has been really magnificent. We are all most grateful to them.

"I should also like to say how much I appreciated the help and advice of Lieutenant Colonel J. E. Swetenham, which he gave unstintingly throughout the operation. I hope we shall be fortunate enough to have them with us again in the future.

Signed: C. M. Coleman"

Major-General Ross passed this tribute on to our own GOC of the 7th Armoured Division:

"Dear Verney,

"It is with great pleasure that I forward to you the attached tribute, which I can personally enthusiastically confirm.

"160 (SW) Brigade is my old Brigade which I commanded for some two and a half years. I knew them well. Since the battle I have had the chance of talking to a great number of the men and have heard their experiences. One and all are loud in their praises of the tank support they received throughout the action—and they are the chaps who really know.

"During most of the battle Swetenham was in support of 160 (SW) Brigade but he also supported 158 Brigade whose officers and men are equally emphatic. The dash of the squadron along the railway embankment to the support of the battalion of 158 Brigade who had obtained a footing in the town by a night advance, when there was every reason to believe the enemy was still in strength on both sides at about 400 yards range, was magnificent and typical of the dash and élan of the whole regiment throughout the action.

"The complete success of the 160 Brigade, as they are the first to admit, was in no small measure due to the magnificent support they received from the regiment, whose one thought was to get the infantry on and who were apparently entirely oblivious of the dangers to tanks that lurk in hedgerows, street corners etc.

"I only hope, as does Coleman, that we will be lucky enough to have their support again in the future.

Signed: Bobby Ross."

On October 27th, having had a two-day stay in Muggenhoek and Boxtel, the Regiment was again in action. In the Recce Troop, a 4th Troop had been added and placed under command of Lieutenant Peter Duckworth, who had been posted in from another regiment. He had seen plenty of action and rapidly impressed his subordinates. Second and Third Troop turned north in support of 'B' Squadron and then advanced eastwards. In the thickly wooded country, Third Troop (Recce) took a wrong turning. A bazooka was fired at them but fortunately missed. Sergeant Tom Broad shot the firer. This showed them at least where they ought not to have been. They were joined by Fourth Troop.

A Troop of the Cherrypickers (11th Hussars) was observed firing into the end of a large wood. Fourth Troop made its way to the opposite end. Sergeant Ted Glynn's tank suffered a complete electrical failure and Sergeant Tom Wagstaff pulled past him to take the lead. Immediately, a bazooka man stood up and fired at 'Waggie's' tank from point-blank range and scored a direct hit on the turret. The driver immediately put his tank into reverse, but a second bazooka struck the front. This was followed by a phosphorous grenade which burst on the hull. The tank ran backwards, completely out of control, and ran off the track. The carrier crew, commanded by Corporal Ginger Proudlove, shot up the attacker and then raced after the tank with a fire extinguisher to put out the fire. But the damage was done: Sergeant Wagstaff, who had been a personal friend for many years, Trooper Sid Parr, and 'Ginger' Percival had been killed instantly and Trooper 'Nipper' Daley died from his wounds.

Hardly had the troops recovered from this disaster before a sniper took advantage of the situation and shot and badly wounded Corporal Bob Edwards. Recce Squadron was withdrawn to regroup but, during the withdrawal, an anti-tank gun fired a shot in front of and behind Tom Broad's tank. Ted Glynn's tank, driven by Corporal Ted Hughes, was found to have some burned-out wiring and had to be recovered after dark. It had been a dark day for the Squadron. To add to their misery, it rained all night and they were shelled periodically.

After the liberation of Tilburg and the easing of the supply position there followed a mopping-up operation to clear German troops from west of the Rhine. That was still a formidable task, for the Germans were fighting on their own soil. There were a few days' relaxation, some to take advantage of the hospitality of Malines, where an ex-officer of the Regiment, Major Bill Barraclough, ran a leave centre. Brussels was in a liberation mood. There was again time to write those letters of condolence to give what comfort one could to those who were bereaved.

Eight men were buried in the Uden cemetery and each had played a major part in the battle. Major Gibson wrote this letter to the parents of Trooper Wood:

"Dear Mr Wood

"It is my painful duty to have to tell you that your son is wounded and has been missing since September 26th, but I know that there were Germans about where the incident occurred and I believe they would have given him all the medical attention possible. As far as I am aware they have always treated our wounded well.

"The incident occurred when we had been fighting all day and a German carrying a Red Cross flag had been wandering about the battlefield, presumably dressing the wounded. His actions, however, were suspicious and when I saw him walking off with four apparently able-bodied Germans, I thought it my duty to investigate further. I accordingly sent the Troop to which your son belonged to apprehend them.

"When they were some 100 yards from them and 50 yards from a thick hedge, your son's tank was hit by a bazooka and caught fire, but this caused no harm to the crew inside. As they were getting out of the tank they were machine-gunned by the Boche and your son was hit in the leg and could not get away.

"The Troop Leader immediately volunteered to go and bring your son back. He got to within 50 yards of the tank when his own was hit and the crew had to bale out. Two of the crew from your son's tank had managed to crawl a little way from their vehicle and made a dash towards the Troop Leader's tank. During the course of this, one of them was badly hit and the Troop Leader, without regard for his own safety, went forward on foot and carried the man back to safety. I am glad to say that the Troop Leader and his crew came back safely.

"In the meantime, your son had dropped down from his own tank on which he was sitting and into a ditch in which there were Germans.

"As you will realise from the above, we were up against a particularly strong force and it was humanly impossible to get your son back. We are all deeply concerned over the affair and offer you our deepest sympathy, I would like you to know that your son has been quite splendid throughout this campaign, during which time he has been employed as a gunner and wireless operator. He has always been cheerful, co-operative and reliable, and was most popular with everyone. He is a great loss to the Squadron and particularly his many friends, but I am full of hope that when this war is over you will see him safe and sound once again. I have told you the simple truth and hidden nothing from you as I feel sure that you would like the fullest details possible."

N.B. The Troop Leader was again Sergeant Archie Carr who carried LCpl Charlesworth to safety.

Mr Wood replied:

"I am grieved to inform you that I received a letter from the Royal Armoured Corps Record Office notifying me of the death of my son on September 26th. The report is to the effect that he was killed in action on September 26th, 1944."

Major Creagh Gibson answered:

"It is with a heavy heart that I write this letter. I have to tell you that your son was killed on September 26th. We discovered his body some days later. This was the first day we were able to get up to his tank. It may be some consolation to you to know that we are of the opinion that he must have been killed almost immediately after he dropped into the ditch.

"I did not tell you in my first letter, but shortly after we saw him do this, a shell pitched just where he dropped and, from the evidence, it is clear that this must have caused his instant death, so I do not think he suffered very much at all.

"I have written many sad letters since this campaign started, but none has grieved me as much as this. If I may say so, your son was of the kind that makes England the kind of country she is. I cannot pay him higher compliments than to say he possessed all the qualities that go to make up a brave Englishman.

"If I am spared this war I should very much like to meet you when it is all over. I will retain your address and as my wife comes from close to where you live I will take the first opportunity of calling on you.

Creagh Gibson."

There had been another terrible tragedy in which one of our most popular NCOs, Sergeant 'Darky' Bowley, was killed. Tiredness, fatigue, familiarity with dangerous weapons, all played some part in a freak accident. Darky was standing on the engine cover of his tank whilst other crew members were checking their areas of responsibility—drivers looking at tracks, operators netting their radios, and gunners making last-minute adjustments and oiling guns. Suddenly, from one of the tanks near that of Sergeant Bowley's, came a loud explosion as the 75mm was fired accidentally. the shell struck poor Sergeant Bowley and he died almost instantly.

How do you describe such tragedy to a wife, and later to a child, and how does the gunner and commander of the tank who had failed to ensure that the safety catch was applied, live with that responsibility?

# The Noose Tightens

Hitler had threatened to wring our necks after Dunkirk. Winston Churchill had responded, in one of his most famous wartime speeches: "Some chicken . . . some neck". London was still being pounded by V2 rockets launched from further up the Dutch coast, but air attacks had ceased and the battle for the seas had eased. Convoys were getting through without loss and our aircrews were meeting less resistance from the Luftwaffe.

In the autumn of 1944, some street lights were permitted and blackout boards removed in the northern and western counties of Britain. Our hospitals were filled to capacity with the wounded of both sides. The Italians, now fighting with the Allies, were allowed to travel to and from their camps quite freely and were employed on the farms and manually in other industries. Our troops in Italy were fighting hard and winning.

In eastern Europe, the Russians were forcing the Germans back into their own country and at much the same pace as ourselves in the west. We did not know of the terrible atrocities which would be unearthed in the concentration camps, a polite name for extermination centres.

Hitler and his henchmen were doomed men and knew it. It is not surprising that he ordered his generals to fight and hold the Rhine crossings against all odds. Those in the fighting line still had concern for their families at home and had to face the news of "dead or missing" telegrams relayed from home. There was an urgency and desire to get on with it and to get home and back to normal life.

In the Far East, the Japanese were also suffering defeat from our 14th Army and the Americans, but they occupied a vast continent and there was a lot to be done to clear them from the many islands they held in the Pacific.

The Regiment, after a short break, was moved south into the small neck of Holland sandwiched between Germany and Belgium. Comfortable billets were found and the Dutch people were magnificent. It was now December 21st and some thought could be given to a Christmas celebration.

Munstergeleen is a mining area and the pit-head baths were far better than our own in Britain. The modern facilities were put to excellent use and much enjoyed. Lieutenants Peter Duckworth and Ben Tottenham produced a Regimental Revue, at which they gave an excellent impersonation of the "Western Brothers" in a monologue "It's frightfully 5 DG". John Pilborough, Tony Price and Bob Sawtell wrote their own monologue, "Push on, Recce, Push on". A dance was arranged and, yet again, the girls were discouraged by a local priest. He enjoyed only limited success in this contest, the girls being as eager as the troops to have a party.

Winter was upon us and freezing conditions prevailed. Hurricane lamps were left burning in turrets all night and engines had to be run every two hours to prevent freezing. The oil on machine-guns froze and had to be removed. All crews were issued with white clothing to camouflage them in the snow and even the tanks were painted white. Some fresh rations of meat, rice and flour made a change from the Compo rations, though some appointed cook for the day made a blunder or two. It is reported that one man made porridge with flour in lieu of powdered milk and another had a go at pancakes but, unfortunately, reversed the quantities of baking powder and flour. The result was a great puff-ball.

Major Bill Barraclough's leave centre in Malines was very popular if only to act as a base for those who spent their time in Brussels. Goods appeared in the shops, giving troops a chance to send presents home, including nylon stockings, which had been long out of supply in the UK.

Crews were now clothed in "Oversuits, tank-crew" and a white smock. The oversuit was a one-piece, well-lined articles of clothing with many pockets and zips which allowed the whole thing to be opened up from top to bottom. Though a little cumbersome to run in, it offered good protection against the cold. The radio head-set could be worn under the hood and at night, it served as an excellent extra blanket.

There was some excitement when the Luftwaffe made an unexpected appearance on New Year's Day, 1945, as part of their last attempt to counter-attack in the Ardennes. Our divisional gunners brought down eight aircraft in a day. The main attack was against the bridges across the flooded Maas. The cinema at Sittard, the town to which the Regiment had moved in readiness for the next stage in our advance, also received some attention from guns which were reported to be situated in the much-publicised Siegfried Line.

The enemy, using captured US equipment, had some success in a drive to split the Americans in the south and our own forces in the north. The target was Brussels. Jeeps carrying supposedly American soldiers were treated with suspicion, as were our own troops in the American area. The renewed attack by the Germans served as yet another reminder that there was no room for complacency.

Germany is a large country and would have to be cleared house by house. There would be no friendly greetings there. On January 10th, 1945, the Regiment moved to villages nearer to the front at Grevenbicht and Papenhoven. The ice and snow made the journey a lengthy one. The Recce Squadron had hardly parked their tanks in readiness for a meal when one of the troops was briefed for a night foot patrol to man an outpost on the Juliana Canal. It was a bitter night, the coldest of the year, and the outpost consisted of a dugout in the bank of the canal, on the enemy side and half a mile from the nearest crossing. A bottle of rum helped to keep out the cold. At this time, the enemy positions were unknown, and the outpost was manned for a number of nights.

The Regiment was to support our Divisional infantry in clearing a triangle, the apex of which was Roermond. Movement over the frozen fields was very slow and even land mines, which we sometimes ran over, were so frozen that they failed to detonate. The Germans could not dig holes to bury these mines in the hard ground and often left their long, box-type 'Regal' mines on the road surface, covered with snow. The only way to remove them was to attach a length of wire to a handle, the other to a tank, and drag them clear. Anti-lifting devices often set them off.

It was quickly established that the area was defended by parachutists. There was a fairly large town, Echt, to be cleared, then St Joost and Montfort, a largish town crowded with refugees.

The operation, code-named 'Op Blackcock', started on January 16th. The 1st Royal Tank Regiment pushed into Echt and soon met heavy resistance from well-placed anti-tank guns and bazooka men. They lost a number of tanks. The Regiment was to pass through Echt and, supported by 1/5th Queen's, to capture and hold Montfort. 'A' Squadron moved via Schilberg and Hingen, 'B' via Steil and Aan der berg, a crossroads in the northern outskirts of Montfort (forever to be called Aandenberg by 'B' Squadron).

Many bridges were found to have been destroyed but, since they spanned narrow gaps they could be replaced by 'Scissor bridges' though this slowed the pace. The Recce Squadron was ordered forward to relieve the 8th Hussars at a stream half a mile from Montfort. 'B' Squadron relieved other troops of the Hussars but could not advance until the Engineers arrived with more bridging kit. It was late afternoon on January 22nd when the bridge was finally in position and a Troop of 'B' Squadron crossed. Supported by men of the Rifle Brigade, they moved forward to capture Aan der berg. Montfort and the suburbs had been heavily bombed by the RAF and presented an eerie sight in the light of burning houses and the reflection of light from searchlights off low cloud, nicknamed 'Monty's Moonlight'.

4th Troop, 'B' Squadron, commanded by Lieutenant Roger de Grey, was Sergeant Syd Swift's troop, but it moved forward without him because his tank had been in collision with a truck during the move forward and his traversing gear had been damaged. Nor did they have the promised supporting infantry from 1/5th Queen's but, instead, had a platoon from the Rifle Brigade. The Troop edged forward and into a desperate battle with the German paratroopers: burning houses, the crackle of small-arms fire, shouting, and the crash of mortar bombs. At 2200 hours the leading company of the Queen's arrived and joined the night battle. The leading tank of 4th Troop was struck by a bazooka and caught fire killing Barry

Goulding, Larry Fison, and Jimmy Reid. The Troop Leader, Lieutenant de Grey and Crew Commander, Corporal Starr, were wounded. Syd Swift mourned his men with this poem, in which he wrote:

A tree looked on with sorrowing sigh,
As with heavy hearts we carried them by.
Grieving, we laid them down to rest,
Three flowers of youth, who had given their best.

The frozen earth had been made to yield,
To provide a grave in a foreign field.
In the cold, cold soil we left them there,
With the sorrowing tree, leafless and bare.

Farewell gaunt and weeping tree.
Guard well the gift of our comrades three.
We cannot, like you, remain in sorrow,
There will be more war and a battle tomorrow.

We bade our comrades a last farewell,
Our sorrowing eyes, our grief to tell,
Choked and unhappy, we stumble away,
The weeping tree left to softly sway.

As we move away across the snow-covered plain,
The space in the Troop leaves an aching pain.
I think of that tree, its branches undressed,
Guarding our comrades in eternal rest.

Rest you well, my comrades three,
Beneath the shade of that sorrowing tree.
I will remember you, young and gay,
While we grow older, day by day.

The Recce Troop sent forward to reconnoitre the small bridge leading into Montfort also suffered casualties. They reported the destruction of the bridge and asked for a Scissors bridge to span the gap. Lieutenant O'Dowd led the troop back to farm buildings beside a ruined castle, parking his scout car beside the old ramparts while the Troop searched the area. In the half light they found Dutch civilians who had been sheltering in cellars for the three days since the RAF bombed Montfort. Informed by them that there were no Germans left, the Troop prepared breakfast while Lieutenant O'Dowd, Corporal Bob Sawtell and Troopers George Webster and Paddy Byrne, his driver, took a closer look at the old castle. Suddenly there was a loud explosion, followed by a long burst of machine-gun fire as enemy troops fired from the castle wall. A bazooka struck the empty Scout car.

Sergeant Bert Moule and the remainder of the Troop emerged from the farm, uncertain in the poor light of the whereabouts of the other party and were caught by Spandau fire while in the open.

'Busty' Woolley was hit in the stomach. Others made a dash for the tank and brought it round to deal with the unseem enemy. The walls of the castle were three feet thick and impervious to the 37mm and Browning machine-gun fire. But it was effective enough to keep the enemy heads down while Woolley was loaded on to the 'Sawn-off' and returned to where the Scissors bridge was being laid and our medical half-track vehicle was positioned.

Attempts to recover the abandoned Scout car, which still contained maps and codes, were met with concentrated enemy rifle fire, so it was decided to destroy the vehicle. John Pilborough fired one round from his 37mm and it caught fire at once.

Later in the day, when our infantry could be brought in, the area was cleared and the whole of the Recce Squadron used the farm and castle as a billet for further operations. The following morning shellfire, reported to be coming from the Siegfried Line, registered a direct hit on one of the barns and wounded Sergeant 'Ginty' Gilliland, Trooper Jeff Ward, and Lance Corporal Tony Price. Tony died three days later from his wounds.

It was at this time that I rejoined the squadron, having recovered well after four months hospital treatment. On January 18th, I with a draft of crew commanders was taken from Crowborough, Sussex, to join a tank landing craft at Tilbury. On the first night, a strong wind prevented the ship from leaving dock. It also snowed, and we were ordered to remain in the watertight compartments around the side of the cargo deck. I have never found out where the ship took us, but a journey which should have taken a few hours lasted four days, during which we were only allowed to leave our accommodation for meals. German E-boats were still operating from around Dunkirk and we supposed that we had taken a long, zig-zag course to confuse them as well as ourselves.

There was yet another event played out in the Vilvoord transit camp which could have prevented the completion of this book. During my stay in hospital and convalescence, I was sent a certificate signed by the Adjutant requesting that I should be returned to my own regiment. Captain Maurice Peters, mentioned as the RSM in pre-war years, and Corporal Bill Peate, awarded the MM on the day I had been wounded, were also on the draft. There was a lot of antiaircraft fire during the night as German planes flew low along the coast to supply their troops cut off along the French coast. In the morning, however, we were assembled and as vehicles arrived from numerous armoured regiments, we were relieved to see that one had been sent for us. RSM Woods, in command of the parade, was passed a list of names. We had presented our certificates and quietly waited for our names to be called.

The RSM was giving no priority to anyone and compared his first list with a second one, which obviously gave numbers required to reinforce each regiment. He started with the 1st Royal Tank Regiment, and, to our amazement, ordered us to board the vehicle from that regiment. "No", we protested. "We are to return to the Skins." "Place your kit in the truck," came the firm order. At this point Maurice Peters came down the rear of the parade and quietly said, "Follow me". He climbed into the cab of the truck from the Regiment and told us to get in the back. We left the camp hurriedly and with RSM Woods making enough noise to frighten the Germans in Berlin. We comforted ourselves with the certain knowledge that we had obeyed the last command, and that of an officer!

[In 1949 I was supporting the Cheshire Yeomanry at a Brigade football match when there was a bellow from a supporter on the opposite touchline. I noticed that it was the RSM of the opposing team and was immediately reminded of the Vilvoord incident. I discreetly enquired what his name was. "RSM Woods", I was informed!]

Our truck slithered slowly down the long road towards the front in a bitter cold that caused us to stamp about to keep warm. Whenever there was a halt of any length, we dismounted and walked ahead. In the early evening we arrived in a village somewhere on the Belgian-Dutch border where our 'B' echelon was billeted and where we had a happy reunion with old friends and were brought up to date with casualties and the dangers ahead.

Bill Peate and I had settled down with a liberal ration of rum when someone came into the room and a hush fell upon the gathering. In the poor light I could see that it was an officer—it was my old friend and scourge of the idle, Jack Robinson. He greeted us warmly, particularly Bill Peate, who had been closely associated with him during the cavalry days. Both were excellent horsemen. I enquired where Captain Fred Robson was and was told that he had been badly injured in a Jeep accident.

The following day I was in a very nice billet with a Dutch family. The gunfire from the front was continuous and I was beginning to wonder how I would cope with all that again. I hoped for a day or two in the billet teaching the family English! At 4 p.m., however, Corporal Cyril Lomas, an old friend and despatch rider arrived to take me in a Jeep to join the Recce Squadron. I now had a nice warm tank suit with a hood, so the journey was easier than the one we had endured the previous day.

Arriving at the old castle I found my old friends Sergeant Reg Worman, Captain Robert Crockett, and many others, and was taken into the farmhouse and met the other members of the Squadron, who included four new officers—Lieutenants Peter Duckworth, Tony Rickards, Desmond O'Dowd, and the mad Belgian, Charles de Selliers. I was brought up to date with the fate of old friends, particularly Tom Wagstaff and Ginty, who had been wounded with Tony Price in this very building that morning. The officers sized me up and were very friendly and I was delighted to be back among real men, feeling that there was a job to do again after the long lay-off in the UK. They listened intently to my stories of V2 damage and of the delight in having lights restored in the North and North-west. I had met other wounded friends who would never be fit enough to return.

In the morning Robert Crockett sent for me, he went over the story of the death of Tom Wagstaff and his entire crew, then pointed to a "Sawn-off" Stuart. "That was his tank," he said. "Now it's yours. Get it sorted out." I knew nearly all the men in the Troop under the command of Desmond O'Dowd. My crew would be my old friend Jock Ramsey, Bob Sawtell who had driven the Sherman on the move in France, and Taffy Willingale. The others soon noted that we all had something wrong with us: Jock had a bad speech impediment, Bob wore rather thick spectacles, Taffy was very deaf, and I still limped a bit. There were friendly gibes about a load of invalids and enquiries as to whether we would like some walking sticks. We carried on regardless. The guns were sorted out, the radio checked, and I drew up some local maps. A final but very important piece of equipment—a small primus-type cooker—was cleaned to perfection and given a test run. Now we were ready for whatever was to come.

I walked across the small Scissors bridge into Montfort, which was now firmly in our hands. The destruction and smell there was awful. More than 200 civilians had been killed in our bombing and shelling and others now faced the bitter winter cold without fuel or food and would have to be evacuated. The 'B' Squadron tank was still where it had been knocked out and burned, and there was the smell of death about the place. This was war again, in all its evil. Montfort would have to be rebuilt.

Early in the afternoon, Desmond O'Dowd told us to prepare to move, to take a look at a large house on the west side of a little village right up on the Roer. Our own tanks were in action and there had been casualties, particularly from mines. It was made plain to me that I was going to have to prove my ability, but I was more concerned with proving it to myself. It was almost like the first days in action in Normandy and I accepted the challenge and set off in the lead.

We soon came to the tell-tale lumps in the road that we knew to be 'Regal' mines. We brushed the snow off the first of them and I carefully lifted the lid, only to find that the mine itself was frozen to the road and, for all we knew, could still have an anti-lifting device under it. We removed the fuses, tied a length of signal cable to a handle, got well out of the way and let the tank pull it clear. Five mines in all were removed in this way and placed on the side of the road.

We set off again, this time across country and towards a belt of trees which lay between us and our objective house. I halted the tank beside a pile of earth, resembling a potato or swede clamp. From behind this cover I could just see the house which showed no signs of life, though the rattle of tank machine-gun fire over to the right told us that something was there. When the other tanks arrived and took up a similar position, Lieutenant Desmond O'Dowd called crew commanders over to his vehicle and asked: "How do we do this, Corporal Boardman?" I was flattered to be asked. "We can't take the tanks any closer," I replied. "They are too noisy and, in any case, the drive-way is probably mined. We'll have to do it on foot." "OK" replied Desmond. "You lead the way." Leaving the operators of each vehicle to cover us, while the remainder peered cautiously over the top of the potato clamp, I slid down the other side and ran flat out for the nearest tree. Nothing happened, though I seemed to have made a lot of noise, so I ran to the next tree, again without arousing any signs of life. Another move forward took me about 50 yards into the wood, which I judged to be the limit of my lone advance. As I looked back, expecting someone to come up and join me, Desmond stuck his head over the mound and waved at me with his pistol, indicating that I should go on. Feeling very isolated, I moved to the next protective tree and again waited. The next move would bring me to the house, so I looked back and waved to indicate that someone should come forward to cover me. Bob Sawtell and Paddy Byrne came up. "What's the matter with everybody?" I asked. "Mr O'Dowd said that he doesn't want more than one casualty on this job," was the reply.

A dead German lay face down in the snow outside the door. I made a run for the house, followed by the other two, still without reaction from the enemy or my back-ups. We gathered by the wall and I cautiously pushed the door open to reveal a terrified family—a man, woman and two children—huddled in the room. Bob and Paddy, who had picked up a smattering of Dutch, learned from them that there were no Germans around, so the remainder of our party arrived to search the house and the other buildings, which were on three sides of a courtyard. We found evidence to suggest that the Germans had used the place as a medical clearing station. One room had a large quantity of Colgate talcum powder, a tin of which I pocketed. There were also gramophone records and a lot of office equipment—rubber stamps and documents—which were placed in a box.

We were searching the second floor, and our nerves were getting a little edgy, when there was a loud bang outside. We dived for the floor and waited for a minute before peering over the window sill, only to see Desmond O'Dowd, who was calmly standing in the centre of the courtyard, trying to bag a pigeon. Chick Strickland, now a sergeant and only recently returned from hospital, expressed his annoyance to Mr O'Dowd and reminded him in no uncertain terms that we were a very isolated group and could do without drawing attention to our presence. Back in our farm billet we handed over our collection. It had been a good and successful exercise for me and I felt confident and pleased with myself. My friends were pleased, too. I felt accepted.

The following morning, a message from the intelligence officer congratulated us on the information we had gathered and asked if there was any more. We thought there would be, so we were immediately despatched in search of it. With our tanks established in St Odilienberg, half a mile away, we followed the same route in more confident mood. The dead German was still lying in the snow and I opened the door. A German helmet was rocking on the kitchen table as though it had just been placed there. We withdrew quickly judging this to be a fighting job which would take more men than we had to occupy the whole house and its outbuildings. To our relief we were told over the radio to come back.

That would have been the end of the story had we not taken a party of veterans back to the area in 1984. I wrote to the Burgemeesters of Echt, Montfort, and St Odilienberg, telling them of our interest, and of our wish to meet again the civilians we had encountered so briefly in the war. To our astonishment and embarrassment, all three towns gave us a welcome we will never forget, treating us as liberators when we thought we had destroyed what little they had left. We had played a part in the killing of so many civilians that we could hardly expect any form of celebration. Yet there was a civic reception, conducted tour, luncheon and a banquet, all with speeches of welcome. Even the small town band of Echt turned out.

I had received a letter from a Dutch doctor who told me that he had been at the house in St Odilienberg, called Hoosten, and had written a book which, translated into English, was called *Doctor in the Front Line*. In this he gave an account of our patrol crashing through the front door on the occasion of our first visit. We were taken back to the old castle and found the same family living there. We also learned that the farmer had been arrested and taken away for interrogation because he was suspected of knowing Germans were still in the castle. He was released after an intervention by a Belgian—presumably Charles de Selliers, who as a Resistance leader would have read the danger in such an arrest.

It was alarming, after all those years, to learn that Dr Harry Stapert had 23 badly injured civilians in the basement of the house we searched, and at least one wounded German. He said the Germans were also hidden somewhere in that house and he was praying that we would not meet. A battle there would certainly have caused more suffering to his patients. He was not at all surprised that we had found a helmet rocking on the kitchen table during our second visit. "You were lucky" he informed us.

Another of his wartime experiences had a very happy ending. He told of how a British airman landed by parachute in his garden. He had a badly injured ankle and was very shaken. The police, it seemed, already knew of the incident, so it would be only a matter of time before the Germans arrived. The doctor had learned the poem *The Village Blacksmith*, at school, and now tried to recall the words.

The airman filled in the gaps, and thus they formed a relationship. The airman gave his hosts some items as souvenirs, and also gave his home address.

After our return to the UK in 1984, Harry Stapert wrote to me, saying he had thoroughly enjoyed our new-found friendship and now had a yearning to find the airman, whose name he remembered was Bernard Dolby and whose address was something like The Bakery, Huntingdon. I wrote to the RAF and had the story broadcast over the BBC, but there was no response. Then a letter arrived from another ex-prisoner-of-war, an air gunner as Bernard Dolby had been, who subsequently sent me a copy of a book which he had written, *The Diary of a POW*. In this book was a small map drawn by an inmate in the POW camp in Fallingbostel, Germany. His friends had written their names and addresses round the map and drawn lines pointing to where they lived. There was just the one I was looking for—B. H. Dolby, The Baker, Great Gidding, Hunts. I 'phoned the local police immediately and was directed to a councillor who had lived in the area during the war and knew of the Dolby family, but not their present whereabouts. Through Ken Cockerill, a regimental friend who had been on the trip and who had a relative in the area, a scan of the local telephone directory and a few calls located Bernard. Since then, Harry Stapert, Bernard, and members of his family have had a very happy reunion.

*Lieutenant Hugh Craig-Harvey*, brother of Andrew, who explained his experiences at the outbreak of war and was subsequently imprisoned in France, was leading a troop of tanks in 'C' Squadron. He relates his experience during the battle for St Odilienberg:

"It was to be very much a set piece attack by two troops of 'C' Squadron: I commanded First Troop and Henry Woods Fourth Troop. We had, in support, two companies of infantry, Flail tanks, and some Crocodile flame-throwers, with some other odds and ends.

"The Americans were expecting to take over the area the following day; and since this was the only serious battle being fought in the area on that day, a great number of senior British and American officers, came to watch: our Colonel, two Brigadiers, the General and Corps Commander and, for all I know, Percy Hobart, too, as we were using his Flails and Crocodiles. The American party certainly included a number of one- and two-star generals and, I believe, even a three-star General. Although we had been clearly told what we had to do before we started, we thought it would impress our senior officers and allies if we were to hold a proper 'O' group before the battle.

"The attack was due to begin at 1000 hours—presumably to allow travelling time for our visitors—so the 'O' group began at about 0930 hours with our Squadron Leader, Major John Ward-Harrison, in the chair, surrounded by we subalterns and the platoon commanders of the supporting infantry. Our little group stood in front of this enormous crowd of Allied Brass and their satellites. I felt like the victim of a Batman drawing. It was thus that I met my downfall!

"From Normandy onward, my wireless operator, friend and keeper had been one Pete Spink (remember, he was the sentry in France who mistook the Germans for his relief). After a series of collisions with higher authority due to my arriving late or without proper maps, chinagraphs or pencils, Spink, like the perfect butler, made sure that I attended every 'O' group properly equipped, even down to a pen-knife to sharpen my chinagraphs. He would even come with me to ensure that I didn't lose anything on the way!

"On the day before this attack we had been issued with up-dated aerial photographs. Why, I was not sure, because the village only had two streets and was bounded on the east side by the River Roer. Even I could not have got lost, and the future Major-General Henry Woods certainly could not. Anyway, the powers-that-be set great store by these photographs. On the preceding day, I had the misfortune to be mined and had left our tank in a hurry, which meant that for this great battle, I was having to use someone else's tank and had not the good services of Trooper Spink. These two factors combined to form the prelude to disaster. My new operator knew nothing about the aerial photographs and, not unreasonably, assumed that I was capable of looking after myself. Where those photographs went, I never did find out. Perhaps we had left them in the damaged tank.

"Of course, the first words uttered by Major Ward-Harrison were: 'Have you all got your aerial photographs?' Those who knew my Squadron Leader will remember what happened next!! The ice fell off the trees, the snow melted on a farmhouse some distance away, and I was left standing on a bit of charred earth while our important onlookers listened with delight and admiration. Several junior officers hid behind trees.

"The storm eventually blew itself out, the 'O' group continued, and battle finally commenced, though somewhat late as battles usually do. During it I was wounded and sent to hospital. Two days later, when resting in a general hospital, an officer in the next bed, who I had never seen before, sat up and said: 'I know you. You're the chap who left his aerial photographs behind!' "

Regimental history records the action more formally and describes the short battle thus:

> "The approaches to the little town of St Odilienberg were known to be heavily mined, and thus the advance was led by the Flails. They effectively breached the minefield short of the town and First and Fourth Troop then took up the running. But there were more mines in the town, and three tanks of First Troop were disabled. Undaunted, the Troop Leader, Lieutenant Hugh Craig-Harvey, continued into the Market Square on his own. Lieutenant Woods, leading Fourth Troop

> on the right, had to clear 'Schu' anti-personnel mines in the street with the help of the infantry and arrived at the Market Square as the last surviving tank of the First Troop went up on a mine. Lieutenant Craig-Harvey was blown up four times in five hours (five if you count the misplaced photographs). He and his crew survived to finish the day on their feet, still attacking the enemy. He was awarded an immediate MC for his bravery."

Second Troop of the Reconnaissance Squadron, patrolling north-west of Montfort ahead of 'B' Squadron, also had a hectic day. The ground they had to cover was flat and snow-covered and menaced by woods on the flanks. Their objective was a group of farmhouses about a mile away and in the open. The patrol stopped short of the buildings and Sergeant Ted Glynn, with Troopers 'Cracker' Noble and Cranfield, dismounted and went ahead. They found German helmets and rucksacks in the outhouses and felt certain that the place was occupied. It was too quiet: that absolute, shuttered kind of stillness which always precedes trouble. Sure enough there came a long burst of Spandau fire from a cellar window. They dodged among the buildings and, crawling and running, made for the vehicle. The Scout car came forward to pick them up and promptly struck a mine. Lieutenant Rickards was unhurt. Paddy Boyle, who thought they had been hit by a shell, leaped out of his Scout car and landed already running and dashed for cover. There was a mad scramble for the Sawn-off which began to reverse. One mishap followed another. The Honey, withdrawing down a track, also struck a mine. Trooper 'Pompy' Brown was wounded in the leg and the crew took a shaking. Trooper Jimmy Clarke courageously stuck to his radio and transmitted accurate reports of the situation. The enemy clearly had the advantage now but failed to take it and withdrew.

Third Troop of the Squadron had been approaching St Odilienberg from another direction and they were some distance ahead of our forward troops when a civilian stopped them to warn them that there were Germans in the house ahead. The Dutchman climbed aboard the Sawn-off and they moved cautiously on. As they approached farm buildings they saw a Red Cross flag pushed out of an outhouse. The ground was pitted with foxholes and, from one of them, a German paratroop sergeant-major emerged with his hands up. At the sight of this, the Dutchman leaped from the tank. The Germans headed for cover, one firing a shot which whipped away Ken Horsfield's aerial. Lieutenant de Selliers grabbed some hand grenades and his Sten gun and ran ahead. He fired a burst through a window and the occupants left hurriedly through the back door. He was then joined by Lieutenant Peter Duckworth, and the pair of them were doing a real Audi Murphy act when our own artillery joined in. The troop hurriedly pulled back without further casualties. Honours about even, they felt.

The battle to clear the area west of the Roer had succeeded and the whole Regiment withdrew to the area west of Echt, where there were plenty of empty houses and we were able to live warmly and in comfort for two weeks: trips to the mines for a bath, letter-writing again, new clothing, maintenance galore, and even some sport. There was a move to Opoeteren, near Bree, and there was more short leave to Brussels. While we were preparing for battle, the Canadians and Americans were clearing the area up to the Rhine and the Americans had captured the bridge at Remagen.

British troops were fighting a bitter battle in the Reichwald Forest, through the battered streets of Cleves and Goch. The last barriers were gradually being broken down and the stage was set for the Rhine crossing. Finally, the Regiment moved to the Someren area to complete preparations. Major-General Lyne, our Divisional Commander, assembled all officers and NCOs in a cinema in Bree and told us of the battle to come. It would not be easy, he warned. Every German house was built with a cellar capable of defence. There was a new German tank in operation, the King Tiger, reported to be bigger and better than the ordinary Tiger. It was a matter of waiting for good weather reports before starting the final run for Berlin.

A youngish sergeant from the permanent staff of the Gunnery School at Lulworth, was sent out to talk to the Recce Squadron and was horrified to see that we had welded a case to hold the ammunition box directly on to our Brownings and thought that someone would be in trouble! This poor, ill-informed NCO went on to explain that the school desperately wanted to get hold of a King Tiger intact and that, if we saw one, we were not to shoot it up but capture it. The gathering fell about the floor laughing. The replies he received are unprintable.

Two troops of the Recce Squadron were billeted in the local convent in Someren, where we helped the nuns to remove furniture and fittings and wintered comfortably through what remained of February and into March. I celebrated my 21st birthday in Eindhoven.

Robert Crockett, now a Major, appeared one morning and introduced us to a very smart and bright-eyed Dutchman who wore a light coloured mackintosh and spoke excellent English. We made a steady collection of nationals during the campaign and used them as interpreters. This latest arrival was *Johanness C. C. de Vaal* who would be attached to us with the customary rank of sergeant. He was called Hans, of course, and soon made friends. We were told that he had been found hiding under a heap of coal, but this was later discovered to have been a small hide-out made from peat. His story is a reminder of the determined resistance put up by those suffering German occupation:

"When the war broke out I was aged 17, a high school student and a troop leader in the Boy Scout movement. The war machine rolled over us quickly and unexpectedly since Jerry's aim was to capture the Continent by surprise. Initially there was no ill-treatment or hardships but the Quislings, usually low-down misfits, ex-criminals, dropouts or passed-over ideologists, who would have never made the grade in normal society, became our main problem. Now they turned out in fancy uniforms, chanting and barking like their 'friends', but were ridiculed by everybody, invaders included. There was faith in the country that the war could not last long. How mistaken we all were.

"Gradually the screws tightened. Collaborators moved into civil servant positions, newspapers were censored, our radios were confiscated, Jews were to be identified and later isolated, the first floggings and arrests occurred, and many more restrictions were imposed.

"Early in 1941 the Boy Scout movement was forbidden, since it was regarded as a semi-military, British inspired organisation. The night before the announcement all troop houses across the country had been sealed tight by the police with everything inside. This action made us very angry and, within 24 hours our group leader and myself, knowing every inch of our hut, decided to try to salvage our precious logbooks, membership rolls, trophies and other memorabilia, plus the boys' private belongings, before they could be placed on an inventory and confiscated. We broke in very professionally during curfew hours, without touching the 'war-seals', and cleaned the place out. Although there was no relatiation, we found out later that we now had the first black mark against us.

"In 1942 we lost our first friend. He had only just joined the Military Academy when the war broke out but was taken as a POW and then released. He was itching to get out of Holland and join the Free Dutch Forces in England, and was into the escape route when he and three others were caught and executed when only a few miles from the French-Swiss border. These executions, broadcast as a warning to all Dutchmen, had the very opposite effect. They were showing us blood which made ours boil. We started a campaign of passive resistance, petty sabotage and other underground activity. We 'Voortrekkers' became involved. Some raided distribution offices and stole ration cards for those in hiding (Jews and politicians). Others gathered information for Allied agents dropped into Holland.

"In 1943 the Germans ordered that students were to be used as labourers. Colleges were raided, but the catch was meagre and the reaction violent. To pacify us again, those who had been taken were released. Instead, we were asked to sign a kind of declaration of loyalty. By not participating in demonstrations and working voluntarily on the Atlantic Wall during summer vacation, we would be guaranteed continuation of our studies. We would not accept this and 90 per cent refused to sign.

"Subsequently, all men of age were required to register at the Labour Office, destined for slave labour camps across the border.

The Germans embarked on a round-up which, at first, was confined to the larger cities. I had dodged one of the raids on my college, and had since been involved in guiding fugitives, among them some Allied pilots who had been handed to us from 'somewhere' and had to be taken 'somewhere'. From my Boy Scout days I knew the area between Arnhem and the Zuidersee like the back of my hand and felt pretty secure. But I thought it better to lie low. Nevertheless, my dad was tipped off and told that my name and those of some friends were on a list of people to be 'invited' to report to the Labour Office. I realised that this would be an interrogation, and was afraid that I would expose my father and the other members of my family—four younger brothers and a sister. We had some very serious discussions about what I should do and my father not only supported but actually urged me to disappear and join the ranks of the hunted. So I was now taken from 'somewhere' to 'somewhere'—by a nice young woman who carried my bag (no male chauvinism then). I arrived in Someren, a place I had never, until then, heard of. There was no running water, no gas, no electricity in the small farmhouse, but it was occupied by the warmest of people. They had no idea who I was, nor of my reason for visiting. The farmer, with a family of seven children, took the same risk as my dad. For this reason, I never slept in the house but built my 'nest' in the open.

"I was employed by a land reform organisation which had Underground connections. This gave me a legitimate reason for being around. We dug ditches, moved earth with a wheelbarrow and attended to the payroll and administration from a small cabin out in the 'sticks'.

"My identity card had been crudely altered by the Superintendent to make me a few years older and to show my occupation as a 'Junior Surveyor'. This was in fact a big error because my name was listed in the dreaded 'Black Book' which the Quisling Police carried with them at all times. If I were now to be caught, I could expect the worst.

"When my father heard of this (we had occasional contact) he talked to a trusted 'clean' official in our town hall who agreed to issue me with a new card and to replace my completely unreadable card which had been soaked in water. There was one risk: I would have to appear in person to sign the card and be finger-printed. I took the chance and was in and out of the office in one minute. I actually went home for two days. It was now April, 1944.

"A week later my parents' house was raided by Quisling Police at 0200 hours in the morning. They had been informed that I had fled from a German factory in Bielefeld (I had never been there). My dad reacted coolly and pretended that we had fallen out over my studies and that I had left home a year earlier and threatened to join the Dutch SS. He said my mother was heartbroken and, if the police found me, would they ask me to write a letter home. They searched the house from top to bottom and, as they padded around my mother, who was still in bed and about to faint with fear, they told her: 'Don't worry, Madam. Your son may or may not be on our side now, but if we find him, we will force him to write you a letter.'

"A month later I had another close call. My farmer host had an eye injury, so I took him to hospital in Eindhoven and decided to run the farm in his absence. Two days later, the cabin where I would normally have been doing the payroll was raided but they only found my boss who was having to do the job himself. I never returned to that cabin again.

"As soon as we heard of the invasion in June, there was much work to be done with the Underground and things got very hot by August and September. Jerry was getting desperate and ruthless. We had a Ball!! The prospect of freedom inspired us to take risks, which we took with pleasure. We carried out acts of sabotage wherever we could and almost came into the open when the Allies were halted on the Albert Canal, only 25 miles away. We did not know of the supply problems until contact was made with the Princess Irene Brigade. We lost a few friends, but on September 21st, 1944, our village was free. It was a year to the day since I had first arrived there. It was heaven.

"My own home was on the outskirts of Arnhem. The disaster there prevented my returning, though I tried to join forces with the Guards Armoured Brigade. I then volunteered for the Dutch Army, but there wasn't much excitement and I was delighted to have the opportunity to serve with the British Army as an interpreter. It was May, 1945—Mother's Day—before I saw my mother and family. She looked thin after the miserable winter and the bombardments. They had never left the house, but their spirit was unbroken. My youngest brother hardly knew me but was delighted to accept all the chocolate I could provide."

[Footnote: In March 1947, my wife, Joan, and I spent a wonderful four days with the de Vaal's at their home in Velp. We were there to witness the Orange Day celebration and the birth of the youngest addition to the Dutch Royal Family. Arnhem was still a mess: the knocked-out vehicles and remnants of the Paras at Oosterbek were still there, as was the large cemetery on ground presented to Britain. The Union Jack flew over the plot and most touching of all, the rear of each headstone bore the name of a Dutch child whose responsibility it was to tend the grave.

The de Vaal family proudly told of the pranks they had played. The 12-year old brother of Hans had hidden in a ditch beside the road and, with a wheel brace, unscrewed the wheel nuts of German trucks. Sand had been thrown into petrol tanks of parked lorries. When the 'Drop' came, they believed they would be liberated and ran out into the street to cheer the tanks passing their house, but they were German tanks and there would be terrible reprisals carried out in Arnhem before freedom finally came. They proudly showed us the loose floorboards in the wardrobe where they kept a radio to listen to the news from Britain. They were a warm, happy family again. Hans remained with the Regiment until 1948 carrying out many useful tasks associated with interpreting.]

# Across the Rhine

Dawn broke on March 24th as a curtain-raiser for the final assault on Hitler's Germany. Wave after wave of Dakota aircraft, some towing gliders, passed low overhead with paratroopers waiting for the signal to drop. Some waved from their lofty and dangerous perches near the exits. There would be heavy casualties, and many of those we saw were probably dead or badly wounded only minutes after passing.

Our Generals were not risking a second Arnhem. The 15th Scottish Division had made a river assault during the night and were holding positions on the eastern bank. Only the width of the Rhine separated leading troops and the drop zone, though the river was a swift and formidable obstacle, 300 yards wide at the chosen point at Xanten, a few miles north of Wesel. The order to pack up and move came almost immediately. We were to make a long approach march to cross the Maas at Roermond and then to Venlo and a wooded area near Xanten. It was bad terrain for tanks and we spent what remained of the day extracting ourselves from boggy ground. The 4th Armoured Brigade had already been ferried across but the 7th Armoured Division, with ourselves in the lead, would be the first Armoured Division to break out. We were well supported by our friends from the Durham Light Infantry and the Rifle Brigade.

The pontoon bridge was successfully pushed across to the eastern bank and we were ready to cross. This delicate structure would have to carry hundreds of heavy vehicles, and a break-up would cause the separate pontoons to break quickly away and float down-river to points where they would not easily be recovered. Our A1 Echelon and some heavy artillery were first to use the crossing. This would ensure a supply point on the eastern bank, and ammunition and rations to support the attack. One member of that Echelon, *Corporal Joe Treadwell,* expressed his thoughts in verse:

*The Crossing of the Rhine 1945*

Oudenarde and Ramillies,
   And bloody Malplaquet,
Will your stalwarts ride amongst us
   As we cross the Rhine today?

Salamanca and Vittoria,
   And Bleak Sevastopol,
Your foes are now our allies,
   Do you find that rather droll?

Did you who wore these badges,
Heard 'Boots and Saddle' blow,
Feel this same gutsy flutter
When the time was nigh to go?

Perhaps if I were Christian,
There would be a little help.
As it is I'll just cross my fingers
Not to join you over there.

You Balaclava heavies,
Whom all but we forget.
Lend us some of your spirit,
We hope not to join you yet.

Once the column's rolling
It will be far too late to pray.
We ask. "Whose bell is tolling?"
On this, our Crispin's day.

The Recce troops had been reorganised yet again and I was a member of First Troop under Lieutenant Charles Snell and Sergeant Chick Strickland. We had a wager with Third Troop that we would capture the first live prisoner. We drove slowly over the pontoons, each section sinking low into the water as we crossed. The current of this fast-flowing river was adding extra strain to the mooring lines. Royal Engineers were moving about the construction, constantly checking the lashings and adjusting where necessary. Once over, we moved forward quickly and soon arrived among paratroopers and their broken gliders. It was a giant devil's toyshop—broken and destroyed aircraft, bodies of those who had been killed on impact or in the air before landing, some swinging in their harness from trees, others badly wounded and awaiting evacuation. Many Germans lay dead too.

The problem appeared to have been caused by the restricted size of the landing area. Some of the aircraft had landed on top of others, or collided on landing. A glider, having once cast off its tow, has only one course—down. Split second decisions had to be made, and many had little choice but to crash-land as near as possible to their own group.

We soon passed through the Airborne troops and on to tracks in very close country. A badly wounded German tried to rise to give himself up but failed. With the thoughts of that wager with Third Troop and Ginger Proudlove in particular, a message was sent over the radio claiming the prize. (I cannot now remember what it was to be). No prisoner could have received better treatment. If he did survive, I am sure he will tell a story of compassion second to none. Had it not been for the wager we would have left him because he was an encumberance. A troop of the 11th Hussars joined us and then, from our right, came a burst of fire from a high-velocity machine gun, not unlike the Spandau. Another troop joined us—men in Jeeps and with Vickers 'K' guns. They introduced themselves as SAS (Special Air Service). Few of us had ever heard of this organisation and we viewed them with suspicion. They said they had been swanning around for two days. 'B' Squadron was over to our left and one of the tanks, uncertain of our identity, fired a shot which fortunately passed between us. We felt it was time for someone else to do some apologising and quickly sent a message through the network. Syd Swift, now with a new Sherman, was leading the 'B' Squadron advance and wrote of his experience. under the title 'The Brew Up':

"The fighting for the bridgehead had been fierce; on both sides of the Rhine were scenes of destruction—buildings with gaping holes in their walls and roofs and some burning. To clear the way, burnt-out vehicles and any other obstacles had been bulldozed into the rubble.

"At the eastern end of the bridge, ruined buildings gave way to open country. We passed through the carnage of the DZ (dropping zone). Once more the constant message from higher formation was to 'push on'. I urged 'Smudger' my driver, to 'step on it'. We speeded up and soon came to the area where the gliders had landed. It was shortly after this that we made our first contact with the enemy. It was now almost dark. I was relieved when we were ordered to leaguer for the night.

"Early the following morning we pushed along at the head of the Squadron but I dropped back to second tank in the line of march. We were held up momentarily in the small village of Gemen. I have good reason to remember that village. It was here that I saw a pig eating a dead German soldier by the roadside.

"During a lull in the advance, we stopped near some farm buildings and I had a chance to take a hurried look inside. At once I had a feeling about the place. 'Jerries in here', I thought. We had developed a nose for them. A platoon of the Queen's Regiment came forward, searching buildings and I told the commander of my suspicions. Sure enough, they emerged some ten minutes later with a batch of German prisoners which included a high-ranking officer.

"The pressure to 'get a move on' continued. We turned off the main road, down a small side road. I can see it all so clearly, even after 40 years—a narrow road seemingly leading to nowhere. After a short distance I saw a farm-house, lying just off the road to my right. As we came in sight of it, I spotted a group of Germans crouching in a ditch near the hedge on the left of the road. Our machine-guns pounded into them and we then gave our attention to the house. I ordered the gunner to fire at it. Out came the enemy soldiers with their hands held high, dirty white flags fluttering from their fingers. As I watched, I saw others make a dash across open country to the rear of the farm. The turret Browning caught them as they ran. One by one they stumbled, fell, and remained still.

"We moved down the road to where a small track led off to the left of our advance and through a plantation of young saplings. I was not happy with the approach which led through wet, boggy woodland. I thought that, should we be attacked on that track, we would be trapped. Again came the radio message to 'push on', so we complied. The track became more impassable; the leading tank became bogged. I managed to find a way round it by driving through the young trees, the trunks of which made a grip for our tracks. Once more we were in the lead. I was relieved to see that the other tanks in the troop were able to use the same route and pass the bogged vehicle. Ahead, the wood was thinning out and I could see that there was open country again.

"Almost at the end of the track, I stopped to inspect some distant buildings and observed, through my binoculars, what appeared to be a small village with rows of houses, a church and a farmhouse. I also thought I saw enemy troops running into one of the houses. We opened fire, but nothing more was seen. The voice over the radio was there again: 'Push on'. I ordered the driver to advance. I was still screened by the trees in the plantation. Ahead was the village and, on my right, open ground. As we moved forward there was a terrific explosion and I was flung high into the air. I recall being astonished to see the blankets, stowed on the outside of the tank, blazing. I hit the ground with a bump. I was momentarily winded but one thought possessed me as I struggled to my feet: Dick and Smudger were still inside the tank, which was burning fiercely as I clambered up to the turret. Dick was struggling to pull himself out, his face blackened and cracked and his hair scorched. I managed to get an arm under his shoulder and haul him out, together, we fell off the tank.

"As I dragged him clear and to the rear, I was tormented by the thought of 'Smudger', still inside that inferno. The flames were now belching from the engine compartment and the turret, and I hoped desperately that they had not reached the driver's compartment. I was also fearful that the gun barrel would be over the driver's hatch and prevent his escape. Leaving Dick with the operator who, with me, had been blown clear, I dashed back. As I did so, 'Smudger' appeared through the smoke, staggering as though blind. I called and he ran towards me as though pursued by the devil himself. Thankful that he was safe, I returned to the ditch and took a look at Dick. He was in a bad way, his boyish face blackened and burned by the flames. But he was conscious and he managed to tell me he had a pain in his chest. I had been able to get to one of the external first-aid kits, so I injected him with morphine and smothered his burns with soothing burn cream. There was no sign of blood on his clothing and I though it best to keep him warm and clothed. 'You are going to be all right', I assured him, and he managed to smile at me. He enquired about Smudger. 'Smudger has just gone up the track like Sidney Wooderson,' I assured him. There was a flicker of a smile on his blackened face. The operator was wounded in the leg but his injuries were not serious.

"We lay in a shallow ditch, the tank between us and the enemy. Behind, the other tanks in the troop were still in the trees, doubtless trying to locate the gun positions of the enemy.

"Realising that we would have to get medical treatment very soon, I began to drag Dick along the ditch to the safety of the trees, but each movement caused him pain. I sent the operator ahead and he soon came back with other tanks. As we made the slow and, for Dick, painful journey, I began to feel pain in my left leg and for the first time realised that I, too, was wounded. Slowly, keeping low in the ditch, I pulled Dick along, giving him a running commentary to cheer him up. He calmed down as the morphia began to take effect. It seemed a long journey to the protection of the trees and once there I ran to the nearest tank for a blanket to wrap Dick in.

"We learned that the medical half-track was on its way and as we waited there, I realised that we were about to make our last journey together as a crew. We had travelled from the beaches of Normandy and had come to know and respect each other. We had shared dangers, discomforts and pleasures and, in the close confines of the tank, had learned to live with each other. If we had never been brought together by war, there would have been a little less colour in the weave of our lives. The half-track arrived and we placed Dick on a stretcher for the rough ride across country to where a proper ambulance could pick us up. I never saw Dick again. He died in hospital.

"We who survived are left to remember and grow old. When I think of him, I always remember him as he was; his youthful face, a ready smile which came from his eyes and was supported by the lips; warm, friendly, trusting. A smile on a face which will never grow old."

* * * * *

*Sergeant Bob Price,* now commanding his own troop, recalls his experiences then:

"My strongest memory of the leap across the Rhine is the terrific artillery bombardment which preceded it, the smoke screen which obscured the preparations and the air drop reminding me of the Arnhem battle. It was lovely weather when 'C' Squadron set off for our objective, Borken. Apart from a bullet in the heel of one boot (my own fault for nipping out of the tank to collect some parachute material for my wife), being missed by an anti-tank gun and being shot up by a light, quick-firing ack-ack gun, and being soft with a prisoner, it had not been a bad day—sunny and warm. There was also a moment of concern when a quartet of rocket-firing Typhoons looked as though they were about to use us for target practice until

I, with much haste, produced our luminous orange-coloured identity strip. A waggle of wings from the leader said, 'Sorry'. I could only shake the panel in reply."

* * * * *

All Recce troops were out checking bridges. Third Troop spent the whole night guarding one which was to be the main centre-line of our advance the following day.

For me it was to be a night to remember, too. We took over a sort of grain loading-bay for the night. We were all, except for Third Troop, in one building, and instead of having a tank as a guard point, I was in charge of three sentries. Other troops were in buildings near by. Trooper George Webster, who had been given the task of guarding three SS prisoners, leaned out of an upstairs window asking to be relieved. I told him to wait until we had replenished the tanks with rations and ammunition. When I eventually joined him, George told me that his prisoners were locked in a small room. I opened it and looked. "I thought there were three?". "There were", he said. A hole in the roof told the story. Only moments later, a sentry for Tac HQ of the DLI was shot. Whether it was our escapee or another, we never knew. The two remaining prisoners were too tired to do anything and I took them downstairs and into the large room we were using. There was a trap door in the floor, leading to the floor below, which was flooded. My prisoners must have spent a very uncomfortable night sleeping on the stairs below me.

We were all settling down for what was left of the night when the sentry came in saying that he had another prisoner. I went to look. He was a very old and very irate prisoner, who stuck a piece of paper under my nose. It appeared he was demanding something, but what? The sentry woke up one of our interpreters—Dobkin, I think—who told me: "He is the post NCO from an ack-ack site up the Rhine and he collects his mail here every night," I was informed. "Who does he think we are?" I asked. The poor man was very shocked to learn that we were British, and was further angered when we applied a new rule—to run over bicycles.

We made an early start next morning and it was still very dark when we passed over the bridge which Third Troop had held during the night. Commanding the leading vehicle, I was required to check a track running parallel with the road and leading to the small village of Brink. Leading at any time is hazardous, to say the least, and was even more strenuous in the dark, trying to read a map without lights, unable to see what sort of threat lay left, right or in front. There was some consolation in the realisation that the enemy would be in much the same position and would not know whether we were his own troops. We halted about 100 yards short of Brink and, as soon as it was light enough we moved forward and into the narrow roads of the village. First, a door opened on the right and a chair with a piece of white cloth tied to it was hurled into the road. I told Bob Sawtell to watch that side while I would watch the left. Then a figure came from a cowshed which I had already passed. He ran down the hedge and was only the width of a garden away from me when I saw that he was carrying a bazooka. He had not seen me because I had no turret and he was obviously intent on trying to ambush Sergeant Strickland, who was close behind me. At ten yards' range, and without even bothering to sight my Browning, I gave him a long burst and he fell behind the hedge. We were in a very narrow road and, with buildings on each side, could be heading for trouble. So we reversed out and back to our original position, where we intended to move out into the field and at least put some distance between ourselves and possible bazooka men. There had been considerable noise already and, if the enemy had mistaken us for their own troops in the dark, they were unlikely to do so now.

'B' Squadron now came up behind us, Sergeant Pat Whitmore leading. He had seen us firing at something and then reverse out, assuming that the village was being defended. I also had an experience similar to Syd Swift, in that a pig was about to eat the man I had shot. I told 'Taffy' Willingale, the forward gunner, to shoot the pig, which he did. All this activity enhanced the impression that we were having a pretty tough fight. Pat opened up with his guns and soon the thatched houses were ablaze. There was probably only that lone German in the village, and he had been caught napping. The Germans now shelled us and added to the total destruction of that small village. We were told that we could stand down and get some breakfast.

On our radio came a report that Third Troop had left the bridge and been sent to liaise with a troop of the 11th Hussars. They headed through wooded country for some miles without sighting the 'Cherry-pickers'. They halted at cross tracks where a loaded bazooka and a bicycle lay in the road. A rifle, fired at point-blank range, shot Corporal Ken Horsfield through the neck. Ginger Proudlove accounted for the attacker. Fortunately, the shot did no permanent injury and Ken would recover.

The Regiment was now heading towards Raesfeld, and believing themselves to be on virgin territory, but Lieutenant Ben Tottenham, who had been seconded to Brigade Headquarters as a liaison officer, was about to make the headlines in *'The Times'*.

A reporter from that newspaper who was well up with the forward troops, subsequently included all his reports in a book *Berlin '45; the Grey City*. Ben, believing that our troops were already well forward of Raesfeld, entered the town by a side road. He soon discovered that we had not yet arrived, but that the Germans had vacated it. He was able to radio back and tell us that he was already in occupation and that he was about to return via the route of our approach.

'C' Squadron now took the lead through Raesfeld and towards

Weseke. 'B' Squadron was fired upon by SPs from an area east of Weseke. 'C' Squadron, with a company of 9 Durham Light Infantry in Kangaroos (armoured personnel carriers) were ordered to take the town. Fourth Troop, 'C' Squadron, dashed down the road at full speed while 'K' Battery shelled the SPs who had the road covered. The platoon of the DLI roared after them in their APCs. The village was secured after the infantry had cleared the houses and the tank guns had demolished a road block.

'A' Squadron now took over and led along the main centre-line to Weseke and Sudlohn. 'C' Squadron fanned out to the right and on to tracks in open countryside, reaching Stadlohn just after 'A' Squadron, who had caught some German lorries on the road. There was a small, single-track railway line through the town and, more important, a bridge still intact. Fourth Troop 'C' Squadron moved on to the track and crossed but it was a lengthy task because the bridge was not intended for such weight and the tanks, once on to the line, could not leave it until they came to a road crossing. Any diagonal movement could lead to a track being shed. They continued their advance in darkness and towards Stadlohn, where the Rifle Brigade were held up and without tank support. Lieutenant Woods commented in his report that "A tank is rather like a blind rhinoceros at night, dangerous if it knows where the enemy is, but otherwise only too aware of its blindness". Fourth Troop shelled the first few houses at a range of 600 yards.

The infantry made their way down and completed the clearing. The enemy replied with an SP or tank which tried to fire at Fourth Troop, but both sides were aiming at gun flashes and in total darkness. The infantry commander decided to hold his position until dawn. It was a tense three hours with regular bursts of Spandau and mortar fire and other noises. At dawn a troop of 'B' Squadron tanks led by Lieutenant Meredith-Hardy arrived and permitted them some rest. Our centre-line was to be Ahaus, Heek, Metelen, Wetteringen, Neuenkirken and Rheine. There was plenty of resistance but the German population in general had suffered more than enough and most houses displayed white surrender flags from their windows. We had expected some form of resistance movement and sabotage attempts on our supply lines, but there was nothing of the sort: the average German was pleased to see us go past and seemingly resigned to the idea of occupation. Lack of sleep was becoming our main problem. Late nights, all-night moves, and guard duties followed by an early start, were beginning to have an effect. It was, for me, another unique experience which I would not wish to repeat. I had spent that first night over the Rhine dealing with the guard situation, the second night as a guide for tanks making their way round Stadlohn, and a third night on the move. Fortunately, the other members of my crew had managed some sleep and were able to carry on, but on the morning of the fourth day, despite sitting on sharp edges and trying to stand up instead of sitting, I suddenly just fell asleep. Bob Sawtell rolled me in the camouflage net on the back of the engine deck, and there I stayed for a couple of hours while patrolling was continued. Nothing could have kept me awake any longer. Lack of sleep to that degree is very dangerous. Nothing matters except to be able to close your eyes. It could be fatal!

My troop was given the task of checking a road parallel to the main centre-line and leading into Rheine. We came upon a carrier troop of the Herefords of 11th Armoured Division who had been manning a road block all night and were pleased to see us. They had seen very few Germans and moved their road barrier to allow us to pass. Only a mile down the road we came upon three young German airmen burying a fourth in a ditch. They were very tired and raised their hands as we approached. I was the second vehicle in the column of three. The leading tank had hardly moved off when it struck a mine and slewed into the ditch only 20 yards further on. Our three prisoners were at that time sitting on the back of my tank and looking very despondent. I ran forward to Sergeant Strickland's tank as he climbed out. Trooper Bill Whitcombe, the driver, was slumped in his seat, and I could see that the tank's bottom plate had been blown upwards. When they started lifting Bill from his seat, I could still see the heel of his boot protruding from under the vehicle. I feared the worst. He was still conscious despite the loss of a foot. The other foot was so damaged as to be almost unrecognisable. There was also very little blood, which was not a good sign. Both his arms were broken and he had a very badly broken nose. We used bivouac poles to splint his arms and, as his foot was just hanging by skin, we had to cut it off. It was a gruesome business.

As Paddy Byrne went back up the road in his Scout car to get aid from the infantry, Bill repeated several times, "Don't forget my parachute." Most of us had by this time collected one and intended to take the coveted silk home as a present for someone. It was to be a wedding dress for his intended bride. When the Carrier arrived with a stretcher, Bill was placed carefully on the vehicle, which was turning when it struck yet another mine. This time Bill was killed instantly and the crew of the Carrier became casualties. Bill, who had been in the Recce Squadron for a long time, was a very quiet chap from Bristol and his loss was a sad one. The prisoners who had sat unattended on my tank while all this went on, now became the centre of aggression. There was a feeling that they must have known about the mines and should be shot. Some of us pointed out that, as we had not been taking much precaution against attack while dealing with our casualties, perhaps they were of greater value to us alive. But it was a very close thing for those three. As we rejoined the centre-line and moved up the long column of tanks my three prisoners wept. They were totally beaten and I felt compassion for them. We spent a night and a full day resting in a mill in Rheine.

The 11th Armoured Division, supported by the 6th Airborne, was coming up fast towards Osnabrück. We saw for the first time the latest tank now in service with the 15/19th Hussars—the Comet, a little larger and heavier than the Cromwell, but of similar design. The northern flank of this advance was being threatened by strong resistance from the hills running west to east and known as the Teutoburger Wald. We spent the night in a valley to the south of Ibbenbüren.

# Ibbenbüren

The approach into Ibbenbüren from the south was a winding road between high ground and heavily wooded country. On one side of the road was a deep gully which would prevent tanks from leaving the road at any point south of the outskirts of the village. It was quite definitely a death trap. The artillery gave the wooded areas their attention, but anyone dug in would and could survive. The area had been well prepared for defensive action and staff from the officers' school at Hanover had been brought there to defend the ridge running east to west from Detmold to well beyond Osnabrück. These troops, although older than most we had met, were professional soldiers.

The day started normally with a patrol from the Recce Squadron carefully motoring up the road and taking up a position of observation to the left of our main advance. There was no reaction from the enemy and they sent back a report to the effect that the area was clear. 'A' Squadron then drove up to the point with a company of DLI—Sniper action from those prepared positions soon caused a number of casualties. Only the heads of crew commanders and operators were slightly above the turret cupola but it was sufficient for such experts. Small-arms fire pinned down the infantry, and the tanks could not venture into thickly wooded areas alone.

April 3rd was a bad day for 'A' Squadron and little progress was made. We had moved forward to the southern part of the town and spent the night near the railway station. The artillery again gave the wooded areas their undivided attention throughout the night and, at dawn, further patrols were sent forward. My troop in the Recce Squadron motored across a field to the east to try to cut off the main road from Ibbenbüren to Osnabrück. A dead German lay in the field about 50 yards from my position. The single track railway was on an embankment which hid from our view all activity on the eastern bank.

Someone on our right reported that enemy troops were creeping along the bank to get just in front of our position which we tried to protect from sudden attack, by throwing hand grenades over the embankment at irregular intervals. On our left, a long trench defending the approach into the town was full of dead German troops who had fought to the last man. I counted 61 of them slumped in various positions, some still clutching their rifles. More than 100 yards ahead of the rail embankment was a wood and we could see troops moving about. We called for the Artillery to shell it. Three ranging shots came over and were corrected. As in Lieutenant Peter Kiddle's experience in Geffen, when the whole battery was firing, one gun was dropping short. One round fell on our right and another on the railway just ahead of us. Our tanks came up and fired at vehicles we had observed using the road out of the town, and a factory which was still belching thick smoke. We were less protected in a Sawn-off and kept our heads down. Lieutenant Charles Snell, our troop leader, called me over to his Scout car just to our rear and asked me to take a look at the dead German behind us. I was not best pleased with this task, seeing little point in it, but could think of no good reason for not complying. Pointing out that I had no personal weapon on me, he told me to take his, which was lying across the back of his neck in a canvas cover. I grabbed it rather roughly and, as in Lisieux, it fired a number of rounds which must have missed Charles by inches. He was not at all pleased. I tried to exonerate myself by making a run for the body in the field. I took out the dead man's wallet from which fell evidence of happier days—a photograph of himself in civilian clothing sitting on a motor-cycle combination with a girl and child. I opened his tunic from which fell a number of bullets which had gone through him. There was nothing else of interest, but it left me something to think about. He, like me, had lived in another world.

We decided to move forward and cross the railway. The wood which had been shelled was now on our right. We could see some Germans digging on the edge of the road some 400 yards ahead and gave them a burst. While this was going on another troop, led by Lieutenant Charles de Selliers, had probed further east in a long, circular movement. They met a civilian who claimed to be a Czech but, as soon as they had passed, he picked up a bazooka and fired at them. It missed and Corporal Ginger Proudlove shot him.

The Honey became bogged and, while they were trying to drag it clear, they saw German infantry crawling down the hedge towards them. They fired at the positions until all their ammunition was spent, and still the enemy came on. We listened to this drama on our radio and were already moving towards their position when we received the order to go to the rescue. There was a frantic call from Ginger repeating "Don't shoot, don't shoot, we are coming down towards you." The crew of the Honey had mounted the other vehicle and had beaten a hasty retreat.

Lieutenant Bill Shelton with his troop from 'B' Squadron came to the rescue (again). His own tank was bogged but the others came forward. We joined them to recover the Honey and a hectic exchange went on before we succeeded. We had withdrawn almost to the point of our start behind the railway line when we received a message from TAC HQ to return and try to get into the town via the main road from the east. It was already getting dark and we wondered what we were going to achieve by this since we could not consolidate the ground and would not be able to see.

Being the last vehicle during the withdrawal, I now found myself

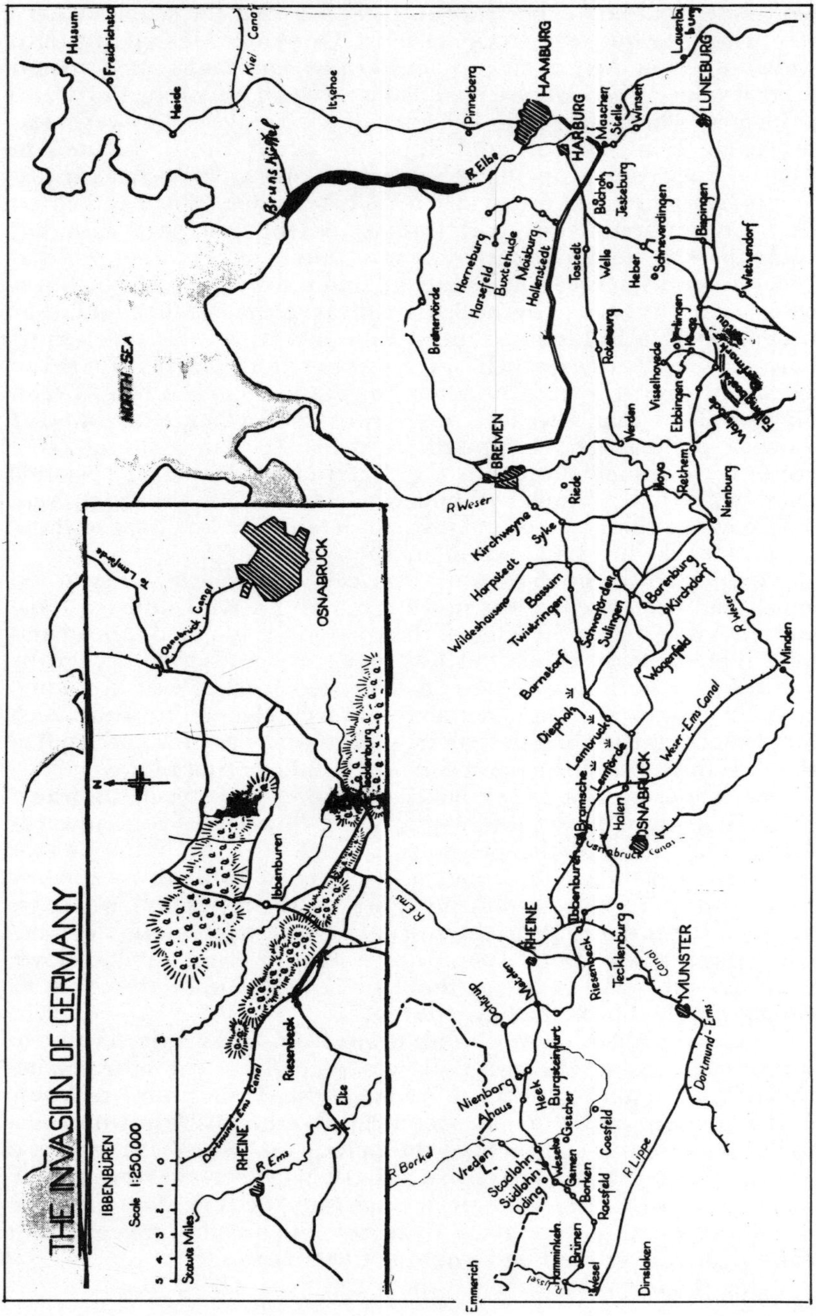
THE INVASION OF GERMANY
IBBENBÜREN
Scale 1:250,000
Statute Miles
OSNABRUCK
Osnabrück Canal
R Lemförde
Ibbenburen
Tecklenburg
Riesenbeck
Dortmund-Ems Canal
RHEINE
R Ems
Elbe
NORTH SEA
Husum
Friedrichstadt
Kiel Canal
Heide
Itzehoe
Brunsbüttel
Pinneberg
HAMBURG
HARBURG
R Elbe
Maschen
Stelle
Winsen
Lauenburg
LUNEBURG
Bremervörde
Horneburg
Harsefeld
Buxtehude
Moisburg
Hollenstedt
Tostedt
Welle
Buchholz
Jesteburg
Heber
Schneverdingen
Bispingen
Wietzendorf
Rotenburg
Visselhoevede
Ebbingen
Verden
BREMEN
R Weser
Riede
Hoya
Rethem
Nienburg
Kirchweyhe
Syke
Harpstedt
Bassum
Wildeshausen
Twistringen
Schwaförden
Sulingen
Barenburg
Kirchdorf
Barnstorf
Wagenfeld
Diepholz
Lembruck
Lemförde
Minden
Weser-Ems Canal
Bramsche
Holen
OSNABRUCK
Osnabruck Canal
Ibbenburen
RHEINE
Riesenbeck
Tecklenburg
MUNSTER
Dortmund-Ems
Ochtrup
Metelen
Burgsteinfurt
Nienborg
Heek
Ahaus
Gescher
Coesfeld
Vreden
R Borkel
Stadtlohn
Südlohn
Oding
Weseke
Gemen
Borken
Raesfeld
R Lippe
Hamminkeln
Brünen
Wesel
Dinslaken
Emmerich

in the lead. The road was heavily wooded on each side and posed all sorts of dangers, so we were relieved to receive a message ordering us to return. As we did so, we saw a figure emerge from the woods and run towards us. It was impossible to see properly in the gloom, but the pent-up emotions of the day were spent in giving this poor chap a burst of machine-gun fire over his head to make him crawl and grovel. He went down on his knees and put his hands up. Another burst passed just above him and he fell on his face. Three men ran out to get him, believing that he was at least wounded. To our complete horror and total embarrassment, we found that he was a British fighter pilot who had hidden there for two days awaiting our advance. He could hardly talk because of the reception we had given him. Should that man ever read this account, may I, on behalf of the whole patrol, express our sincere apologies and regrets.

On the outskirts of the town, the Sabre Squadrons had a bad time. Lieutenant Martin Fitzgerald, who had fought so bravely throughout the campaign and particularly at Geffen, had been a casualty from a sniper's bullet which had gone through his neck. He died from loss of blood before he could receive medical attention. Lieutenant H. J. Elkins was also shot through the stomach and died.

* * * * *

*Sergeant Bob Price* recalled:

"Ibbenbüren remains in my mind as the most horrible experience a tank troop leader could undergo while supporting infantry. It was so frustrating for us and so demoralising for the PBI. As far as military tactics go, it emphasised that you could so easily be seen and heard when on the move. Here was a comparatively small number of oldish soldiers holding at bay a much superior force, their only weapons being a rifle and a few mortars.

"My troop was sent forward to assist 'A' Squadron, who were losing tank commanders rapidly. My Squadron Leader, Major John Ward-Harrison, finished his orders to us with the words 'For God's sake be careful. Do what you can.' I did account for five snipers whom I spotted through the thick, swirling smoke. We may have killed or injured others since we fired at every possible point where they might be located. We used both our main gun and the Besa machine-guns. One man appeared only 20 yards from the tank after my forward gunner had raked a pile of hedge trimmings. Whether he was hit on the 'funny bone' I shall never know, but he rose up shedding twigs in all directions, gyrating as though in an ecstatic dance routine. Just nerves, I suspect, for as quickly as the dance commenced, he fell and lay very still.

"We were mortared. I reached up to close my hatch and, in the moment that my hand appeared, a bullet struck the upright hatch between my thumb and first finger. The bullet shattered and cut my hand, and a piece of it entered my mouth and broke two teeth without touching my lips.

"The infantry casualties mounted. Our troop fired smoke and sprayed the area where we suspected the enemy to be but we just could not advance under those conditions. I reported the situation and was told to return to the farmyard in which we had made a temporary sanctuary. We loaded all the casualties on to the tanks under cover of a smoke screen from our dischargers and withdrew, feeling we had achieved very little. The Platoon Commander, travelling on my tank tapped me on the head and told me that one of the wounded had been hit again. I offered him the internal first aid kit, but he just shook his head. I gave the order, 'Driver, speed up'."

* * * * *

My good friend, Corporal George Elliott, who had attended the Bovington course with me and had spent many happy evenings with my future wife's parents in Ashington, had been in the centre of the battle. While trying to empty the container which catches the empty cartridges from the machine-gun, George had dropped it onto the engine deck. He made a dash to recover it but a German close by fired at point-blank range and killed him outright.

George Boxford, originally a member of my troop in the Recce Squadron had been caught by snipers. In all there were 16 casualties in that little town which had earned the title "Happy Valley".

We have revisited the area in recent years. The railway line is no more, but a fast autobahn runs to the south of what is now a very flourishing town. Tucked away in the woods is a German military cemetery, each grave giving the name of the soldier buried there and his date of birth. On one of the visits, I was accompanied by a young officer from the Regiment who commented that the dead had all been born before the turn of the century and must have been over 40 at the time. He was right, of course, which proves that well-trained soldiers, and particularly old soldiers, can give a very good account of themselves. They earned our respect. The Battle Honour, Ibbenbüren, was equally theirs.

The Echelon and mail arrived. I received my usual letter from my future wife, Joan, which told me that she had at last been to visit Mrs Elliott and that she had a lovely child which George had never seen. I managed to write a sad reply, urging her to make yet another visit.

We were withdrawn from the area to allow the infantry to mop up and the Regiment made a long, sweeping move to the south of Osnabrück, heading north towards Bassum and Twistringen. A freak shot fired by an anti-tank gun at a leading tank in 'A' Squadron struck the road and the ricochet hit the turret of a tank well down the column, killing Lieutenant Wallworth who had also served so magnificently in 's-Hertogenbosch. The anti-tank gun was quickly knocked out and the crew, hardly more than boys, were killed.

Twistringen was a small town on an arterial roadway linking Osnabrück and Bremen. My troop was ordered to move south on a long, straight road and to link up with troops of the 11th Armoured Division coming from the south. The route was tree-lined, but with open ground on both sides. The cobbles could easily be mined and, even more threateningly, there could be anti-tank guns in the woods some 300 yards to left and right. There were also a few houses dotted along the route to make the task even more unpleasant.

Sergeant Chick Strickland, impatient with my slow advance at 15 mph, suddenly shot past me in his Scout car. I thought he had gone mad or seen something which I had missed. He stopped abruptly and opened fire on a horse-drawn column of troops to our left. They had all their equipment on a wagon and were walking very slowly behind, obviously very tired men. They scattered and we moved on.

Our tanks joined us as we waited for the 11th Armoured Division to come from the opposite end of the town. German troops kept running across the road ahead of us, trying to escape before being cut off. They were probably the same ones we had shot up. As we moved closer a shot went through the Browning ammunition box just beside Bob Sawtell's head. The belt in the box began to smoulder and he had difficulty in getting it out without revealing too much of his body. We tried to reverse back up the road, taking our direction from the lines of telephone poles in order to put a little distance between ourselves and the enemy. I spoke to Sergeant Ralph Chalmers, who put a few rounds of HE into the area.

*Sergeant Bob Price*, who later wrote his account of the war years, adds some interesting thoughts on the Twistringen action which I feel are sentiments worth repeating in full:

"Writing these reflections in 1987, 42 years afterwards, I am indebted to books written by members of the Regiment: *Change and Challenge* written by General Sir Cecil Blacker and Major-General H. G. Woods; and *First In. Last Out.* the Recce Squadron story written almost immediately after the war and republished in 1986.

"Until reading these works, my own activities had sunk almost into oblivion . . . or so I thought. There is nothing like the rural life of a gamekeeper to ruin one's memory, especially of mankind in conflict. I have read much of what has been written about the Second World War, but both these books revived names and faces of characters I soldiered with when I joined the regulars; worked and chatted with on tank parks in England; and fought beside during the war years. What is more important, they revived all manner of experiences; and the sequence of them. Prior to reading these accounts they had become a hotch-potch of unrelated incidents.

"Just the same, memories written years later cannot be totally dependent upon official documents. No two participants in the same battle will share exactly the same experience. Nor, during or after the event, will all be known about the movement of others who may have influenced the battle in a positive way. When in action there was very little, if any, coffee-house type of chat. There was too much going on. Often, we were just too tired or hungry to be concerned with the experiences of others. It was sufficient to be out of the limelight for a while to be permitted to rest and recuperate. I cannot remember any 'idle chat' then.

"In *First In. Last Out.* excellently written by John Pilborough with realism and typical Skin-like sense of humour, I found the atmosphere of those days in action recaptured since it was written soon after the war, when memories were fresh. At this time, many of us had already handed in our blankets and drawn demob Trilbys. During the final stages of the operation in Germany, one sensed an air of competition, of friendly rivalry, which shows the sort of spirit by which our Regiment won its Battle Honours. On Page 87 of *First In. Last Out.* my eye caught that remark about 'standing astride the arterial road between Osnabrück and Bassum'. It also mentioned that 'Depleted Third Troop, one Sawn-off and a Scout car entered Twistringen alone'. There was a touch of the liberation spirit about Twistringen. The people there were devout Catholics and had not been well treated under Nazi rule. Also there was a hospital."

For this and subsequent actions, Bob Price was awarded a Military Medal. The citation submitted by Major J. M. Ward-Harrison read:

> "Sergeant Price has been troop sergeant of Second Troop, 'C' Squadron, throughout the campaign in NW Europe and throughout that time has been noted for his tactical skill, judgment, and coolness in action. During the action at Borken on March 28th, 1945, his troop commander had to be evacuated, and from that time to the present he has commanded the troop. As a Troop Leader he has been outstanding. He has taken part in all the operations in which the squadron has been engaged.
>
> "Typical of his performance were his actions at Borken, Ibbenbüren and Twistringen. In the first two of these, he had the task of flank protection and in both cases he showed the same qualities of coolness when under fire, skill in manoeuvre, leadership and determination to close with and destroy the enemy, which in both cases he succeeded in doing.
>
> "At Twistringen, he was the leading troop and by his dash, speed of action and skilful, appreciation, he entered the town some two hours ahead of the remainder of the squadron, dominated the main exits, prevented the re-entry of certain parties of enemy attacking from the south west and west, took numbers of prisoners, and ensured the successful occupation of the town by the Squadron Company Group before nightfall.
>
> "Sergeant Price has proved himself unquestionably the best troop leader in my squadron. His unfailing willingness, his personal courage, coolness and judgment and his technical and

tactical efficiency, have throughout been an inspiration to the men under his command. No other troop leader in my squadron, or NCO, has made a greater single contribution to its successful operations."

* * * * *

The Regiment now directed its attack upon Bassum. A number of isolated incidents occurred before the town was cleared. We were diverted north-westerly towards Wildeshausen, not appreciating that this town was essential to the enemy to maintain supplies to their troops still fighting in the north of Holland. Sergeant Chalmers, with his troop from 'C' Squadron ran into a bazooka attack as soon as they entered the town.

After harbouring overnight, my troop patrolled forward and soon came to his knocked-out tank which had caught fire. Trooper Batty who was thought to have been killed when the bazooka struck, was lying in the road beside the burned-out vehicle. He must have climbed out and been machine-gunned. We drove past and into the town.

Once on to the main road, we headed north and through the built-up area. Immediately clear of the town was a river and, behind that, a thickly wooded area. I could see much debris on the bridge and, as we approached, a German ran from underneath it and into the woods, We fired, but I think he escaped. Examining the rubbish on the bridge from about 20 yards distance, I could see two sets of fins protruding from two enormous holes in the road. They must have been at least 1000-pound bombs or rockets, and the very sight of them was enough to make us call a halt and report back. The whole lot could easily go up before our eyes and, the more I looked at the fins, the more I felt we were too close to them for safety. I reported the situation and was informed that Holdfast (Royal Engineers) would come forward to take a look.

While we were waiting, a gun—probably a 50mm—was firing at the column of tanks but, miraculously, the shots were passing between my vehicle and that commanded by Sergeant Tom Broad immediately behind me. I was keeping very low in the tank when a casual voice outside called out: "What's the matter, then?" I looked over the side to see a very young sergeant standing there. "That mess in front is the matter", I replied. When told that there were two bombs resting on the river bed and that a German had been seen to run away, he replied "Right", and walked unconcernedly on to the bridge, kicked some rubbish off the road, went down the bank, reappeared on the bridge again, and crossed to the other side. We were full of admiration and quite certain that we were witnessing an award of a VC. At last he emerged, stood on the bridge and shouted "OK".

I was still not entirely sure that we would not disappear into eternity once on the bridge and, for want of something more constructive to say, I asked him about all the other rubbish lying about. He kicked that off, too, so we had no choice but to cross, lifing our feet in the air as we went over.

On the other side, the road ahead divided, and I took the left fork while the following troop veered right. No further than half a mile ahead there was another small bridge. I halted and was examining it through my binoculars when my hero from the Engineers came bounding up in his Scout car and enquired cockily: "Do you want me to look at this one, too?" "Well, since you're here, you might as well," I replied. No sooner had he started to move forward than volleys of rifle fire peppered us. The Sapper reversed smartly and was never seen again. "Some sort of nut case," commented a member of the crew. He was probably fresh out from England, determined to make a name for himself in what little time remained. He was a very lucky man, and an heroic one, whoever he was.

Sergeant Fred Heaps came forward with a troop from 'A' Squadron and dealt with the riflemen, twelve in all. Another mile up the road, we were observing the open country ahead when the gunner OP tank came up and, as though taking orders for drinks, asked if there was anything he could do. We looked around, trying to find him a target, when a German staff car suddenly appeared, crossing the open field from right to left. "There you are," we said, "have a go at that." He quickly traversed his six-pounder on to the car and fired. The shot went well over the top of the target and we heard the remark to the gunner: "I always knew this bloody thing was not properly 'T and A'd!" His shot had the effect of making the passengers dive into the ditch and one of our vehicles went out and brought in four high-ranking officers complete with maps and documents. (We received a pat on the back for that later.)

We soon realised that our presence was not expected in that area. First we encountered a member of the German Home Guard wearing an armband displaying the words "Volksturm". Our attempts to convince him that we were British met with protests of "Nein, nein." He believed us when we ran a tank over his bike! Then a youth came up the road on a bicycle. We arrested him, but he escaped and rode away furiously into the woods. Jock Ramsay and I crawled forward with a Bren gun around a bend ahead of the tank when a woman came along, also on a bicycle. I wasn't sure whether she had seen us or not, but just as she drew level, she dived her hand into her shopping bag and fell off. She was ushered to the rear of the tank and taken away.

Two Germans on a motor-cycle now appeared on the bend about 200 yards ahead. I told Jock to hold his fire and see what they would do. They spread their maps out on the fuel tank and studied them, then started the bike and came towards us. I told Jock to leave the tank to deal with them, but they stopped in the road right in front of our position and he could contain himself no longer. After all, the poor drivers seldom had an opportunity to have a shoot at anything. The pair almost left the road and went over the hedge opposite. We followed and found there was a pond on the other side from which we pulled one of the Germans. The other we never found. We were very unsympathetic when we discovered that the motor-cycle was one of our 7th Armoured Division machines.

This was one of those days when you seem to be in an "all win" situation, but over to our right the other troop of Recce had reported 17 German tanks in a wood. We had not seen so many tanks in any one place since Holland, and the rocket-firing Typhoons were called in to shoot them up. Within a quarter of an hour they came in, all guns firing, and we heard the deadly woosh of the rockets as they went home.

It was now dusk and time to withdraw. As we re-entered Wildeshausen we were met by a relaxed Sergeant Ted Glynn, who directed us to the local school which would be our billet for the night. "Get yourselves cleaned up," he said. "We have captured some hooch and we are going to have a party." We told him there were 17 German tanks just up the road, but he replied "Don't worry. The Norfolk Yeomanry are in position all round the town and we can stand down."

We were having a meal when we heard a sudden shot and a round went through the roof of the school. "Bloody fools", said Ted. "Some stupid bastard has started on the booze and fired his main armament." The shot was followed by another and another, and a lot of Spandau fire. "Mount up", came the shout, and we were back on our vehicles and hearing radio reports that German tanks and infantry had followed us in. The Norfolk Yeomanry had assumed that they were with us.

The leading German tank had a hey-day and simply shot at unmanned tanks as he drove down the road. The only crewmen in a tank were the regimental headquarters radio operator, who was maintaining a link to Brigade, and 'A' Squadron Leader's gunner, who knocked the leading German tank out at point-blank range. The German infantry were in among us and we could not distinguish between friend and foe. Our own artillery was called down upon our own positions and we were very lucky to escape with the loss of two Scout cars and one tank slightly damaged. The DLI had lost their regimental aid post and six medical orderlies who were taken prisoner, though they escaped and returned a few days later. Had the attack come an hour later when the parties had started, the situation could have been far more serious for us all. We were still learning, even at this late stage! I believe there is a memorial to the German officer who led that attack somewhere in Wildeshausen. He earned it!

3 Division took over the responsibility for securing Wildeshausen. The Regiment was withdrawn and moved to a concentration area west of Nienburg. The bridges over the Weser had been blown,

which gave us a three-day rest to make proper meals, wash, and change our clothing. We moved on April 16th, crossing the Weser at Rethem and halting three miles west of Walsrode and Fallingbostel. The following morning we moved out at 0500 hours to clear the centre-line from Dorfmark to Soltau.

General Patton's army was driving towards Czechoslovakia and the Russians were at the gates of Berlin. Where would we meet the Russians? There was grim news filtering through via the BBC on 6.2M/cls: the 11th Armoured Division south of us had liberated Belsen. I remember thinking very seriously about the German race. There was a strong feeling that this bastard race would have to be exterminated. Perhaps Hitler and his Nazis felt the same way about the Jews! The news had a very telling effect upon us all and was partly responsible for Soltau being so heavily attacked. It was defended, but not at any great strength. It seemed to us that nothing we could do would punish the enemy for the atrocities we had heard about.

We moved quickly, Sergeant Chick Strickland leading and I as back-up. Lieutenant Charles Snell decided to travel in my Sawn-off instead of his Scout car, which followed behind. Both Bob Sawtell and I were large men and fully occupied the hole where the turret had been. Charles was equally large, and his presence restricted movement in a confined space. A civilian—a Frenchman who had been working on a farm nearby—told us that there was a gun in the wood on the outskirts of Soltau. From his description, it sounded like a 37mm type or ack-ack gun which could be used as an anti-tank gun. Chick edged forward and was looking through his binoculars in the direction indicated by the Frenchman when there was a large puff of smoke and both he and John Pilborough were blown out of the turret. They both made for the ditch to the left of the tank. Albert Wilde, who had only arrived with the Squadron on the previous day, scrambled out of the co-driver's seat and joined them.

I fired my smoke discharger over the top of them as heavy machine-gun fire cracked around our heads. Charles stood up in the centre of the turret and was so engrossed in reporting the contact that he seemed oblivious to the shots above our heads. I hit him hard on the back of the legs, which brought him down to join Bob and me. He looked at me and inquired indignantly, what I thought I was doing. I pulled his head-set off and pointed upwards. He soon realised why we were all in a heap in the bottom of the turret.

A squadron of Flame-throwers came up on our left and started to squirt fire at the woods to our front and towards the source of the machine-gun fire. We dismounted and ran forward to the crew of the Honey, but Pat Ledwith was still inside. One look at the front of the tank convinced us that he was unlikely to be alive and, in any case we could not get at him without being cut to pieces. We evacuated the other three to join our own Headquarters. Captain James Ussher, who had replaced Robert Crockett as our leader just before crossing the Rhine, listened to our tale of woe but, like his predecessor, was fairly unsympathetic. He told us to get back up the road, get Ledwith out, and stay with the tank until it could be cleared of maps and codes. The woods and a farm just in front were well ablaze as a result of the flaming, but there was no further fire from the enemy positions. Chick and I crawled forward into the wood to our right to get a better look at the gun which had fired at him. Suddenly Pat Ledwith, badly wounded in the head, fell out of the driver's hatch of the knocked-out tank and we carried him to the rear. He was to survive for 20 years though badly injured. "Taffy" Willingale was left on the radio and Jock Ramsay attended to Pat.

We suddenly found ourselves on the edge of the most intense artillery barrage from all the guns which could be brought to bear on the field and woods in front of us. We were pinned down and dared not try to run back to the tank. Taking refuge in a slight indentation in the ground, our main hope was that Taffy would see our predicament and radio back and get the barrage lifted. It must have been ten minutes before it stopped as suddenly as it had started and we made a dash for the tank. As previously reported, Taffy was known to be very deaf. "Did you stop that?" we asked. "Stop what?" he enquired. "The stonk," we said, scarcely believing that he had not noticed. "I didn't hear anything!" he replied. In due course, a pale-faced James Ussher came forward full of apologies for arranging the artillery when we were in the line of fire, but he was not to know that we would creep forward. Headaches apart, we were unhurt except for minor injuries to Chick's hands. His binoculars were twisted and smashed but he, yet again, had been given a lucky break.

'C' Squadron came up and moved ahead while we watched with amazement as the town fire brigade came from the opposite direction to begin an extinguishing operation as though dealing with a normal fire. We shared a house with a family of Germans that night. Normally they would have been thrown out to fend for themselves, but there were so many of them and nowhere that they could go. They stayed well out of our way and hid in the cellar. There was no sympathy for these people, and a feeling of gay abandon as we parked the tank in the front garden. The following morning, we moved through the devastated town and on to the autobahn, the first time we had seen such a road. Hitler is reported to have built them to enable his armour to speed west in 1940. It may have served him well, but for us it was a raised road and provided any well-placed 88mm gun with a marvellous target. We were glad to get off it and head to the north-west, halting in Tottensen to send patrols out.

I was recalled to our HQ and introduced to a sergeant wearing an Airborne beret. Captain Jimmy Ussher introduced him as an official war correspondent who wanted to get some pictures of Hamburg, which could be seen from hills to our right. I was to take him in my tank. As he climbed aboard, I explained that there was an SP firing from the edge of the wood below us and out of sight. I invited him to take the Bren on the front of the turret while Bob Sawtell and I manned the side brownings. "I know nothing about guns" he said, and declined my offer. "I thought you were Airborne," I said. "Not likely!" he said. "I'm a photographer." We felt that we definitely had a passenger.

We crawled to a point where the photographer could best get his shots and waved to him to come forward. He refused to move and went lower into my tank. What a wasted journey, we thought. We had an excellent view of the low ground up to the Elbe and could watch movement with ease. A German soldier suddenly rose from a hole some 200 yards ahead and walked casually down a fence carrying a shovel. He was clearly going to answer the call of nature and would have been properly caught with his trousers down, except that we did not want to disclose our commanding position. I wondered how often any of us had been followed through a gun sight and not been fired at?

# The Final Days of War

Individual stories are scarce and I have to rely upon the account written by John Pilborough, and my own vivid memories, to complete the last few days of hostility. The war was not over for all Germans, and they obeyed the order to fight to the last. Casualties would have been far higher on both sides if the Allies had not played a waiting game. The Regiment was ordered to withdraw from the approaches to Hamburg and veer north-west towards the German Naval Headquarters at Buxtehude. A report had been received that the plans of the North Sea mined areas would be held there, and we were to support staff officers and some Royal Marine Commandos to obtain access to the barracks.

We set off at 0500 hours and soon arrived at the large barracks, which to our delight, we found to be occupied by a large number of German Women's Naval Services, the equivalent to our Wrens. They were hardly out of their beds and made a nice change from the sort of prisoners we had grown used to! We were not allowed very long to ogle this sight and left the Marines to search the place! We spent a day gathering in pistols and bazookas which were taken to a large sports field and destroyed.

Moving to the small village of Apensen, we established ourselves in farms and the local school. There was news of an armistice in Italy and, though unbeknown to us at the time, Monty was just to our south making arrangements for a meeting with the Germans on Luneberg Heath. We settled down to daily patrols up the same route, lifting mines from the cobbled roads which were replaced by the Germans at night.

We had received a number of new and fast American light tanks—the M24 (Chaffee), which had a 75mm gun, five forward and reverse gears, fully automatic transmission, and a wide track to permit travel over soft country. It was roomy and bristling with weapons. If only we had had them for the Normandy campaign! We had no training on these vehicles and spent much time reading the instruction book that came with them. It looked as though we would never use them in anger. On the first day out, we were determined to fire at something, so the leader T and A'd his sights on to the window frame of a nearby house. A Frenchman, who said he had escaped from a labour camp, came up and pointed out that the house was the home of the local Volksturm (Home Guard) Commander. It was a good enough target and excuse enough for a testing round. The first round was a direct hit and the house collapsed. We soon learned that, like the Sherman, the engine had to be running at high revs to keep the batteries up as the traverse system was powered totally by electricity. Now the batteries were flat and we had to have a tow start.

The following morning we returned to the village from the opposite end and went to look at the target house, now a smouldering ember, to check the effectiveness of the round fired. A young girl of about fifteen was collecting items in a sack which already included her pet rabbit. The interpreter discovered that she had lived there with her grandparents, both of whom had been badly injured. We looked at her tearful face and I think that none of us were without compassion for her and felt some degree of shame.

We were still encountering mines and had to be very careful. Most were laid in the verges and not difficult to see. Ginty did his own clearing by attaching a cable to one of them and ordering the tank to pull it out of the ground. Unfortunately, Corporal Johnnie Dixon had not heard his warning and walked round the side of the tank just as the mine blew up. He was wounded in one arm and in the body but, fortunately, not seriously. Ginger Proudlove ran over another with his Sawn-off, and so ensured an honourable end for it. An Engineer corporal came up to look at mines which we had uncovered and I took a walk through the village with him and found more.

That evening, back in the school, Tom Broad came in late and informed us that the village had contained a company of German infantry. More care would be necessary. We went forward more cautiously the following day and found the Bürgermeister, who was ordered to collect all the weapons and cameras. We gave him three hours. At about 1800 hours, Chick Strickland and I crawled along a ditch from the eastern end of the same village. We were some 200 yards away from our vehicles when a telephone cable broke and curled down the road. We had not heard any shot which might have broken it, but it made us cautious. Then, from behind an unmanned road block immediately in front of us, we heard a heavy mechanical rumbling and were relieved to see it was a farmer towing a urine spreader up and down a field. It was a very normal sight, but completely out of place in this situation. We entered the village and the Bürgermeister handed over a box of weapons he had collected.

A patrol of the 11th Hussars was reported to be meeting heavy resistance and one of the patrol had been killed. On another occasion, we occupied a house with a sort of observation room on the first floor. From here we had a very clear view right up to the Elbe and watched our aircraft attacking shipping on the river. One largish ship raised a white flag and, as the Spitfire flew over, gave it a burst and took the flag down again. Other aircraft put in an attack. We ran a long lead from our tank radio and tuned one of the sets in to the BBC to find out what was going on. The announcers said: "Units of the 7th Armoured Division are occupying positions overlooking Hamburg and the Elbe." We were in the news!

Horneburg, a few miles north, was quite a large town and we did not wish to fight for it. Probing around the southern approaches, we soon found that the Chaffee was not as bogproof as we had been told. Chick was stuck. I was about to tow him out when I saw three very sad-looking Germans standing patiently on the path behind us and waiting for one of us to take notice of them. We reported back that we had three prisoners. The CO ordered us to send one of them back into the town and tell the senior German officer that if his garrison did not surrender by 1500 hours, we would attack it. The prisoners were very reluctant to go back but, at the prod of a pistol the oldest was directed back over the railway line. We saw him disappear through a hedge, and waited. Nothing happened, and a message came through that the other two should be brought to the Tac HQ, where there was a vehicle to take them away. One of the prisoners, convinced he was going to be shot, was down on his knees begging for mercy. I could not convince him that he was safe. He continued to tell me about his wife and children and was too frightened to walk. I put my pistol away and helped him along. Arriving at Tac, I herded my two into a truck and there, sitting contentedly, was the first one we had sent into the town. Other troops had seen him come through the hedge and immediately re-bagged him! Another prisoner indicated that the level crossing and a bridge were wired to very nasty-looking sea mines and could be blown from switches in a distribution centre. He was set to work to defuse them.

On May 3rd, Hamburg surrendered and we were given strategic positions to occupy. My tank was to park in the car park of the Harburg police station; others were on the Harburg-Hamburg bridge and at other government offices. That evening we moved over the bridge and, at about half past five, a message came over the Regimental net saying that hostilities were to cease and that we could put our side lights on. We did not think very much of that because we were certain that all Germans were not on our frequency!

We then saw the terrible destruction in Hamburg. The roads were badly pothholed and piles of rubble on each side had been made into temporary homes. We were later told that the Germans dare not try to clear the debris because so many bodies were buried under it and they had no medical supplies to fight the epidemic which would follow. Some 80,000 people had died in one night when a fire ball had been created by the extensive bombing. We moved through to the northern suburbs and into Pinneberg. That drive through devastation will never be forgotten. We now built our hopes on continuing our advance up the peninsular of Schleswig-Holstein and over the Danish border. It would be wonderful to be among liberated civilians again and to be away from these sullen, defeated Germans.

Thousands of German troops surrendered and created a major problem. We herded them into fields and collected arms and equipment. Feeding points had to be arranged, and many required medical attention. We pushed on and up to the Kiel Canal, where our instructions were to prevent any more potential prisoners from coming south. They must remain where they had been before the surrender. My troop motored up to a small, hand-operated ferry capable of carrying small vehicles. There was a German ack-ack troop on the southern side and another troop over the canal. Two large cargo boats were tied up at a jetty, one of which, we learned contained a cargo of confiscated radios from Norway and Denmark. It was not very long before a truck arrived from the Echelon and it was loaded. We personally selected sets for ourselves.

My moment of triumph came when we arrived at the camp. I saw a young officer who spoke very good English and told him to get everybody on parade and to have all weapons placed in a heap. I thoroughly enjoyed inspecting the two dozen dejected Germans and having all the weapons removed. I told the officer that he was to remain in the camp and that they were to feed themselves until they could be moved. Lieutenant Charles Snell came up just as a party from the opposite bank was coming over for a meal. "Where are they going?" asked Charles. We were now beginning to use a few German words in our vocabulary, and I replied: "They are going to essen," (German for food). Charles went red and roared that nobody was to go anywhere, and certainly not to Essen!

Our next problem was caused by all kinds of foreign labour, enforced civilians who now felt free to plunder, rape, and generally attack the German population. Who could blame them? There was a mixture of Poles, Russians and Czechs, and all were half starved. We gave them what rations we could and they were very grateful but just hung around the tanks begging for more. We remained at Bendorf for about a week. We now had confiscated shotguns, sacks full of ammunition, and had time to enjoy shooting game. Someone shot a very nice deer and we persuaded a kind German lady in the house we occupied to cook it. I was out with a tank acting as a road block on the edge of the canal when Captain James Ussher came to tell me that I had been promoted to Lance Sergeant, back-dated to early March. The same kindly German woman in the baker's shop stitched some new stripes on for me. Rank had not counted for much when in action: we all had a job to do and sometimes the most difficult tasks and decisions were made by very junior ranks. But at least I knew I was in good books!

This lush and productive area of Germany had not suffered greatly from the effects of war, and there was little hostility to our presence. On the contrary, we seemed to be viewed as liberators, which assured us that we were not likely to encounter underground activity. There was one other interesting patrol here when we were briefed to proceed to a farm north of the canal where Himmler, the Deputy Führer, was reported to be hiding. We proceeded with all haste only to find that he and his SS bodyguard had moved some 20 minutes earlier. Later that day he was apprehended on a bridge in Hamburg and, while awaiting interrogation, bit a cyanide pill and died instantly. SSM Charlie Gower, who had drilled those early subalturns in Colchester, proudly announced over the air that he had captured the German heavyweight boxer, Max Schmeling. He was dressed in civilian clothing and driving a car towing a trailer full of souvenirs. Charlie and his crew were told that he would be taken prisoner and escorted to a proper interrogation centre.

The whole Regiment moved to occupy Brunsbüttelkoog, the port on the western end of the Kiel Canal. German naval vessels, including submarines, lay at anchor as we again occupied strategic positions and rounded up suspects. I was given the distasteful task of collecting six very attractive girls, all of different nationalities, who had been brought from the ships. They had been the mistresses of the captain and were the best-dressed women we had seen for a very long time. I cannot remember what we had to do with them, but I can remember that we did not give much for the chances of the Russian girl among them.

*Lieutenant Ben Tottenham,* still carrying out liaison duties at Brigade, was also sent to Brunsbüttelkoog to act as a sort of 'Gauleiter"! He wrote the following report:

"With me was Dickie Brett-Smith and Dick McAdam, troop leaders in the 11th Hussars. Dickie, who later became the defence correspondent of the *Daily Telegraph*, describes very amusingly in his book, *Berlin, Grey City*, how Major-General Wittkopf, in command of 2,000 POWs. presented himself and surrendered to me as the senior British officer present! We were a somewhat shabby and unusually dressed trio by contrast to the General, who was immaculate in field grey, red stripes and gold braid on his ample form. However, our drill was impeccable, thanks to the recent administrations of RSM 'Bosom' Bland at Sandhurst. Having thereby established moral superiority, and with the willing co-operation of a friendly Bürgermeister, I rapidly sorted out the logistic problems of absorbing 2,000 POWs and controlling the town.

"A few days later I took tea with the German naval officer in command, Kapitan zur Zee Heyer, whose flag lieutenant, Frigaten Kapitan Friere von Egensburg, chatted away about capercailzie in Austria and socialites he had known in pre-war London. As a memento, the Kapitan handed me his binoculars (in advance of my confiscating them). I have always treasured them, not particularly as a memento of the artificial bonhomie of the meeting, but because Zeiss glasses with rubber eye pieces are perfect for night vision and tank work."

*　*　*　*　*

The spoils of war were many. There was a small motor-boat which we used for trips up the Kiel Canal. The Commanding Officer appeared on a splendid German horse as he rode around the areas under his command. Radios from a ship tied up at Beldorf were everywhere. Cameras and film seemed plentiful, and trading in cigarettes commenced. They were the only worthwhile currency. Marks were quite valueless.

The 11th Armoured Division had captured Lübeck and the Royal Dragoons had been allocated the coveted task of liberating Denmark. We envied them that. There was a final round-up of German soldiers still wandering about south of the Danish border, and they were given a time to report to the main centre of Meldorf, a small market town some ten miles north. Tac HQ tanks were placed on the edge of the market square and Recce tanks closed the exits. At 1000 hours on about May 10th, the vanquished came marching in, one German regiment complete with a band at its head and seemingly defiant. A burst of Browning above them soon knocked that final act on the head.

A DP (displaced person) reported that a German General lived not very far away and I was despatched with the civilian to investigate. The interpreter went into the house and soon came out with an old man who looked well past his best. His wife and daughter also came out and pleaded with us to spare him. I assisted him on to the tank and, with my assurance that he would soon be returned, we rejoined the gathering of German servicemen, some complete with wives or girl friends. I helped the General, who I believe was a General Mann, to alight and was told by the second-in-command, Major Bridgewater, to take him home and ensure that he next appeared in uniform.

We returned and two men accompanied him into the house to ensure that he did not attempt suicide. Some 20 minutes later a very smart German appeared, straight as a ramrod and very indignant. He had obviously decided that if they wanted a General, he would act like one. This transformed figure declined my offer of assistance to mount the tank and, once in the market square again, berated the nearest German officer, clearly telling him that his men were a rabble and to get them smartened up. Men lounging about sprang to their feet, buttons were done up, cigarettes extinguished, and they aligned themselves in ranks ready for loading on to our vehicles. The General had a conversation with the interpreter and also with our Pedro Sharpe from whom we learned that he had served on the German Embassy Staff in Buenos Aires and spoke very good Spanish. The General's wife and daughter arrived and joined in the friendly conversation. The General also amazed us when, after asking what regiment we were, immediately gave us the name of our Commanding Officer. He had opposed us as a brigade commander in Normandy.

This round-up was, in reality, the last warlike duty we performed. We were quartered in barracks in Itzehoe, a very nice town, untouched by war and really very friendly. We were at first allocated tasks to round up and transport SS men to one of the islands off the coast and to guard the DPs who were wandering around aimlessly. The Recce troops were running a camp full of every nationality in the Eastern Bloc. It was a matter of feeding them and keeping them occupied until they could be returned to their own countries. Many, for obvious reasons, had no wish to be repatriated. Every man, woman and child in Itzehoe was ordered to provide a complete set of clothing, and these items were distributed.

After a few weeks, we moved a few miles east and were billeted in farming areas at Mühlenbarbek, Lohbarbek and Lockstedt Lager. There was an immediate release for all those who had experience in the building trades and for those who had been pre-war reservists. Replacements for those we were to lose came from those regiments which were originally in the Territorial Army and the regiments formed in 1941.

Lieutenant Colonel Teddy Swetenham, who had led us throughout with calm and consideration, was taken off to command the Royal Scots Greys. Lieutenant Colonel Perry Harding replaced him for a short while before being promoted to Brigadier and creating a vacancy for Lieutenant Colonel Alec Scott to return. The Regiment soon found the nucleus for a strong riding team equipped with requisitioned German horses and set about show jumping. For the other ranks there was sport and plenty of high-class athletics, shooting, riding and motor-cycling on commandeered German machines. The German population, left without food and accommodation, depended very heavily upon the forces for work. Despite General Montgomery's order that there should be no fraternising with the vanquished, there had to be, and life as an occupation force was pleasant.

For me, as a young sergeant, there was much to learn about peacetime soldiering. My Squadron Leader, Major Maurice Peters, who had been the pre-war RSM, saw to it that I got it. He realised that I still had at least six years to serve on my present engagement, and sent me on course after course: a month's drill in the 7th Armoured Division Battle School near Brussels, Chaffee gunnery and driving in Brünswick, and a sniper course on the first class German ranges at Sennelager. During one of these periods, when away from the Regiment, there was a move to a new barracks in Münster. As the individual stories commenced with one by Lieutenant Andrew Craig-Harvey, who was later taken prisoner, I thought it fitting to round it all off with a story by his brother, Hugh (who lost his aerial photographs at St Odilienburg). It emphasises a few of the problems associated with Occupation:

"It happened while we were at Münster, some time in 1946. The Commanding Officer, Lieutenant Colonel R. P. Harding, suddenly discovered that he was Military Commandant of the area. Determined to exert his authority, he one night despatched Major Monckton and myself with a patrol to catch any German out after curfew without a pass. Münster was pretty flat at that time but we duly established ourselves at a crossroads amid the ruins and waited hopefully. At about 2200 hours we established a road block. As you might expect, absolutely nothing happened except that a few rabbits came out to nibble the grass growing through the stones of the cobbled streets. Eventually a solitary cyclist arrived who stated that he had been visiting his wife in hospital. He had no pass, so we kept him with us and resumed our vigil. By midnight we were getting pretty bored and felt that our lone German was little to show for the CO to exert his authority! However, just as we were thinking of packing it all in and going home, around the corner came a British three-tonner, without any regimental or divisional markings. Worse, it was being driven by a civilian. It halted at our road-block and the passenger beside the driver, also a civilian, leaped out and started to abuse us in German (the war had only just ended)! I hit him with my stick and Major Monckton threatened him with his pistol. We had him doubling up and down the road until he was quite out of breath. I think he was ex-SS as he responded excellently to this treatment and was now standing rigidly to attention and being much more polite. There was plenty of 'Ja, Herr Major' and 'Ja, Herr Oberleutnant'. We made everybody get out of the truck, male and female, and lined them all up. They had not a pass or identity card amongst them, nor did the vehicle have a work ticket. To our joy they turned out to be a band from the Control Commission Officers' Club! The army did not like the Control Commission. Politely we referred to them as 'Green Lizards', from the flashes on their epaulettes; less politely as 'Barnacles on the posterior of Victory'! Delighted with our catch, we put them into cells in barracks, where there was much wailing and gnashing of teeth. Our Colonel was equally delighted with our haul but was not too sure what to do with our prisoners, so they were left in the guardroom for the night.

The Control Commission usually stopped for lunch about 12 noon when they went to their club. They were much concerned to find themselves without their band. By 12.30 they had discovered where it was and came round to our barracks demanding its release. This the Colonel refused to do, pointing out that he was military commandant of the area and that his Regiment had found a dozen Germans wandering about Münster at midnight, in a British truck without a work permit and which he presumed was stolen. The conversation, according to Rupert Kettle, the Adjutant, became acrimonious. Higher authority was brought in, with the result that, at about teatime, the Commander-in-Chief himself came on the 'phone and ordered our CO reluctantly to release the band. Such were the duties of a regiment, carrying out occupational duties."

NB: To be fair, the Control Commission, Germany, had a difficult task to perform, with little food or accommodation, almost nothing to treat the many injured and sick civilians, no transport system and a very weak police force. It is understandable that any soldier who had fought through the war and had long dealings with the population, should resent the intrusion of a lot of civilians sent out from Britain to try to establish a civilian government. Army commanders were cautious about handing over any authority to what appeared to be a very dubious lot.

To their credit, the CCG did establish a form of Government quite quickly and, above all, gave direction towards establishing trade unions. By having far fewer of them, conflict between rival unions was avoided, and the result is to be seen in the German economy today.

The Regiment was to settle in Münster for almost two years, and in Paderborn for a further three years, before again coming under active service conditions in a different war—Korea. This was to be fought as a unit of the first United Nations Force and under far different circumstances from those experienced in Europe.

# Envoi

As I complete these individual memories, I feel the same sense of urgency as well as the same satisfaction and sense of achievement which we shared during the closing stages of the war. My friends who served at that time are at least sixty-four and some are well into their eighties. There is constant news of the death of one or other of them which has urged me on with renewed vigour. Since I started writing, many of my closest friends have died (from natural causes, I am pleased to say).

Two of my troop leaders, Captains Jack Bissill and John Milligan, have died recently; my close friend, Corporal John Pilborough, who dedicated the last months of his service to record the tales of the Recce Squadron in *First In. Last Out,* suffered a second heart attack and died suddenly. Ginty, the mad Irishman and close friend with whom I served for many years after the war, lost a leg five years ago and was taken into hospital on Christmas Day, 1988, threatened with a second amputation. I visited him in Scunthorpe Hospital and found him still able to joke about his illness. He constantly sat up in bed to look at the monitor at the foot. Noting that it was not doing very well, I tried to divert his attention from it and asked: "Why do you keep looking at that thing?" "Because when it stops bobbing up and down, I know I'm dead," he replied. It was typical of him. He died two days later.

It is partly to preserve these memories that I have completed the book. I hope that their nearest and dearest will feel pride in the stories I have related on their behalf. Some of them will, I am sure, seem completely out of character with the men they knew. They returned to take up employment in less active occupations, to being normal people who, probably like me, still view roads through woods or in open ground as awful ground to have to fight over. Perhaps they, too, avoid crushed animals on the road!

Corporal Joe Treadwell, had he lived, would have more to write about the alliance we have with Germany, now our staunchest ally and Russia. Whatever Joe's belief, his wishes in his short poem before crossing the Rhine were granted for most of us. My own awful feelings about the German race have changed completely. I have many, many close German friends and a German daughter-in-law who has presented us with two delightful grandchildren. But it was the circumstances of the war, and its outcome, which have made that possible, and I value it as part of the happy outcome.

Facts about the war which we have learned since, compare with feelings expressed by Wellington after Waterloo, when he stated: "It was a close-run thing." Those young officers who stood and listened to Chamberlain, telling the nation in 1939 that we were at war with Germany, would follow varied careers. Three of them—Captain Charles Keightley, the adjutant; Captain D'Arcy Anderson, who was to go off and serve as a Brigade Staff Officer during the retreat to Dunkirk and later as Commanding Officer of the Sherwood Rangers; and Lieutenant Monkey Blacker—would serve on to become Generals and to occupy commanding positions in the army.

Major Perry Harding, pre-war amateur steeplechaser, Lieutenant Gilbert Monckton, Captain John Ward-Harrison, and Lieutenant Henry Woods, would serve on to become Major-Generals. Colonel Mike Ansell was to receive much publicity and honour for pioneering British show jumping and taking it into the TV era. He also continued to inspire the blind to live an active life and to partake in sport and activity previously thought beyond the ability of a handicapped person. His own books are an inspiration which will live on.

Captain Bryan Marshall, the first officer to be wounded in Normandy, returned to the horse-racing world and was to ride the winner of the Grand National twice and in successive years. In 1953 on 'Early Mist' and 1954 on 'Royal Tan'. The three wartime Commanding Officers—Jack Anstice, Hook Sangster and Teddy Swetenham—also enjoyed quieter lives among the farming community before they died.

Many others were to command the Regiment in later years. Major Arthur Carr, who had been posted to the City of London Yeomanry and was taken prisoner after being wounded in Normandy, was to take the Regiment to Korea in 1951; and then be promoted to Brigadier and to continue his interest in equitation. He with Captain Alec Scott, who had been transport officer and failed to provide a three-tonner to take the silver to the bank in 1939, were two of the three who made up the British show jumping team in post-war years. Alec was to command the 2nd Fife and Forfar Yeomanry before returning to command the 5th Royal Inniskilling Dragoon Guards in 1946.

Lieutenant John Ward-Harrison, pack-master of that peculiar gathering of hounds in France, would later command the 10th Royal Hussars and retire as a Major-General Commanding North-East District. His character, like others, remained unchanged though diverted in another direction. His final act before he died was as a fund-raiser to rebuild the South West Trancept of York Minster.

Major Maurice Peters was to play a more active part in my personal career. Having sent me on all those courses immediately after hostilities as a young sergeant when still only just 21 years old, he put me on the right course for the future. He left the Regiment as Quartermaster when the Korean war called for our services, to be a pioneer of the newly-created Junior Leader Regiment of the Royal

Armoured Corps at Bovington. Always a keen sportsman and champion of youth, there could have been no better choice. It was a great sadness to us all when Maurice, who had become the unchallenged father figure of the Regiment, died in 1977.

The two Craig-Harvey brothers ran successful stud farms in the West Country, while Captain Neville Ussher, who suffered so much after being wounded in 1940, had to wait until 1943 for repatriation. He was fit enough to serve on as ADC to the Earl of Athlone, Governor-General of Canada. After the war, he completed his studies at agricultural college and farmed for a few years before taking an appointment as land agent to the Earl of Harewood, whom he served for 31 years. Despite those awful injuries, he has survived where other apparently fitter men have died.

Sergeant Charlie Bevan, one of two who received the double award of a DCM and MM, was not permitted to serve in France again for very obvious reasons, but he did serve in the Middle East. He retired to Uttoxeter to raise a family and to be a frequent visitor to our Home Headquarters in Chester and my own home. It was a sadness when he died in 1979, and I believe that his suffering had much to do with his war injuries. As a final tribute to Sister Marie, he named his eldest daughter Marie.

Lieutenant Ian Turner, who had such a worrying time defending that pontoon bridge in Belgium, was later wounded during the retreat to Dunkirk but recovered to be posted to a tank regiment in the Middle East. He had only served in the desert campaign for three weeks when his tank was struck by an anti-tank missile and he was killed.

Ginger Livingston, the natural clown who dug latrines from Normandy to the Kiel Canal, disappeared into the confines of Blackburn. Though not seen in Regimental circles or even reported upon, I suspect that the tales others have told about him have influenced the creators of many film and TV characters. There is always one like him.

Major Gus Newport, who survived that escape from Greece in 1941, served on with horses and mules in the Middle East and then retired to become an authority on greyhounds, breeding many outstanding dogs. He died three months before this publication.

Of my friends in the Recce Squadron, the Squadron Leaders survive. Robert Crockett ran a stud farm for many years; Jimmy Ussher became a grain merchant and Guy Glover farmed with Knox Chapman in Hertfordshire. Sergeant Chick Strickland, who probably had more narrow escapes than any other member of the Regiment, retired to farm in Lincolnshire. Rearing sheep and poultry is a much less exacting task than the service he gave to the Regiment during the war. Corporal John Pilborough, whom I mentioned previously, became a deputy headmaster of a York school. I could not have made this book worthy of publication had he not written so much immediately after the war.

Lance Corporal Pedro Sharpe, who travelled from Argentina to fight with us, married an English girl and returned to his native country. We have all retained a link, though relations with Argentina have suffered considerably. Trooper Taffy Willingale probably wears a deaf aid. We know he was working as a manager in a South African gold mine. Trooper Fang Bent worked for the Post Office as a telephone engineer and, as an enthusiastic radio "ham", maintains a weekly link with Ginger Marley, who had a successful career in insurance. The master escaper, Sergeant Harold Suggitt, was awarded the MM for his attempts and returned to become a leader of Hull Council.

Sergeant Ted Glynn, the joint holder of the DCM and MM, with Charlie Bevan, traded in textiles in Northampton and seems as youthful as ever. Sergeant Tom Broad is one who did not settle to a quiet life. He took employment with the Hereford Fire Brigade, rising to high rank, but the cries of children and people trapped in car accidents took its toll and he suffered a nervous breakdown. He is recovering steadily.

Captain Peter Duckworth found fame as an outstanding athlete, winning the modern pentathlon in many high-class events including the Olympics. He served in Korea, and later at Sandhurst, before retiring to run a market garden.

The courageous Belgian, Captain Charles de Selliers, became a successful businessman in Ghent and still lives in Brussels. Lieutenant Ben Tottenham, who made that nostalgic journey to see his sister in Paris and then found himself the liberator of Raesfeld, left the Regiment in 1947 but joined the Territorial Army, where he was to command The Kent Yeomanry. He is still a very active master of hounds at Sandhurst. Captain Charles Snell emigrated to the United States and took employment with an aircraft manufacturer, where he became operations manager.

Sergeant Eric Roodhouse, wounded at St-Georges-du-Vièrve, eventually returned to the Regiment to hold the rank of Squadron Sergeant Major before retiring in 1962 to run a tyre supply company. He died in 1984. Sergeant Reg Worman, who was so effective as command operator in keeping us all informed, was one of those to receive an early release to return to his father's building business. He was eventually joint inheritor of the firm.

Sergeant Bob Sawtell, whom I first met in Normandy when ordered by JR to move a Sherman, gave up studies as an architect and became a director of a Devon textile firm. Trooper Alf Stoker, "lover of dogs", became a butcher in Morpeth, Northumberland. Corporal Max Cooke was suddenly granted a commission when in Holland and joined the Green Howards. He was to spend some years with that regiment both during and after the fighting. He later emigrated to Canada but was disappointed there and returned to own and manage a Post Office in Southampton.

Corporal Ginger Proudlove, who settled in St Helens and was

employed by the Tootal clothing company, died in 1970. Tosh Baker, the legendary SSM of Headquarters Squadron, eventually retired in 1947. He still retained a great interest in horse-breaking while at the same time, working for the Hampshire Water Authority. He died suddenly in 1984.

Of the wartime squadron leaders, only two survive, Major the Lord Gerald Kildare, who has inherited his late father's title and is now the Duke of Leinster; and Major Tony Leavey, who after a lengthy business career in the City still works for the welfare of soldiers with SSAFA. Lieutenant Peter Kiddle, who gave a vivid account of the Geffen incident, served on until 1952 and then also worked in the City. Captain Mick Murland, who supplied the article about the raising of John Ward-Harrison's hounds in France, transferred his services and technical knowledge to REME, where he earned his promotion to Colonel before returning to Northern Ireland. Captain Charles Maple, our own mechanical officer, continued to serve with REME to become a Brigadier. After retirement he became the sales manager of British Leyland. Cancer accounted for his untimely death in 1988.

Sergeant Ralph Chalmers, having been awarded a well-deserved, DCM, retired to his native Northern Ireland to become a manager with Courtaulds. He was the victim of a sudden heart attack in 1969. Sergeant Archie Carr, DCM, retired to the quiet village of Malton in Northampton to become the village postman. His number two, Albert Morris, most unexpectedly became the manager of parks and cemeteries in Newcastle-under-Lyme.

The much-mentioned Captain Jack Robinson DCM was to become a Quartermaster to the Cheshire Yeomanry, our affiliated TA regiment, and then to work for British Aerospace. But he was not a fit man and fought against ill health for many years before he died in a Chester hospital. I was flattered when his wife 'phoned to tell me that he had been taken into hospital and that he was not expected to live very long. He told her: "Tell Boardman. He'll know what to do."

SSM Jack Clayton MM served on and fought in the Korean campaign. After serving a period as Regimental Sergeant Major he retired to run a pub in Colchester and then to work for the army once again as a unit accountant. Sergeant Bob Price has written a very interesting biography of his own life. His love of game-keeping in Gloucester returned him to the occupation he so enjoyed. He says in his biography that he used many of the skills from that trade during his active service days. I am sure he was equally able to use skills obtained in war to further his professional ability as a keeper.

Corporal Slim Ingley, who wrote the article about the Dunkirk Evacuation, emigrated to Australia, where he still lives. He was wounded in September, 1944, and those wounds still give him problems. Sergeant Sam Hayward, the driver who punched holes in his exhaust to make his tank sound as though it were larger, became the Mechanist Sergeant to 'A' Squadron and spent more time patching-up engines. Alan Merson, having finally rid himself of the dye from the vats in Swarland blanket factory, returned to his native Devon.

Captain George Archibald, pre-war jockey, took his talents to America where he runs a successful stud farm. Lieutenant Derek Philo took a long time to recover from his Normandy injuries, but eventually returned to become Technical Adjutant. He now runs a guest house in Oxfordshire. That happy and uncomplaining despatch rider, Trumpeter Syd Shepherd, became a milkman—just the employment to suit his talents. I am sure many depressed housewives in the Barnet area owe much to Syd for his cheerfulness, reliability and good humour. Lieutenant Bill Bradfield MC returned to study medicine and re-enlisted into the Territorial Royal Army Medical Corps to become a Colonel. He now practises in Harley Street.

This leaves me to cover the lives of two very close and helpful friends, Sergeants Pat Whitmore and Syd Swift. Both contributed so much to this writing. Pat went up to Oxford and then became a master at the City of London School, Blackfriars. He continues to maintain a link with the Services through the City of London Cadet Force. He and I have shared many delightful returns to the Normandy battlefields, now so peaceful and colourful.

Syd, an outstanding soldier because he gives of his best in anything he does, transferred to the Royal Army Service Corps and served on as a Barrack Accountant. He then took up a new career as a Ministry of Defence policeman, becoming an inspector. I long ago gave up any attempt to compete with him since he is an expert in art, woodwork, pottery, marquetry, writing, poetry and gardening. His gardening talents led to his own garden being featured on a TV programme.

I enjoy the company of both of them as often as I can. Pat, who is a fluent French linguist, has been so important to us all in the planning and operation of our returns to those *Tracks in Europe*, though some are no longer there, and others have become motorways. They are always, and will always, be part of our lives.

For me there would be continued service until 1970, and then the Regimental Secretary post which has enabled me to compile these letters and reports. My service has given me an understanding of youth. I see the same spirit in the young men in today's army as those who served 50 years ago. Should they ever be called to arms, they will give the same account of themselves as the men who served at Waterloo and Balaclava and during two world wars. I hope they are never put to the test, but readers may rest assured. Those who survived the ghastly period covered by this book will, I am sure, feel that they are better men for having endured and shared the suffering.

# Roll of Honour
# British Expeditionary Force 1940

| *1940* | | | *Cemetery* | *Burial place, if known* Plot | *Row* | *Grave* |
|---|---|---|---|---|---|---|
| 17th May | 203871 | Tpr B S Brewin | Berchem-Ste-Agathe | | | 2706 |
| 18th May | 321101 | Tpr T H Angell | Berchem-Ste-Agathe | | | 2706 |
| | 7880467 | Tpr R C Arnold | Langemarck | XVII | B | 1 |
| 19th May | 409242 | Cpl E O Griffiths | Langemarck | XVII | B | 1 |
| | 321740 | Tpr F Tingle | The Dunkirk Memorial | Col 2 | | |
| 22nd May | 404717 | Tpr A Jackson | The Dunkirk Memorial | Col 2 | | |
| 23rd May | 7882624 | Tpr H O J Gillard | The Dunkirk Memorial | Col 2 | | |
| | 5434070 | Tpr E A Geach | The Dunkirk Memorial | Col 2 | | |
| | 321341 | Tpr C Coyle | Morbecque | V | B | 6 |
| 24th May | 321583 | Tpr B W Edgerton | Boéseghem Churchyard | | | |
| | 548061 | L/Sgt E G Lockley | The Dunkirk Memorial | Col 2 | | |
| 26th May | 4971890 | Tpr S Slater | Tannay, Thiennes | V | F | 13 |
| | 321082 | Tpr E Sawyer | The Dunkirk Memorial | Col 2 | | |
| 27th May | 68115 | Lieut F V Beaumont | Hoogstadt Church | | | 100 |
| | 7880602 | L/Cpl N Horsfield | Estaires | V | E | 6 |
| 28th May | 6711736 | Tpr J Charman | Bailleul | III | G | 203 |
| | 321455 | Tpr A I Latto | Bailleul | III | G | 196 |
| | 321472 | L/Cpl E Smith | Bailleul | III | G | 202 |
| | 3592846 | TSM J Crawley | Outtersteene | 5 | A | 73 |
| | 321188 | Tpr L Carrington | The Dunkirk Memorial | Col 2 | | |
| | 409307 | Tpr J E Rogers | The Dunkirk Memorial | Col 2 | | |
| | 321103 | Tpr J E Simpson | The Dunkirk Memorial | Col 2 | | |
| 29th May | 4858199 | Tpr B G Hammond | The Dunkirk Memorial | Col 2 | | |
| | 405310 | Sgt L W Workman | Pihen-les-Guînes | II | B | 1 |
| | 3386055 | L/Cpl J Connolly | Pihen-les-Guînes | II | B | 2 |
| | 321138 | Tpr B E Bamber | Pihen-les-Guînes | II | B | 3 |
| | 7882243 | L/Sgt B Anderson | The Dunkirk Memorial | Col 2 | | |
| | 408920 | L/Cpl V H Meadows | The Dunkirk Memorial | Col 2 | | |
| | 6978479 | Tpr E J McAteer | The Dunkirk Memorial | Col 2 | | |

These lists do not include those men attached from other Regiments.
There are no lists of those made Prisoner of War nor the wounded from this period.
It is recorded that 4 officers and 15 other ranks were taken prisoner.

The following are known to have died while Prisoners of War or when serving with other formations:

Brigadier R N Cartwright. Died when serving with the Royal West African Forces.
Major E A Widdrington M.C.
Captain W R Turner. With the Royal Tank Regiment, Middle East.
Captain A D Beirne O'Ryan
Lieutenant J Hethey
Lieutenant J R Hornby
Lieutenant G M M Mathews, Middle East.
Lieutenant B A O'Meara
Corporal A H Collinson
Corporal G Keogh
Lance Corporal L Buckley
Lance Corporal A Miller
Lance Corporal W A Ryan
Trooper J Clydesdale
Trooper W Crosby
Trooper T H Dean
Trooper C King. From illness in BMH Woolwich

Died during the period of re-training, pre Normandy Invasion

Captain B C Fleury-Teulon
Trooper P Maher

## ROLL OF HONOUR

# 1944 — 1945

| | | | | *Burial place, if known* | | |
|---|---|---|---|---|---|---|
| ***1944*** | | | *Cemetery* | *Plot* | *Row* | *Grave* |
| 20th Jul | 191487 | Capt (Rev) J A Newson | Bayeux | | | |
| | 295417 | Lieut G A Rawlins | Bayeux | I | E | 6 |
| | 7955277 | Tpr P H Bloom | Bayeux Memorial | Col 2 | | |
| 28th Jul | 90278 | Lieut D G P Leavey | Bayeux | II | L | 7 |
| 1st Aug | 14222659 | Tpr J G Jones | Hottot-le-Bagues, Tilly-sur-Seulles | IX | D | 8 |
| 2nd Aug | 14412350 | LCpl J R Booth | Bayeux | XIX | C | 19 |
| | 317433 | Tpr G Hodgson | Bayeux | XIX | C | 18 |
| 4th Aug | 7906864 | Cpl C W Ray | St Charles-de-Percy | XV | G | 3 |
| 9th Aug | 170597 | Capt M D Williams | Tilly-sur-Seulles | IX | G | 9 |
| 11th Aug | 7945291 | Tpr A Sutton | Tilly-sur-Seulles | VII | B | 1 |
| | 7960422 | Tpr H A Moore | Tilly-sur-Seulles | VI | E | 3 |
| | 304678 | Lieut B Berry | Tilly-sur-Seulles | VII | E | 13 |
| 12th Aug | 7931632 | Tpr J Campbell | Banneville-la-Campagne | XVI | B | 20 |
| 21st Aug | 14514393 | Tpr R A O Fuller | Bayeux | XXIV | B | 2 |
| 26th Aug | 7955939 | Tpr D Grieves | St-Désir, Lisieux | II | B | 4 |
| | 7939415 | Tpr L Elson | St-Désir, Lisieux | II | B | 3 |
| | 4231086 | LCpl W J Turner | St-Désir, Lisieux | II | B | 2 |
| | 14220270 | Tpr L K Makepiece | Bayeux Memorial | Col 2 | | |
| | 3608003 | Tpr J Huntington | Bayeux Memorial | Col 2 | | |
| | 7880442 | Tpr J E Paige | Boissey-le-Châtel Church | | | |
| 3rd Sep | 265689 | Lieut T D Sedgwick | Dunkirk Town Cemetery | II | II | 12 |
| 4th Sep | 7907106 | Tpr J H Hewitt | High Wood, Langueval | XIII | G | 29 |
| 5th Sep | 14297134 | Tpr T Marshall | St-Sever, Rouen | | M | 17 |
| 22nd Sep | 410505 | Sgt W Bowley | Miero War Cemetery | VI | C | 1 |
| | 14201230 | Tpr H Sissons | Miero War Cemetery | VI | C | 2 |
| 23rd Sep | 14317852 | Tpr H G Thaxter | Walkenswaard | 1 | A | 4 |
| 26th Sep | 319498 | Sgt J Kennedy | Uden | IV | C | 13 |
| | 14317391 | Tpr L Riley | Uden | IV | D | 13 |
| | 7906041 | Tpr A E Thickpenny | Miero War Cemetery | VI | B | 3 |
| | 14422152 | Tpr A Wood | Uden | IV | D | 12 |
| 20th Oct | 256500 | Lieut W J M Crocker | Uden | 3 | H | 1 |
| 22nd Oct | 14307767 | Tpr W F Everett | Uden | II | H | 11 |
| 23rd Oct | 7903169 | Tpr H Hannah | Uden | II | B | 13 |
| 24th Oct | 5614890 | Tpr C P Young | Uden | III | F | 10 |
| 27th Oct | 7940869 | Sgt T C F Wagstaff | Bergen-op-Zoom | IX | C | 13 |
| | 4539578 | Tpr S Parr | Bergen-op-Zoom | IX | C | 15 |
| | 14219311 | Tpr T Percival | Bergen-op-Zoom | IX | C | 14 |
| 29th Oct | 3771162 | LCpl W A Dunn | Bergen-op-Zoom | IX | C | 10 |
| 31st Oct | 14514239 | Tpr N A Daley | Sterksel Monastery | | A | 18 |
| ***1945*** | | | | | | |
| 18th Jan | 14436407 | Tpr K Priestman | Bergen-op-Zoom (Canadian) | VIII | F | 3 |
| 22nd Jan | 14408542 | Tpr W Bottomley | Mook-en-Middelaar | II | D | 12 |
| | 14441022 | Tpr L de V Fison | Mook-en-Middelaar | II | D | 8 |
| | 14424647 | Tpr B T W Golding | Mook-en-Middelaar | II | D | 9 |
| | 144220286 | Tpr H J Read | Mook-en-Middelaar | II | D | 11 |
| | 7896508 | Cpl T Stark | Mook-en-Middelaar | II | D | 10 |
| 4th Feb | 14427005 | LCpl AJ Price | Thorpe Cemetery, Egham, Surrey | | | |
| 12th Mar | 7945754 | Cpl J Wiseman | Durnbach, Germany | III | D | 10 |
| 30th Mar | 6405142 | Tpr S W Pollard | Reichwald Forest, Cleves | LXII | B | 10 |
| 1st Apr | 7960238 | Tpr W H Whitcombe | Reichwald Forest, Cleves | IV | F | 3 |
| 2nd Apr | 7955810 | Tpr D W Smith | Venray War Cemetery | I | D | 9 |
| 3rd Apr | 14432362 | Tpr G W Boxford | Reichwald Forest, Cleves | XLVI | A | 4 |

*1945 continued*

| | | | | | | |
|---|---|---|---|---|---|---|
| 4th Apr | 7926960 | Cpl G R Elliott | Reichwald Forest, Cleves | XLVI | A | 6 |
| | 1453398 | Lieut M Fitzgerald MC | Reichwald Forest, Cleves | LV | C | 13 |
| | 14231926 | Tpr J R Gower | Reichwald Forest, Cleves | XLIII | D | 13 |
| 5th Apr | 324105 | Lieut H J Elkins | Reichwald Forest, Cleves | XLVI | J | 18 |
| 8th Apr | 304675 | Lieut P T Walworth | Beckengen, Saltau | XV | A | 1 |
| 9th Apr | 4547444 | Tpr H Batty | Bechengen, Saltau | X | C | 7 |

# Wounded

*1944*

| | | |
|---|---|---|
| 28th Jul | 7881869 | Sgt A Piper |
| 1st Aug | 7909271 | Tpr F Perry |
| 2nd Aug | | Captain B A Marshall |
| | | Captain D A Philo |
| | | Lieut R A Irwin |
| | 7936683 | L/Cpl S Burns |
| | 14352411 | Tpr H Tuckwood |
| 3rd | 408479 | Sgt R Carr |
| | 321645 | Tpr E Wilson |
| | 14424302 | Tpr R Fisher |
| 4th Aug | 7952796 | Tpr C Marley |
| | 14418623 | Tpr J Blatchford |
| | 321137 | Tpr J Leah |
| | 321108 | Cpl P Cooper |
| 5th Aug | 7955853 | Tpr C Lewis |
| 6th Aug | 3494841 | Tpr W Kennedy |
| 8th Aug | | Lieut J S Milligan |
| 10th Aug | | Captain G A Glover |
| | 7957761 | Tpr D Williams |
| 11th Aug | 721067 | Cpl A Johnson |
| | 14215703 | Tpr G Fuller |
| 12th Aug | 7942292 | Tpr A Dodgson |
| | 1434935 | Tpr L A C Steed |
| | 14220170 | Tpr V Verrell |
| 13th Aug | | Major The Marquess of Kildare |
| 14th Aug | 5045702 | Sgt A Chesters |
| 18th Aug | 7926452 | Tpr J Riggs |
| 21st Aug | 321367 | Tpr W Pocklington |
| | 4622543 | Tpr R Smith |
| 22nd Aug | 4616345 | Tpr H Broadbent |
| 23rd Aug | 407151 | Sgt E C Roodhouse |
| | 14407854 | Tpr C Taylor |
| 26th Aug | 321614 | Sgt A R Daglish |
| | 322377 | Cpl C J Boardman |
| | 410700 | L/Cpl G Udall |
| | 144344860 | Tpr R P Hawkes |
| | 4622705 | Tpr L S Hume |
| | 7938938 | Tpr R P Ryan |
| | 7956513 | Tpr A Hillman |
| | 7962897 | Tpr V F Doyle |
| | 7958828 | Tpr A M Wheeler |
| 27th Aug | 7907109 | Tpr S F Jones |
| 28th Aug | 7963438 | Tpr C Chatswood |
| | 321525 | Tpr G Berry |
| | 14222916 | Tpr K H Woodrow |
| | 7908341 | Tpr F G Evans |
| 30th Aug | 409079 | Cpl T J Rishton |
| | | Lieut D K O'Meara |
| | 2598647 | Cpl E Burrows |
| | 4524449 | Cpl W Rumble |
| | 7920878 | Tpr L Coots |
| 3rd Sep | 14324922 | Tpr P J Wynn |
| | 14432554 | Tpr H C Blewitt |
| | 1437807 | Tpr M R Wingate |
| | 7962708 | Tpr J Skeggs |
| | 321108 | Cpl P Cooper MM |
| | 7906874 | Cpl W Green |
| | 321409 | L/Cpl D Ingley |
| | 7920708 | Tpr H Bent |
| 4th Sep | | Lieut D B D Dickson |
| | 3910026 | L/Cpl H Swain |
| | 14297134 | Tpr T Marshall |
| | 398883 | Sgt R S Knaggs |
| | 14216129 | Tpr C King |
| | 14232084 | Tpr J Tring |
| 6th Sep | 406301 | SSM J Clayton MM |
| | 4616282 | Tpr S Addyman |
| 7th Sep | 14498558 | Tpr L E Coomes |
| 19th Sep | 558497 | Cpl C W Abbott |
| 20th Sep | 4623437 | Tpr A Gale |
| 22nd Sep | 7899108 | L/Cpl C A Wood |
| 24th Sep | 7907001 | Cpl A L Webb |
| 26th Sept | | Lieut J E Gillett |
| | 79044904 | Cpl L Charlesworth |
| | 4389248 | Tpr A A Brown |
| 2nd Oct | 7900063 | L/Cpl D S Wright |
| 3rd Oct | 7945299 | Sgt P A Strickland |
| 9th Oct | 321661 | L/Cpl D Ryan |
| 22nd Oct | | Lieut W M Ackroyd MC |
| | 7926433 | L/Cpl B W Law |
| | 7900063 | L/Cpl D S Wright |
| | 7952431 | L/Cpl J B Powell |
| | 321691 | Tpr L Rudd |
| | 556411 | Tpr R Weir DCM |
| | 14437350 | Tpr R Nunn |
| 24th Oct | 404957 | L/Cpl J Read |
| | 14414843 | Tpr A E Stoker |
| | 796282 | Tpr C King |
| | 7013550 | Pte P Ireland |
| 27th Oct | 14437740 | Tpr C K Field |
| | 7884993 | Tpr D C Kempson |
| | 321965 | Cpl J MacFarland |
| | | Lieut W B Cowdy |
| | 14222692 | Tpr G Thomas |

| | | |
|---|---|---|
| 29th Oct | | Lieut P G Lewis |
| | 4624324 | Tpr A C Day |
| 1st Nov | 7962961 | Tpr R E Edwards |
| 7th Nov | 14514647 | Tpr P M Halladay |

*1945*

| | | |
|---|---|---|
| 13th Jan | 14412066 | Tpr B J Fitzsimmons |
| 14th Jan | 7933664 | L/Cpl A J Lees |
| | 79336644 | L/Cpl A Harris |
| 18th Jan | 14231954 | L/Cpl A W Hodges |
| | 7901881 | L/Cpl G W Breaks |
| | 14432362 | Tpr G W Boxford |
| | 14435516 | Tpr G Rowan |
| 20th Jan | 321390 | L/Cpl E G Jordan |
| 22nd Jan | | Lieut R de Grey |
| | 7920278 | L/Sgt A Stewart |
| | 14219972 | Tpr R B Sanderson |
| 23rd Jan | 4617812 | Tpr G E Woolley |
| | 4342779 | Tpr T S Coser |
| | 14499998 | Tpr J J Ward |
| | 14310794 | Tpr G W Haggerwood |
| 24th Jan | 14688500 | Tpr S B Gelfarb |
| 25th Jan | 409236 | Sgt W Gilliland |
| | 7888009 | Cpl C E Etheridge |
| | 14499333 | Tpr P Brown |
| 27th Jan | | Lieut H F Craig-Harvey |
| | 321478 | Cpl W West MM |
| | 7963288 | Tpr F Gibbons |
| | 14499512 | Tpr K J Ellis |
| 28th Mar | 320163 | L/Sgt J Oldham |
| | 7955736 | Tpr W M Upton |
| 29th Mar | 4610796 | L/Sgt S F Swift |
| | 14430514 | Tpr R Brookes |
| | 7955922 | Tpr K Horsfield |
| 2nd Apr | 7961458 | Tpr E S Sharpe |
| 3rd Apr | 5948246 | Sgt W Starr |
| | 7887243 | Cpl W Barton |
| | 5625875 | L/Cpl A E Clarke |
| 4th Apr | 7938868 | Cpl A W White |
| | 409249 | Cpl D Lines |
| | 7897243 | Cpl H Rhodes |
| | | Lieut H G Woods MC |
| 5th Apr | 14435800 | Tpr A D Krill |
| 8th Apr | 7903092 | Sgt E Robinson |
| | 321158 | Cpl C Dransfield |
| | 14713153 | Tpr E C Roff |
| | 321130 | Tpr K Brooke |
| | 7902101 | Tpr E Lomas |
| 9th Apr | 409323 | Sgt R W Chalmers DCM |
| | 14213984 | L/Cpl W N Davies |
| | 4616483 | Tpr E Bodsworth |
| | 14499412 | Tpr K J Ellis |
| | 14433348 | Tpr J S Clark |
| 12th Apr | | Captain L F York |
| 17th Apr | 14413868 | Tpr P Ledwith |
| | 14310643 | Tpr J Pilborough |
| | 409177 | Tpr A W Wild |
| 24th Apr | 7938111 | Tpr A M Brenhan |
| 28th Apr | 14232807 | Tpr L A Windeatt |
| 29th Apr | 14497162 | Tpr J Dixon |

# Evacuated Sick

| | |
|---|---|
| | Captain R B Kettle |
| | Lieut W M Ackroyd MC |
| 7873851 | SQMS W Birkett |
| 409323 | Sgt R Chalmers DCM |
| 4743992 | L/Sgt H Carr |
| 4539241 | Cpl T Steel |
| 321108 | Cpl P Cooper MM |
| 321679 | Cpl C Benge |
| 7926442 | L/Cpl J Nuttall |
| 14429597 | L/Cpl K Grudgings |
| 157438 | L/Cpl H Richards |
| 410700 | L/Cpl G Udall |
| 4615711 | L/Cpl E Dennell |
| 1153864 | Tpr F Barker |
| 4626648 | Tpr P Byrne |
| 14401922 | Tpr J Cooke |
| 14415303 | Tpr T Gardner |
| 14445098 | Tpr H Haines |
| 14426226 | Tpr A Jiggins |
| 14431750 | Tpr R Lloyd |
| 14405161 | Tpr W Lawson |
| 14310634 | Tpr P Musk |
| 14423620 | Tpr W McCathie |
| 4746180 | Tpr R Methley |
| 7952495 | Tpr H Palethorpe |
| 3607440 | Tpr J Richards |
| 14309925 | Tpr H Southard |
| 13041590 | Tpr B Stannard |
| 7952514 | Tpr J Troop |

# Honours and Awards

## C.B.E.

Major J D A'Anderson D.S.O.

## O.B.E.

Major F J S Whetstone

## D.S.O.

Major J D A A'Anderson
Lieutenant Colonel M P Ansell
Lieutenant Colonel J A Anstice
Major R P Harding
Major C F Keightley
Major A B J Scott
Lieutenant Colonel J E Swetenham
Major R D C Vigors
Major T C Williamson

## M.C.

Lieutenant W M Ackroyd
Major W Barraclough
Captain J Bissill
Captain C H Blacker
Lieutenant W Bradfield
Lieutenant H F Craig-Harvey
Lieutenant M Fitzgerald
Major A C Gibson
Captain E M Kilbane
Major W W G Lavery
Captain G W R Monckton
Lieutenant H F Phillips
Captain R C M Shelton
Major A B J Scott
Captain C de Moranville de Sellier
Captain J M H R Tomkin
Captain H. C. Walker
Major J. M. D. Ward-Harrison (with bar)
Captain E A F Widdrington
Captain H G Woods

## M.B.E.

Sergeant J McMahon
Major G T Newport
Major M Peters

## D.C.M.

Sergeant C W Bevan
Sergeant T H Broad
Sergeant R Carr
Sergeant R C Chalmers
Corporal E Glynn
TSM E Imms
TSM J R Robinson

## M.M.

Trooper R C Arnold
Sergeant C W Bevan, DCM
Trooper A Brown
Trooper H Carr
SSM J Clayton
Corporal P L G Cooper
Trooper J Eden
Sergeant E Glynn, DCM
Corporal R M Hancox
Corporal W J Hill
Trooper G T Jones
Corporal G Litchfield
Trooper W Melvin
Lance Corporal S J Osborne
Corporal W L Peat
Lance Corporal W G Pochin
Sergeant R Price
Trooper H A Sims
Trooper J Smith
Sergeant H V Suggit
Sergeant J Tartt (now Gerrard)
Trooper W A West
Lance Corporal R Wright

## Mentioned in Despatches
**(Officers)**

Captain J D A'Anderson, DSO
Major J A Anstice, DSO
Captain G W Archibald
Captain J P Bissill
Captain G T Blundell-Brown
Captain H K Chapman
Major J S Collings
Major D S L Gregson
Lieutenant Colonel C F Keightley
Major T J F Killick
Captain P R Kiddle
Major J A Leavey
Captain F O G Longstaff
Major E G B Oates
Captain F A Stockdale
Major J E Swetenham
Captain J N B Ussher
Lieutenant Colonel F J S Whetstone
Lieutenant E A F Widdrington
Major T C Williamson

## Mentioned in Despatches
**(Other Ranks)**

Trooper R C Arnold
Trooper H Cass
Sergeant H Chesters
Trooper J Eden
Trooper C J Escritt
Sergeant F Heaps
Corporal W J Hill
Troop Sergeant Major E Holt
Corporal J Huntley
Trooper C J Killow
Lance Corporal S J Osborne
Bandsman S W Shepherd
Trooper J Smith
Lance Sergeant S F Swift
Sergeant P A Strickland
Sergeant P J S Whitmore

## Croix de Guerre
**(Belgium)**

Lieutenant H S L Tottenham
Sergeant R Chalmers

## Order of Leopold II

Lieutenant H S L Tottenham